The Crusades, 1095–1204

Second Edition

Jonathan Phillips

Routledge
Taylor & Francis Group

LONDON AND NEW YORK

Second Edition published 2014
by Routledge
2 Park Square, Milton Park, Abingdon, Oxon OX14 4RN

and by Routledge
711 Third Avenue, New York, NY 10017

Routledge is an imprint of the Taylor & Francis Group, an informa business

First published 2002 by Pearson Education

British Library Cataloguing in Publication Data
A catalogue record for this book is available from the British Library

Library of Congress Cataloging in Publication Data
A catalog record for this title has been requested.

ISBN: 978-0-415-73636-7 (hbk)
ISBN: 978-1-405-87293-5 (pbk)
ISBN: 978-1-315-79821-9 (ebk)

Typeset in 10/13.5pt ITC Berkeley
by Graphicraft Limited, Hong Kong

MIX
Paper from
responsible sources
FSC
www.fsc.org   FSC® C013604

Printed and bound by CPI Group (UK) Ltd, Croydon, CR0 4YY

T

This new and co .... edition of The
couples vivid narrative v ...... a clear and accessible analysis of the key issues
that prompted the conquest and settlement of the Holy Land between the
First and the Fourth Crusade.

This edition now covers the Fourth Crusade and the Sack of Constantinople,
along with greater coverage of the Muslim response to the Crusades from the
capture of Jerusalem in 1099 to Saladin's leadership of the counter-crusade,
culminating in his struggle with Richard the Lionheart during the Third
Crusade. It also examines the complex motives of the Italian city states during
the conquest of the Levant, as well as relations between the Frankish settlers
and the indigenous population, both Eastern Christian and Muslim, in times
of war and peace. Extended treatment of the events of the First Crusade, the
failure of the Second Crusade, and the prominent role of female rulers in the
Latin East are also featured.

Underpinned by the latest research, this book also includes:

- a 'Who's Who', a Chronology, a discussion of the Historiography, maps,
  family trees and numerous illustrations
- a strong collection of contemporary documents, including previously
  untranslated narratives and poems
- a blend of thematic and narrative chapters that also consider the Military
  Orders, kingship, warfare and castles, and pilgrimage.

This new edition provides an illuminating insight into one of the most
famous and compelling periods of history.

Jonathan Phillips is Professor of Crusading History at Royal Holloway,
University of London. He has written widely on the subject, including *The
Second Crusade: Extending the Frontiers of Christendom* (2007), and *Holy Warriors:
A Modern History of the Crusades* (2009); he has also appeared in numerous
television programmes, such as *The Crusades: The Crescent and the Cross*.

Introduction to the series

History is narrative constructed by historians from traces left by the past. Historical enquiry is often driven by contemporary issues and, in consequence, historical narratives are constantly reconsidered, reconstructed and reshaped. The fact that different historians have different perspectives on issues means that there is also often controversy and no universally agreed version of past events. *Seminar Studies* was designed to bridge the gap between current research and debate, and the broad, popular general surveys that often date rapidly.

The volumes in the series are written by historians who are not only familiar with the latest research and current debates concerning their topic, but who have themselves contributed to our understanding of the subject. The books are intended to provide the reader with a clear introduction to a major topic in history. They provide both a narrative of events and a critical analysis of contemporary interpretations. They include the kinds of tools generally omitted from specialist monographs: a chronology of events, a glossary of terms and brief biographies of 'who's who'. They also include bibliographical essays in order to guide students to the literature on various aspects of the subject. Students and teachers alike will find that the selection of documents will stimulate discussion and offer insight into the raw materials used by historians in their attempt to understand the past.

Clive Emsley and Gordon Martel
Series Editors

For Jonathan Riley-Smith and Peter Jackson

Contents

Preface to the second edition

I am very pleased to take this opportunity to produce an updated and extended edition of this book, over a decade after the writing and publication of the first edition (2002). The history of the crusades and the Near East are dynamic areas of research that have, in many respects, expanded and moved on during this time; I hope (constraints of format allowing) they have been done some justice in the following content. My own interests and academic contacts have developed and some of the material utilised here reflects this too; I have also sought to respond to requests to enlarge particular sections, such as the failure of the Second Crusade. The most obvious change from the first edition is the expanded time period, now encompassing the Fourth Crusade and the capture of Constantinople, an inclusion that reflects many teaching syllabi. Another notable advance has been increasing availability of translations from Arabic, something that allows a much better insight into the impact of the crusades in the Near East and the response of the Muslims; some of the texts here have not been published before in English.

Growing numbers of historians and archaeologists work on the crusades and related subjects. This huge volume of work is represented here in, for example, new sections on: pilgrimage; interaction (peaceful and violent) between Franks, Muslims and Eastern Christians; on the motives of early crusaders; the involvement of the Italian city states, and the origins of the First Crusade. The scope of crusading, now recognised to encompass arenas other than the Holy Land too, as well as the long and complex legacy of the crusading age are also given some coverage here while acknowledging that they are outside the prime concerns of this book.

Acknowledgements

I would like to thank Mari Shullaw of Longman for inviting me to write this second edition and for her patience in waiting for it to arrive. Similarly, my gratitude goes to Stacey Carter and Laura Mothersole at Routledge who have been so positive and welcoming towards this text. I have continued to enjoy evolving much of the subject matter in my 'Crusades and Eastern Mediterranean' classes at Royal Holloway, University of London, and I am thankful to those students for their lively and challenging response to the material over the years. Louise and Jonathan Riley-Smith, Carole Hillenbrand, Mike Routledge, Marcus Bull, Susan Edgington, Caroline Smith, Osman Latiff, Martin Hall and Peter Edbury very kindly allowed me to use their translations in the documents section. The help of Jonathan Harris, Bernard Hamilton, Jonathan Rubin, Simon John and Konrad Hirschler has been much appreciated too. I would also like to thank Hereford Cathedral archives, Professor Benjamin Kedar, Alistair Duncan and the Bibliothèque Municipale, Boulogne-sur-Mer for the use of their illustrations. The advice of both Dr Paul Loxton on the effects of leprosy, and Graham Byfield of Baldwin's Numismatics, London, on medieval coinage has been invaluable. As usual I am indebted to Meg Davies for her indexing skills. Once again all my love to my wonderful Niki, Tom and Marcus.

One happy side-effect of working in such a vibrant field of study has been the opportunity to talk to many others who teach and learn about the subject. I have been made immensely welcome at a large number of university departments, colleges and schools across Britain and Ireland. I am very grateful to all these staff and students for their interest and enthusiasm in the subject of crusading history. Everyone involved in education is acutely aware how important it is to inspire their students and it is my privilege to dedicate this book to Professor Peter Jackson, whose tremendous undergraduate teaching did much to encourage me to further study, and to Professor Jonathan Riley-Smith whose academic rigour, enthusiasm and patient support took me through my doctoral thesis and beyond.

List of illustrations

FIGURES

MAPS

Chronology

1099 *7 June*	Crusaders arrive at Jerusalem
1099 *15 July*	Capture of Jerusalem
1099 *22 July*	Godfrey of Bouillon is chosen to rule Jerusalem as Advocate of the Holy Sepulchre
1099 *12 August*	Battle of Ascalon
1099 *August–September*	Many First Crusaders return home to the West
1100 *18 July*	Death of Godfrey of Bouillon
1100 *25 December*	Coronation of King Baldwin I
1101 *17 May*	Capture of Caesarea
1101 *August–September*	Crusaders are defeated in Asia Minor
1104 *7 May*	Battle of Hauran – Franks heavily defeated
1104 *26 May*	Capture of Acre
1106	Bohemond of Antioch tours France seeking support for a crusade against the Greeks
1107 *October–September* **1108**	Bohemond invades the Byzantine Empire, but is defeated. Treaty of Devol
1109 *12 July*	Capture of Tripoli
1110 *13 May*	Capture of Beirut
1110 *4 December*	Capture of Sidon by a force including Norwegian crusaders led by King Sigurd
1113	Papal bull *Pie postulatio voluntatis* recognises Hospital of St John in Jerusalem
1118 *2 April*	Death of King Baldwin I on campaign in Egypt
1118 *14 April*	Consecration of King Baldwin II as ruler of Jerusalem
1119	Foundation of the Knights Templar
1119 *28 June*	Battle of the Field of Blood, northern Antioch
1120 *January*	Council of Nablus
1122 *April–August* **1123**	Captivity of King Baldwin II
1124 *7 July*	Capture of Tyre
1127–29	Mission of Hugh of Payns to the West to recruit men for the Damascus crusade and to secure ecclesiastical authorisation for the order of the Temple
1129 *May*	Arrival of Count Fulk V of Anjou to marry Melisende, heiress to Jerusalem

1129 *November*	Failed Frankish attack on Damascus
1130 *February*	Death of Prince Bohemond II of Antioch – rule taken over by Princess Alice
1131 *21 August*	Death of King Baldwin II of Jerusalem. Coronation of Fulk and Melisende
1134	Revolt of Count Hugh of Jaffa
1136 *April*	Arrival of Raymond of Poitiers and his succession to the principality of Antioch
1137	Birth of Saladin
1137–38	Emperor John Komnenos of Byzantium threatens Antioch
1142–43	Second expedition of John Komnenos to Antioch. Death of John (March 1143)
1143 *10 November*	Death of King Fulk
1144–45	Byzantine army forces Raymond of Antioch to travel to Constantinople and acknowledge Byzantine overlordship
1144 *24 December*	Fall of Edessa to Zengi of Aleppo and Mosul
1145 *1 December*	First issue of *Quantum praedecessores*, crusade appeal of Pope Eugenius III
1146 *31 March*	Bernard of Clairvaux preaches the Second Crusade at Vézelay to King Louis VII and the French nobility
1146 *14 September*	Death of Zengi, succeeded by Nur ad-Din
1146 *September–January 1147*	Bernard tours Flanders and the Rhineland recruiting men for the crusade
1146 *24 December*	King Conrad III of Germany takes the cross
1147 *May*	Fleet of Anglo-Norman, Flemish and Rhinelanders sets out for the Holy Land via Lisbon
1147 *June*	Armies of Conrad III and Louis VII set out for the Levant
1147 *28 June*	Start of the siege of Lisbon
1147 *July–September*	Wendish Crusade
1147 *17 October*	Genoese and Catalan fleet capture Almeria in southern Spain
1147 *21 October*	Capture of Lisbon
1147 *September–October*	Armies of the Second Crusade at Constantinople
1147 *25 October*	German army defeated in Asia Minor
1148 *7 January*	Defeat of the French army at Mount Cadmus in Asia Minor
1148 *March–May*	Louis VII at Antioch
1148 *24 June*	Council of Palmarea decides to attack Damascus
1148 *23–28 July*	Siege of Damascus fails

1148 *July–30 December*	Siege and capture of Tortosa in northern Spain by crusaders from Genoa, Barcelona and southern France
1149 *29 June*	Death of Prince Raymond of Antioch at the Battle of Inab
1149 *15 July*	Inauguration of the new Church of the Holy Sepulchre
1150 *March–May*	Failed attempts to launch a new crusade in France
1151–52	Struggle between Baldwin III and Melisende for control over Jerusalem
1153 *22 August*	Capture of Ascalon
1154 *April*	Nur ad-Din takes control of Damascus
1157–58	Crusade of Count Thierry of Flanders and the attack on Shaizar (December 1157)
1158–59	Manuel Komnenos in northern Syria
1158 *September*	Marriage of Baldwin III and Theodora, a niece of Manuel Komnenos
1163 *10 February*	Death of King Baldwin III
1163 *18 February*	Coronation of King Amalric
1163 *September*	Amalric's first expedition to Egypt
1164 *August–October*	Amalric's second expedition to Egypt
1167 *January–August*	Amalric attacks Egypt with a Pisan fleet; he captures but then concedes Alexandria
1167 *29 August*	Marriage of Amalric and Maria, grand-niece of Manuel Komnenos
1168	Construction of the concentric castle at Belvoir by the Hospitallers
1168 *October–January* 1169	Amalric's fourth expedition to Egypt; Nur ad-Din takes control of Egypt
1169 *October–December*	Amalric's fifth expedition to Egypt
1169–71	Mission of Archbishop Frederick of Tyre to the West; he visits King Louis VII and King Henry II of England
1169 *29 July*	Papal appeal *Inter omnia* of Pope Alexander III
1170–*c.* 1184	Composition of *Historia* of William of Tyre
1171	Amalric visits Constantinople and swears homage to Manuel Komnenos
1174 *15 May*	Death of Nur ad-Din
1174 *11 July*	Death of Amalric; succession of Baldwin IV
1174 *November*	Saladin takes control of Damascus
1176 *17 September*	Manuel Komnenos is defeated by Seljuk Turks at the Battle of Myriocephalum
1177 *25 November*	Battle of Mont Gisard – Saladin is defeated

1177–78	Crusade of Count Philip of Flanders
1178–79	Construction of the castle of Jacob's Ford; it is taken by Saladin in August 1179
1180 *April*	Marriage of Guy of Lusignan and Sibylla
1180 24 *September*	Death of Manuel Komnenos
1181 *January*	Papal appeal of *Cum orientalis terrae* of Pope Alexander III
1182 *December–February* 1183	Reynald of Châtillon's expedition to the Red Sea and attack on Medina
1183 *February*	General tax enacted in the kingdom of Jerusalem
1183 12 *June*	Saladin takes control of Aleppo
1183 *September–October*	Saladin invades – the Franks shadow him and the Muslims retreat
1183 *October*	Removal of Guy of Lusignan from the regency
1184–85	Mission of Patriarch Heraclius and the masters of the Templars and Hospitallers to the West
1185 *May*	Death of King Baldwin IV; regency of Count Raymond III of Tripoli
1186 *May–September*	Death of King Baldwin V (precise date unknown)
1186 *September*	Coronation of Guy and Sibylla
1187 *January*	Reynald of Châtillon attacks a Muslim caravan in Transjordan
1187 1 *May*	Battle of Cresson
1187 1 *July*	Saladin invades the kingdom of Jerusalem
1187 2 *July*	Saladin lays siege to Tiberias; King Guy decides to march to Tiberias
1187 4 *July*	Battle of Hattin
1187 *August*	Arrival of Conrad of Montferrat at Tyre
1187 *July–November*	Saladin moves through the kingdom of Jerusalem taking towns and castles
1187 *October*	Fall of Jerusalem
1187 *October–November*	*Audita tremendi* issued by Pope Gregory VIII – a call for the Third Crusade
1188–90	Crusade preparations in western Europe
1189	King Guy lays siege to Acre
1189 *May*	Emperor Frederick Barbarossa sets out on crusade
1189 *July–May* 1190	Frederick moves successfully through the Byzantine Empire and also defeats Seljuk Turks of Iconium (May 1190)
1190 10 *June*	Death of Frederick at Silifke in Asia Minor

1190 July	Richard the Lionheart and Philip II Augustus of France set out for the East
1190 September–April 1191	Richard and Philip winter in Sicily
1191 May	Richard captures Cyprus
1191 12 July	Capture of Acre by crusaders and settlers
1191 3 August	Philip returns to France
1191 7 September	Battle of Arsuf
1191 October–January 1192	March to Jerusalem – crusaders turn back
1192 April	King Guy steps down from throne of Jerusalem, but is given Cyprus by King Richard
1192 28 April	Murder of Conrad of Montferrat
1192 May	Henry of Champagne is crowned king of Jerusalem
1192 June	Second march on Jerusalem fails
1192 5 August	Battle of Jaffa – Richard defeats Saladin
1192 2 September	Truce is arranged between Richard and Saladin
1192 9 October	Richard leaves for home
1193 4 March	Death of Saladin
1194 December	Death of Guy of Lusignan, ruler of Cyprus
1195–98	German crusade; recaptures Beirut (24 October 1197)
1197 10 September	Death of King Henry of Jerusalem
1197 October	Aimery of Lusignan, ruler of Cyprus, secures a crown from the German Empire for the island. He also marries Isabella, heiress to Jerusalem, and becomes king of Jerusalem
1198 8 January	Election of Pope Innocent III
1198 August	Issue of *Post miserabile*, the papal appeal for the Fourth Crusade
1199 November	A crusade preached against Markward of Anweiler in southern Italy
1199 November	Fourth Crusade preached at a tournament at Ecry-sur-Aisne, Champagne
1201 March–April	Northern French envoys reach Venice and agree terms for the transportation of the crusade by sea; 'The Treaty of Venice'
1202 Spring to August	Crusaders start to gather in Venice
1202 October	Fourth Crusade sets out from Venice, destination: Zara
1202 13 November	Start of the siege of Zara; city surrenders 24 November
1203 January	Negotiations between representatives of Prince Alexios of Byzantium and the crusaders at Zara

1203 *April*	Simon de Montfort leaves main crusade and goes to the Holy Land
1203 *June*	Fourth Crusade and Prince Alexios arrive at Constantinople
1203 *5 July*	Crusaders cross the Bosphorus and land on Galata shore; first siege of Constantinople begins
1203 *17 July*	Confrontation outside northern walls of the city; Emperor Alexios III retreats and overnight flees
1203 *18 July*	Crusaders enter the city and their ally, Prince Alexios is crowned Emperor Alexios IV
1203 *Autumn*	Crusaders help Emperor Alexios IV consolidate his lands around Constantinople
1203 *Winter*	Tensions grow between the crusaders and Emperor Alexios IV
1204 *1 January*	Byzantines try to destroy the Venetian fleet using fire ships
1204 *27 January*	Coronation of Emperor Nicholas Kannavos
1204 *27 January*	Coronation of Emperor Alexios V Mourtzouphlos
1204 *8 February*	Murder of Emperor Alexios IV
1204 *March*	'The March Pact': Agreement between the Venetians and the crusaders for the division of spoils should they take Constantinople
1204 *9 April*	First assault on Constantinople – fails
1204 *12/13 April*	Second assault on Constantinople succeeds
1204 *13–17 April*	The Sack of Constantinople
1204 *9 May*	Election of Count Baldwin of Flanders as the first Latin Emperor of Constantinople
1205 *14 April*	Disappearance of Baldwin at the Battle of Adrianople Death of Doge Enrico
1205 *May*	Dandolo in Constantinople

Genealogies of the rulers of Jerusalem and Antioch

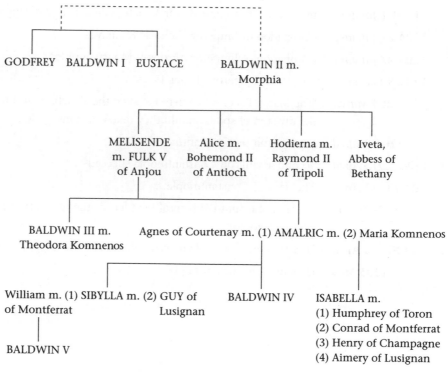

GODFREY   BALDWIN I   EUSTACE

BALDWIN II m.
Morphia

MELISENDE
m. FULK V
of Anjou

Alice m.
Bohemond II
of Antioch

Hodierna m.
Raymond II
of Tripoli

Iveta,
Abbess of
Bethany

BALDWIN III m.
Theodora Komnenos

Agnes of Courtenay m. (1) AMALRIC m. (2) Maria Komnenos

William m. (1) SIBYLLA m. (2) GUY of
of Montferrat   Lusignan

BALDWIN IV

ISABELLA m.
(1) Humphrey of Toron
(2) Conrad of Montferrat
(3) Henry of Champagne
(4) Aimery of Lusignan

BALDWIN V

Royal house of Jerusalem (simplified)

Rulers of the Principality of Antioch (simplified)

SELJUKS OF
RUM

CILICIA

Tarsus

Adana

Anazarba

COUNTY
OF
EDESSA

Edessa

Pyramus

Baghras

Antioch

Harim

Aleppo

Euphrates

PRINCIPALITY OF ANTIOCH

Orontes

Latakia

Jabala

Margat

Shaizar

Hama

CYPRUS

Tartus

Homs

Krak des Chevaliers

COUNTY OF TRIPOLI

Tripoli

Jubayl

MEDITERRANEAN
SEA

Beirut

Sidon

Damascus

Banyas

Tyre

Safad

Acre

Hattin

LAKE TIBERIAS

Tiberias

Caesarea

Nazareth

Belvoir

Arsuf

Nablus

Jaffa

Lydda

Ramla

Jerusalem

Jericho

Ibelin

Bethany

KINGDOM OF JERUSALEM

Ascalon

Bethlehem

Gaza

Darum

Hebron

DEAD SEA

Blanchegarde

Kerak

0		80		160 km

0		50		100 miles

Montreal

Map 1 The Eastern Mediterranean

1

Introduction

WHY STUDY THE CRUSADES?

The study of the history of the crusades is flourishing in schools and universities, in academic research (in Europe, the Middle East and North America); it is also a subject that attracts considerable interest from the general public. In part this is a consequence of the enduring fascination fostered by such a dramatic and important aspect of the histories of western Europe and the Middle East, of Christianity and Islam and, to a lesser extent, Christianity and Judaism. The sense of adventure in trying to conquer and hold a distant and unknown land still exerts a powerful pull on the imagination of the modern West; the perceived glamour of men such as Richard the Lionheart and Saladin has great allure too. Alongside this, there is, to some modern western eyes at least, curiosity and confusion as to how and why people could fight and kill in the name of God.

There is also the historical legacy of the crusades – a legacy of brutality and fanaticism that has cast a deep shadow across relations between Christianity and Islam, Christianity and Judaism, and amongst Christians themselves. From the sixteenth century onwards, first the Protestant Church and then an increasingly secular European society began to relegate the crusades to a distant and exotic escapade carried out by barbaric and foolhardy knights. During the nineteenth century, however, the crusades found new resonance. The colonial empires of Europe spread into North Africa and the Near East, reviving memories of times gone by while the emergence of nationalism as a powerful force during this period meant that people looked back positively to past successes and times of unity (such as the First Crusade). In the world of literature the phenomenal international success of historical writers such as Sir Walter Scott, author of *Ivanhoe* (1819) and *The Talisman* (1825) did much to spawn artistic and musical material that glorified the age of chivalry, including the crusades. World War I proved a fertile ground for combatants on all sides to depict their struggle as a righteous fight against the devil and to use crusading language and imagery. During the 1930s bishops who supported General Franco's Nationalist forces invoked divine help and Franco described himself as a crusader. The unprecedented horrors of World War II and the nuclear age largely expunged any sense of romanticism in warfare and in the West the ideas and imagery of the crusade have largely faded from an explicitly military context. One grim exception to this was the appalling massacre perpetrated by the Norwegian extremist, Anders Brevnik, in 2011 whose manifesto invoked a crusading message in his hatred of Muslims.

Recent academic scholarship has formulated a more sophisticated picture of the crusades as a complex and central element in the history of medieval Europe. In discovering how this legacy has endured though the centuries, it is evident that the origins and meaning of the word have become obscured. From the nineteenth century the term 'crusade' has also been used in a non-military context in western society such as by the Women's Temperance Movement of 1873 in Ohio, or participants in the Jarrow March who bore the banner 'Jarrow Crusade' in 1936. Today it has become casualised and secularised. It is used readily in everyday life: a crusade to cut hospital waiting lists, a crusade for fair play in sport. Given the fact that, ultimately, the crusades to the Holy Land collapsed, the continued deployment of the word in such ways shows how far removed it has become from historical reality. Why do people want to identify with something that failed? In its contemporary, generic meaning, therefore, people are embracing a sense of moral right, and/or a quest for justice. Such sentiments have their roots in the medieval usage and this broadly positive meaning explains why the word still has such currency.

In the world of contemporary Islam, however, the crusades have retained a much sharper and more vivid presence, in large part because the outline of events in the medieval period have a number of pertinent parallels to the present. In 1099 the armies of the First Crusade (representing the Catholic Church of western Europe) captured Jerusalem and were popularly reported as wading ankle-deep in the blood of their slain Muslim foes; in the wake of this conquest the Crusader States were formed and Christian rule was established in the Levant. By 1187 Saladin had drawn together the Muslims of the Eastern Mediterranean region under the banner of the *jihad*, or holy war. The forces of Islam retook the city of Jerusalem and relegated the Christians to a strip of land on the Mediterranean coast until their eventual expulsion in 1291. For the Muslim world of modern times the ingredients seem familiar: violent western incursions, slaughter and oppression of the faithful and the loss of the holy city of Jerusalem. These are among the reasons why the crusade still has such a high profile in the Muslim Middle East. Emerging scholarship shows that, contrary to previous claims by historians, the memory of the crusades and the standing of Saladin as a man of admirable virtues, had not (as previously thought) disappeared from view but remained clearly perceptible down the centuries and grew stronger once the western Europeans began to invade the region with Napoleon's attempted conquest of Egypt in 1798.

At the start of the twentieth century, as the Arab Near East began to shake off the shackles of western imperialism, their predecessors' struggles against the crusaders seemed especially relevant and this is a perception that has continued. Even more significantly, Saladin provided a redily available role model: a devout Muslim who had succeeded in driving out the invaders. Such a figure has obvious attractions in the modern age and contemporary political leaders have often sought to appropriate his legacy. In the late 1950s President Nasser of Egypt clashed with the British and French over the Suez Canal. He also created the United Arab Republic (1959–61) which joined Syria and Egypt together – just as Saladin had done in the twelfth century. Nasser frequently invoked the sultan in his struggles against the West and drew parallels between the defeats of the crusaders and his actions in Suez and his hopes for the recovery of Jerusalem. President Saddam Hussein of Iraq also compared himself to Saladin, not least because they were both born in Takrit in northern Iraq. A mural depicting Saddam leading his Iraqi tanks into battle against the West alongside Saladin who rode at the head of his mounted warriors conveyed the appropriate message. Similar representations appeared on more prosaic and mass-produced items, such as bathmats, showing the wide circulation of such an image. Saddam, therefore, identified himself as someone who, like Saladin, would defeat the westerners and drive them from the Middle East. In 1992, the late President Hafiz Asad of Syria commissioned a large equestrian statue of Saladin in Damascus. The emir is shown riding to victory, guarded by Muslim holy men as defeated crusaders slump behind his horse. Placed just outside the old citadel of Damascus, Saladin is, of course, symbolically protecting the city, while the West bows to him.

A further, important parallel with the age of the crusades exists for Muslim militants in the form of the state of Israel. Although the First (and subsequent) crusades were responsible for numerous atrocities against the Jews of Jerusalem (in 1099) and in western Europe (1096, 1147, 1190), the close identification of Israel with the USA, and, in the eyes of some, as an enemy of Palestine and occupier of the holy city, means a perception that the crusader kingdom of Jerusalem was a forerunner of the modern Israeli state. Some Muslim polemicists argue that the creation of Israel was the West's revenge for the failure of the crusades and they point out that the Christians were eventually expelled from the Levant: inevitably, therefore, they argue that the Jews will suffer the same fate. The militant Islamic groups in the Middle East, Hamas and Hizbollah, both invoke the struggle between the crusaders and *jihad* in their efforts to liberate Palestine.

1. Statue of Saladin outside the citadel of Damascus

Undoubtedly the most high-profile use of the word 'crusade' in recent times was when, after the terrible attacks of 11 September 2001, President George W. Bush stated that 'this crusade . . . this war on terror is going to take a while'. Once the implications of the word were revealed to him, Bush tried to distance himself from the comment but it was too late. In calling the fight against bin Laden a crusade he had created the historical parallel the Islamist leader had long claimed existed and offered an opportunity to tap into the emotional tinderbox of centuries of conflict: 'So, Bush has declared in his own words: "crusader attack." The odd thing about this is that he has taken the words right out of our mouth . . . So the world today is split into two parts, as Bush said: either you are with us or you are with terrorism. Either you are with the crusade or you are with Islam. Bush's image of him today is of him being in the front of the line, yelling and carrying his big cross.' Just to complete the circle, the head of the CIA unit charged with hunting bin Laden described him as: 'an Islamic hero, as the faith's ideal type, and almost as a modern-day Saladin' (Phillips, 2009: 348).

THE PURPOSE OF THIS BOOK

This book is concerned to move back from the modern constructs and possible misconceptions of the crusades to explore the origins and development of the idea in its historical context. It will outline the key events and issues in the history of the crusades to the Holy Land down to the end of the Fourth Crusade. The work sets out to show the roots of the First Crusade; to consider the various motives of the First Crusaders; to reveal the challenges of conquest and settlement in the Levant; to indicate the complexities of dealings among the Frankish settlers and also their relations with the indigenous people of the Near East, as well as contact with their co-religionists in western Europe. It will also assess the impact of the crusades in the Eastern Mediterranean and follow the Muslim response to the crusades through the rise of the *jihad*. The mixture of narrative and thematic chapters is designed to analyse and tell the story of events, but also to provide an insight into new areas of research and to synthesise them into a mainstream textbook. The Documents have been chosen from as wide a range of sources as possible with material from the Latin West and the Frankish East, as well as Muslim, Byzantine and Jewish writers. Narratives, official documents and letters, charters, poetry, songs and art are all represented. It is hoped that this selection will, in some small way, demonstrate the breadth of evidence available to the historian and also help to bring this intriguing subject to life.

HISTORIOGRAPHY AND DEFINITION

The historiography of the crusades continues to develop rapidly, both in terms of approach and interpretation. The first recognisably modern analysis of the crusades was produced in the early nineteenth century by the Frenchman Joseph-François Michaud who wrote (1811–22) a multi-volume narrative based on extensive, if uncritical, use of many original texts and without the judgemental tone of Protestant or Enlightenment authors. Michaud's account was immensely popular being revised and reprinted many times, widely translated and also produced in a schools' edition. He portrayed the crusades as a glorious episode of French history, fighting, as Tyerman neatly summarises, 'against the barbarism of Islam, [demonstrating] the superiority of western culture and vindicating conservative religious and political values . . . the idea of the crusades as a witness to western supremacy reflected and informed the creation of the colonial mentality in France' (Tyerman, 2011: 108–9).

The aftermath of World War I and the creation of the French mandates in Syria and Lebanon provoked further comparisons with the past and scholars, such as René Grousset in his three-volume history, published 1934–36, portrayed the Frankish East as a forerunner of French colonial enterprise. The next phase of scholarship, represented, for example, by the multi-volume history edited by Kenneth Setton (Setton, 1969–89), was strongly grounded in detailed narrative and looked towards economic motives for the crusades, ignoring much of the evidence for contemporary religiosity. The most important work to come out of this period was Sir Steven Runciman's *A History of the Crusades*, 3 volumes (Runciman, 1951–54), which is still in print today and has exerted an enormous influence over the subject and the image of the crusades ever since. Runciman's beautifully written work does much to capture the excitement of the crusades, but as well as the issues just noted in Setton's work, it has a further, significant flaw. The author was, first and foremost, a historian of the Byzantine Empire and for him, the sack of his beloved city of Constantinople by the Fourth Crusade in 1204 was the ultimate act of betrayal by a bloodthirsty and misguided movement. The contrast with the sophistication of Byzantium and Islam could not have been plainer and the crusaders were seen as ignorant thugs. The violence of the crusading age cannot, and should not, be denied, although any comments about the medieval age being especially brutal in comparison to the modern world can, after the briefest of reflections on present day conflicts, be set aside. Warfare in the twelfth century must be seen in the context of western European society of the time and through proper examination of contemporary motives and values. Furthermore, medieval Byzantium and Islam were hardly immune from perpetrating acts of savagery on their own and other peoples too. Without the constricting judgement imposed by Runciman, we can see that a complex, and at times innovative, society emerged in the Levant and crusading itself was an adaptable and sophisticated concept that developed over both time and space.

The next body of crusading history is represented by the work of Jean Richard (1979), Joshua Prawer (1980), Jonathan Riley-Smith (1973) and Hans Eberhard Mayer (1988), and has done much to illuminate the judicial, constitutional and structural form of the institutions of the Latin East and is now absorbed into many mainstream texts.

Since the early 1980s several significant developments have emerged in crusading studies. The first and most important is a conceptual one: previously, 'true' crusading had tended to be regarded as taking place only in the Eastern Mediterranean and was something that effectively finished in 1291 with the fall of Acre and the end of the Catholic hold on the Levant. In other words, the expeditions to the Baltic, the reconquest of Spain, the attacks on Albigensian heretics in southern France, the wars against political opponents of the papacy, expeditions against the Ottoman Turks in the fifteenth century and even the Spanish Armada against Protestant England were distortions of the original idea and were to be treated as separate species. Based on an analysis of the temporal and spiritual privileges (the Indulgence) granted by the papacy, and on a closer examination of contemporary assessments of this issue, crusade historians now accept a much broader (pluralist) and more flexible definition of the subject to encompass these other theatres of war as equals to the crusade to the Holy Land in all but prestige. A workable definition of a crusade is thus: 'An expedition authorised by the pope on Christ's behalf, the leading participants in which took vows and consequently wore crosses and enjoyed the privileges of protection at home and the Indulgence, which, when the campaign was not destined for the East, was equated with that granted to crusaders to the Holy Land' (Riley-Smith, 2009: 5). This present book is primarily concerned with crusade and settlement in the Levant down to 1204, and therefore the distinction between expeditions to the Latin East and elsewhere does not perhaps seem immediately relevant. But, this concept is crucial in understanding the broader development of crusading (particularly in the thirteenth century and beyond) and does have significant connections with several episodes concerning crusades to the Eastern Mediterranean, connections which, by their very existence, serve to underline the validity of the pluralist understanding of the subject.

Christopher Tyerman, in his *The Invention of the Crusades* (Tyerman, 1998), questioned the whole development of crusading during the twelfth century. He argued that because the distinctive institutions and definitions of the crusade were not in place until the legislative programme initiated by Pope Innocent III (1198–1216), the notion of 'crusade' in the twelfth century is a construct of modern historians. He claims that the word *crucignatus* does not appear until the later decades of the twelfth century, although Vertannes notes that it was used by Peter the Deacon at the abbey of Monte Cassino in the 1130s or 1140s (Vertannes, 2013). This view has found little favour for a number of reasons, however. First, simply because a movement lacks formal and defined institutions does not mean that contemporaries failed to understand what was happening. The distinction between a pilgrim and a crusader that historians sometimes struggle with was evident enough to those contemporaries who wrote pilgrim guides to the religious sites of the Holy Land or answered a papal appeal to fight the infidel in the Levant. It is true that in some cases the evidence is hazy: the practice whereby a western noble would fight in defence of the Holy Land for a year (see below, p. 101) was not linked to a call for a crusade, but more to a sense of Christian honour and duty – although the spiritual rewards for such an act are not specified in any surviving material. By the time of the Second Crusade (1145–49), however, the picture was clearer and, as the relevant chapter shows, this expedition confirms crusading to be a geographically flexible concept, but with the key ideas, privileges and rewards plainly defined to all. When Pope Eugenius III (1145–53) or Pope Alexander III (1159–81) put out crusade appeals to the Holy Land (five separate calls in the latter's case), their audiences knew what they were committing themselves to and the range of privileges and benefits that they would receive: Eugenius and Alexander were working through an idea with consistency and logic. Furthermore, their care in guarding the preaching of such expeditions reveals papal concern over the concept of crusading and an understanding of what lay inside and outside its boundaries. Tyerman also neglects two further points. First, crusading in the Iberian peninsula. The series of privileges and bulls issued here (see below, pp. 87, 203–4) indicates again the development and regulation of the idea from the time of the First Crusade. Furthermore, he ignores the foundation of the military orders – institutions inexorably linked to crusading whose growth again indicates a more rapid maturation than Tyerman allows.

The second notable advance in crusading studies over recent years is a concern with the spiritual motivation of crusaders and the roots of this in the society of eleventh-century Europe. The use of charter evidence (see below) by Jonathan Riley-Smith (1997) and Marcus Bull (1993a) has revealed the importance of connections between the local nobility and ecclesiastical institutions and has demonstrated a strong religious drive among the secular knights of the West. The role of relics and pilgrimage formed a central and ongoing aspect of this contact between the Holy Land and Europe during the crusader period. The use of charter evidence has also shown the existence of family networks of crusaders and the importance of crusading traditions in certain families as shown between the First and the Second Crusaders by Phillips (2007). Paul (2012) took this a step further in tracing how these traditions were maintained through literature and objects to form a collective memory of the crusades and to contribute to dynastic identities and the culture of the contemporary nobility.

Such was the astonishing success of the First Crusade that contemporaries across the Latin West were prompted to record this seemingly miraculous event on a scale unseen for other episodes in the medieval period. Historians are now reappraising these texts, in part to produce up-to-date editions of them (which in turn often reveal more manuscript copies than hitherto known), but also to place them in a proper cultural context in terms of their composition, transmission and reception. More importantly, this work will show how the successive narrative accounts could frame and impact upon memories of the crusade (Bull and Kempf, 2014).

Further important developments are emerging from exciting archaeological work, principally in Israel. The discovery and analysis of human skeletons at the castle of Jacob's Ford (Vadim Jacob) have added real value to our understanding of warfare at the time, while excavations at the same site have also enabled an unparalleled insight to the process of medieval castle-building. Other work at, for example, Acre, Blanchegarde and Petra (in Jordan) has illuminated various aspects of Frankish rule in the Levant too; similarly, Ellenblum's work on rural settlement has transformed our picture of the Franks' relations with the indigenous population, particularly the Eastern Christians (Ellenblum, 1998, 2007; Boas, 1999, 2001; Mitchell et al., 2006).

Finally, there is the Islamic Near East. Long-obscured to western crusade historians by the barrier of language, the landmark work of Carole Hillenbrand (Hillenbrand, 1999), along with an increasing number of key narrative texts in translation (notably those by Richards, 2001 and Cobb 2008) are changing this. Scholars such as Cobb (2005), Talmon-Heller (2007), Mourad and Lindsay (2013) and Latiff (2013) have taken this work beyond narratives and looked at poetry, at didactic texts, collections of literature extolling the merits of Jerusalem, *hadith* that preserved the sayings of the Prophet pertaining to *jihad*; and from such material we are beginning to assemble a much fuller and clearer appreciation of the impact of the crusades in the Eastern Mediterranean.

SOURCES

There survives a wide range of evidence to reconstruct the history of the crusades and the Latin East. The historical record is, however, uneven, with some events such as the First Crusade attracting considerable attention, while others, such as the history of Frankish settlement or the unsuccessful Second Crusade, are harder to trace. Quite naturally, all writers and record-keepers had their own agendas and were subject to contemporary influences and biases when compiling their work. This can both help and hinder our studies and, where relevant, such traits will be indicated. Alongside written material there remains artistic and archaeological evidence that can add much to our understanding of the period.

Given the geographical area touched by the crusades, the origins of available source material are indeed broad. The Documents here include work by contemporary writers from the Latin East, western Europe, and the Muslim, Byzantine and Jewish worlds. A brief outline of the career of the most important of these writers is included in the Who's Who section or via bibliographical references as appropriate. In basic terms, the majority of writers from the Latin world were churchmen because literacy was largely confined to the clergy. Naturally enough, this can sometimes result in a particularly strong theological slant to their analyses, and where possible, alternative or complimentary forms of evidence, such as crusaders' letters (Barber and Bate, 2010), or the narrative of the layman Caffaro of Genoa (Hall and Phillips, 2013), are brought into play to provide another perspective. In conjunction with narrative texts there is documentary evidence in the form of charters and official documents. Charters, which usually survive from ecclesiastical institutions, are often deeds of land transactions, in the form of mortgages or agreements, and in these cases designed to raise funds for expeditions to the Levant. To us, land deeds of today are dry and formulaic documents, but in the eleventh and twelfth centuries they had not been subjected to the strict conventions of bureaucrats and some included lengthy explanatory passages which (in those concerned with the crusade) outline the donor's motives for taking the cross and his hopes, fears and aspirations. These documents, which are often precisely dated and survive in tens of thousands, allow us an insight into the financing and motivation of crusaders and have helped to deepen our understanding beyond the narratives into contemporary ideas and actions. For a good introduction to the subject see Bull (1997). Official documents can survive in the form of papal calls for the crusade and also legal arrangements concerning diplomatic or feudal obligations. Letters written by important individuals may also remain, either in collections or incorporated into narratives. One further form of evidence worth noting is that of songs, often written by laymen, which provide an important insight into the concerns and ideas of secular society.

CONTEXT

Many of the elements that came together to form the idea of the crusade were familiar aspects of European society in the late eleventh and early twelfth centuries. To understand the origins of the First Crusade it is useful to have a brief, schematic overview of western Europe at this period and to highlight those points that bear upon the origins of the crusade (see also Map 2).

In many respects this was a very different world from our own. It was highly localised with poor roads and communications networks. Today we watch international conflicts unfold live on the internet. Back in the age of the crusades news of events in Jerusalem probably took a *minimum* of ten weeks to reach northern Europe: up to two months of sea travel to Genoa, Venice or Pisa (although ports were closed between October and February because of the dangerous winter seas), and then weeks of hard riding through Italy and France on old Roman roads. Modern-day leaders contact their enemies and confidants by the internet and they can respond to events almost immediately. A medieval leader had to dispatch messages by horse – another slow and cumbersome process – and the recipient would then have to ride back or send a messenger in reply.

In some respects, the physical landscape would appear different from that of today; for example, there was far more woodland than now. This period saw significant population growth and, while agricultural techniques were improving, famines were frequent and devastating (one every seven years in twelfth-century Flanders, for example). The vast majority of the population lived in the countryside; urban centres were relatively few and in northern Europe particularly, they were small and underdeveloped; Paris is estimated

Map 2 Europe at the Time of the First Crusade

as having a population of *c*. 20,000 at the end of the eleventh century, today it is at least 2.3 million. The intellectual landscape was different too. Monastic writers and other churchmen produced highly sophisticated works of theology and history and the study of science, law, logic and government would all take off rapidly in the twelfth century. We take the ability to read and write for granted, but these skills were rare at the time of the First Crusade. Education was limited to the monasteries and the elite households, although by the middle of the twelfth century cathedral schools such as Laon in northern France were flourishing and the Italian cities of Bologna and Salerno were centres of learning in law and medicine respectively. While literacy was very limited in *c*. 1100, it would expand rapidly over the next century and written record-keeping and the formal offices of Church and State (such as chanceries) also emerged strongly over this time. A rise in trade – in part encouraged by the opening of the Eastern Mediterranean through the crusades – further stimulated literacy and numeracy with bills of exchange and accounting records becoming ever more essential.

In a society dominated by violence and religion the role of women was often limited to that of a wife and child-bearer. Women could not carry arms in battle and church teaching on the sins of Eve meant that women were viewed as a prime cause of sin and temptation in all walks of life – even in a religious vocation far fewer openings were available for female spirituality than for that of men. While a select few women could have great standing as carriers of a royal blood-line (such as Melisende of Jerusalem), a lack of legal status and education also prevented women from holding power outside the home. That said, women did play an important part in crusading, especially as regents during their husband's absences, as well as taking on many different roles, across all levels of society, during campaigns.

Aside from the overarching bond of Christian faith, loyalties at the time of the First Crusade were much more localised than today. Modern European societies revolve around nation states, but medieval allegiances tended to be with one's lord and the local saint and church, rather than with a king or emperor, or the papacy in Rome. During the twelfth century this did start to change with a growth and consolidation of central power apparent in both the secular and ecclesiastical spheres. In consequence of this, many people began to look towards such figures for direction, for protection and for justice, thereby further increasing their leaders' authority.

Marcus Bull has pinpointed two prominent aspects of eleventh-century society and indicates their crucial influence on the attraction of Pope Urban's appeal of 1095 (Bull, 1995). First, the violence so endemic in the medieval West. The weakness of central authorities at this time meant that renegade castellans and robber bands could ravage an area and cause chaos. Localised warfare was a perpetual danger, so much so that the Church attempted to control it through the Truce of God movements which, for a certain period, bound warring parties to keep the peace as a way of trying to instill some sense of order. If the vows were disregarded, then knights working on behalf of the Church would punish the oath-breakers with force. Second, and linked to this culture of violence, was the importance of religion. Western Europe in the twenty-first century is a fairly secular society and it is often difficult to grasp the centrality of religious belief to medieval men and women. God's favour dictated much of their lives and explained many events, both natural and man-made. Miracles, that to us might seem doubtful, were often accepted as manifestations of the divine. For example, at the Battle of Antioch in 1098, 'There also appeared from the mountains a countless host of men on white horses, whose banners were all white. When our men saw this they did not understand what was happening or who these men might be, until they realised that this was the succour sent by Christ and that the leaders were St George, St Mercurius and St Demetrius. This is quite true for many of our men saw it' (*Gesta Francorum*, tr. Hill, 1962: 69). The matter-of-fact comment at the end of this passage indicates the implicit acceptance of God's hand in this. Medieval people should not, however, be seen as simple or credulous because their belief-systems accommodated concepts and values to which we no longer hold. It is not necessary for us to accept their viewpoint, but it is essential that we recognise it and appreciate its impact upon their lives and actions: only when this is understood can we begin to comprehend episodes such as the crusades. As a coda to this issue we should note that during the twelfth century ecclesiastical authorities kept an ever closer eye on claims of the miraculous and showed a real determination to safeguard orthodoxy. In fact, to many contemporaries, Peter Bartholomew's failure to survive his trial by ordeal after the discovery of the Holy Lance was a sign of fraud (see pp. 29–30 for the background to this case).

A prime concern of medieval man was to avoid the terrors of the afterlife – eternal damnation in the torments of hell so vividly depicted in the frescoes and sculptures that adorned every church and survive today in their most sophisticated and fearsome form at Autun and Conques in France. Religious observance, led by the monastic empire of Cluny, was growing rapidly. The lay nobility formed close ties to a particular institution and in their quest for salvation often provided increasing levels of financial support for the local church. Pilgrimage was also extremely popular as people visited saints' shrines in search of help, protection, cures and forgiveness. The cult of saints was a prominent aspect of religious life. Saints were formerly humans, who had led exemplary lives (virgins, martyrs) and were almost certainly in Heaven. They were used by medieval people as intercessors to God – in other words, as intermediaries who, if properly approached and venerated (not worshipped, or else the sin of idolatry was committed), might secure an

2. The Entry into Hell, Abbey Church of St Foy, Conques

individual, a family or a community divine favour. Saints were tangible evidence of the divine and were present in the form of relics, which were fragments of their bodies, or objects associated with their lives, placed in highly decorated crosses or caskets (known as reliquaries) and kept in churches. The gathering of relics was especially valued and the crusades meant that many more items connected with the life of Christ and the Apostles could be brought back from the Holy Land (see pp. 34, 142–3).

The need to atone for one's sins – sins that were committed in thoughts and deeds of avarice, greed, envy, lust and violence – was a message hammered home to Christians. The ability of the Church to communicate this message was given a powerful stimulus by the rise of the Reform Papacy. By the middle of the eleventh century the papacy had become a localised and inward-looking institution concerned with politics in Rome, rather than the leadership of the Catholic Church. In 1046, however, Henry III of Germany removed the three rival candidates for the see of St Peter and installed the first of a series of reform-minded outsiders who were determined to purify the Church itself and also to offer direction and spiritual advancement to their flock.

A brief tour of Europe reveals the fragmentation of the area and also demonstrates an important trend in the political map. The bulk of the Iberian peninsula had been conquered by Muslims from North Africa in the eighth century, but the Moors, as they were known, were eventually checked. By the middle of the eleventh century, the small Christian kingdoms that had grown up in northern Spain were firmly established and the first stirrings of the *reconquista* (the reconquest) were being felt. Moves to regain Christian lands and to establish control over more territory saw a major advance in 1085 with the success of King Alfonso VI of Léon-Castile at Muslim-held Toledo, and at the time of the First Crusade further progress was anticipated. What we would recognise today as France was, in theory, under the authority of the Capetian King Philip I (1060–1108), but his sphere of influence extended barely 35 kilometres outside Paris and the nobles and castellans in his lands could challenge his authority with relative impunity. Other lords in France held greater areas of land, although, with one exception (see later), they lacked Philip's cachet of being a king – an anointed monarch – and therefore blessed by God. The duke of Aquitaine and the count of Toulouse, for example, controlled substantial territories, but were geographically remote from the Capetians and were also separated by language (the southern French spoke a tongue called Occitan) and culture, with their nexus based around the Pyrenees and the Mediterranean. In the north of France, the counts of Anjou and Champagne were very strong, but it was the dukes of Normandy who, through the conquest of England in 1066, had the greatest prestige and, of course, a royal title. They also had far more money than the Capetians, although in the 1090s their land was divided between Robert Curthose duke of Normandy and William Rufus in England. The counts of Flanders held an important economic and strategic position on the North Sea coast and to the east their lands bordered on the German Empire. This vast dominion, covering Germany, the duchy of Burgundy (in the south-east of modern France) and northern and central Italy (down to just north of Rome), was the most powerful and prestigious territory in Catholic Christendom. The emperor was anointed by the pope and claimed superiority to kings. From the mid-1070s, however, a bitter schism between the papacy and the emperor had broken out (known as the Investiture Controversy) as the two leading powers in the West tried to delineate the extent of their authority in this fast-evolving society. The struggle reached such a pitch that Emperor Henry IV was declared an excommunicate (in other words he had been cast out of the Church by the pope) and hence was unlikely to work with Urban II on the crusade. Furthermore, many of the powerful German nobles who regularly challenged Henry's power were also looking to their own affairs, rather than any external enterprise. The only exception to this concerned their interest in the regions to the east of Germany (the eastern side of modern Germany and Poland), which were inhabited by pagan tribes and, in conjunction with the Church, were subject to the gradual extension of Christian influence. The kingdom of Hungary began the process of conversion early in the eleventh century and missionary work took place further north in Poland and Pomerania. Scandinavia was already largely Christian by this time.

In Italy, the papacy governed a belt of land around Rome, and to the south the Normans ruled their territories in Apulia and Calabria, taken from the Byzantine Empire by the 1060s, along with Sicily, conquered from the Muslims by c. 1090. To the east lay the Byzantine Empire, successor to the Roman Empire and seat of the Orthodox Church. The emperor was a figure of enormous authority within the Byzantine system of government and, unlike the pope, his position was not challenged by churchmen. In 1054, however, as the papacy tried to establish its pre-eminence over the patriarch of Constantinople, a schism was declared and various liturgical and doctrinal differences were highlighted. The schism was still in existence at the time of the First Crusade (and remains to the present day), and would complicate the relationship between the Greeks and the West throughout the age of the crusades. The emperor also had to deal with many enemies on his extensive borders, including the pagan tribes of the Balkans and the Muslims of Asia Minor. In 1071 the Greeks suffered a terrible defeat at the Battle of Manzikert and as a result had lost control over most of the land mass of Asia Minor.

These interlinked ingredients of a rejuvenated papacy, the laymans' need to atone for the consequences of sin, ecclesiastical direction of violence through the Peace of God, and the ties between the lay nobility and the Church were all essential elements in the background to the First Crusade. With the conquests of Iberia, Eastern Europe and southern Italy and Sicily, it is apparent that Catholic Europe was expanding, and while the stimulus for this was largely political, rather than religious, it was a trend that would be another important element in the background to the First Crusade. Taken together, the context provided by this outline of the social, political and economic issues of the day forms the setting for Pope Urban to introduce a startling innovation to a layman's chances of attaining salvation during his historic speech at the Council of Clermont on 27 November 1095.

2

The First Crusade

O n 27 November 1095, at the end of a great church council at
Clermont in central France, Pope Urban II launched the First
Crusade – a call to free the holy city of Jerusalem from the hands of
the Muslims. The response to his appeal was quite remarkable: spectators at
Clermont interrupted his speech with cries of 'God wills it!' and hundreds
begged to join the expedition. News of the crusade spread rapidly through
Christian Europe; Fulcher of Chartres, a participant in the expedition, wrote
that people 'of any and every occupation' took the cross. Once the crusaders
had assembled he commented: 'whoever heard of such a mixture of languages
in one army, since there were Franciens, Flemings, Frisians, Gauls, Allobroges
[Savoyards], Lotharingians, Allemani [Swabians], Bavarians, Normans, English-
men, Scots, Aquitanians, Italians, Dacians [Danes], Apulians, Iberians,
Bretons, Greeks and Armenians' (Fulcher of Chartres, tr. Murray, 2011: 107).
Representatives of the last two groups probably joined the expedition *en
route*, but the remainder had been attracted by Urban's initial call to arms.
The crusade therefore appealed to people from almost every level of society
right across Christian Europe.

THE APPEAL OF THE FIRST CRUSADE

Why had Urban's message provoked such a reaction? The pope had managed
to draw together a number of key concerns and trends in late eleventh-century
society and synthesised them into a single, highly popular idea. As we noted
in the introduction, spiritual issues were a prominent factor governing peoples'
lives at the time of the First Crusade. It was an intensely religious age: the
number of saints' cults was increasing, along with interest in relics and the
observation of feast days. Pilgrimage – both local and international – and
monastic life flourished. Sin was ubiquitous in everyday life, particularly in
the violent society of the late eleventh century and the need for all people –

whether rich or poor, nobles or labourers – to atone for their actions is vital in explaining the level of enthusiasm for the First Crusade. Pope Urban was astute enough to pull together these familiar points: contemporary religious zeal, the popularity of pilgrimage, concern for the afterlife and the problem of knightly violence, to form the core of the idea of the crusade. He also offered something new, innovative and highly attractive. A decree from the Council of Clermont records the essence of his message: 'Whoever for devotion alone, not to gain honour or money, goes to Jerusalem to liberate the Church of God can substitute this journey for all penance' (Riley-Smith and Riley-Smith, 1981: 37).

In other words, in return for fighting God's enemies on earth and completing the pilgrimage to Jerusalem, a person would receive a spiritual reward of unprecedented magnitude. For properly confessed sins, these actions would constitute a sufficient act of penance to wipe away the consequences of those crimes. Urban laid great emphasis on crusading as a penitential act – and this concept would always remain at the heart of the idea; it can be seen in the appeals for the Second and Third Crusades (see Documents 11, 20), and in other crusade writing such as the Second Crusade narrative, *The Conquest of Lisbon* (tr. David, 2001). What the Indulgence (as Urban's promise is technically known) meant was that the average layman had opened to him a new way of attaining salvation when previously the only route to such a reward was by joining a monastery (see Document 1 ii). With the lay nobility of France so concerned for their spiritual welfare it was an opportunity not to miss. Pope Urban himself came from a French noble family and he saw how the crusade fitted the skills and aspirations of the knightly classes: as fighting men they were being presented with a set of circumstances in which they could carry on doing what they did best, yet still receive a spiritual benefit. From Urban's perspective there was a further bonus in that they would direct their energies against the infidel, rather than the Church and people of France.

Before considering the planning and progress of the crusade, two important questions need to be answered. First, how could the pope, as a churchman, justify violence, and second, what was the actual aim of the crusade?

Recent events provided some precedents for the justification of violence and papal direction of military forces. Pope Leo IX had fought the Normans of southern Italy in 1053 and in 1074–75 Pope Gregory VII tried to summon the military classes from both sides of the Alps. He wanted knights to help protect the papacy from the Normans in southern Italy, to go to Constantinople and assist the Christians against the Muslims, and even to carry on to liberate Jerusalem. Those who died in these campaigns would be considered martyrs. These plans achieved very little and the elements of a vow, pilgrimage, the indulgence, and protection privileges were absent; that said, Gregory's ambitious plans form a noteworthy backdrop to the ideas of Urban II.

In theoretical terms, the main justification for the practice of war came through reference to authoritative texts. By using the writings of Saint Augustine of Hippo (354–430) it was possible to construct a case whereby Christian violence could be commanded by God through his representative on earth – the pope – and if it was performed in the right circumstances (a just cause) and with the right intent (proper motivation) it was an act of Christian love. Part of this just cause was Urban's call for a war of Christian liberation. Liberation was an idea very much in vogue at this time. The Reform Church was trying to free itself from the control of secular authorities in the struggle known as the Investiture Contest. Also, as we saw earlier, Sicily and parts of the Iberian peninsula were captured by Latin Christians (Catholics) in the latter half of the eleventh century. In 1095, however, Urban was proposing to liberate two things. First, those Christians living in the East who were said to be persecuted by the Muslims of the region (see Document 1 i). It is likely that such reports were greatly exaggerated in the preaching of the expedition, although it was probably necessary to provoke a sense of outrage to prompt people to such a drastic course of action as taking the cross. Regardless of the accuracy of the pope's claims, the idea of aiding the suffering of fellow-Christians certainly helped to attract support. Second, Urban wanted to liberate a place: Jerusalem. The pope argued that it was subject to pagan abominations and he called for his audience to weep for the devastation of the Holy Land (see Document 1 i–iii) and to act. Jerusalem was a site sanctified by Christ, the focal point of the Christian faith and therefore of huge importance to everyone in the West. By making the holy city the goal of the expedition Urban was also, of course, able to give the crusade the character of a pilgrimage because as Christ's burial place the Holy Sepulchre was the ultimate goal for such a journey. There is evidence that the image of Jerusalem as the location of Christ's death and also, in the future, of the Last Judgement, was increasingly familiar to the people of the West through psalms, songs and relics. It was also the target of rising numbers of western pilgrims during the eleventh century; for example, Duke Robert I of Normandy died on his return journey from the Holy Land in 1035, and in 1064–65 c.10,000 Germans, led by bishops and nobles, marched to the East. More contemporary examples could include the pilgrimage of Count Robert I of Flanders in c.1089, or the journey of William, the elder brother of Count Raymond of Saint-Gilles, who died en route to the East in 1093. When Urban spoke of the suffering of pilgrims to the Holy Land he was connecting with a recognisable experience (in terms of the dangers of pilgrimage in general) and an aspiration to reach the East shared by many. He also spoke of the need for vengeance, which was another familiar notion to nobles in the feud-ridden society of the West. Pope Urban's message had to be carefully crafted because of the immense commitment that he was asking of people: to leave their families, friends and homes for a journey of perhaps 3,500 kilometres, at enormous expense, to an unknown land and to fight a fierce and passionate enemy. The effectiveness with which he touched upon so many ideas and values of importance to the people of the Latin West is evinced by the scale of the response to his appeal.

An undeniably powerful spur to Pope Urban's actions came from another quarter. In March 1095 messengers from Emperor Alexios I Komnenos, the Byzantine emperor (1081–1118), arrived at the Council of Piacenza to request military help. The significance of this in shaping Urban's thinking has been much debated by historians. In the 1930s the German Carl Erdmann argued that Urban used the lure of Jerusalem to attract support for an expedition that he intended primarily to assist the Greeks. In doing so the pope also hoped to facilitate closer relations with the Orthodox Church following the schism of 1054. Frankopan (2012) has recently re-examined the role of the Greeks in the origins of the First Crusade and shows that Urban and Alexios had been on positive terms for several years prior to the Council of Piacenza. Thus in 1091, for example, the pope sent troops to help the emperor resist an invasion from north of the Danube by the Pecheneg steppe nomads, as well as encouraging dialogue between the papacy and the Orthodox on disputed ecclesiastical matters. Both men were under considerable pressure – Urban via the Investiture Contest and Alexios from various political rivals. More seriously, as Frankopan rightly emphasises, there was a resurgent threat from the Turks; in 1091, for example, Nicomedia, located only 50 miles from Constantinople, was lost. By 1095, therefore, Alexios really did need help and he made a fresh call for military support, probably envisaging a response numbering a few hundred knights. Alexios was also aware of the importance of Jerusalem in the West and thus he elided the danger to Constantinople with the condition of the holy city which, as noted above, was a point Erdmann claimed Pope Urban duly repeated.

While it seems clear that there was far greater pressure on Alexios than many historians have allowed, the idea that Urban's top priority was to help the Greeks is hard to sustain. While he made some reference to the situation of the 'Eastern Christians', he made stronger and clearer appeals to recover Jerusalem, 'the navel of the world' and especially, Christ's tomb, the Holy Sepulchre. This message was repeated in his letter to Flanders, written within a month of Clermont (see Document 2 i). Erdmann suggested that when the pope asked people to liberate the Eastern Church he meant Byzantium, rather than Jerusalem. Since the 1980s, however, historians such as Riley-Smith (Riley-Smith, 1986, 1997) and Bull (Bull, 1993a, 1997) have used a further source of evidence, namely charters – documents which record the crusaders' sale or mortgage of lands or rights – to demonstrate conclusively that the participants considered that they were going to liberate Jerusalem (see Document 3). In addition, the anonymous eye-witness account of the *Gesta Francorum* includes numerous references to 'the journey to the Holy Sepulchre', and relates Bohemond of Taranto's command to 'charge at top speed, like a brave man, and fight valiantly for God and the Holy Sepulchre' (*Gesta Francorum*, tr. Hill, 1962: 36–37). The holy city was such a potent image that the pope could not seriously have used it as a decoy to cover a campaign designed solely to help the Greeks and to facilitate a union with the Orthodox Church. It should not be denied that Urban would have welcomed both of these things as a consequence of the crusade, but they should be seen only as secondary aims. It was the ideas of liberating the Christians of the Levant and the city of Jerusalem that stirred the hearts and minds of those who planned the expedition and those who took the cross.

It will never be possible to ascertain the precise motives of individual crusaders and, while the bulk of the evidence suggests a strong religious drive, other, more secular aspirations cannot be ignored. In spite of Urban's call for the crusaders to proceed for 'devotion alone', even the pope must have had some awareness of the need for a group of men to settle in the Holy Land after it was conquered. Clearly, this would be a material advantage, although one might argue that the defence of Christ's patrimony had a prominent spiritual aspect too. The inducement of land and profit was even held out in one account of Urban's speech (see Document 1 i) and this broad principle must have inspired some crusaders – the determination of Bohemond of Taranto to set up the principality of Antioch is the most obvious example of this. There was also a need for money to offset the cost of the crusade and to pay for expenses incurred *en route*. An expedition of this duration was cripplingly expensive and had, what in modern terms we would describe as huge running costs. The *Gesta Francorum* caught this sentiment perfectly: 'We passed a secret message down our line, praising God and saying, "Stand fast all together, trusting in Christ and in the victory of the Holy Cross. Today, please God, you will all gain much booty" . . .' (*Gesta Francorum*, tr. Hill, 1962: 20). The writer saw no contradiction between these aims, and in any case, it was permitted in canon law for soldiers to receive a fair wage and to take booty, but *not* to excess: presumably, this would have constituted greed and would incur God's disfavour. The Old Testament contains several references to both fighting the Lord's wars and obtaining booty. For example, in II Chronicles 14, 9–15, King Asa of Judah defeated the Ethiopians, despoiled their cities and seized a large quantity of moveable goods. A letter from Count Stephen of Blois to his wife, Countess Adela, shows a layman's comfortable assimilation of religiosity and securing wealth. In late March 1098 outside Antioch he wrote: 'know for sure my love, that I now have twice as much gold, silver and other riches as you gave me . . . We fought and won seven battles [with the Turks] with the cooperation of the Lord God (Count Stephen of Blois to Countess Adela, *Letters from the East*, 2010: 22–23).

As we will see below (pp. 24–6) the crusaders came from many different areas, including northern Italy. The emerging trading cities of Genoa, Pisa and Venice conducted considerable business with Islamic lands in the Mediterranean basin and their livelihood was based around the making of money. Yet their cities were also full of churches and their religiosity cannot, therefore, be doubted. The First Crusade was preached in Genoa and the inhabitants responded with enthusiasm, being signed with the cross on their shoulders. We are fortunate to have an eye-witness participant from the 1101 campaign to Caesarea, a man named Caffaro (see 'Who's Who' section), who led a distinguished career as a diplomat and civic consul and who also wrote histories of his own city (the Annals of Genoa) and the crusades (The 'Liberation of the Cities of the East' and 'The Capture of Almeria and Tortosa'). After Caesarea was taken he reported that: 'The [Genoese] first set aside one-fifteenth of the booty in the camp for the galley crews. The remainder they divided among eight thousand men, and gave to each as his share forty-eight *solidi* in the coin of Poitou, and 900 grams of peppercorns, except for the rewards due to the consuls, the sea-captains, and men of quality, which were substantial. They started their journey back to Genoa on the Eve of St. James the Apostle [24 July]; and they arrived back in the month of October, 1101 in triumph and covered in glory. [As] with the first Frankish army against Antioch in 1097, in the African expedition in 1088

3. Caffaro of Genoa dictates his 'Annals of Genoa'.
© Bibliothèque nationale de France

[correctly 1087], in the first expedition to Tortosa [in Spain] in 1093, and when Jerusalem was taken in 1099' (Hall and Phillips, 2013: 56). Thus we see here the motives of profit, of honour for his home city and the advance of the Christian cause all expressed in a comfortable continuum. The last of these includes an interesting spread of campaigns outside the Holy Land and before Urban's appeal of 1095, again indicating a different perspective on conflict with the Muslims from that usually put forward by northern-European ecclesiastical writers.

Other motives for crusaders may have included a wish to escape from legal proceedings in the West, or simple curiosity of the wider world. Finally, as will be seen later, membership of a noble household probably brought about the involvement of some crusaders, although they too may have been motivated by any of the ideas outlined here.

What we should recognise, therefore, is a broad range of possible motives with some having greater hold than others. The particular influence of, say religion or honour, might vary according to rank and social status, according to an individual's personality. Similarly, as Caffaro of Genoa shows us, a crusader's place of origin must have exerted some effect on the broader context of their aims and experiences. In other words, historians should resist the temptation to ascribe a single motive to the campaign and to treat its participants as a single group with a consistent pattern of behaviour.

PREPARATIONS FOR THE CRUSADE

After his speech at Clermont Urban wrote letters to elicit support for the crusade (see Document 2 i) and he toured parts of southern and central France himself to seek recruits for the expedition. The pope carefully scheduled his tour to coincide with local saints' days and other important festivals to ensure as large a gathering as possible. After his sermon, people came forward and were signed with the cross. They also received the pilgrim's staff and scrip (wallet) and were taken under the protection of the Church. This was a voluntary and binding commitment and could usually only be released by fulfilling the vow or death. Incidentally, the 'voluntary' nature of the vow may have been a little tenuous in the case of a noble's household; if their lord decided that he was going on crusade, his entourage, including squires, servants and domestic attendants, would have had little option but to join him, willing or not.

What preparations were required to set out for the Holy Land? First, there was the need to organise the guardianship and running of one's house and property. As Park (2013) shows, the crusade created an opportunity for the wives of participants to exercise power as regents while their husbands were away. In theory, a crusader's lands and family came under the protection of the Church – an innovation in part intended to allay the fears of potential crusaders. Yet a series of legal cases from the early twelfth century reveal that many who went to the East had their territory and rights encroached upon during their absence. The question of finance was another key issue because crusading was a hugely expensive business. To buy chainmail, horses and supplies for oneself would cost a great deal – some estimates suggest over four years' annual income for most knights. People would have had some idea of the resources needed to fight a large-scale military expedition and the recent experience of the Norman Conquest of England (1066), for example, had provided just such an insight. The land market became flooded with crusaders trying to raise money and churches were forced to melt down valuables to provide gold and silver. The issue of cost is one reason why the old cliché of the crusaders being freebooting younger sons in search of land and money is deeply flawed, simply because such men would have been unable to afford to set out in the first instance, other than as hangers-on. Furthermore, charter material reveals family networks (see below) of crusaders comprised of fathers and sons, brothers, uncles, cousins, eldest sons, youngest sons, with no sense at all of a monolithic body of youthful adventurers. The evidence also indicates that the suggested desire for land in fact applied to very few crusaders. The fact that the Frankish States were chronically under-manned throughout their existence demonstrated that relatively few crusaders chose to settle in the Levant.

THE CRUSADE SETS OUT

It is estimated that c. 60,000 people set out from western Europe in the course of 1096. Of these only about 10 per cent were knights; the remainder were servants, pilgrims and hangers-on – women, children, the poor, the old and the sick. These last groups were a major handicap to the main forces because they needed feeding and protecting, but such had been the attraction of Urban's appeal that they still took part. At first the crusade did not move as one great army, but marched in regional contingents which planned to assemble at Constantinople in the spring of 1097. These forces were led by members of the senior nobility and it appears that some family groups were particularly receptive to Urban's call. Riley-Smith has traced the remarkable involvement of the Montlhéry clan (Riley-Smith, 1997: 169–71). One member, Miles of Bray, was accompanied on the First Crusade by his son, Guy, his brother-in-law Walter of St Valéry and two of Walter's sons, his nephew Baldwin (later King Baldwin II of Jerusalem), and two other nephews – Humberge of Le Puiset and Everard III of Le Puiset – all of whom had taken the cross in 1095/96. We should also note that some crusader families had an existing tradition of pilgrimage to the Holy Land which may have formed a further reason for their taking the cross. For example, both the great-grandfather and the grandfather of Adhémar III of Limoges had been to Jerusalem in the course of the eleventh century. In addition to the forces of the higher nobility there were also smaller groups under lesser lords as well as independent knights who would join or leave the major contingents according to the support that they received. We may notice that no kings took part in the expedition. Urban regarded the crusade as a papally directed enterprise and had not explicitly invited any secular monarch to become involved. In any case, King Philip I of France was an excommunicate on account of his adulterous relationship with the countess of Anjou; Emperor Henry IV of Germany was the papacy's principal opponent in the Investiture Contest, and William Rufus was too entangled in the government of England to be particularly interested. It was not until the crusade of Sigurd of Norway in 1110 that a king participated in a campaign in the Holy Land, although it should be noted that the rulers of Spain had long fought in the *reconquista*.

The leading figures in the First Crusade came from the area of modern France or its borders. Contingents were led by: Count Hugh of Vermandois, brother of the King of France; Duke Robert II of Normandy; Count Robert II of Flanders; Count Stephen of Blois; Raymond of Saint-Gilles, count of Toulouse; Godfrey of Bouillon, duke of Lower Lotharingia (territory subject to the Emperor of Germany); and the southern-Italian Normans, Bohemond of Taranto and Tancred of Lecce. It was in the late summer of 1096 that the main armies set out. Preparations for the expedition were marked by a burst of solar activity and the first good harvest for years – a favourable blessing. Before following the progress of the larger contingents it should be noted that a first wave of crusaders had departed from France in the spring of 1096, led by the charismatic preacher Peter the Hermit and the knight Walter the Penniless (Sansavoir). Another group proceeded down the Rhine led by Count Emicho of Leiningen and this latter force was responsible for the first atrocities of the campaign (see Document 4). They twisted the idea of fighting God's enemies in the East to include those whom they saw as his enemies at home: the Jews – those responsible for Christ's death and, incidentally, a very wealthy section of society. Fired by religious hatred and a need for money, this army perpetrated a series of terrible massacres on the communities of Speyer, Mainz, Trier and Cologne. As they moved on to Constantinople the armies of Peter and Emicho struggled to secure supplies. Outside the city itself the leaders were advised to wait for the remainder of the crusading forces, but as their men became increasingly restive they crossed into Asia Minor where they were very quickly annihilated by the Turks – a fate that some western chroniclers viewed as thoroughly deserved given their earlier behaviour. Until recently, these armies have generally been assumed to have been a peasant rabble, but in fact research indicates that there were a number of knights in their contingents and it was simply overzealousness and indiscipline that brought about their downfall, rather than the inherent weakness of a group of peasants.

The armies of the great nobles arrived at Constantinople between November 1096 and May 1097. When forces of such diverse backgrounds assemble problems of discipline are inevitable and old squabbles resurfaced along with practical matters such as communication (Murray, 2011: 107–19). The language barrier, for example, meant that it was unlikely a man from Toulouse could understand a man from Flanders. There was also the issue of rivalry between the different contingents and a contemporary chronicler, Ralph of Caen, related an episode which serves to illustrate the tensions that could break out in the course of the campaign. As morale sagged during the siege of Antioch (October 1097 to June 1098), gangs of northern and southern French formed up on linguistic lines to forage for supplies. They assaulted or freed those that they captured according to the language they spoke, and those responding in tongues other than Occitan or a northern French dialect were spared as neutrals (Ralph of Caen, 2005: 117–18).

There was also the question of leadership. Stephen of Blois claimed the other nobles chose him to be the overall commander but his desertion at Antioch in June 1098 obviously ended that. It may well have been the papal legate Adhémar of Le Puy who wielded the greatest influence on the expedition. In part this reflected the pope's role as the initiator of the crusade, in part because of Adhémar's strength of personality. Yet complete harmony was never going to possible and long before his death (1 August 1098 after the capture of Antioch) there had been serious differences of opinion between the leaders, a situation that was first exposed at Constantinople.

It seems that the Emperor Alexios had been expected to join the crusade and possibly to lead it, but the trouble caused by Peter the Hermit's crusaders and the size and strength of the main forces caused Alexios real anxiety lest the army turn against Constantinople itself. The presence of Bohemond of Taranto, an old enemy of the Byzantines, increased the emperor's fears. Yet given Alexios's role in triggering the crusade he also saw the expedition as an opportunity to push the Turks back. He tried to get each leader to swear that they would return to him all the lands they captured which had once belonged to the Greeks. Much of the Levant had been under Byzantine rule until the seventh century and Antioch had been a part of their empire as recently as 1084. Furthermore, Asia Minor had only been lost after the Battle of Manzikert in 1071 and given the route of the crusade it was likely that some territory there would be recovered. Alexios also tried to extract oaths of homage and fealty from the crusaders in order to ensure their obedience. Most agreed to this and some were rewarded with generous gifts. The most notable dissenter was Raymond of Saint-Gilles who refused, claiming that an oath of fealty was not compatible with his crusading vow to serve God. After much hard negotiation and threats to withdraw food supplies, Raymond took a less binding oath to maintain the emperor's life and honour. Nevertheless, the crusade had got off to an awkward start – the westerners were reliant on the Greeks for supplies and had anticipated full military support. Such arguments did not bode well for long-term co-operation; and this was before they had started to confront the Muslims.

THE MUSLIM NEAR EAST

The situation in the Islamic world was complicated and turbulent; in essence, however, it was very much to the crusaders' advantage. There was the basic division in the Islamic faith between the Sunni and the Shiite as to who was the rightful successor to the Prophet Mohammed after his death in 632. The Sunni regard themselves as the holders of orthodox tradition and uphold the choice of the Prophet's immediate elected successors as the head of the Islamic community (the caliph), the Shiite support the claim of Ali, the Prophet's cousin and son-in-law (and his successors) to be the caliph; from this split various doctrinal differences also followed. By the eleventh century the Sunni Orthodox controlled Asia Minor and Syria and their spiritual leader was the caliph of Baghdad; the Shiite ruled Egypt through the Fatimid dynasty and had their own caliph based in Cairo, yet such was the bitterness between these two groups that they were prepared to ally with the crusaders against one another, rather than form a common front against the Christians. A further factor in favour of the crusaders was the political turmoil that had afflicted both Sunni and Shiite lands in the early 1090s when a number of important leaders in both camps died, often in mysterious circumstances. The year 1094 saw a particularly heavy mortality rate among caliphs and viziers and a later Arabic writer, Ibn Taghribirdi, described it thus: 'This year is called the year of death of caliphs and commanders' (Hillenbrand, 1997: 132). In contrast to the powerful rule of the Seljuk Sultan Malikshah (d. 1092), by 1097–99 there was a power vacuum in Asia Minor and northern Syria. This meant that when Christians reached the area they were confronted by a series of small rival lordships more concerned with fighting each other than in defeating the crusade. The leadership of the Sunni world remained in Baghdad, distracted by conflicts closer to home and largely unconcerned by appeals for help from the distant Levant. It was far easier for the westerners to defeat opponents in this sort of condition than a well-established and strong ruler such as Malikshah; in fact, given the difficulties encountered by the crusaders anyway, had they faced such an enemy it is probable that they would have failed to cross Asia Minor. A final point to the crusaders' advantage was that the Muslims, unsurprisingly, failed to recognise the crusade as an army of religious colonisation, and evidence suggests that they saw it as another raid from the Byzantine Empire rather than an army set on the capture and settlement of land.

THE CRUSADE IN ASIA MINOR AND THE SIEGE OF ANTIOCH

In May 1097 the crusaders began the siege of Nicaea in Asia Minor. By mid-June Greek forces had joined the western armies and the city soon surrendered and was taken into Byzantine hands. Later on that month, at Dorylaeum, the crusaders faced another test when they were attacked by a large Turkish army, but in spite of their unfamiliarity with the Muslims' tactics (see below, p. 99), once again the Christians triumphed. In mid-September 1097 the crusade began to split up. Bohemond of Taranto's nephew, Tancred, raided areas of Cilicia (on the south-eastern coast of modern-day Turkey) and captured a number of towns, including Tarsus and Adana. Baldwin of Boulogne, Godfrey of Bouillon's brother, headed further east towards the city of Edessa. This territory was controlled by the Christian Armenians who welcomed the crusaders' support against the Muslims that surrounded them. Baldwin was soon adopted as heir to the county, although he quickly sidelined the Armenian rulers and by March 1098 he had set up the first of the Latin settlements in the Levant. The county of Edessa was a fertile region located astride the Euphrates river and during the forty-six years the crusaders held the area it would provide important food and resources for their other lands. There was also a substantial amount of inter-marriage between the Franks (as the Latin settlers became known collectively) and the Armenians, the two noble classes finding that their warrior ethos and way of life had enough in common to overcome any doctrinal differences between them.

The main crusading army had pushed on across the Anatolian plateau and in October 1097 arrived at the city of Antioch in northern Syria. Here the expedition was to undergo its most testing period. The city itself was strongly defended with a powerful ring of walls, it was well provisioned and had a formidable citadel high above the main settlement. It was also a site of great religious importance for the crusaders as (at times) the home of Saint Paul, Saint Peter, and the likely birthplace of Paul's companion, Luke the Physician, who wrote the third Gospel and The Book of Acts. The latter says that 'the disciples were first called Christians in Antioch' (Acts 11:26), a point of particular significance in the evolution of the Christian faith as it began to distinguish and separate itself from its Jewish origins. Antioch was also the seat of one of the five patriarchal seats in the Christian Church.

The siege of Antioch would last almost eight months and the crusaders endured terrible conditions, including the bitterly cold Syrian winter. The Franks constructed their own fortifications and made sporadic attacks on the city but it was too big to blockade effectively and the defenders continued to receive supplies. The crusaders themselves ran short of food and were forced to mount increasingly lengthy foraging expeditions. Many of their horses died and the cost of all foodstuffs became hugely inflated. Cold and rain debilitated people further and tents and equipment rotted. Unsurprisingly pestilence broke out and many of the crusaders died or deserted. The Franks explained their situation by reasoning that they had incurred God's disfavour. Adhémar of Le Puy proclaimed a three-day fast, banned all sex, gambling and swearing in an attempt to pull the expedition together and to regain God's support. The siege dragged on with engagement and counter-engagement. Finally, in June 1098 the crusaders gained some success. Bohemond of Taranto intended to ignore his oaths to Alexios and to set up an independent principality at Antioch based upon the recently held Greek lands. Bohemond contrived a plot with a renegade Armenian to betray the city to the crusaders. Concealing his intention, he tried to persuade the other leaders to let him keep the city if he could engineer its fall, although Raymond of Saint-Gilles was unhappy at reneging on the oath to Alexios. Meanwhile the military situation was worsening as the Muslims of Mosul marched towards Antioch to relieve the city. Bohemond then revealed his plan to his colleagues who, in spite of Raymond's objections, urged him to act. Before dawn on 3 June 1098 a rope was lowered from the walls of Antioch and the crusaders began to swarm over the walls. They poured into the city killing many of the inhabitants and seizing a considerable haul of booty but the defenders withdrew to the citadel which meant, in effect, the crusaders had taken only the outer shell of Antioch.

Soon after this morale reached its lowest point. The crusaders themselves became besieged when the forces from Mosul arrived outside the city walls to trap them between the relief force and the Muslims in the citadel. The crusaders suffered extreme privation and the *Gesta Francorum* recorded, 'So terrible was the famine that men boiled and ate the leaves of figs, vines, thistles and all kinds of trees. Others stewed the dried skins of horses, camels, asses, oxen or buffaloes, which they ate. These and many other troubles and anxieties, which I cannot describe, we suffered for the Name of Christ and to set free the road to the Holy Sepulchre; and we endured this misery, hunger and fear for twenty-six days' (*Gesta Francorum*, tr. Hill, 1962: 62–63). More of the Franks deserted, including Count Stephen of Blois. This had another damaging effect on the crusade because during his retreat across

Asia Minor he met Alexios, who was coming to assist the westerners. Stephen convinced the emperor that the Franks were doomed and so the Greeks, also fearful of the threat to their home city from the Cumans (steppe nomads raiding southwards from the Danube region), turned back to Constantinople. One consequence of these events was that Bohemond claimed that the Byzantines had broken their agreement to provide military support and this, in turn, released the crusaders from their obligation to return captured lands to the Greeks.

The crusaders were in such a desperate situation that only a miracle could save the expedition; and that, in effect, is what happened. A pilgrim named Peter Bartholomew claimed to have had a vision in which St Andrew revealed to him where the Holy Lance, the lance which had pierced Christ's side

4. The Capture of Antioch. © Bibliothèque Municipale, Boulogne-sur-Mer

during the crucifixion, could be found. St Andrew promised that whoever carried this in battle would triumph. On 14 June the relic was discovered and this engendered such religious fervour that morale in the Christian army was transformed. A contemporary wrote in a letter home: 'the discovery of this precious treasure gave new life to all our men' (Letter of Anselm of Ribemont in *Letters from the East*, tr. Barber and Bate, 2010: 29). Whether such a discovery was genuine or not – and some contemporaries doubted its authenticity – the crusaders faced their enemy with new determination. On 28 June 1098 the Franks lined up outside the city in their now customary squadrons. By this point they were also becoming used to Muslim tactics:

'In their usual fashion they [the Muslims] split up into groups, occupying the hills and making for the roads wherever they could in order to encircle us, because they thought that they would be able to kill us all that way. However, our many battles against them had taught us to recognize their ruses and trickery, and helped by the compassion of God we forced them to regroup, despite our very small numbers in comparison with theirs. With God's fighting hand we routed them . . .' (Letter of the Crusade leaders to Pope Urban II, September 1098: *Letters from the East*, tr. Barber and Bate, 2010: 32). Thus the battle-hardness and cohesion acquired during three years on campaign paid off and the Muslims fled. Seeing no relief, the defenders in the citadel soon surrendered and Antioch was taken. Bohemond was able to establish his principality, but the breaking of his oath to Alexios frustrated the Greeks' long-term plan to re-establish their influence in northern Syria and this meant that future relations between Antioch and Byzantium were marked by episodes of considerable tension.

THE SIEGE OF JERUSALEM

After a period of rest the crusaders moved south. In December 1098 they besieged the town of Ma'arrat an Nu'man. Once again supplies were a major problem and a contemporary letter back to the West mentioned that the crusaders were compelled to resort to cannibalism to sustain themselves. Some have claimed this was a demonstration of extreme religious hatred; in fact, simple desperation was the reason: history is filled with examples of similar behaviour in the most extreme of circumstances, such as the siege of Stalingrad in World War II or during the Russian Civil War. The first months of 1099 were marked by a series of squabbles between the leaders of the expedition and also an underlying pressure from the rank and file of the army who were desperate to press on to Jerusalem and to fulfil their vows. This resolute sense of purpose was a clear display of religious devotion as the principal factor in driving them onwards. It was around this time that Godfrey of Bouillon began to appear most clearly as a figure of influence. He was widely recognised as a great soldier although he had been incapacitated for several months by injury. As the crusade moved southwards he re-emerged as a dynamic warrior who attracted support.

On 7 June 1099 the Franks finally reached Jerusalem; by this stage their numbers had fallen to *c.*1,300 knights and 12,500 footsoldiers. The city was controlled by Egyptian Shiite forces (they had displaced the Sunnis the previous year) and, as at Antioch, the Christians made little progress in the early stages of the siege. Jerusalem was encircled by strong walls and with a moat protecting the northern section and natural valleys to the south and east it was a difficult place to take. Raymond of St Gilles set up his men in the south-west corner, Godfrey and Tancred to the north-west. The arrival of Genoese ships provided a supply of wood and this prompted the construction of two fine siege towers, catapults and a ram, but the defenders remained resolute.

Yet now they had finally reached their goal the crusaders' spiritual strength was renewed. A fast was proclaimed for 8 July and barefoot, carrying the relics of saints, the bishops and the clergy led the army in procession to the Mount of Olives and implored God's help. Still progress was slow and the prospect of the arrival of an Egyptian relief force further increased the pressure for a breakthrough. On the night of 13 July, Godfrey made an audacious move: he had noticed an area of the wall a few hundred metres further to the east that looked weaker and under cover of the darkness he had his siege tower dismantled, moved and reassembled. By nightfall on 14 July a day of intense fighting had brought the crusaders to the foot of the walls. On 15 July Godfrey's men managed to fill the moat and bring their tower to stand above the curtain walls. Amidst a hail of fire and projectiles Godfrey led his men from the front. Blazing arrows compelled the Muslims to leave a section of the walls and Godfrey ordered the tower's drawbridge to be lowered and his men began to take the walls. With this bridgehead created ladders were laid against the walls and more crusaders began to cross the ramparts and swarm into the city.

After years of effort and toil the accumulated tensions of the march spilled over into an appalling sack of the city's Muslim and Jewish defenders. Many of the former took sanctuary in the Dome of the Rock where Tancred promised them protection. Yet on 16 July other crusaders slaughtered these people. Tancred was livid because this breached his oath and because, as a southern Italian whose family had both fought and used Muslims in their armies over recent decades, he saw this as an opportunity to secure a large sum of ransom money. The combination of religious fervour and extreme brutality is conveyed in these later comments by William of Tyre:

It was impossible to look on the vast numbers of the slain without horror; everywhere lay fragments of human bodies, and the very ground was covered with the blood of the slain. Still more dreadful was it to gaze upon the victors themselves, dripping with blood from head to foot. . . . Then, clad in fresh garments, with clean hands and bare feet, in humility they [the crusaders] began to make the rounds of the venerable places which the Saviour had deigned to sanctify and make glorious with His bodily presence . . . with particular veneration they approached the church of the Passion and Resurrection of the Lord. . . . It was a source of spiritual joy to witness the pious devotion . . . with which the pilgrims drew near to the holy places, the exultation of heart and happiness of spirit with which they kissed the memorials of the Lord's sojourn on earth.

(William of Tyre, tr. Babcock and Krey, 1943: 1.372–3)

Without in any way wishing to belittle this appalling event, stories of crusaders wading in blood up to their knees, or even the bridles of their horses, so favoured in popular histories down the centuries are likely an exaggeration and a (hugely effective) literary flourish. The use of such imagery derives from the apocalyptic Book of Revelation 14:20. A little-used contemporary Muslim source (and hence hardly likely to minimise the killing), Ibn al-Arabi, who was in Egypt at the time, gives a figure of 3,000 slain. This contrasts with the 10,000 given by William of Tyre, the 65,000 of the Armenian writer Matthew of Edessa and the 75,000 of the thirteenth-century Muslim, Ibn al-Athir; thus it seems that as time passed and the religious and emotional impact of the event gathered greater significance the number killed also grew (Hirschler, 2014 provides a close analysis of the Muslim response). Some of the Jews were ransomed and the Fatimid garrison in David's Tower managed to negotiate their freedom too. That said, if Ibn al-Arabi's figure is at all correct it still represents a truly grim figure given the city's likely population of up to 30,000 inhabitants (Kedar, 2004, who also offers an excellent analysis of the western accounts of the siege).

The crusaders' victory was by no means assured. Three weeks later a large Egyptian force under-estimated the battle-hardened crusaders and was heavily defeated, leaving the Christians to secure their hold on Jerusalem (at least in the short term) and to gain substantial amounts of booty. This marked the end of the main thrust of the First Crusade and the Holy Land was regained for Christianity. The capture of Jerusalem was a remarkable achievement and the crusaders believed that God must have blessed their expedition for it to have succeeded. Their incredible determination, principally borne out of a desire to free the Holy Sepulchre from Muslim hands, their growing military cohesion, and the deeply divided state of the Islamic world all contributed to their success. Pope Urban, however, did not live to see the victorious outcome of his creation because he died before he heard news of the fall of Jerusalem. In the short term, many of the crusaders left for home, exhausted by their labours, but exultant at having accomplished their vows in the face of seemingly insurmountable odds. These men returned to the West as heroes, fêted for their achievements (see Document 6 iii), although often worse off in physical and financial terms. There is only limited evidence of people coming back from the crusade with newfound riches. Caffaro was pleased to record that the Genoese crusaders of 1099 secured huge treasures of gold, silver and gemstones from the Battle of Ascalon (Caffaro, tr. Hall and Phillips, 2013: 117). Others brought back relics from the Holy Land. Lord Riou of Lohéac, for example, acquired a fragment of the True Cross and bequeathed it to his local church when he died in 1101. When they reached home many of the crusaders had to reclaim lands and rights encroached upon in their absence. Those Franks remaining in the Levant had to start trying to stabilise their new possessions and to establish a rule of government.

In the Muslim world there was shock, and in some quarters outrage, at the crusaders' success. Document 5 indicates the deep emotion generated by contemporary poets protesting at the failure of the Islamic people to react. As we will see shortly, the Seljuk sultan was preoccupied with events in Persia and did not lead an army to confront the westerners; Hillenbrand concludes, 'The fate of Jerusalem was sealed, therefore, in Isfahan' (Hillenbrand, 1997: 135). This neglect of his co-religionists was crucial because it gave the Franks the chance to conquer and then to consolidate their presence in the Levant – the birth of the Latin East.

3

The early decades of the Latin East, c. 1097–c. 1152: establishment and consolidation

T he period 1097 to late 1144 was, in general, a successful time for the
Franks. They consolidated the achievements of the First Crusade and
founded four fully viable Latin states, although the loss of Edessa to
Zengi in December 1144 was a most serious setback. Two particular features
stand out when reading contemporary narratives of this time. First, the
huge energy and effort required to establish the Frankish hold on the Holy
Land is immediately apparent. The need for almost ceaseless campaigning –
against a series of enemies – and exhausting marches and counter-marches
is striking; the dynamism of King Baldwin II is especially worthy of note.
Second, there were only four appeals to the West for crusades (1101, 1106–8,
1120–24, 1127–29) compared to at least fifteen for the period 1149 to 1186.
This emphasises the Franks' strength in this first phase of settlement and also
reflects the relative weakness of their enemies.

THE 1101 CRUSADE AND THE EARLY YEARS OF CONQUEST

The first appeal to the West in 1101 was really a continuation of the First Crusade.
Throughout the expedition the crusaders had been aware of people in Europe
who had taken the cross but had failed to set out. Given their own losses, the
crusaders sent home a series of messages desperately urging their co-religionists
to join them. Papal letters restated this point and threatened shame and
excommunication on those who did not fulfil their vows. A second spur for
these people to act, and for others to join them, was provided by the news
of the capture of Jerusalem. God's apparent blessing of the crusade must

have prompted a flood of people hoping to benefit from the success and fame of the campaign. Other, more worldly, attractions were put forward too. Godfrey of Bouillon boasted, almost certainly in part for propaganda purposes, of the vast fortune that he had acquired in the East. That said, as we saw earlier, there is evidence from Caffaro of Genoa of the wealth secured after the Battle of Ascalon in 1099, and Caffaro and Fulcher of Chartres, both of whom were present, mention the substantial amount of booty taken at Caesarea in 1101.

The 1101 expedition also provided an opportunity for those who had deserted the main armies in 1097–98 to return to the Levant and to complete their vows. Among these was the former crusade leader, Count Stephen of Blois, whose wife had famously berated him for his cowardice and insisted that he redeem his honour. Two main armies were formed: a Franco–Lombard army (Italians, northern French and Burgundians), and an Aquitanian–Bavarian force led by Duke Welf IV of Bavaria and Duke William IX of Aquitaine. As they crossed Asia Minor both of these armies suffered a series of heavy defeats by Muslim forces and a much-depleted crusader army reached Jerusalem in the spring of 1102. It did, however, provide a large cavalry contingent for the Battle of Ramla in May 1102, although many men, including Stephen of Blois, were killed there. An infantry army fought at Jaffa in 1102 and this engagement marked the end of the crusade. In light of the size of the armies involved (probably 10,000 men in the Franco–Lombard army alone) the 1101 crusade achieved little, although, as Mullinder concludes, its involvement at Ramla and Jaffa was a significant contribution towards the survival of the fledgling kingdom of Jerusalem. Some of these crusaders also chose to remain in the Levant as settlers (Mullinder, 1998).

The need for the 1101 crusade can be vividly illustrated by outlining the extent of Frankish landholdings at the start of Baldwin I's reign in 1100. The king held only the cities of Jerusalem, Bethlehem and Jaffa (his sole port). When Baldwin was crowned, Fulcher of Chartres noted that the king would need energy to 'conquer the Muslims in battle, or . . . compel them to make peace'. Fulcher also commented, with a sense of wonder that, given the Christians were so few in number, it was surprising that the Muslims did not attack them. Antioch, the other main centre of Christian strength, was c. 450 kilometres away and its leader, Prince Bohemond, had just been captured by the Muslims (July 1100). In spite of this unpromising situation, the hope of a new crusade and sheer necessity drove the Franks in the south to act. They recognised the need to capture further ports to allow new crusaders to arrive and to generate money from trade and pilgrim traffic because without this the Latin States would simply perish. The Italian mercantile states of Genoa, Pisa and Venice were all involved in the conquest of the Holy Land and were granted property (usually an area in a city known as a 'quarter' – see pp. 63–4) and legal and fiscal (tax) privileges. In May 1101 a force comprising of the troops of

King Baldwin I and the Genoese besieged and captured Caesarea and here we can see, in microcosm, the process of conquest and settlement. Caffaro, who was present, reported that the patriarch of Jerusalem urged the Christians to victory, promising them both spiritual and material rewards (Caffaro, tr. Hall and Phillips, 2013: 54–55). The Genoese, whom we must remember were crusaders signed with the cross and not, as might be mistakenly characterised, solely out for commercial advantage, stormed the walls, led by William Testad-imaglio ('Hammerhead'). The city was quickly taken and another eyewitness, Fulcher of Chartres, recorded that during the siege most of the Muslim men fled or were killed, but the women who remained were spared 'to turn hand mills' (Fulcher of Chartres, tr. Ryan, 1969: 154). The Franks were, therefore, clearly aware of the need to use local labour, of whatever faith, to maintain food production and to sustain the local economy. King Baldwin also chose to ransom the emir of Caesarea as another way to raise money and the city itself provided substantial levels of booty. The Genoese alone were able to give their men (8,000 in number) 48 *solidi* each in cash and 900 grams of peppercorns – a fine reward. They acquired relics too, most notably the beautiful green emerald bowl still in the Cathedral of St Lawrence in Genoa as well as a church in Caesarea that was dedicated to St Lawrence, their patron saint. Finally, the settlers appointed an archbishop to impose their religious authority on the region. Thus we can see aspects of economic, administrative and religious issues organised to facilitate a permanent Frankish settlement.

The main threats to Christian lands at this time were to the south from Fatimid Egypt and to the north-east from Aleppo. A series of intense and bloody campaigns was fought in both theatres of war and Frankish resources were stretched very tightly indeed. Fulcher observed: 'We were afraid that our foes might take one of our cities while it was denuded of manpower' (Fulcher of Chartres, tr. Ryan, 1969: 183). Much of the time the Franks were victorious, although there were setbacks. At the Battle of Harran (in northern Syria) in May 1104 Count Baldwin of Edessa was captured and many other Christian knights were killed. In consequence of this defeat huge tracts of land were lost and the area controlled by the principality of Antioch was reduced by almost 60 per cent. Remarkably, the settlers recovered most of this territory within a decade, illustrating the extraordinarily flexible nature of boundaries in northern Syria during the early years of the twelfth century (Asbridge, 2000).

THE 1108 CRUSADE – A HOLY WAR AGAINST CHRISTIANS

When Bohemond was released from captivity he resolved to bolster the long-term security of Antioch against both Muslim and Byzantine threats by seeking support in the West, first from the pope and then in France and England. As a leader of the First Crusade and probably its most accomplished warrior, Bohemond enjoyed a tremendous welcome when he arrived in Europe in late 1105 with some in southern Italy reported as hoping to catch a glimpse of their hero, as if they were about to see Christ himself. Bohemond's purpose in the West was twofold. He wanted a wife and a new crusade. His new-found status meant that he could seek a bride at the highest level and in 1106 he married Constance, the daughter of King Philip I of France, thus cementing his prestige and establishing the ruling house of Antioch as one of real standing. Bohemond contacted Pope Paschal II on his way through Italy and by the time he reached northern France he was accompanied by a papal legate to help raise support for a new crusade (Whalen, 2010 discusses this episode). The first target of this expedition, intriguingly, was the Byzantine Empire and only after a campaign against the Greeks did the crusade plan to proceed to the Holy Land. Bohemond had been a long-time adversary of the Byzantines and he intended to take the initiative himself by invading the empire and asserting his rights to act freely in northern Syria. There is little doubt that full spiritual rewards were offered for these campaigns and the presence of legate Bruno of Segni indicates papal awareness of this aim. For a crusade to be preached against Christians – albeit the schismatic Greek Orthodox ones – was a significant, and often overlooked, development in the history of crusading ideas. Pope Urban's original concept of an expedition to free the Holy Sepulchre from the forces of Islam had, in just over a decade, been adapted to include warfare in the Iberian peninsula (see below, pp. 87, 203–4) and here, against fellow-Christians. In spite of its focus on the Greeks, some contemporaries also saw the 1108 crusade in a continuum with the First Crusade. Orderic Vitalis, an Anglo–Norman writer of the time, described it as 'the third expedition to Jerusalem' (Orderic Vitalis, tr. Chibnall, 1978: 6.68–73). Bohemond recruited a large army to follow him and in October 1107 he sailed for western Greece and besieged the port of Durazzo (on the Adriatic coast, in present-day Albania). He was soon defeated, however, and by the 1108 Treaty of Devol he became an imperial vassal, relinquished his lands in Cilicia and agreed to hold Antioch and Edessa from the emperor. Bohemond was also granted Aleppo in fief should the Christians capture it and he was forced to accept the principle of the restoration of a Greek Orthodox patriarch in Antioch. Part of Bohemond's army continued on to Jerusalem where some men settled, but the prince himself returned to Italy where he died in 1112. His nephew, Tancred, had ruled Antioch in his absence and he rejected the terms of the Treaty of Devol. Fortunately for him, distractions elsewhere in the Byzantine Empire soon caused the Greeks to turn their attention away from northern Syria. Bohemond and Tancred had shown a determination to establish an independent principality and, while their aggression was tempered by the defeat at Devol, in the short term at least, circumstances enabled the Antiochenes to rule free of immediate Greek influence.

MUSLIM–CHRISTIAN RELATIONS: WARFARE AND ALLIANCES

One factor in the Franks' favour, and a theme that would run through most of the first fifty years of settlement, was the disunity of the Muslim world; each of the major powers of the region had other priorities and demands upon their attention. They had, as noted earlier, failed to recognise the First Crusade as a campaign of religious conquest. It seems also that the fusion of interests between the religious and secular leadership that so characterised the attraction and the energy of the crusade in western Europe was not present in the Muslim Near East at that time; a crucial difference.

In 1100, a delegation from Damascus went to Baghdad to try to convince the sultan to respond but he was too embroiled in local political concerns; his people, it was later reported, 'remained aloof'. Eleven years later, a group from Aleppo made a much more dramatic protest in the sultan's mosque. 'They drove the preacher from the pulpit (*minbar*) and broke it in pieces, clamouring and weeping for the misfortunes that had befallen Islam at the hands of the Franks', and prevented the congregation from praying (Ibn al-Qalanisi, tr. Gibb, 1932: 111). They staged a similar event at the caliph's mosque the following Friday. The symbolism of the destruction of the *minbars* was plain: the sultan and the caliph had failed in their duty to defend Islamic lands from the infidel and did not deserve to be honoured during Friday prayers. While these events prompted the dispatch of an army to Syria, it made little impression on the broader attitude of the leadership.

Poetry was one of the most important forms of communication in the Arab world and through this we can find some evidence for the impact of the crusade. A writer from the northern Syrian town of Ma'arrat an-Nu'man, a place that was heavily hit by the First Crusaders, wondered if the remains of his house had been transformed from a dwelling place into the pasturage of savage beasts and lamented the injustice of this fate. Writers such as Ibn Khayat (d. *c.* 1125) and al-Abiwardi (d. 1113) sought to convey their anger through powerful images of the violation of women to symbolise what had happened during the Frankish conquest (Document 5 ii).

Probably the clearest insight into the situation comes from a sermon composed *c.* 1105 by as-Sulami, a Damascene preacher (see Document 5 iii). He lambasted the ruling classes for their laziness, their fixation with fighting one another and their failure to engage in the *jihad* in the way a good Muslim should.

Jihad and crusade are often perceived as synonyms and, as we will see, while they certainly share some similarities, this is not a parallel that should be overstretched. For example, *jihad* means 'struggle' and has been a part of the Islamic faith from its origins in the seventh century. In contrast, the idea of the crusade was invented by Urban II in 1095. The notion of holy war is found in the Qur'an and *hadith*, the sayings of Muhammad, and they both stress the virtues and celestial rewards of the *jihad* (two instances where there are similarities, of course). The *jihad* has two elements, the 'Greater' and the 'Lesser' *jihad*. The former (*al-jihad al-akbar*) is the struggle against a person's lower self; an individual's fight against immorality and sin. This is of the utmost spiritual value, and regarded by many as a necessary precursor to the lesser *jihad* (*al-jihad al-asghar*). The latter is a perpetual obligation on all Muslims to strive to extend the House of Islam (*Dar al-Islam*) until all mankind accepts the faith or submits to Muslim government. Non-Muslims (such as Christians and Jews, although not polytheists) living within the House of Islam must be protected although are subject to a tax. Land outside the House of Islam is the House of War (*Dar al-harb*) and in theory there is a permanent state of hostility between the two Houses until the former is victorious. Truces of up to ten years could be allowed.

As-Sulami was a perceptive observer and he seems to have recognised that the Franks were driven by religion (he described them as being engaged in a *jihad*). He also saw that they were far from their homelands, few in number and reliant upon their horses for military strength. As-Sulami urged his co-religionists to pull together and to respond, holding out the prospect of spiritual rewards and – in contrast to most Christian preachers – a clear worldly incentive in the form of women and money. For all his passion, as-Sulami met with practically no response, he preached to an audience of perhaps three or four scholars in a mosque on the edge of Damascus (Mourad and Lindsay, 2013: 33–46). His ideas would come to be closely mirrored by the preachers of Nur ad-Din and Saladin in the second half of the century, but in his own lifetime, they fell on rocky ground.

Ongoing conflict amongst the northern Syrian Muslims was of particular advantage to the Christian settlers. This is not to say that such groups, as well as the Fatimids of Egypt did not pose a significant threat to the Franks but the fragmented nature of this danger did much to dilute its menace.

Two other features stand out concerning the Frankish–Muslim conflict in this period. First, the Franks were strong enough to impose annual payments of tribute from local emirs such as that rendered on occasion by Aleppo and Shaizar in the second decade of the twelfth century. Second, as we saw earlier, there were times when the settlers were in conflict with each other and this, remarkably, led them to seek allies in the Muslim world. In 1105, for example, both Tancred of Antioch and King Baldwin I had Turkish allies in

THE BATTLE OF THE FIELD OF BLOOD (1119)

Soon after Baldwin II's accession in April 1118 he had to deal with a major crisis in northern Syria. A period of Frankish expansion had created a semi-circle of Christian-held settlements around Aleppo, some no less than 25 kilometres from the city. This unprecedented threat provoked deep anxiety in the Muslim camp. Il-Ghazi of Mardin was called in to take control and, with the forces of Tughtigin, he led an aggressive push to the west. On 28 June 1119 Prince Roger of Antioch's army was surrounded near Sarmarda (c. 45 kilometres west of Aleppo), and during the ensuing battle he was killed and almost all of his 700 knights and 3,000 footsoldiers were either slain or captured. Ibn al-Qalanisi, a contemporary Damascene chronicler, rated this victory as 'one of the finest of victories, and such plenitude of divine aid was never granted to Islam in all its past ages' (Ibn al-Qalanisi, tr. Gibb, 1932: 160–61). Matthew of Edessa, a contemporary Armenian Christian, noted the Turks 'ravaged all the country . . . bringing bloodshed and enslavement, while the whole Frankish army was practically annihilated' (Matthew of Edessa, tr. Dostaurian, 1993: 224). Il-Ghazi took back a number of towns on the Muslim–Christian frontier and raided the environs of Antioch itself. While the area of land lost was far smaller (although strategically more important), than that lost after Harran in 1104, the real crisis was caused by the death of so many of the Antiochene nobility. Baldwin II marched northwards and took command of the situation. He provided for the defence of the city of Antioch and remarried the widowed to his own men. The king needed to travel north several more times in subsequent years, but in the short term he had succeeded in preserving the viability of the principality at a moment of extreme pressure.

From the Muslim perspective, the Battle of the Field of Blood also marked the first time that *jihad* imagery began to be used with any frequency in the age of the crusades. We might also note the presence of an Aleppan preacher in the Muslim army rousing the troops to greater efforts. Thus we can see the religious classes beginning to get involved in the holy war even if close engagement with the political classes remained patchy. Prompted by the events of 1119, however, *jihad* references (including some from the Koran) start to appear in the surviving evidence, principally in epigraphic sources (inscriptions on buildings or tombs). This material is also useful because it is often precisely dated and we may note that no similar quotations are found elsewhere in the Islamic Mediterranean at this time. Tughtigin was described in 1122 as 'protector of those who fight the holy war'. Another memorial dating from 1130, the year after his death, called him 'the prince, the one who fights the holy war, the one who perseveres assiduously on the frontier, their struggle with each other. In 1114 Roger of Antioch fought alongside Tughtigin of Damascus and Il-Ghazi of Mardin to fight off the threat of Bursuq, commander of the sultan of Baghdad's army. Set alongside the hyperbolic emotional register of the calls to the First Crusade, this seems incredible but such deals represent the practicalities of divided Muslim and Christian powers living alongside one another, a reality that we will see manifested in several other forms too (see below, pp. 55–7). Walter the Chancellor saw the 1114 agreement as 'an alliance of Belial [the devil]', yet it served both Antiochene and Muslim interests well and accomplished its aim of fending off a more powerful outside force (Walter the Chancellor, tr. Asbridge and Edgington, 1999: 95). In any case, such deals were nearly always shortlived and the parties involved might soon be at war with one another.

THE KINGDOM OF JERUSALEM AND THE SUCCESSION OF BALDWIN I

If the early decades of the principality of Antioch can be characterised as turbulent and unstable, then events to the south saw the Franks establish themselves more steadily and effectively. The process of taking the coastal cities continued with Acre falling to the Christians in 1104, the county of Tripoli coming into being in 1109, and Beirut and Sidon being taken in 1110 (the latter with the help of a large force of Norwegian crusaders under King Sigurd). The armies of the kingdom of Jerusalem fought almost annual battles against the Egyptians and sometimes against the Damascenes, although the latter regarded the Muslims of northern Syria as their most serious enemy and often chose to ally with the Franks or at least remain neutral. The settlers expanded their territories inland with, in 1115, Baldwin I's construction of the huge castle of Montreal in Transjordan to 'dominate the country in the interests of the Christians' (Fulcher of Chartres, tr. Ryan, 1969: 215). The control of this region east of the River Jordan and the Dead Sea, and extending down to the Red Sea port of Aqaba, meant a valuable increase in revenue because traders between Damascus and Egypt had to pay taxes to traverse the area.

Baldwin I's reign can be viewed as a successful period for the Franks. As a monarch he held his nobles in close control for much of his reign until the issue of his succession finally came to a head (see below, pp. 125–f Baldwin died in April 1118, returning home from a campaign in Eg He was determined to be buried in the Church of the Holy Sepulchre a his deathbed the king instructed his cook to attend to his corpse p the intestines were to be removed and the body embalmed to fulfi' wish. The army hurried back to Jerusalem and the king was duly to his brother, Godfrey.

the warrior' (Hillenbrand, 1994: 66). Balak of Aleppo died fighting the Christians in 1124. He was portrayed as a martyr and the appropriate Koranic inscription adorns his tomb: 'Think not of those who are slain in the way of Allah as dead. Nay, they are living. With their Lord they have provision' (ibid.: 67). This evidence, although limited, indicates that in northern Syria at least, in conjunction with the Muslims' first real success against the Franks, the seeds were being sown for the later propaganda campaigns of Nur ad-Din and Saladin.

THE 1120 COUNCIL OF NABLUS

In January 1120, the leading churchmen and secular figures of the kingdom of Jerusalem gathered at Nablus in Samaria. The atmosphere was sombre; only six months earlier, the forces of Il-Ghazi had crushed Prince Roger of Antioch's army at the Battle of the Field of Blood, while in April 1119 around 300 pilgrims had been killed near the River Jordan. The settlers discussed how they could improve their situation; perhaps their moral failings had brought God's anger? King Baldwin I's bigamous marriage to Queen Adelaide of Sicily, or the liaisons of Patriarch Arnulf of Jerusalem (1099, 1112–15, 1116–18) with, first a married woman, and then a Muslim woman with whom he had a son, were prominent recent examples. The assembly at Nablus enacted a series of laws which can give us an insight into the Franks' situation and their concerns (see Document 6 ii). The general tenor of this legislation was particularly harsh and it is likely that its main purpose was a deterrent, rather than illustrating widespread behaviour at the time. That said, some broader observations can be made. Of the twenty-five decrees, almost half derive from earlier, but still widely circulated, Byzantine law codes (Kedar, 1999). Along with the issues of shared religious observance and settlement patterns (see below, pp. 141–2, 55–7), this is a reminder of cross-cultural influences between the indigenous Orthodox of the Levant and the Frankish settlers, a significant feature of the Crusader states.

Some of the individual measures are particularly interesting. There was clearly a fear that sexual relations with Muslims brought divine disapproval; there was also a strong stand against sexual impropriety in a variety of forms with notably harsh punishments being set out for transgressors. Franks were permitted to marry local Christians, and even Christian converts from Islam, but union with a practising Muslim was evidently out. The issue here was not race or ethnic heritage, but religion. Protection for non-Latins against sexual violence was, however, built into the legislation too (canons 13–14).

Canon 20 was notably original and ran against all contemporary legislation in the West. The idea of clerics bearing arms had long been rejected but given the recent traumatic events in Antioch where, with the knights and nobles dead or imprisoned, armed clergy had guarded the city walls and 'acted the part of military service wisely and vigorously . . . and kept the city intact from the enemy' (Walter the Chancellor, tr. Asbridge and Edgington, 1999: 139–40). This canon was, therefore, a reflection of life in the Levant and was designed to permit just such a reality. As we will see later, the Council of Nablus was also an important moment in the foundation of what became the Knights' Templar and enacting legislation that permitted clerics to fight could be seen as preparing the ground for such a group.

THE 1120–24 CRUSADE AND THE CAPTURE OF TYRE

The Council of Nablus may also have sent an appeal to Pope Calixtus II (1119–24) for a new crusade. While no text of the papal encyclical survives, it seems that letters were dispatched to France and Germany encouraging people to take the cross. The response to this plea was limited, although a number of western nobles are known to have travelled to the Levant at this time, possibly in response to Calixtus's call. The kingdom of Jerusalem also approached Venice because negotiations for a joint naval and land campaign were opened – again with papal encouragement. This resulted in the siege of Tyre which, along with Ascalon, was the remaining Muslim-held port on the coast. By early 1124 the Franks had gathered all the resources that they could muster, even pledging ornaments from the churches of Jerusalem to raise cash, and the attack began. After five months the Fatimid defenders could do no more and on 7 July 1124 the city surrendered. Charters of the agreement between Jerusalem and Venice survive, both the texts confirmed by Patriarch Gormund of Jerusalem (because Baldwin II was in Muslim captivity in the north) and the king himself once he was free. As we can see from Document 8 the arrangements covered an extensive range of territorial, legal and fiscal rights. Land was to be held freely (known as an allod) and full legal and fiscal rights existed over Venetians and non-Venetians in houses owned by the Italians. Intriguingly, much of the *Pactum Warmundi* concerns Acre rather than Tyre, reflecting the former's greater commercial importance and the Venetians' concern to secure an advantageous position there. Contrary to most previous interpretations, Jacoby has shown that these privileges were not so sweeping as previously thought, in part because Baldwin II cut back on the terms earlier agreed by Patriarch Gormond. For example, the Venetians' legal rights did not extend to the higher aspects of criminal justice (such as murder) because no medieval ruler would consider resigning such a prerogative. Jacoby has also shown that Venetian lands in the lordship of

Tyre were fiefs (held from the king), rather than allods as originally agreed, and thus owed the crown knight-service (Jacoby, 1997: 157–66). While such clauses were important to Baldwin the end-result of this agreement was still of considerable benefit to the Venetians as well. The settlers had secured one of the two remaining Muslim-held ports on the Mediterranean and the Venetians had gained possessions and important privileges to encourage their full involvement in the commerce of the Eastern Mediterranean.

THE CAMPAIGNS OF KING BALDWIN II

The reign of King Baldwin II was characterised by vigorous military endeavour. Baldwin led at least nineteen campaigns in his thirteen-year rule, which included a period of sixteen months in captivity (April 1123 to August 1124). He was forced to ride from Antioch to Jerusalem no less than six times, a round trip of c. 900 kilometres, and from 1119 to 1126 he had to act as regent in the principality and in 1130 he was required to restore order there again after the death of Prince Bohemond II. A glimpse of the intensity of Baldwin II's activities can be seen in his itinerary of August 1124 to January 1126. He was released from prison in August 1124 and capitalised on the momentum of the Franks' success at Tyre to continue to take the offensive; he also needed to re-establish his own authority in the eyes of his nobles. By October that year he had gathered sufficient forces to engage in a five-month siege of Aleppo, the sole occasion Christian forces ever seriously threatened this key Muslim city. In February 1125 he returned to Jerusalem, only to ride north to Antioch again in April. Fulcher of Chartres noted that he had only a few men of Jerusalem with him because 'in the present and preceding year they had been much exhausted' (Fulcher of Chartres, tr. Ryan, 1969: 278). He then fought and won two big battles at A'zaz and Zerdana. Baldwin went to Damascus and Ascalon in 1125 and, in January 1126, back to Damascus, with success in all instances. The year 1126 saw further victories at Raphania and Egypt and there was another visit to Antioch. It was Damascus, however, that held the key to his next moves because, although he had been victorious in the battle of January 1126, it is evident that he had more ambitious plans for the city.

In 1127 three issues came to the fore and required the king to make important choices. First, as we will see later, he encouraged Hugh of Payns, master of the Templars, to travel to the West to gain papal endorsement for the order and then to raise men and money for the brothers. Hugh was also entrusted with another task: to recruit men from Europe for a new crusade. Baldwin's raids on Damascus had shown the king that he could only threaten the city – to capture it he would need outside help. This crusade would be wholly aggressive in purpose and was to expand Christian territory (the justification of defending the holy places could not really be applied here); such a plan showed Baldwin II's confidence and his belief that the Christians could conquer a major Muslim city. There is no surviving papal bull to endorse the crusade or any record of preachers other than Hugh being delegated to generate support. That said, we do have unambiguous and contemporary evidence of people taking the cross to journey to Jerusalem for the remission of their sins and to fight the Muslims. In other words, this was a crusade. The origins of most of these individuals are linked to the third element of Baldwin's decision-making – that concerning his succession. By 1127 his wife had died and he was left with four daughters. It was essential that the eldest, Melisende, should marry to provide the kingdom with a military leader and to father future rulers. With the unanimous agreement of the nobility of Jerusalem, Baldwin chose Count Fulk V of Anjou as his prospective successor. Fulk was already known to the settlers because he had spent a year in Jerusalem (1120) as a *confrater* (lay associate) of the Templars. The pope offered his approval of the marriage and an embassy from Jerusalem led by William of Bures, lord of Galilee, travelled to Anjou. The missions of William and Hugh of Payns coalesced in the person of Fulk because, if he could be persuaded to marry Melisende, when he travelled to the East, it made sense to try to draw a crusade along with him as well. Fulk agreed to these proposals and led a substantial contingent from Anjou, while Hugh of Payns is said to have recruited men from England and Scotland too. The army sailed to the Holy Land in 1129 and in late autumn joined with forces from Antioch, Tripoli, Edessa and Jerusalem to march on Damascus. The Christians' campaign was dogged by bad weather and poor discipline and broke up having achieved nothing of note. Fulk, however, married Melisende, and their first child, Baldwin, was born in 1130; in addition, a number of his Angevin associates remained with him in the Levant.

THE REIGN OF KING FULK (1131–43)

King Baldwin II died in August 1131. Fulk succeeded him, although as Chapter 9 reveals, the early years of his rule were marked by a struggle for supremacy between the newly arrived Angevins and the native Levantine nobility. Two other features marked Fulk's reign. First, the Franks took action to contain the threat from Egyptian-controlled Ascalon to the south of their lands (as discussed below, p. 102 and Document 19). Second, hostile Christian and Muslim forces exerted considerable pressure on the principality of Antioch. In the 1130s King Leon, the Christian ruler of Armenia and a former ally of the Franks, became antagonistic and he recaptured the southern Cilician towns of Tarsus, Adana and Mamistra taken by the First Crusade. In part, Leon exploited the state of near civil war in Antioch caused by the actions of Alice, widow of Prince Bohemond II. When her husband died Alice had decided that she wanted to rule in her own right until their infant daughter, Constance, came of age. On no less than three occasions, first Baldwin II (in 1130), and then Fulk (1133 and 1135) were forced to march north to answer calls from disaffected Antiochene nobles who wanted Alice to wed again or to be replaced. Finally, Raymond of Poitiers married the eight-year-old Constance in 1136 to bring some stability to the situation (see also, p. 129 below for more on this episode).

In 1137–38 and 1142–43, the prince had to contend with the appearance of John Komnenos (1118–43) and a Byzantine army. The emperor was furious that he, as overlord of Antioch, had not been involved in choosing Constance's husband and that through her marriage to Raymond an opportunity to increase Byzantine influence in the area had been missed. He arrived at the gates of Antioch in 1137 with a huge army and demanded the city should submit. John was wary of open conflict with the Franks because it would almost certainly provoke a crusade against him. Nonetheless, he wanted his authority recognised. The threat was sufficient to compel Raymond to swear homage to the emperor and to acknowledge that his land was subject to Greek overlordship. Furthermore, if Christian forces should take Aleppo and Shaizar (presently held by the Muslims), then he would receive these towns and, in return, hand over Antioch to the Byzantines. In 1138 the Greeks and the Franks besieged Shaizar to try to fulfil this agreement, but the siege was unsuccessful. John then tried to coerce Raymond into handing over Antioch regardless of the failure to take Aleppo and Shaizar as agreed the previous year. Raymond asked for time to consult his people and staged an anti-Byzantine riot which forced John to depart. Any further trouble was stayed by news of unrest elsewhere in the Byzantine Empire and John returned to Constantinople. Yet tension persisted and the Antiochenes had still to acknowledge Byzantine overlordship to John's satisfaction. In 1142 he menaced the principality anew. Once again the Antiochenes managed to play along the emperor sufficiently to delay a full-scale assault on the city. To the Franks' great good fortune, when John's forces withdrew to Cilicia for the winter he suffered a fatal hunting accident which lifted the immediate threat to the settlers.

ZENGI AND THE FALL OF EDESSA (1144)

The Greeks and the Armenians were not the only danger to Frankish lands in northern Syria. During the 1130s, Zengi, the atabeg of Mosul and Aleppo, had developed sufficient strength to mark himself as the most serious challenger yet to the Christians of the Levant. Hillenbrand has revealed a ruthless personality who inflicted terror and cruelty on his army and his subjects, as well as the Franks (Hillenbrand, 2001). Ibn al-Adim, a thirteenth-century Aleppan writer, noted, 'When Zengi was on horseback, the troops used to walk behind him as if they were between two threads, out of fear that they would trample on the crops. If anyone transgressed, he was crucified' (ibid.: 123). Zengi spent many years establishing his power in the Muslim world as well as raiding Frankish lands. In December 1144, however, he besieged the Christian city of Edessa. Zengi set up a close blockade and dug a complex series of mines to bring down one of the walls. This allowed him to enter the city which fell on 24 December. The Muslims came to see this as the turning of the tide against the Christians. Ibn al-Athir later wrote, 'Islam became like the full moon after it had been obscured'. Zengi's feat was lauded in contemporary poetry, which depicted him as a *mujahid*, or holy fighter, and for the first time the *jihad* became a truly active force to push towards the ultimate reconquest of Jerusalem. Zengi himself had few associations with men of religion, but his achievement was rewarded by the caliph of Baghdad, the spiritual head of Sunni Islam, with a string of honorific titles: 'The adornment of Islam, the King helped by God, the helper of the believers' (ibid.: 119). For the Franks, the loss of one of their key cities was the greatest setback that they had yet faced and Muslim forces followed up their success to take much of the county to the east of the River Euphrates. The Edessans sent messengers to Antioch and Jerusalem pleading for help and this, in turn, resulted in the appeals to Europe that prompted the Second Crusade.

THE REGENCY OF MELISENDE AND THE ACCESSION OF BALDWIN III

When news of the fall of Edessa reached Jerusalem it was the regent, Queen Melisende, who ordered a relief force north. On the death of her husband, King Fulk, in 1143, the throne passed to their son, Baldwin III, but he had not yet come of age and so the queen governed on his behalf. She had shown her political acumen in the Hugh of Jaffa affair (see below, pp. 126–8) and she undoubtedly played a prominent part in ruling Jerusalem during the remainder of Fulk's reign. William of Tyre was a particular admirer of Melisende and described her as a 'woman of great wisdom'. He observed that she 'dared to undertake important measures' (William of Tyre, tr. Babcock and Krey, 1943: 2.139–40).

Such was Melisende's power that when Baldwin came of age (at 15) in 1145, she continued to govern. In June 1148 the leaders of the Second

Crusade would meet both Baldwin and Melisende at Palmarea (near Acre) in the great council that decided to attack Damascus, although as a woman Melisende did not accompany the army on campaign. She continued to play the leading partner, however, much to Baldwin's increasing displeasure. By 1152, when the king was aged 22, he had gathered enough backers – in part through his effective military exploits in northern Syria and the Hauran – to try to force his mother to step down. The situation polarised the kingdom's nobility; both camps formed their own chanceries and issued charters in their own name and each established their supporters in positions of power. The struggle had reached the point of armed conflict when Baldwin besieged a castle controlled by Melisende's constable (her chief military leader). At first the kingdom was partitioned between the two rivals, but given the growing Muslim threat this was impractical and, in any case, Baldwin wanted to exercise full authority. He besieged Melisende in the citadel of Jerusalem and forced her to surrender her lands, except the city of Nablus, and to promise to abstain from politics. In fact, Melisende excerted a considerable influence in public life until her death in 1161.

Melisende was more than an astute political player, she was also a great patron of the Church and art. She founded a convent for religious women at Bethany (her youngest sister Iveta was the first abbess), and gave many estates, precious vessels and ornaments to provide for their development. She was a generous donor to the *Templum Domini* church, the convent of St Anne's, the abbey of St Mary Jehosophat and the Holy Sepulchre. Melisende's mother had been an Armenian and this was one reason why the queen was a supporter of the Eastern Christian church of St James in Jerusalem. She is also associated with an exquisite psalter (a book of private prayers, reading and meditation), known as the Melisende Psalter, that is still preserved in the British Library. Roughly the size of a paperback book, it is beautifully illustrated with images from the New Testament and the Zodiac and its contents include the Psalms and prayers. The ivory covers themselves are an amazing blend of styles: English, French, Byzantine, Arab and Levantine, a reflection of the polyglot society of the Frankish East. The front cover concentrates on the Old Testament ruler King David, and it has roundels studded with turquoise, ruby and emerald stones, showing images that depict his strength, fitness to rule, his humility and interest in harmony. The king on the back cover performs the six acts of mercy listed in the Book of Matthew. This monarch sits under a bird, labeled 'Herodius', also known as a 'fulica' in medieval bestiaries, that is, a falcon. The name is, therefore, a pun on Fulk and signifies him as the patron of a work that must have been hugely expensive. The themes of peace and reconciliation are appropriate to an attempt by the king to apologise for the political and personal failings he displayed during and after the revolt of Hugh of Jaffa (see below, pp. 126–8).

Melisende was one of the most memorable figures in the history of twelfth-century Latin Christendom. In spite of the endemic warfare in the Levant, and the fact that the prime function of a medieval ruler was as a warrior, she overcame her inability to participate in warfare by her formidable political skills and her position as the carrier of the blood-line of the royal house of Jerusalem. There were precedents in the medieval West for women to exercise power, most notably Queen Uracca of León-Castile (1109–26), although the near-contemporary failure of Empress Matilda to take the crown of England showed that female rulers were not always accepted.

She was involved in high-level politics for almost twenty years, and she had ruled, effectively in her own right, for the best part of a decade. It is a vivid testimony to Melisende's power that she had the strength to hold on to the crown for seven years after Baldwin III had reached his majority. While at first there may have been some misgivings over the king's youth, the excuse to remove Melisende could have been brought into play much sooner had there been doubts as to her abilities. She attracted the blessing of Bernard of Clairvaux, the most important churchman of the age, who described her as 'a strong woman, a humble widow, a great queen', while William of Tyre adjudged her the equal of her ancestors as a ruler. On her death in September 1161 she was buried in the church of St Mary at Jehosophat where her tomb chamber remains today.

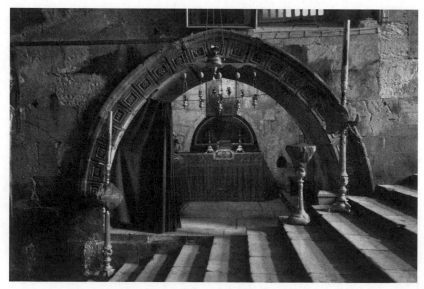

5. Tomb chamber of Queen Melisende, Jerusalem

CONCLUSION

The first five decades of the twelfth century had seen the Franks establish themselves in the Levant. The ruling houses of Antioch and Jerusalem had taken root, although not without the need to adapt and incorporate outside influences such as Fulk of Anjou and Raymond of Poitiers. The Italian mercantile communities had played a central part in the conquest of the coast. Their rewards of land and privileges cemented their involvement in the Frankish East and ensured a flow of pilgrim and commercial traffic from the West. The idea of the crusade had expanded to include Bohemond's campaign against the Greeks in 1108 and also saw papally authorised expeditions (marked by letters and the award of privileges) against the Muslims of the Balearic islands in 1114 and mainland Spain in 1116 and 1118. By the end of this period, however, the Muslims of the Levant were beginning to develop some cohesion in their opposition to the Christians and the *jihad* was truly underway.

4

The challenges of a new land: Frankish rule and settlement

In the early years of the twelfth century the Frankish settlers faced a daunting series of problems if they were to establish themselves permanently in the Levant. In part they required the same determination, religious devotion and military success that had propelled the First Crusade to victory. Yet further attributes were needed because, if the First Crusade had confronted a formidable challenge, that of the early generations of settlers was, by reason of the diversity and the duration of their task, even greater. Interestingly, we see this recognised in contemporary western sources (see Document 6 iii). Among the issues that the settlers had to resolve were: first, to complete the conquest of unfamiliar lands inhabited by a culturally, ethnically and politically heterogeneous group of peoples (for the events of the conquest, see Chapter 3); second, to establish a rule of government over these regions – in other words, to form a relationship with the indigenous population and to create or take over administrative systems; third, to prevent internal revolts and to fend off enemy attacks; and finally, to settle themselves in both rural and urban areas. All of this had to be achieved far from their homeland. The Christian kingdoms of Spain were taking over Muslim lands at this time, but their own territories were contiguous with existing Catholic possessions which provided a base to work from. Similarly, during the Norman conquest of Muslim Sicily (c. 1060 to c. 1091), the nearby southern Italian mainland could supply men and resources and was close enough to retreat to if necessary. For the nascent Frankish States in the Levant, geographically distant from the West, there were no such luxuries. The awareness of this is powerfully conveyed by Fulcher of Chartres's eye-witness report of King Baldwin I's speech just before the Battle of Ramla in September 1101: 'If you should be slain here, you will surely be among the blessed. Already the kingdom of Heaven is open to you. If you survive as victors you will shine in glory among all Christians. If, however, you wish to flee remember that France is indeed a long distance away' (Fulcher of Chartres, tr. Ryan, 1969: 157–58).

RELATIONS WITH INDIGENOUS PEOPLES

Because of its rich history and ongoing importance to Christianity, Islam and Judaism, the indigenous population of the Levant was extremely diverse. The Franks had to confront, assess and establish friendly or hostile relations with ethnic groups and faiths whom, in some cases, they were unlikely to have encountered before. Walter the Chancellor, who wrote in the principality c. 1115 to c. 1122, related that the population of the city of Antioch contained 'Franks, Greeks, Armenians, strangers and pilgrims' (Walter the Chancellor, tr. Asbridge and Edgington, 1999: 81); there were large numbers of Greek Orthodox and Muslim farmers in some areas as well. The county of Edessa was predominantly Armenian in population; the county of Tripoli had enclaves of Greek Orthodox and other eastern Christians (such as Maronites), as well as Sunni and Shiite Muslims (the renegade Shiite sect known as the Assassins). The kingdom of Jerusalem was particularly mixed, with Muslim villages, eastern Christian settlements and roving Bedouin tribesmen. While many of the Jews in Jerusalem had perished in 1099, small communities reappeared in urban areas across the Latin East once the initial turmoil of the conquest had subsided.

The outstanding feature of Frankish settlement was the newcomers' numerical inferiority. Population figures are very hard to establish, but a peak ratio of one Frank to three of the indigenous populace (Eastern Christian or Muslim) seems a consensus, although in the early years of settlement the gap would have been much wider. In 1101 Fulcher of Chartres recorded that only 300 knights remained in the kingdom and while new crusaders and settlers continued to arrive the Christians still had to make a calculated judgement as to what area of lands they could hold without overstretching themselves. It was not viable for the Franks to remove all non-Christians; equally, it was not practical for all of the native peoples to leave their farms and to start afresh elsewhere. In any case, their services were more valuable to the Franks than in Muslim-ruled lands, therefore a *modus vivendi* was established in order to satisfy the basic needs of day-to-day life. The sack of Jerusalem and the bloody aftermath of other sieges, such as Caesarea in 1101 or Beirut in 1110, have to be balanced with the surrender of other cities such as Sidon (1110) where the inhabitants were offered a choice of leaving or remaining under Frankish rule. It was reported that Baldwin I let the farmers stay at Sidon 'because of their usefulness in cultivating the land' (Fulcher of Chartres, tr. Ryan, 1969: 200). In the same year, Tancred of Antioch was sufficiently concerned that native labourers should remain on his lands that he arranged for their wives to return from Aleppo where they had fled for safety. It must be remembered that Tancred and his Norman associates in Antioch were of the same dynastic line as the Normans who had completed the conquest of both Byzantine southern Italy and

Muslim Sicily as recently as 1091. There was, therefore, a body of men amongst the crusaders with recent experience of taking over territories with large Greek Orthodox (southern Italy) and Muslim (Sicily) lands and who, similarly constrained by lack of numbers in the same way that the Franks of the East were, had adopted a low-key approach that did relatively little to disturb the majority of the urban and rural populace. The conquest of Sicily was proving durable and in the early twelfth century it seems that after the initial conquest a similar policy was often operated in the Latin East.

One demonstration of this engagement with the indigenous population can be seen through the Antiochene coinage. In an age prior to mass communications, one way to get an image or a message across to as many people as possible, was on money. The Norman rulers of Antioch were familiar with using local language coupled with carefully chosen iconography on their coinage in southern Italy and Sicily and they did the same in their new conquest which had a large Orthodox population not least because it had been part of the Byzantine Empire until 1084. Two examples can show this:

1. Prince Tancred, type 1. This has an image of St Peter on one side, and on the reverse, in Greek, the inscription 'O Lord, come to the aid of thy servant Tancred'.
2. Prince Roger, type 3. This shows St George slaying the dragon. St George was an important figure in eastern traditions who had also figured in accounts of the First Crusade as offering assistance to the Christians during the battle of Antioch in 1098. The idea of good defeating evil is also pertinent. The reverse (not shown here) has an inscription, again in Greek, which says, 'Roger, prince of Antioch', although technically he was only the regent for the young Bohemond II.

It is noticeable that after the death of the Norman Sicilian Bohemond II in 1130 his successor, Raymond of Poitiers, chose to end the production of these coins and struck money bearing his own image and with Latin inscriptions.

(a)   (b)   (c)

6. Coins of Prince Tancred (a), Prince Roger of Antioch (b) and Kingdom of Jerusalem, gold bezant (c)

A wish to establish his own identity as distinct from his predecessors, coupled with rising antagonism towards the Byzantine Empire meant that such a change was appropriate.

The coinage of the kings of Jerusalem also shows adaptation to local conditions, in this instance with regards to gold coinage. There were no gold coins in contemporary western Europe (except in Sicily), but the conquerors of the Holy Land now ruled an area where Islamic gold dinars were familiar to the local merchants. The Franks could have put Christian designs on the coins but for reasons we do not know, they simply carried on producing the existing gold dinars with the name of al-Amir (the Fatimid caliph between 1101 and 1130) from mints in Acre. Baldwin III, probably in the early 1150s, reformed the gold coinage and introduced a modified gold coin, or as the Franks called them, bezants (see illustration 6c on previous page). They looked like dinars but were lighter and had a lower gold content and were exchanged at a rate of 4 bezants to 3 dinars. Perhaps commercial familiarity (and hence confidence) in the design overrode a wish to change their appearance; it is certainly an oddity given the care the kings gave to the design on their silver coins (see below, p. 131).

Details of the treatment of Muslims under Frankish rule are hard to ascertain because very little material survives. Document 10 contains two accounts. Ibn Jubayr was a Spanish Muslim on pilgrimage to Mecca who stayed in the Latin East for around four weeks in 1184 and visited a limited area of the kingdom of Jerusalem. The Hanbali peasants described in Diya al-Din's thirteenth-century work were a hardline minority religious group who saw exile from the Frankish lands as a positive achievement and have left a source that reflects a particularly tense (and probably unrepresentative) element of the relationship between the settlers and the Muslims. In spite of these limitations, both writers, in conjunction with other evidence, enable us to indicate that Muslims were allowed to practise their faith and to worship at shrines that formed part of Christian churches. The mosque in Tyre was in full Muslim possession, but the status of those elsewhere is unclear. The payment of a poll tax of 1 dinar and 5 *qirats* (24 *qirats* to 1 dinar) as a subject people, plus the yield of up to half of their crops was, in fact, lighter than that demanded in Muslim lands – a reflection of the Franks' wish to keep the farmers reasonably content. The Muslim *Rais* or headman, would deal with a Frankish estates steward and also had jurisdiction over minor disputes within Muslim communities. In more serious cases (such as physical injury) the dispute was brought before the Frankish Court of the Burgesses and in cases between members of different communities the Court of the Market (*Cour de la Fonde*) was the relevant forum, although it was chaired by a Frank and had four eastern Christian and two Frankish jurors. The omission of Muslim representation showed them to be at the bottom of the legal ladder, with the eastern Christians above them and the Franks at the top.

Usama ibn Munqidh (see 'Who's Who') gives several other insights into relations between the Muslims and the various Christian groups. On one occasion he sent a representative to Antioch where a Greek Orthodox friend of Usama's invited the latter's man to join him for lunch at the house of an old Frankish knight who had lived in the Levant for several decades (see Document 10 iii below). This scene shows that the old knight was happy to share his table with a Muslim and an Orthodox Christian, that he had an Egyptian cook and (presumably as a consequence of this) that he did not eat pork; he was, therefore, well integrated into the local culture. Soon after the lunch ended, Usama's man was walking along the street when he was accused of having killed a Frank. He seemed about to be lynched, yet the same old knight (his lunchtime host) identified him as a merchant, not a warrior, and saved the Muslim's life. As Usama noted, some of the Franks were well acclimatised and kept the company of Muslims, as in the example just given. Yet he also related instances of recent arrivals being aggressive towards the local population, indicating that westerners tended to be more prejudiced in their attitude to the Islamic inhabitants of the region.

The danger of a revolt by indigenous peoples must have been of real concern in the early decades of settlement. After the calamitous defeat at the Battle of the Field of Blood (1119), when most of the Antiochene nobility had been killed, Walter the Chancellor recorded that the native populace 'could greatly oppress our people by betrayal . . . because that is how the scales of justice change; for indeed the people of Antioch had been deprived of their goods by the force and deviousness of our people' (Walter the Chancellor, tr. Asbridge and Edgington, 1999: 138). Given the profile of the population of Antioch, this statement probably refers to the Eastern Christians and shows how a heavy-handed approach to government – especially at times of military weakness – might provoke a rebellion against the Frankish minority. Muslim uprisings could also take place, especially if they believed the Franks were on the verge of defeat. Fulcher of Chartres noted that in 1113 the Saracens who were subject to the settlers around Nablus deserted them at a time of Muslim invasion. However, it should be emphasised that such episodes were extremely rare and that, in general, the Franks managed to maintain full authority over the indigenous people in their lands, largely through military presence supported by provision of justice and a reasonable burden of taxation.

FRANKISH RURAL SETTLEMENT

The nature of Frankish rural settlement has been a highly contentious issue amongst historians and it is a matter which touches further upon relations with the indigenous population (more with the Eastern Christians than with the Muslims), as well as the policies of the Franks themselves. The form and extent of this practice has long been debated and until recently two basic models had been put forward. The first, constructed by French scholars in the late nineteenth and early twentieth centuries, argued that the Franks became highly assimilated with the indigenous population of the Levant and adopted many of their customs and practices, thus becoming 'orientalised'. Relations with the locals were good, with Ibn Jubayr's description of a Muslim workforce living contentedly under Christian rule providing the main evidence for this. A second, and completely contrary, view emerged in the 1950s. Prawer and Smail claimed that the Latin East was a highly segregated society in which the ruling Franks, separated by religion and language, lived in their castles and cities, aloof from contact with an untrustworthy local populace (both Muslim and native Christian) and fearful of external attack from the neighbouring Muslim powers (Prawer, 1980; Smail, 1995). Both of these models have been challenged recently by the work of Ellenblum (Ellenblum, 1998). Through the use of archaeological evidence – to supplement the written sources employed by earlier historians – he has put forward a new and largely convincing interpretation of the nature of Frankish settlement, although his study applies only to the kingdom of Jerusalem and not to the more northerly regions. In essence, Ellenblum argues that a substantial element of the Frankish population lived in the countryside, but they chose to inhabit only certain areas of land and seemed to avoid others according to the identity of the indigenous people *in situ*.

THE ORIGINS OF THE FRANKISH SETTLERS AND THEIR WAY OF LIFE

The reasons for Frankish rural settlement in the Levant were varied and multi-faceted. The rulers of the Latin East granted their nobles areas of land in return for military service (see Document 17) and the barons then protected and administered these regions to the best of their ability. The rural districts under their control might already have an indigenous populace, but would also be subject to immigration from western farmers and workers. The spiritual resonance of living in the Holy Land would have attracted a number of settlers, while some crusaders must have chosen to stay in the Levant after completing their vows, doubtless attracted by the prospect of acquiring property and financial privileges. Others may have been obliged to remain with their lord if he had chosen to settle. Economic motives would have been a vital inducement for westerners to uproot themselves from their native lands and to seek a new life in the distant orient. It should be remembered, however, that this was an age of population growth with areas such as the

Low Countries experiencing overcrowding and frequent famines. It was also a time when migration was not at all uncommon: as Christendom expanded its borders into Eastern Europe and Iberia, land agents offered new opportunities which many thousands of people accepted. We presume that similar recruitment drives were mounted to persuade people to live in the Levant, where, as noted, there was a spiritual dimension to the settlement, but there was also the risk of enemy attack and unfamiliar and sometimes hostile agricultural conditions. As with the motives of a crusader, we are dealing with a combination of the religious and the secular and it is impossible to determine the precise nature of the mix, although given the needs of daily survival it seems likely that in the case of the average farmer it was the more practical aspect that dominated.

Some evidence survives concerning the terms upon which settlers were offered land. In the mid-twelfth century King Baldwin III of Jerusalem (1143–63) gave newcomers at the fortified village of Casal Imbert (*c.* 12 kilometres north of Acre), long-term leases on houses, an exemption from annual rent and plots of arable land. In return, the settlers were to pay the king one-seventh of all their crops, 25 per cent of the produce of the vineyards and orchards, and 40 per cent of the produce of the communal olive grove. Other rights pertaining to the tenants were exemptions of tax on moveable products sold in the market at Acre and free use of a nearby mill. One-fifteenth of the bread from the village oven was due to the king, along with 10 per cent of the proceeds from the bathhouse. At around the same time the Church of the Holy Sepulchre conferred upon settlers at Nova Villa (north of Jerusalem) land for building a house and for planting gardens and trees, rights to free use of the local flour mill, oven and other such facilities, and the right to cultivate the church's local vineyard. In return the settlers had to pay tithes to the archbishop of Jerusalem, give him 25 per cent of the annual grain and vegetable production, 20 per cent of the produce of the vineyards and olive groves planted in the village and 25 per cent of the olives from older olive groves. Finally, all the produce and tithes were to be stored in the church's storehouse in the village. Ellenblum explains the difference in rights between Casal Imbert and Nova Villa as a consequence of the latter settlement being sufficiently long-established and successful that it could demand more from settlers than the newer site in the north (Ellenblum, 1998: 72). Regardless of detail these examples show the basic pattern of land tenure for newcomers.

From around the same period we have an insight into the place of origin and the occupation of two groups of settlers in the Latin kingdom. A document pertaining to the village of Magna Mahomeria allows the identification of forty-four westerners. The majority of these individuals came from France (with central France best represented and northern France absent) with a few

Italians and Catalans (northern Spanish). A document from Bethgibelin enables a further nineteen settlers to be identified and here there is a bias towards southern and western France and again a dearth of people from northern France. This perplexing point may be a quirk of our evidence, but in any case, it seems certain that the settler villages were of a mixed western composition. The range of occupations mentioned includes builders, agriculture, animal husbandry, metalworking, a butcher and a baker, thus forming a coherent rural community appropriate to the social and economic conditions in the Levant.

As the Franks began to settle they had the option of creating entirely new villages (*villeneuves*), or establishing themselves within and alongside native villages. The latter tended to be of a more random layout, reflecting irregular growth over time, but archaeological work also reveals Frankish villages (i.e. *villeneuves*), built to a consistent plan and connected to other settlements by new roads. These villages, such as the recently excavated site of Ramot, about 6 kilometres north-west of Jerusalem, were constructed on either side of a road with strip fields (again, of a uniform size) running behind them. Linear villages such as Ramot were commonly found in medieval Europe, which indicates that the Franks imported a pattern of settlement familiar to them. These villages usually had a fortified building, probably the residence of the lord or his representative, which might offer security and storage facilities. Houses in Ramot feature wine-treading basins, olive presses and an oven inside them. The religious needs of the populace might be catered for in a new church, either in the village or in the locality. At the fortified village of Sinjil, for example, the parish included several nearby Frankish villages whose landlords paid the church tithes to support it. In settlements established alongside a native Orthodox population the Franks often took over a local church, but still permitted the locals to use it to some extent, as at the church of St George above Tiberias.

In addition to rural communities the Franks also constructed isolated manor houses or farms – again a familiar sight in western Europe. Some of these were quite substantial buildings that obviously represented a serious investment in the working of the land. They would need to be connected to other sites by new roads, and often consisted of a barrel-vaulted hall, a residential tower and big reservoirs linking irrigation channels to a series of terraced fields that could support crops such as bananas, indigo, dates and sugar cane. At Khalat Salman (*c.* 15 kilometres north-west of Jerusalem) the farm is located on a terrace above a wadi with irrigated fields spreading down below the house and adapted to the terrain to exploit the flow of water. Some of the irrigation systems were quite sophisticated and probably relied upon local advice and labour for their construction. The Franks obviously assimilated this technology quickly, although those from the dryer regions of southern Europe and the reclaimed marshlands and waterways of Flanders would have had some experience of hydrographics, if not the farming of unfamiliar crops such as sugar cane. The importance of irrigation is made plain in legal documents that outline agreements concerning the flow of water from springs owned by one institution to the lands of other farmers.

The administration of a Frankish lord's lands was through his representative or *dragoman*. This man lived permanently on the estates of his lord and might be a native Christian. His upkeep was provided for by contributions from the farmers and the produce of his master's lands. In return he had to accompany his lord on missions that risked incurring losses of men or horses and he might have to provide the lord with a knight as well. The existence of such officials allowed Frankish lords to divide their time between rural estates and their properties in urban settlements.

THE PATTERN OF FRANKISH SETTLEMENT IN THE LATIN KINGDOM OF JERUSALEM

As we noted earlier, there was a remarkably mixed population in the Levant. The majority of the indigenous population was Muslim or native Christian, with strong regional variations between these groups. Frankish rural settlement also seems to have displayed a distinct pattern. Ellenblum has observed that there was intensive Frankish habitation in western Galilee, but almost no Latin settlement in eastern Galilee (Ellenblum, 1998: 253–76). The latter area was characterised by William of Tyre as a lawless region not subject to Frankish law where Jews, Muslims, renegades and nomads lived. We know that a tribe of 100 Bedouin tents was based near Belvoir and it seems that groups of this sort were hard to control and promoted feelings of insecurity among the settlers. Central Samaria was another district with no written or archaeological evidence of Frankish habitation during the crusader period and there are clear indications that Muslim and Samaritan villages covered the region. Yet in southern Samaria (bordering on Jerusalem itself) there was extremely intensive Frankish settlement. Ellenblum concludes that the borders of Frankish settlement were set on cultural lines and that the Latins lived among or alongside the local Christian communities and avoided Muslim areas. He argues that the Franks did little to prejudice the landholding rights of individual native Christians (obviously this was a different matter for ecclesiastical institutions) and, as noted earlier in the case of the church of St George above Tiberias, they might use the same churches too. Thus the original French model of a Franco–Syrian nation needs to be modified to place the Franks and native Christians together, but distinct from the Muslims. Likewise Prawer and Smail's model of an urban-dwelling society fearful of external Muslim attacks and native uprising is flawed by the apparently secure conditions that existed in the kingdom of Jerusalem from the 1120s to the late 1160s. In consequence, there was no need to stay in the towns and cities and this permitted a close degree of interaction with the native Christians. The apartheid state envisaged by Prawer and Smail did not, therefore, exist as far as Latins and local Christians were concerned. Ibn Jubayr clouds matters a little in that his journey from Banyas via Hunin and Tibnin to Acre in 1184 passed through 'continuous farms and ordered settlements whose inhabitants were all Muslims, living comfortably with the Franks' (Ibn Jubayr, tr. Broadhurst, 1952: 316). The first part of this journey matches Ellenblum's identification of eastern Galilee as devoid of Franks, but Ibn Jubayr described Muslim villages in close proximity to Acre in an area where intensive Frankish settlement was found too. Perhaps the sharp regionalisation between Franks and Muslims that was found in central Samaria and eastern Galilee was not so distinct everywhere in the Levant, especially in the fertile coastal regions where a particularly large labour force was needed.

URBAN LIFE

When the Franks conquered the Levant their power was based upon control of the urban centres. The imposition of Christian rule brought a number of changes to urban life, although many of the everyday aspects of city dwelling in the Eastern Mediterranean remained the same. One obvious and visible effect was the conversion of mosques to churches and, as the Franks established their religious hierarchy and Catholic spiritual life took root in the region, new churches and convents were also constructed. The case of the Holy Sepulchre will be discussed later (see pp. 133–4 below), and often other Frankish ecclesiastical buildings were erected on top of existing buildings, such as the church of St Anne in Jerusalem (Anne was the mother of the Virgin Mary and the church marked the home of her parents and her birthplace) where a structure had stood since the fourth century. The settlers also created their own graveyards to bury their dead.

The population of Jerusalem was c. 20,000 in the early twelfth century, rising to c. 30,000 in later decades, although pilgrims would have increased this significantly during the summer months (Boas, 2001: 13, 35). The Franks needed to ensure their security in all the cities they had conquered and there was often a need to repair walls damaged during sieges or to develop new fortifications themselves. Medieval cities featured numerous gates – sites of defensive importance, but also essential in the financial operation of a town as key points of taxation for both people and goods. With rural land potentially subject to enemy raids and therefore an unreliable source of revenue, the king (or other major landholders) often gave knights the rights to the profit of a gate (an arrangement known as a money-fief). Tax levels varied from 4 per cent to 25 per cent and the crown usually kept back a proportion of this for the central treasury.

In all urban centres, certain essential functions were needed. Markets were a focus of commercial life and in 1152 Queen Melisende encouraged this through the construction of a series of properly covered streets, including the notorious 'Street of Bad Cooking', presumably the site of takeaway food vendors. Other streets boasted specialities such as spices, fish, leather, cloth, pilgrims' souvenirs, furs, pigs, poultry, or in the case of Tripoli where there was an important centre of silk production, a silk market. A city might also feature other industries such as mints, blacksmiths, bakers, gold and silver smiths, abbatoirs and tanneries. The inhabitants needed a water supply and the Franks took over existing cisterns and aqueducts and also added their own.

Some Franks took property in the immediate aftermath of the early conquests. At Jerusalem in 1099 Fulcher of Chartres reported that 'whoever first entered a house, whether he was rich or poor, was not challenged by another Frank. He was to occupy and own the house or palace and whatever he found in it as if it were entirely his own' (Fulcher of Chartres, tr. Ryan, 1969: 123). After later sieges the Frankish rulers shared out their gains in a more orderly fashion, but in any case the newcomers' arrival in urban life was made plain. The great institutions, such as the military orders and the principal churches of the Latin East were given their own streets and districts which contained chapels, storehouses and accommodation. The Franks also built their own houses, some of two or three storeys, often with the lowest level used as a shop or storage facility. Other forms of accommodation included courtyard houses and tower houses, and cities would also feature bathhouses, hospitals and, often just outside the gates, a leprosarium.

TRADE

The strategic and economic importance of controlling the ports of the Mediterranean coast has been made clear earlier (see pp. 36–7, 44–5). Acre, Tyre, Tripoli and Saint Simeon (in the principality of Antioch) – were the most active with traders from (especially) Venice, Genoa and Pisa meeting those of the Latin East, Muslim Syria, North Africa, Iraq and Byzantium.

Ekkehard of Aura visited the Holy Land in the immediate aftermath of the First Crusade and he reported that Godfrey of Bouillon 'maintained firm peace for the sake of commerce with Ascalon and Damascus'. While calm could not be assured the whole time it was natural that peace would promote prosperity. The Italian city states had been trading in the Levant prior to the First Crusade, most notably in Alexandria, which was by far the most valueable port in the Mediterranean. As the Christian settlements became more secure the volume of contact between the Near East and the Italian cities (and also Marseille) grew significantly. While it might appear odd that trade between the Islamic Near East and the Franks blossomed during what was, on the surface, an age of irreconcilable enmity, economic realities dictated a considerable contact. Ibn Jubayr, the Spanish Muslim pilgrim, noted in his visit to the region in August 1184: 'One of the most astonishing things that is talked of is that though the fires of discord burn between the two parties, Muslim and Christian, two armies of them may meet and dispose of themselves in battle array, and yet Christian and Muslim travellers will come and go between them without interference' (Ibn Jubayr, tr. Broadhurst, 1952: 300). He recorded that Acre and Tyre both had an indigenous Muslim population and many visiting merchants from Islamic lands. The Italians certainly maintained and developed their presence in Alexandria while more intrepid merchants ventured inland; we know of Genoese trading in timber in Cairo early in the twelfth century or in Damascus in 1156, for example. This is not to say that in times of conflict traders were immune from suspicion or hostility; the Egyptians were wary of spies masquerading as merchants.

We should not see commercial relations between the West and the Levant in a vacuum, of course. The Italians also developed commercial relations with Byzantium, although these were subject to periodic disturbances, most notably in 1171 when Emperor Manuel Komnenos (1143–80) seized all the Venetians and their goods in the Empire and when in May 1182 the actions of the anti-Latin Andronicus Komnenos (regent 1182–83, emperor 1183–85) prompted a massacre of the Italian traders in Constantinople.

The trading cities of the Frankish East must have had an extraordinary buzz of languages in the crowded *souqs* (markets) of the Holy Land as trade flourished throughout the twelfth century. We can see in Document 8 how the Italian trading communities negotiated their own districts (known as 'quarters') with a church, usually dedicated to their patron saint (such as St Lawrence of Genoa, or St Michael of Venice), and their own houses, shops and palaces. The port area itself was the hub of all commercial activity and a brief survey of buying and selling can demonstrate the complexities (and opportunities) of trade and tax collection. At any point in this chain, an individual or community (usually the Italians or southern French) might be granted exemptions from a particular tax (or taxes), often in return for military help. At first glance it would seem the grantor was writing off a substantial proportion of his revenue by this approach. In fact, alongside the strategic benefit of capturing a port, it was intended that the exemptions would give the privileged party sufficient incentive to trade even more and to generate an overall rise in the volume of commerce. Furthermore, taxes paid by other people at other points in the commercial process (see later) would also make up what had been conceded in the first instance. A merchant arriving at Acre, for example, would have had to pay his passage on the ship to the East. The ship needed to make a payment to moor at the outer harbour and then to raise the chain that protected the inner harbour. At Acre this area was known as the 'Ordemer' because of the refuse and excrement floating on the water. The merchant's goods would have to be transferred to the shore (for a fee), and were then taxed according to their value, although in the case of bulk products such as wine, grain, oil and sugar, according to quantity. The goods had to be stored, which again required a fee. The sale of goods would attract a tax and the purchaser would then have to pay to take the goods out of a gate to leave the city. In short, there existed a series of economic opportunities for those in power to secure income and to favour those whom they wished to reward. Acre was the busiest port in the Frankish East and its atmosphere is described by Ibn Jubayr in 1184 as 'a port of call for all ships. It is the focus of Christian and Muslim caravans, and the meeting place of Muslim and Christian merchants of all regions. Its roads and streets are choked by the press of men, so that it is hard to put foot to ground. It stinks and is filthy, being full of refuse and excrement' (Ibn Jubayr, tr. Broadhurst, 1952: 318). Urban life, with its mixture of commerce and religion, must have been an intense and highly involving experience for the settlers, pilgrims and traders alike.

A FRANKISH IDENTITY?

As the Franks set up their new territories at the heart of the Christian faith it is worth noting contemporary views on the sense of identity that emerged in the Latin East. One perspective is provided by Fulcher of Chartres, the French-born chaplain to Count Baldwin of Boulogne (later King Baldwin I of Jerusalem). Fulcher wrote his account of the First Crusade and the early decades of the kingdom in three stages. The first was completed by c. 1107–8 and covered the First Crusade and the early years of the conquest. In October 1100, as Baldwin marched south to take the throne of Jerusalem, the Franks faced a difficult battle near Beirut. Fulcher wrote: 'On all sides we were besieged by our enemies. . . . That day nothing went well. . . . Indeed I wished very much that I were in Chartres or Orleans and so did the others . . .' (Fulcher of Chartres, tr. Ryan, 1969: 139). Although, *de facto*, these men had not returned home after the First Crusade, at this point they had not yet put down emotional or even practical roots to tie themselves to the Levant. Yet in the final part of his work, composed in the 1120s, Fulcher was able to write the famous lines contained in Document 6 i. While, to some extent, Fulcher may have been indulging in an element of recruitment (his *Historia* circulated in the West), he would have been rash to have presented an entirely false picture. He suggests, in fact, that the Franks regarded themselves as permanent settlers and that they had formed a self-image borne out of their common Christian stock and their achievements to date.

We can also see reference to the process of intermarriage with native women. In the county of Edessa, marriage to women of the indigenous nobility was an important way for the newcomers to cement their rule over the local peoples and a similar practice had been employed with great success in southern Italy during the Norman conquests of the eleventh century. In the case of Edessa, the first three Frankish counts married Armenian wives.

Naming practices can also cast light on the mentality of settlement. Jacoby has drawn attention to one Guibert of Jaffa, a house owner in Acre in the early 1120s, who had evidently shed the western surname found among many early Frankish settlers to take on a name that reflected his eastern home (Jacoby, 1997: 160). The Embriaci were a Genoese family who eventually acquired independent control over the coastal city of Jubayl in the county of Tripoli but also had other branches of the clan still in their homeland. By the late 1160s they started to drop their original name and used instead *de Biblio*, that is 'Byblos', the ancient Greek name of Jubayl. This was in part a consequence of disputes with the ruling consuls of Genoa but also a wish to emphasise their permanence in, and affinity to, their Levantine home. Hugh III of Jubayl was amongst those captured at Hattin in 1187 (Mack, 2003).

Shagrir has examined naming patterns for males in the Latin Kingdom of Jerusalem (Shagrir, 2003) and she demonstrates that during the twelfth century the most popular names were William, Peter and John. William represented a royal, dynastic image, linked to leading families in the West (England, Sicily); Peter was consistently popular amongst the burgess classes of medieval Europe and was similarly prominent in this group in the Levant. The name John, along with James and Nicholas, rose steadily in popularity through the twelfth century with John topping the figures by 1190. In these three cases, as well as that of Peter, we should note that the names may also have acquired popularity because they were important in the naming traditions of Eastern Christians. Thus, they were appropriate and familiar names for the children of mixed couples with oriental and Latin parents.

Language was also an important issue. As we saw earlier (pp. 24–6) the First Crusade was made up of many different groups, speaking a broad range of tongues. The majority of crusaders came from what we now call France, although here too there was variation because much of the southern half of France spoke Occitan dialects with German and Flemish dialects used in the north-east. The settlers in the Levant were known as 'Franks', a label given to them by the Byzantines and the Muslims, and one it seems that they adopted for themselves too. Notwithstanding the regional variations in the origins of the inhabitants noted in, for example, the village of Magna Mahomeria (see pp. 58–9 above) the northern variety of Old French emerged as the principal spoken language for the Franks of the Latin East (Murray, 2011).

While they continued to share faith and family ties with their brethren in the West, the crusaders had indeed become settlers with their own independence and a real sense of identity.

5

The military orders

I n the first half of the twelfth century two institutions emerged to protect
and to care for western pilgrims visiting the Holy Land. These functions
soon coupled with the settlers' need to increase their limited military
resources and, when combined with the idea of religiously directed violence
(highlighted by the First Crusade), there evolved orders of warrior-monks
known to us as the Templars and the Hospitallers. This new concept proved
highly popular and over time other military orders were founded in Iberia
and, later, in the Baltic region. The orders played a prominent role in the
defence and extension of the borders of Christianity in both the West and the
Levant, while through their numerous landholdings they had a high profile
across western Europe as well. Bernard of Clairvaux wrote of the Knights
Templar *c.* 1130, 'I do not know if it is more appropriate to call them monks
or knights; perhaps it is better to recognize them as being both, for they lack
neither monastic weakness nor military fortitude' (see Document 7 i). The
Templars and the Hospitallers came to form the core of the settlers' army
during the twelfth century; they were trained fighters who were sworn to
defend the Holy Land against the infidel, but, as Bernard had noted, they
were members of a religious order as well. They took the monastic vows of
poverty, chastity and obedience and lived in communities, yet they also
moved in the outside world to fulfil their duty against the enemies of Christ.
The notion of the warrior-monk was a striking innovation, and one that
fitted perfectly the needs and aspirations of the medieval knight, the Church
and the frontier societies of Latin Christendom.

THE ORIGINS AND DEVELOPMENT OF
THE TEMPLARS

The Templars were founded in Jerusalem around 1119–20 by the French
nobleman Hugh of Payns and a small association of laymen. According to

William of Tyre, their initial purpose was to defend pilgrims in the Holy Land from robbers and lions. The date of the foundation may be significant; an atmosphere of shock ensued after a massacre of 300 pilgrims near the River Jordan at Easter 1119 and the crushing defeat at the Battle of the Field of Blood in June of that same year. By 1120 Hugh and his companions had attracted the interest of a figure of high standing because Count Fulk V of Anjou (later King Fulk of Jerusalem) stayed with them for a year. The group derived its name from the accommodation granted to them in the Temple complex by King Baldwin II of Jerusalem, who, given the settlers' constant need for trained knights, regarded the idea of a body of men committed to the defence of pilgrims as worthy of support. It was soon decided to change the status of Hugh and his associates from that of laymen to professed religious and with this in mind a letter was sent to Abbot Bernard of Clairvaux in France. Bernard provided the Templars with a Rule (a way of life) and worked to secure papal approval for the nascent religious order. In two particular respects the emergence of the Templars reflected trends in contemporary European society. First, the success of the First Crusade meant that the concept of religiously directed violence was generally accepted. Second, the early decades of the twelfth century saw the foundation and growth of a number of religious orders (typified by the Cistercians), many of which had a sophisticated hierarchy capable of sustaining an international organisation – a structure that was to be essential for the Templars' development.

The Rule of the Templars, based on that of St Augustine (which was more appropriate for a group that moved in the secular world compared to the Benedictine Rule used by Bernard's Cistericans), included the key monastic precepts of poverty, chastity and obedience, but also contained a substantial level of practical information on the conduct of knights in battle, the maintenance of discipline, the appropriate levels of equipment and the hierarchy of the order (*The Rule of the Templars*, tr. Upton-Ward, 1992). The Templars were formally approved by the Church at the Council of Troyes in January 1129 and their numbers increased rapidly. While the First Crusade had endorsed the idea of religiously directed violence, the notion of fighting monks was extremely radical and needed to be justified. Bernard of Clairvaux wrote *De laude novae militiae* (In Praise of the New Knighthood) (Document 7 i) on the Templars' behalf, which explained why monks could also be warriors. According to Bernard, this depended – as did all crusading activity – upon the right intention (i.e. the motivation) of the individual. He argued that the Templars were a new sort of knight who fought evil in the world and, by their faith and their efforts, the Holy Land would be preserved in Christian hands. He set out the errors of secular knights – their vanities, their lust for glory and their greed for material possessions – and he contrasted such behaviour with that of 'the knights of Christ', as he called the Templars. He

7. Knights Templar riding out to battle. © Ronald Sheridan/Ancient Art &
Architecture Collection

concluded that for the former group 'to kill or to be killed for such reasons
is senseless'. The Templars, however, would behave very differently: they
lived a communal life of discipline and obedience to their superior; they
were focused on their duties to God and not on the shallow distractions of
the secular world – it was inner faith and trust in God that gave them extra
bravery and commitment in battle. Bernard was aware that the Templars
would not have the time for contemplation accorded to other monks, but he
suggested that their constant proximity to the holy sites would allow them to
reflect on the spiritual aspect of their surroundings. Also, as Barber has suggested, a detailed knowledge of the holy places would allow them to better
explain their significance to pilgrims (Barber, 1994: 45–49).

Hugh of Payns travelled around Europe seeking support for the Templars
and this produced numerous donations of land and money, as well as a stream
of new recruits. Within two years of the Council of Troyes there was a telling
indication of the order's attraction to contemporary laymen in the bequest of
King Alfonso I 'the Battler' of Aragon (1104–34). Remarkably, the king gave
over his entire kingdom to the Templars, the Hospitallers and the Canons of
the Holy Sepulchre. Alfonso was childless and his wish to prevent certain
rivals from taking over his lands may have played some part in his actions;
nevertheless, the king had founded two military fraternities of his own and
he was a committed participant in the *reconquista*. The terms of his testament
were a way of perpetuating his struggle against Islam and, although its execution would be frustrated by the intervention of local nobles, the Templars
secured a series of generous grants and castles by way of compensation.

A trio of privileges issued between 1139 and 1145 reinforced papal endorsement of the Templars. The order secured the right to elect its own master, the exemption from tithes (taxes) payable to the local church; they were also allowed to collect these revenues from their own lands and keep the profits for themselves. The order was permitted to have its own priests, which created greater independence from the local hierarchy. Further legislation set out inducements to encourage support for the order – in essence this meant that a layman making material provision for the brothers would receive a spiritual reward. For example, Pope Eugenius III (1145–53) decreed 'whoever . . . assists them and establishes a community for so holy a brotherhood and cedes to them benefits annually, we grant an indulgence of the seventh part of the penance enjoined upon him'. Another attraction for laymen was the prospect of becoming a Templar towards the end of their lives (thus joining a religious community), and then, when they died, to be buried in the cemeteries the papacy allowed the brothers to set up so that their souls would benefit from the association with the order.

As the military and financial strength of the Templars grew they were given custody of a number of castles and landholdings in the Holy Land. The first of these (in the late 1130s) was around the castle of Baghras in Antioch, a strategically crucial region that controlled the Belen Pass, one of the main routes into northern Syria. Other acquisitions followed, including castles at Gaza (1149–50), Safed (before 1168) and Toron (before 1172). In some areas the Templars held larger areas of land which they ruled virtually independently, such as the territories near Baghras and also around Chastel Blanc (Safita), and the port of Tartus (on the frontier between Antioch and Tripoli). Local churchmen resented the Templars' intrusion on their diocesan authority, but because the order had the support of Rome little could be done. There were times when the brothers clashed with secular rulers too. The most spectacular example of this was in 1173 when Templar knights killed Assassin envoys who were travelling home under a royal safe-conduct after negotiating some form of *rapprochement* with King Amalric of Jerusalem. It seems that the Templars disapproved of such dealings with a Muslim power. The king was furious at this injury to his honour and demanded that the perpetrators be given over to him. In theory, papal bulls gave the Templars immunity from secular jurisdiction in such cases and provided that the culprits be judged in Rome. On this occasion, however, Amalric, who was a very powerful monarch, had the ringleader seized and imprisoned. William of Tyre suggested that had the king lived longer (he died in 1174) the matter of the Templars' independence would have been challenged. In spite of this episode, the Templars' military power remained undiminished and when King Baldwin IV constructed the castle of Jacob's Ford in 1178–79 he chose to entrust it to the order (see below, pp. 151–2). In combination with their contribution to the armies of the Latin East, such responsibilities typified the role of the Templars in the latter half of the twelfth century.

King Amalric was not the only critic of the Templars during this period, however. John of Salisbury, one of the great intellectuals of the age, felt that knightly and clerical functions were incompatible and that the Templars' privileges encouraged pride and avarice. Likewise, William of Tyre, while recognising the central importance of the order in defending the Holy Land, sometimes saw their actions as self-interested, most famously at Ascalon in 1153 when a group of Templars breached the walls ahead of the main army and allegedly refused to let the other Franks join them because they wanted all the booty for themselves. As a result, the knights became trapped in the town and were massacred – a just reward for their greed. William probably influenced the Anglo–Norman cynic Walter Map whose vituperative criticism of the Templars stemmed from his (and William's) antagonism towards the financial and jurisdictional exemptions granted to religious orders by the papacy. More significantly perhaps, the Cistercian abbot, Issac of L'Etoile, expressed concern as to what those of another faith might think of the Christian Church encouraging violence rather than gentleness, and feared that any military activity carried a danger of leading the participants towards evil. While these voices show that the concept and development of the Templars was not universally welcomed (Barber, 1994, pp. 60–63), the substantial level of support that the order enjoyed indicates that, for the majority, the idea of warrior-monks defending Christ's patrimony was a positive step.

THE ORIGINS AND DEVELOPMENT OF THE HOSPITALLERS

The other leading military order of the time was the Order of the Hospital of St John of Jerusalem, known to us as the Hospitallers. Like the Templars they were warrior-monks sworn to defend the Holy Land, but there were important differences between the two institutions. Most notable of these, as indicated by their name, was the Hospitallers' medical function, which would remain a prominent part in their activities throughout the order's history; indeed, today's St John's Ambulance Brigade is a descendant of that legacy.

The origins of the Hospital pre-dated the First Crusade and derived from a hospice run by Amalfitans (Italian traders) who had established themselves in Jerusalem around the mid-eleventh century. The group followed a quasi-religious communal life in caring for sick pilgrims and were based in a building adjacent to the Holy Sepulchre, but after the Latin conquest the Amalfitan interest was replaced by French influence. Godfrey of Bouillon was an early supporter and with the increased flow of western pilgrims coming to the holy city many responded to the Hospital's charitable role by giving donations of property in the Levant or the West. Daughter hospices were founded in Europe, often serving pilgrim traffic, and entire settlements came under Hospitaller authority too. Southern France (1100) and Sicily (1101) saw early expansion, followed by Spain (1108), Italy (before 1113) and England (1128), with Germany following in the latter half of the twelfth century. One noteworthy episode was the creation, through deforestation, of a community of forty villages in the southern French county of Commignes c. 1099–1120. The European estates paid a proportion of their revenue – usually one-third – to sustain the Hospital in the Holy Land and their properties were often manned by knights who had retired from active service in the Levant. The western estates were organised into commanderies that typically consisted of a village, a church, a hospital and farm lands. Commanderies were grouped into provincial units known as priories that included those of England, Catalunya, Lombardy, Champagne and St Gilles (southern France). The officers were answerable to a General Chapter (a meeting of the leading men of the order from all over Christendom), held in the Holy Land, that oversaw the running and development of the order: such a structure was vital to sustain the workings of an international institution. The scale of endowments, donations and exemptions from ecclesiastical taxation meant that the Hospitallers held substantial resources across the West, although, as we shall see, this was essential because the expenses of warfare and medical provision required enormous support. The same issues (excepting medical matters) applied to the Templars.

In its early years the Hospital was associated with the church of St Mary of the Latins in Jerusalem, but in 1113 it became an independent order. Pope Paschal II issued the bull *Pie postulatio voluntatis* which brought the group under papal protection, confirmed its possessions, recognised the brethren as *fratres* and *professi* and, crucially, allowed them the freedom to elect their own master. This point marked the foundation of the Hospital as an international order although there were disputes with the patriarch of Jerusalem and other religious institutions in the Levant (including the Templars) and it was not until 1154 that further papal privileges ensured exemption from the jurisdiction of local church authorities.

The Rule of the Hospital dates from the mastership of Raymond of Puy (1120–58/60) and, like that of the Templars, was based upon Augustinian principles. It set out a series of regulations for a communal life covering the structure and administration of the order, the vows of the brethren, matters of discipline, the organisation of the Hospital itself and the care of the sick and poor. The brothers took vows of poverty, chastity and obedience, and there were also lay brethren, although, as we shall see, there was no direct mention of military personnel at this stage.

THE HOSPITAL IN JERUSALEM AND MEDICAL CARE

The primary function of the Hospital of St John in Jerusalem was the care of poor and sick pilgrims and several descriptions of this great institution survive. According to the German pilgrim Theoderic, who visited in 1169, the number of beds available was around 1,000. At times of crisis, however, the brothers would give up their own beds and the Hospital could cater for many more; we know that after the Battle of Mont Gisard in 1177 Hospitaller field services transported 750 of the wounded back to the main hospital in Jerusalem. In normal conditions, however, the report of a visiting cleric in the 1180s related that there were eleven wards for men, although the number for women is unknown (see Document 7 ii). The sexes were separated, even to the extent of having distinct kitchens for the male and female wards and female staff to care for the women. The writer noted that all sick were admitted, except lepers, regardless of origin, sex or status. This means that, in theory, Jews and Muslims could be helped although, given a lack of corroborative evidence and the emphasis on prayers and processions to fortify the inmates, such cases must have been very limited in number.

There were only four resident physicians in the hospital – a much lower patient/physician ratio than in contemporary Islamic and Byzantine institutions, yet far greater than anything in the West – who made two ward rounds a day and were supported by thirteen attendants on each ward. The doctors checked the patients' pulse and urine and dispensed electuaries (syrups) and other medicines. The main method of treatment was through diet and our sources provide much detail on which foods were considered appropriate – in accordance with medical belief of the time – to balance the body's humours and temperament. Meat was to be served three times a week, but certain foods, such as eels, cheese, lentils and cabbage, were considered bad for one's well-being. Blood-letting, lapidiary (the wearing of stones: for example, a dry stone would counter an excess of moisture in the patient) and the use of herbal remedies were also common. There was a maternity ward and the Hospitallers took care of abandoned infants who were given to nurses who received 12 talents per annum to care for the child and had to bring it to the hospital for regular inspections.

The cost of operating the hospital in Jerusalem must have been enormous and there is evidence that certain priories were directed to provide specific quantities of materials to keep it running; for example, the estates at Mont

Pèlerin and Tiberias were each to send two hundredweights of sugar a year for the making of medicines. It seems that the role of surgery was very limited and the primary task of the hospital was to provide a caring environment for weary and undernourished pilgrims, and to give them the opportunity to recover their strength and to continue their journeys.

THE HOSPITALLERS AND MILITARY ACTIVITY

Alongside this pastoral function the Hospitallers became increasingly involved in military affairs. The exact timing of this and the reasons that lay behind such activity are not entirely clear. Some have suggested that it was in response to the rise of the Templars, others interpret a military element as a natural extension of the Hospitallers' care for the poor and pilgrims. In 1136 King Fulk gave the order the castle of Bethgibelin, and although mercenaries probably formed the bulk of the garrison, the Hospitallers exercised ultimate authority over these men. By 1144 the order was seen as having sufficient strength to take on a substantial estate in northern Tripoli, which included the important castle of Krak des Chevaliers, and in 1148 we first find an individual explicitly described as 'a knight and a brother of the Hospital'. All this information points to a gradual process of militarisation and indicates that concern for the sick remained the order's main concern. In the 1160s, however, there was a change in approach and the level of militarisation accelerated rapidly. Before this time the Hospitallers owned seven castles and helped in the defence of two others, but in the 1160s they agreed to assist in the defence of Sidon, acquired control over eleven or twelve additional castles and gained theoretical rights over a further six. Master Gilbert d'Assailly's (1163–72) enthusiasm for involvement in military matters almost brought the order to financial ruin and provoked serious controversy. In late 1168, contrary to the advice of most of the nobles of Jerusalem and the Templars, Gilbert encouraged King Amalric to break a treaty with the Muslims and to invade Egypt. Gilbert promised to provide the king with 500 knights and 500 Turcopoles, while in return, if Egypt was conquered, he would gain the town of Bilbais, a share of the campaign spoils and the promise of considerable financial advantages. The attack failed, however, and the Hospitallers faced widespread criticism for their greed and accrued a debt of 100,000 bezants. The cost of assembling the forces promised to Amalric and the aggressive policies of Gilbert's mastership plunged the order into crisis. William of Tyre wrote that Gilbert had exhausted all the treasures of the Hospital, borrowed more money and spent that too. Gilbert resigned the mastership and he seems to have suffered a nervous breakdown because he retreated into a cave for a time. Chaos followed; there was a disputed leadership and, more significantly, there was a serious debate concerning the future direction of the order. Pope Alexander III became involved and between 1168 and 1180 he issued a series of instructions reminding the brothers that their first duty was to care for the poor and that arms-bearing should only take place in certain prescribed situations, usually in times of crisis (Riley-Smith, 2012: 32–37).

These pleas had an effect because there was some effort to re-emphasise the Hospitallers' spiritual and pastoral activities. In spite of this concern about militarisation, the Hospitallers continued to develop this role, in part drawn along by the gathering strategic tension in the Levant. The period 1170 to 1187 saw the order involved in numerous battles, skirmishes and sieges and they acquired even more fortifications, including a series of castles in northern Tripoli which came with the promise of full rights over still-to-be conquered land around the city of Homs. In 1186 the Hospitallers took over the powerful castle of Marqab from its lord, Bernard Le Mazoir, and the terms of the agreement reveal their power by this time. Bernard's family received an annual rent for the site, but the Hospitallers held full rights over those secular knights who lived on the castle's lands and the order was not bound by treaties made by the prince of Antioch during their absence. Conversely, however, the prince was obliged to observe any agreements made by the Hospitallers and local Muslim rulers. In effect, therefore, the order had created a semi-independent palatinate (lordship) in the way the Templars held their land around Baghras.

A further sign of the Hospitallers' growing involvement in the secular world was their developing political influence. As major landowners and the providers of a significant proportion of the knights of the armies of the Latin states it was inevitable that their interest in political affairs would rise, particularly during the turbulent reign of the leper-king, Baldwin IV of Jerusalem (1174–85). The master of the Hospital became an increasingly powerful figure at royal councils and in decisions over matters of regency and diplomacy. With their large territories in Tripoli it was unsurprising that the Hospitallers favoured Count Raymond in the political struggle of the 1180s and the order supported him in his advice not to engage Saladin at Hattin in 1187.

THE MILITARY ORDERS IN THE WEST

While the Hospitallers and the Templars were founded for different reasons, they came to share a great many features in terms of structure and organisation. The need to maintain contact with their European estates meant there must have been a steady flow of messengers and information between the West and the Levant. The existence of landholdings in Europe made Templars and Hospitallers familiar figures in the West and they acted as a constant reminder of the struggle in the Holy Land. Evidence of this remains today with place-names such as Temple Meads in Bristol, Temple Cressing in Essex and St John's Gate at Clerkenwell in London which were all properties of the military orders. The iconography of Hospitaller seals also evoked their centrality in fighting for the faith; like coins, seals convey an individual and an institutional identity (Whatley, 2012). Garnier of Nablus was prior of England between 1184 and 1190. One side of his seal depicts a truly dramatic image: a face with wild hair and a long beard, in other words, the order's patron saint, John the Baptist, thus signalling a powerful bridge between both Garnier and John's sacred personality and the order in the West and in the Holy Land. Garnier was castellan of Bethgibelin between 1173 and 1176 and he was grand commander of the order in Jerusalem until his appointment to England. The image he used of John is one found in Byzantine art, making it likely that he imported this to Europe himself.

The Orders' landholdings in the West were sources of income, supplies and manpower for the Holy Land; they could also act as places of retirement for more senior figures later in life. The scale of these holdings required

8. Seal of Garnier of Nablus, prior of the Hospitallers in England by kind permission of Hereford Cathedral Archives

proper structure and hierarchy and the Templars and Hospitallers can claim to be the first international corporations. The Hospitallers, for example, were organised into eight provinces (or *langues*, tongues): Provence, Auvergne, France, Italy, Aragon, Castile, Germany and, from *c*. 1185, England. Within each *langue* was a grand priory (located at Clerkenwell, in the case of England), headed by a grand prior, appointed by the Grand Master of the order. Below this level were priories, then a further subdivision, known as commanderies or preceptories. Grand priors were required to attend a Chapter General held in the Latin East to discuss the condition and the running of the order – a broadly similar model to monastic institutions such as the Cistercians.

This close relationship with Europe meant that the brothers were often used by the settlers as official envoys to convey requests for military help and money. As possessors of the cachet of both monk and warrior, and as defenders of the Holy Land, they were respected and trusted figures. In 1166, for example, Gilbert d'Assailly (before his fall from grace) carried letters of endorsement from the patriarch of Jerusalem as he toured France to persuade men to come to liberate the land and the Church of the East before they were destroyed. In 1169 the mission led by Archbishop Frederick of Tyre included the Hospitaller Geoffrey Fulcher, an experienced diplomat, who had written appeals to Louis VII of France and visited the king in the early 1160s as well as taking part in negotiations with the Fatimid Egyptians in 1167. The mission of 1184–85 was the most high-profile embassy sent to the West and was striking for the presence of the masters of both the Templars and the Hospitallers. This may have been calculated to demonstrate the gravity of the situation and would also show that recent bad feeling between the two orders – which was known about in the West – had been resolved.

The concept of the military order was sufficiently popular that it was soon adopted in the other main arena of Christian–Muslim conflict, the Iberian peninsula. We have seen Alfonso I of Aragon's interest in the Templars and Hospitallers, and after the orders received various properties in Spain the next step was direct involvement in military activities. They may have been reluctant to commit themselves to such a responsibility because it is not until 1143 that the Templars formally participated in the *reconquista*, followed five years later by the Hospitallers. Soon, however, new military orders were founded in the peninsula itself, in part because the idea was so attractive to twelfth-century knights, but also for a number of practical reasons: first, local men and resources would not be siphoned off to the Holy Land as was the case with the Templars and the Hospitallers; and second, there may have been a wish to limit the influence of outside powers in Iberian affairs. The first military order to be founded in Spain was the Order of Calatrava in 1158 and the next two decades saw similar institutions emerge, namely Santiago (1170), Montjoy in Aragon (1173), Alcántara (1176) and Evora in Portugal (c. 1178). As instruments of the *reconquista* these groups enjoyed strong patronage from the rulers of the peninsula and they came to form a central part in the struggle against Islam there.

Relations between Iberia and the Holy Land are little commented upon but their shared fight against Islam and the international nature of the military orders did produce some links. For example, from 1177 the Spanish Order of Montjoy started to have a presence in the Holy Land when it received donations from King Baldwin IV and other nobles. A few years later, Arnold of Torroja, who had been master of the Templars in Spain (1163) and then Provence (1166), built upon this experience, coupled with his standing as a well-travelled diplomat, to become Master of the Templars from 1180, until his death during Patriarch Heraclius's mission to the West in 1184. In essence, attempts to involve the Spanish orders in the Levant never came to reality and they remained focused on the conflict in the peninsula, leaving the Templars and the Hospitallers to take centre stage in the conflict against the rise of Saladin.

CONCLUSION

The military orders evolved to play a leading part in the military and political life of the Levant and they held large areas of territory – perhaps 35 per cent of land in the Latin East. The continued importance of the Hospitallers' medical function should not be ignored, and it must also be noted that the Templars became a powerful financial institution who numbered King Louis VII of France among their debtors as early as 1147. The orders were feared and respected by the Muslims who, on account of the brothers' strict training and their sworn vocation to fight Islam, saw them as their most deadly enemies. For these reasons it was customary to kill Templars and the Hospitallers captured after battle. The report of the Battle of Hattin written by Saladin's secretary, Imad ad-Din al-Isfahni, bears testimony to this point. The Sultan sought out the Templars and Hospitallers who had been captured and said: 'I shall purify the land of these two impure races.' He assigned 50 dinars to every man who had taken one of them prisoner and immediately the army brought forward at least 100 of them. He commanded that they should be beheaded, choosing to have them dead rather than in prison. Saladin saw it as essential to cull the military orders because he viewed them as a profoundly serious threat to Islam – a judgement that reveals how successful the idea of the warrior-monk had become and how important the military orders were to the Latin settlement of the Holy Land.

6

The Second Crusade

On 24 December 1144 Imad ad-Din Zengi, the Muslim ruler of Aleppo and Mosul, captured the Frankish city of Edessa. The settlers in the Levant sent messages to the West appealing for help and the result was what has become known as the Second Crusade (as we saw earlier, the expeditions of 1101, 1106–8, 1120–24 and 1127–29 were also crusades). What was originally designed as a campaign to defend the Holy Land was transformed into a wider movement of Christian liberation that encompassed military activity in the Iberian peninsula and the Baltic as well.

QUANTUM PRAEDECESSORES: THE CRUSADE APPEAL OF POPE EUGENIUS III

In response to the settlers' requests, Pope Eugenius III issued the crusade bull *Quantum praedecessores* on 1 December 1145 (see Document 11). This landmark work is the first papal bull for a crusade to the Holy Land to survive and it formed the basis of crusade appeals for decades to come. Such an important piece of evidence is worth examining in detail, but first we must remember the way in which such a document would have been used. The bull was addressed to King Louis VII of France and his subjects. Doubtless it was read out at great assemblies such as that held at Vézelay on Easter Sunday, 31 March 1146, when the king and many of his nobles gathered to take the cross. These meetings were highly orchestrated affairs, often timed to coincide with important religious festivals and the majority of those present were prepared to be stirred into a frenzy of enthusiasm by men like Bernard of Clairvaux, the greatest orator of the age. In addition to these larger meetings the bull would also be distributed to other preachers who had been officially delegated to recruit for the expedition.

Quantum praedecessores was at the heart of the Church authorities' formal pitch to persuade people to take the cross. It was, therefore, a carefully structured and comprehensive document designed to communicate information to as wide an audience as possible. Using vivid and emotive language, in conjunction with the device of repetition, it conveyed clearly and precisely the reasons why people should crusade and the rewards that they would receive for doing so. A number of key themes emerge. The first of these concerns the originator of the First Crusade, Pope Urban II, who was mentioned by name on three occasions in the document. Eugenius was careful to draw a direct line between his own ideas and those of his 'predecessor of happy memory', thus emphasising the historical weight behind his actions and, more importantly, drawing on the association with the God-given triumph of the First Crusade. Reference to the success of that expedition played a large part in the most striking image used in the bull, that of responsibilities binding 'Fathers and Sons', a theme raised four times, albeit in subtly different ways. Eugenius evoked the efforts of the First Crusaders, their sacrifices and their shedding of blood in freeing the Christian Church in the East. Interestingly, he also noted the work of those 'who strove to defend them [the Holy Places] over the years', a reference to the smaller crusading expeditions that followed the First Crusade, and to the one- or two-year service offered by individuals in defence of the Holy Land. Eugenius's most potent use of the image of Fathers and Sons followed the crux of his appeal: having stirred up outrage in his audience with an account of the devastation wrought by the Muslims, he linked the fall of Edessa with a threat to 'the Church and all Christianity'. Then he issued a challenge, because 'if, God forbid', the Holy Land was lost, 'the bravery of the fathers will have proved to be diminished in the sons'. Eugenius also employed the biblical story of Mattathias of the Maccabees – the leader of a people who rose up against the Seleucids (a Hellenistic dynasty who tried to suppress various Jewish practices in the second century BC) in order to hold on to their faith – to show fathers and sons working together in justified Christian violence.

An implicit part of Eugenius's reference to a threat to 'all Christianity' was the danger to the Eastern Church. Again this reflected an aspect of Pope Urban's appeal in 1095 and was probably meant to include all Christians, not just Catholics, and was an idea mentioned three times in *Quantum praedecessores*. The reward for such actions – the remission of all sins – was spelt out clearly and repeated three times in the course of the document, thereby ensuring that the prime attraction of the crusade was made plain. Other privileges were outlined too: Eugenius promised that those who died *en route* would also gain remission of all sins, thus clarifying what may have been a worry for potential participants, that is, whether their efforts would be rewarded if they failed to reach the Levant. The pope set out the legal protection offered by the Church to crusading families and their property, while interest on debts owed by the crusaders was suspended as well. We know from legal cases that these measures were in place at the time of the First Crusade, but this is the first time we can see them laid out so formally. Eugenius, who was a protégé of St Bernard, was also keen to ensure the moral probity of the crusaders and in tones reminiscent of the Rule of the Templars, written by Bernard, he forbade ostentatious display by the knights and he urged them to seek heavenly rather than secular glory.

It is worth exploring the legacy of the First Crusade and its centrality to the preaching of the 1145 campaign. One way to trace this is through the memorialisation of the crusade in written sources. The seemingly miraculous nature of the capture of Jerusalem in 1099, coupled with the fact that it had involved people from many different regions of the Latin West, provoked an unprecedented burst of historical writing. Eye-witness accounts of the crusade included those of the anonymous *Gesta Francorum*, Peter Tudebode, Raymond of Aguilers and Fulcher of Chartres. The *Gesta* in particular was then sent to the West where, in conjunction with the stories of returning crusaders, it was given a major rework by monastic writers such as Baldric of Bourgeuil, Guibert of Nogent and Robert of Rheims. The latter, in particular, produced a highly popular account of the crusade that was widely circulated. Other writers, such as the northern German, Albert of Aachen, completed a huge history of the crusade and the first phase of settlement that went down to 1119. Other visitors to the Levant wrote about the crusade too, including Caffaro of Genoa, who offers the rare perspective of a layman, or Ekkehard of Aura, another writer from the German Empire, or Ralph of Caen who composed the *Gesta Tancredi* to reflect the deeds of his master during the early years of the principality of Antioch. Some of the principal texts were, by the 1120s and 1130s, used to form the basis of further histories, such as William of Malmesbury's 'History of the English Kings' which included a lengthy section on the First Crusade largely based upon the work of Fulcher of Chartres (see Document 6 iii). All of these texts were in Latin, although we should mention the lost vernacular verse history of Gregory Bechada, a southern French knight.

The appearance of these texts must be placed in a context of (slowly) rising rates of literacy and education, as well as being both a stimulus to, and a part of, a growing interest in writing and recording history as a distinct, self-conscious act.

Alongside these narratives we also know of songs about the crusade. These were not written down until the latter half of the twelfth century but we are aware that they were in circulation beforehand and that people made a living by performing them. The opening lines of the Old French *Chanson d'Antioche* give a nice feel for the reasoning behind these accounts:

> Be still my lords, leave off your chatter now,
> If you want to hear a glorious song be sung.
> No jongleur ever sang a better song;
> Hold this song in your heart and love it deep,
> It tells a story great, and of brave men.
> You ought to love this song and hold it dear;
> In it you'll find examples of brave men
> And other things you'll need to keep in mind.
> No better song is sung, as we all know,
> About that holy city that we praise,
> Where God let weak men pierce and harm His body
> Strike it with lance and hang it on a cross,
> Jerusalem, by right the city's named.
>
> (Peters, 1998: 303)

In this age of a growing sense of shared status amongst the knighthood of the West, the emergence of behaviour and a sense of identity that we shorthand as chivalry, coupled with and including the huge popularity of tournaments, the wish to listen to and to celebrate the deeds of (potentially) one's own family, or regional clan, was considerable.

The circulation of these narratives and songs perpetuated and enhanced the memory of the crusade. To give one example: on the coronation of the young Louis VII of France in 1137, one of his nobles, the admirably named William Grassegals (William 'Bigballs'), presented him with a trilogy of crusade narratives (Fulcher of Chartres, Walter the Chancellor and Raymond of Aguilers) with the purpose of providing exemplars of behaviour worthy of emulation – the First Crusade and its heroes were a benchmark of honour, valour and nobility. It is revealing that in the opening lines of Eugenius's bull for the Second Crusade the pope stated that he had 'read in histories of old', of the deeds of the First Crusaders, thus preparing the ground for their successors to prove themselves of equal worth.

THE PREACHING OF THE CRUSADE

Quantum praedecessores and other official letters were not the only ways to encourage support for the crusade. Popular songs circulated widely. Eleven crusading songs survive from the Second Crusade, ten in Occitan (the language of southern France) and one in French. Obviously the wishes of a patron had to be satisfied in the composition of a song, but the content often reflects many wider preoccupations and offers a blend of the religious and the secular. The anonymous author of the song in Document 12, written *c.* 1146–47, included the familiar notions of feudal obligation, vengeance and a tournament, but placed them in the context of the crusade – God as the overlord, Edessa the venue for the tournament, and salvation the prize. In the chorus we see King Louis acting with the right intent, renouncing earthly riches and striving for heavenly glory.

Visual imagery might also act as a spur to take the cross. It is extraordinarily rare for such evidence to survive, but a series of engravings made before the French Revolution testifies to the presence of a crusading window at the abbey of Saint Denis in Paris. Fourteen roundels depicted, variously, Charlemagne, Constantine, martyrs, pilgrims and the events of the First Crusade. Given stylistic considerations, Louis VII's participation in the crusade and the role of Saint Denis as the venue for a final rally before the expedition set out, it is likely that the window dates from the time of the Second Crusade. Once again, therefore, we can see a commemoration of the triumph of 1099 and its use as a spur to the targets of the preaching campaign of the mid-1140s.

Eugenius delegated recruitment of the crusade to St Bernard and the extraordinary charisma of the abbot of Clairvaux, allied to careful control of official preachers and the circulation of official letters, yielded excellent results. Bernard himself embarked upon an intensive seven-month tour of the Low Countries and the Rhineland – a gruelling schedule for a man often weakened by his ascetic lifestyle. His message laid great emphasis on the need for personal salvation and the opportunity that God had so graciously presented to this 'lucky generation', a generation that would be foolish to spurn such a heaven-sent chance. Many thousands responded to Bernard's appeals and flocked to the cause of the crusade. The atmosphere at his preaching rallies could become highly charged and his tour was accompanied by widespread reports of miracles. Part of his energies were diverted because Ralph, an unauthorised preacher in northern Germany, had re-ignited the anti-semitic feeling seen in the Rhineland during the First Crusade, although the attacks on the Jews were on a smaller scale than those seen in 1096–97. The abbot objected to the crusade being diverted against the Jews because, first, Ralph lacked the proper authorisation to preach and, second, the Bible forbade the killing of Jews in order that one day they might be converted.

In outcome the Second Crusade would fall far short of the aims of its originators, but in terms of recruitment it was a great success. King Conrad III of Germany (1138–52) and Louis VII of France (1137–80) led the main armies overland to Constantinople and then across Asia Minor to the Levant. Their forces included nobles such as the count of Flanders, the count of Nevers and the future count of Champagne, as well as papal legates. They were joined in the East by contingents from southern France and northern Italy who had opted to sail to the Holy Land, and by a group of north European crusaders who sailed around the Iberian peninsula via Lisbon (see later).

THE SCALE AND SCOPE OF THE SECOND CRUSADE

The expedition to the Eastern Mediterranean was not the sole element of the Second Crusade and other campaigns took place in the Iberian peninsula and the Baltic. It seems that the crusade evolved into such an ambitious enterprise through the papacy showing proactive leadership and also responding positively to appeals by secular powers who wanted to harness the spiritual benefits of the crusade to their own territorial ambitions.

The crusade began as a response to the fall of Edessa in December 1144. A year later Eugenius launched the crusade appeal and almost simultaneously Louis VII proposed a campaign to help the Latin settlers to his Christmas court at Bourges. The king's plan was initially rejected, probably out of concern for the young monarch's absence (he had no male heir yet either) – no king of a major western power had yet risked the rigours of a crusade – and because the formal authorisation of *Quantum praedecessores* had not yet arrived in northern France. Once pope and king were properly co-ordinated, recruitment in France began in earnest.

The involvement of King Conrad III and the German Empire is more problematic. Traditionally, Conrad has been seen as a reluctant participant in the crusade, browbeaten into taking the cross by an overbearing Abbot Bernard who had taken it upon himself to bring the German ruler into the equation without even consulting Pope Eugenius. Phillips has shown that, in fact, Conrad was deeply concerned at the widespread turmoil in his lands at this time (no less than four major conflicts according to contemporaries) and that Bernard's success in resolving these crises did much to enable the king to crusade (Phillips, 2007). Historians have long argued that Eugenius III was lukewarm about Conrad's participation in the crusade, a proposition based solely on the evidence of a papal letter that made reference to a claim by Conrad that he could not 'delay' his campaign as the pope advised. A suggestion to 'delay' is not the same thing as an instruction forbidding an action. In fact, the remainder of Eugenius's letter makes it clear that the pope had provided Conrad with much useful advice concerning the planning of the expedition: hardly the stance of a man resolutely opposed to the king's involvement. From Eugenius's viewpoint the recruitment of Conrad had many logical attractions. First, the king was an experienced crusader having been to the Levant in 1123–24. Second, Bernard had warned the people of Bavaria and Eastern Francia against following the example of Peter the

Hermit on the First Crusade and setting out without 'proper leadership'. Conrad would, of course, provide such leadership. Third, recent decades had seen a very positive relationship between the pope and the German ruler (in contrast to the ongoing bitterness of the Investiture Controversy at the time of the First Crusade) and Conrad's involvement in the crusade would fit his role as defender of the Church. An assembly at Aachen in March 1147 established peace throughout the empire and confirmed Conrad's son Henry as his successor, thus safeguarding the throne should the king die on the crusade. Through the spring of 1147 the main armies prepared to set out and in May and June they began to march to the East. Before following the progress of these forces we will look at the other arenas of the crusade.

THE CONQUEST OF LISBON

Bernard's preaching tour had covered the Low Countries and the Rhineland and it was from these areas, as well as Anglo–Norman lands, that a fleet which sailed via Lisbon came to the Holy Land. We are fortunate that a detailed eye-witness account of this campaign, *De expugnatione lyxbonensi* (The Conquest of Lisbon), survives (*The Conquest of Lisbon*, tr. David, 2001), probably written by an Anglo–French priest called Raol. While there are some indications that the text was moulded to present a consistent message that the expedition succeeded because of the right intent and the unity of the crusade force, the account remains fundamentally accurate. One point of interest is the regulations drawn up to ensure discipline among the crusaders (Document 13). With forces assembled from different areas of Europe, and perhaps in consequence of experiences during the First Crusade, we can appreciate the need for such matters to be clarified from the start. The regulations reflected the sentiments of *Quantum praedecessores* with their imprecations against costly garments, and they echoed the mood of the Reform Papacy with the separation of religious from lay assemblies and an emphasis on regular communion. The relative cohesion of the Lisbon crusaders' force shows that these rules must have had some beneficial effect. Such regulations were not unique, however. Odo of Deuil, who provided an eye-witness narrative of Louis VII's expedition, noted the existence of (presumably) similar rules for the landbound crusaders, but reflected sadly 'because they did not observe them well, I have not preserved them either' (Odo of Deuil, tr. Berry, 1948: 21).

The position of the Lisbon campaign within the Second Crusade as a whole is a matter of some debate. In the past historians have argued that the crusaders were simply waylaid by a representative of King Afonso Henriques of Portugal (1139–85), who persuaded them to help him capture Lisbon as a chance by-product of the journey to Jerusalem. In recent years, Livermore and Phillips have suggested that this was less of a coincidence than previously believed and that the leaders of the expedition were already prepared to take part in such an engagement (Livermore, 1990; Phillips, 1997b). A previously ignored letter from St Bernard to Afonso may signify that the abbot had sent his approval for the campaign. We also know that Bernard met some of the senior figures in the expedition during his preaching tour and that Raol, the author of *De expugnatione lyxbonensi*, carried a piece of the True Cross, which could suggest that he was a papal representative because the possession of such an important relic was hardly commonplace. Furthermore, Raol indicates that the appearance of the crusader fleet – which numbered between 164 and 200 ships – was *expected* in northern Spain. We can show that the northern European fleet set out around two months before the land armies; thus it would have arrived in the Levant by the late summer of 1147. This meant at least eight months of costly inactivity before the main forces arrived. A planned campaign at Lisbon would, logically, have helped to fill this gap.

The bishop of Oporto appealed to the crusaders to stay and fight in Lisbon and in powerful and dramatic words he convinced them of the value of performing God's work in the Iberian peninsula, a region that had been Christian-held until the eighth century, but where now 'the Mother Church with her arms cut off and her face disfigured appeals for help; she seeks vengeance at your hands for the blood of her sons . . . be not seduced by the desire to press on with the journey that you have begun; for the praiseworthy thing is not to have been to Jerusalem, but to have lived a good life along the way, for you cannot get there without the performance of His works' (*The Conquest of Lisbon*, tr. David, 2001: 79). Thus the bishop reassured the participants that such a diversion did not detract from the holiness of their crusading purpose – and he also offered them extremely generous financial terms. On 28 June 1147 the siege began and seventeen weeks later, on 24 October, the city fell. Many of the crusaders wintered in Lisbon before sailing on to fulfil their vows in the Holy Land or to fight at Tortosa in eastern Spain. The attackers had faced no relieving force to distract them, they had no problems with supplies, they managed to preserve their discipline, they had good siege equipment and engineers, and they were not debilitated by a long journey. In short, from the perspective of the crusaders, it was a textbook siege. Afonso took advantage of the calling of the expedition to the Holy Land to further the *reconquista* in his locality. He was related to the crusading dukes of Burgundy and he was a keen supporter of the Cistercians and the Templars, both of whom were just establishing themselves in his lands. Asking Bernard for his approval for an attack on Lisbon and inducing the abbot to raise awareness of this in northern Europe suited both the king and the papacy. Christendom would be expanded and Afonso could consolidate his newly emergent kingdom.

THE CRUSADES AGAINST ALMERIA, TORTOSA AND JAÉN

In Portugal, therefore, we can see the Church reacting to contemporary political developments. Similar principles apply to the sieges of Almeria and Tortosa and the attack on Jaén, the three other military campaigns in the Iberian peninsula where a close link between secular and religious advantage may be seen. In the cases of Almeria and Tortosa, as well as an expansion of Christendom and an increase in territory for secular powers, there was the added ingredient of the participation of the Genoese and their acquisition of commercial privileges.

In 1146 King Alfonso VII of León-Castile (1126–57) proposed an attack on Almeria in southern Spain and offered the Genoese one-third of the city in return for their help. The Genoese made a further agreement with the count of Barcelona to besiege Tortosa in northern Spain where again they would receive one-third of the city (Both agreements can be found in Hall and Phillips, 2013: 179–83). On the surface this appears to be commercial opportunism triumphing over religious motives, but we must remember the context of the twelfth century as an intensely religious age and it is impossible for cities such as Genoa to have been immune from the influence of religion. As we saw in the First Crusade, it was a combination of motives that induced people to take the cross and a spirit of religiosity and commercial advantage may not have seemed such a dichotomy as it does today. We know that Pope Eugenius encouraged Italians to crusade and he provided strong endorsement for the expeditions to Spain. Iberia was, after all, a familiar arena for crusading, with expeditions authorised by the papacy in 1113–14, 1117–18 and 1123. The impetus generated by the expedition to the East meant that the scale of activity in the peninsula increased dramatically during 1147–48.

The attack on Almeria lasted from August to October 1147 when it fell to the crusaders, prompting a savage and highly profitable sack of the place. Alfonso's grant to the Genoese was recorded as being given for 'the glory of God and of the whole of Christendom and [because the Genoese] have decided to retain control over it in response to the pressing requirements of the Christians; above all because they recognised that this was conducive to the glory and profit of the commune of Genoa' (Caffaro, tr. Hall and Phillips, 2013: 185). The last phrase reveals a neat combination of motives, showing how secular and spiritual might join. Almeria remained in Christian hands until 1157, but the capture of Tortosa (on 30 December 1148) was to be permanent. Clear evidence that the Genoese attached a religious aspect to their successes can be seen by their creation of frescoes to commemorate the campaign in the cathedral of St Lawrence in their home city.

The work of Barton has brought to light yet another element in the crusade in Iberia (Barton, 2000). Using evidence from Muslim sources and a later Christian writer, he identifies as part of the crusade a hitherto ignored attack by King Alfonso VII on the southern Spanish town of Jaén. This episode, which took place in the summer of 1148, has remained hidden largely because the major Christian source for Alfonso's career breaks off in 1147 and the fact that the campaign itself was a miserable failure. This may well account for its omission from most texts. Pope Eugenius offered encouragement for the expedition in a letter of April 1148 which again demonstrated papal awareness of, and approval for, another part of this wider Christian enterprise.

THE BALTIC CRUSADE

Other than the setback at Jaén, the crusade in Iberia prospered. This progress contrasted with the failure of the Wendish crusade in north-eastern Europe. The formal inclusion of these pagan regions as a target of the crusade was a new development and probably the most radical aspect of the Second Crusade. The north-eastern frontier of the German Empire had a long tradition of both Christian–pagan warfare and missionary work sent out from the north German archbishoprics. Back in 1108 a cleric of the archbishop of Magdeburg wrote a letter that described the inhumanity and cruelty inflicted upon the Christians of the area and he urged people in Europe to liberate the region in a holy war as Jerusalem had been liberated by the First Crusade. This campaign was not a crusade, however, because the papacy did not authorise any preaching. It did, though, demonstrate the potential for the principle of holy war to extend further than the Levant and for the ingredients of reconquest, conversion and vengeance (the death of the Christian missionaries) to be harnessed in this connection. In March 1147, at an assembly at Frankfurt, members of the Saxon nobility approached Bernard of Clairvaux and, according to contemporary writer Otto of Freising, 'refused to set out for the Orient because they had as neighbours certain tribes who were given over to the filthiness of idolatory, and in like manner they took the cross to assail those races in war' (Otto of Freising, tr. Mierow, 1953: 76). The Saxons' prioritising of their own campaign, and Bernard's agreement to their proposal, may indicate that the abbot accepted his powers of persuasion had reached their limits and that he had to adapt his message to suit the arena of war; he may also have seen an opportunity to extend the borders of

Christianity even further. For Bernard, the crusade was about fighting the enemies of God, and the pagans certainly fulfilled that criteria. In any case, a campaign against the Wends would also ensure that further elements of the potentially troublesome German nobility were occupied while Conrad was overseas. Bernard wrote to Eugenius who published the bull *Divini dispensatione II* in April 1147. This confirmed that those fighting the Slavs would receive the same remission of sins as those going to Jerusalem. Bernard himself issued an appeal for support that contained the infamous statement 'We utterly forbid that for any reason whatsoever a truce should be made with these tribes, either for the sake of money, or for the sake of tribute, until such a time as, by God's help, they shall be either converted or wiped out' (Bernard of Clairvaux, *Letters*, tr. James, 1998: 467). Historians and theologians have struggled to explain such an extreme directive – one that contradicts biblical injunctions against forced conversion and does not sit easily with Bernard's other writings. This emphasis on conversion – which was echoed by Pope Eugenius – is particularly interesting and marked an innovation in crusading theory: the missionary crusade. Indeed, Eugenius made the remission of sins conditional upon winning the Wends to Christianity, rather than just waging war on them. There are indications that some targeted by the crusades were apostates, those who had earlier converted to Christianity but then deserted their new faith, an act to be punished by death if such people maintained their error. Others had also been visited by missionaries but were only partially assimilated to Christianity and continued to practise a form of pagan–Christian syncretism – something which again needed to be dealt with. The acceptance of tribute was common practice in the Baltic region and it may be that Bernard wanted a different and more durable result to this usual outcome and therefore tailored his message in such an uncompromising fashion.

The crusader army consisted largely of Saxon nobles and several north German bishops, along with two rivals for the Danish throne. In the summer of 1147 they attacked the pagan settlements of Dobin and Malchow. The defenders of Dobin eventually accepted baptism and the crusaders withdrew. At Malchow the pagan lands were ravaged and a temple and idols were burnt before the crusaders turned eastwards towards the Christian city of Stettin on the River Oder. The bemused inhabitants displayed crosses from the walls and persuaded the army not to attack them. The Wendish crusade broke up in the autumn having achieved the token submission of one chieftain and the capture of some booty. This was a reasonable achievement for an annual raiding expedition, but in terms of the grander ambitions of the crusade it was a dismal failure. An astute enemy and dissent among the leadership – the Danes and Saxons mistrusted one another very deeply – meant that the crusaders were unable to carry their diversity of motives through to victory.

PREPARATIONS FOR THE MARCH TO THE HOLY LAND

While Bernard toured Flanders and the Rhineland the French busied themselves raising men and money for the crusade; diplomatic and military issues needed to be resolved too. It was decided to march through Hungary and the Byzantine Empire rather than taking up an offer by King Roger II of Sicily (1130–54) to transport the army by sea. Enmity between the Germans and the Sicilians, and the Byzantines and Sicilians, meant that it was undiplomatic for Louis to accept Roger's proposal, and in any case it was considered propitious to follow the route of the First Crusade across Asia Minor. Emperor Manuel Komnenos was particularly concerned by the advent of the crusade because, unlike his predecessor Alexios, who had actually requested military assistance back in 1095, the Second Crusade was arriving uninvited and unwelcome. This was particularly so in the case of the French who were known to be friendly with his arch-enemies, the Sicilians. The emperor tried to compel Pope Eugenius to guarantee the good behaviour of the crusaders and (as Alexios had managed) to persuade the westerners to swear fealty to him. He also fortified the walls of Constantinople.

Back in the West, final preparations were made and, in the presence of Pope Eugenius, the French king held a great public ceremony at the church of Saint Denis on 11 June 1147. Louis prostrated himself at the altar and asked for the saint's permission to crusade, he then kissed relics of Saint Denis. He took the oriflamme (believed by contemporaries to be Charlemagne's banner) from the altar and was given the pilgrim's scrip (wallet) by the pope. This powerful display reinforced the connection between the abbey of Saint Denis and the Capetian dynasty and also the position of the pope as the head of the crusading movement.

THE JOURNEY TO THE EAST: THE CRUSADE AT CONSTANTINOPLE AND IN ASIA MINOR

The German army marched ahead of the French through Hungary and into the Byzantine Empire. The Germans seem to have been poorly disciplined and engaged in a series of skirmishes with the Greek troops. Conrad's force suffered only minimal casualties but as they neared Constantinople a flash flood hit the army. Losses of men and equipment were substantial and this marked a severe setback to the German effort. Conrad and Manuel – who were related through Manuel's wife, Bertha of Sulzbach (in Bavaria) – remained on reasonably cordial terms, although the Greek ruler was careful to usher the Germans across the Bosphorus and into Asia Minor as soon as possible. The French contingent seems to have been smaller and better disciplined at this point, but when it arrived at Constantinople a faction in the army tried to persuade the crusaders to attack the city. The reasons for this were based upon small-scale engagements with the Greeks and, more seriously, antipathy founded on the long-standing doctrinal differences between the Catholic and Orthodox Churches as well as antagonism borne out of the recent Byzantine invasions of Antioch; a matter of especial concern because the principality was ruled by Queen Eleanor's uncle, Prince Raymond of Poitiers. The existence of a treaty between the Greeks and their Muslim neighbours, the Seljuk Turks, also aroused the crusaders' suspicions. The plan to besiege Constantinople – which was probably impractical anyway – was rejected, most notably by King Louis himself, but Manuel remained deeply unnerved by the crusaders' presence. His concerns were compounded by a Sicilian invasion of Corfu and the Peloponnese peninsula which led him to fear a joint French–Sicilian attack on his city. The promise of better markets induced the French to cross to Asia Minor and once the barrier of the Bosphorus was between the crusaders and Constantinople Manuel could be less cautious towards the westerners.

Unknown to the French, the German army had already been crushed only a few days into its march. It seems that Conrad made a strategic error in choosing the most direct route across Asia Minor. He had over-estimated the speed at which he could march the *c.* 360 kilometres from Nicaea to Iconium and he had not appreciated just how tough an environment the semi-arid steppe of the Anatolian plateau is. This harsh landscape would yield little forage and the Germans failed to carry sufficient supplies to cope with any delays. Turkish mounted archers harassed the crusaders and the footsoldiers took particularly heavy casualties. Within days the nobles realised the futility of their efforts and the decision was made to turn around and try to regroup, rather than risk a pointless defeat. Conrad himself was wounded by arrow-fire as his forces struggled back to Nicaea. Many of the poor and non-combatants left the army at this point, although Conrad briefly joined up with a shocked King Louis (who had been led to believe that the Germans were enjoying considerable success) before going to Constantinople to convalesce over the winter.

Odo of Deuil wrote that Louis was heading towards Antioch. When this evidence is coupled with evidence from a letter written from Constantinople by Conrad in late February 1148, in which the king stated that he was awaiting re-inforcements so that he could proceed to Edessa, it seems clear that the crusade originally planned to campaign in northern Syria. Because this could damage the interests of the Byzantine Empire by promoting Antiochene independence, Manuel may have been inclined to be unhelpful to the westerners. Niketas Choniates, a later Greek writer, noted this (see

Document 14). The Eastern Christian writer, Michael the Syrian, commented, 'The emperor of the Greeks knew that having crossed over the sea and established their influence, they [the crusaders] would not give it up to the empire of the Greeks and therefore he worked in concert with the Turks' (Phillips, 2007: 206). It should also be remembered that his control over Greek lands in Asia Minor was probably very limited and his allies, the Seljuks, could and did move into Byzantine territory and harass the crusaders from an early stage of their march.

Louis progressed via Ephesus and along the Maeander valley. In late December 1147, the French army scored a clear victory over the Turks and, to emphasise God's hand in their triumph, the presence of a white-clad knight was reported. The French had coped with the usual Turkish tactics of fast attacks and feigned retreats and then managed to deliver an effective cavalry charge against the enemy. In light of the catastrophe that was to follow, this success is usually overlooked, but it is important to note that the main armies of the Second Crusade were not *so* ineffectual that they could not, if managed properly, achieve victory. On 7 January 1148, however, crossing the Cadmus mountains, the crusader force became too stretched out. The vanguard lost contact with the remainder of the army and seeing such disorder the Turks struck. Losses of men, horses and materials were substantial – breaking the strength and spirit of Louis's crusading army. The survivors regrouped and belatedly acted to ensure that discipline was preserved in future. The Templars were given control of the march and the crusaders organised into confraternities – temporary associations, bound together by oath – to keep a proper structure. This was an interesting development because it showed just how seriously the Templars were regarded only two decades after their approval as a religious military order. The effectiveness of this arrangement can be demonstrated by the fact that the crusaders recorded several victories and they reached the southern coast of Asia Minor with few further losses.

THE CRUSADE IN THE LATIN EAST

The French king arrived at Antioch in March 1148. Initially he was greeted with great enthusiasm by Prince Raymond who hoped to use his close family ties with Queen Eleanor to persuade him to fight in northern Syria. Louis was unwilling to do this and the prince became hostile to him. The French army marched southwards, a move accompanied by strong rumours concerning one of the great scandals of medieval history. It was alleged that Raymond and Eleanor had become overly intimate and for this reason Louis had refused to assist the Antiochenes. Whatever the truth in this – and contemporary church writers such as John of Salisbury, who met the French entourage in Rome on their journey home, reported the episode in all seriousness – other reasons existed why the king should not campaign in the north at this time. Louis's forces had been decimated in Asia Minor and he needed time to regroup and to join up with the other crusaders who had arrived by sea. More significantly though, he may have felt disinclined to fight alongside the Antiochenes, who, since 1145, when Raymond had been obliged to travel in person to Constantinople and submit to Manuel's authority, were technically subject to Greek suzerainty. Why should Louis exert himself on behalf of the Antiochenes when it would benefit their Byzantine overlords, the very people who appeared to many to bear much of the responsibility for his losses in Asia Minor?

In June 1148 a great assembly was held at Palmarea near Acre. Conrad, Louis, Melisende and Baldwin III, and the nobility of Jerusalem debated the crusaders' next move. With Raymond's non-co-operation, military activity in the north was now unlikely. In any case a second Muslim attack on Edessa in 1146 had destroyed much of the city and while the Franks still held some territory in the area it may well have been pointless trying to reconquer it. In the south the choice lay between Ascalon and Damascus. The former remained the sole port on the Levantine coast still in Muslim hands. The latter had been the target of earlier Frankish attacks, including the crusade of 1129. It was also the major Muslim power closest to Jerusalem and had recently become hostile to the settlers after a period of truce. The principal reason for this was a growing, if uneasy, *rapprochement* between the Damascenes and Nur ad-Din of Aleppo; a union that the capture of Damascus would prevent.

THE SIEGE OF DAMASCUS

On 24 July 1148 the Christian armies reached the city. Accounts differ as to the development of the siege, but after strong early progress through the dense orchards on the west and south-west of the city, some (Frankish) sources indicate that the Christians moved to the other, weaker, side of Damascus to try to make a breakthrough, but on finding little water they were forced to withdraw only four days after the siege had begun. Following the hopes, expense and suffering of the crusade, to fail so quickly cut deep. The fallout from the collapse of the siege of Damascus was swift, wide-ranging and ferocious. Conrad suspected that the settlers had been paid off by the Damascenes. William of Tyre, writing about thirty years later, offered a range of suggestions, but he reported that there were so many different versions of events he could not be sure what had happened. Explanations ranged from the bribery theory noted by Conrad to the meddling of Prince Raymond of Antioch, to a clash between Count Thierry of Flanders (who wanted control of the city for himself) and the local nobility (who resented a westerner benefiting from their decades of labour in the Levant). Odo of Deuil's account of the crusade stopped short of Damascus, but in his view it was the treachery of the Greeks that had caused the principal damage to the expedition. Odo also noted the problems caused by non-combatants slowing up the main army and advised that they should not accompany future crusades.

In reality other factors should be added to the equation, largely focusing upon the decision to take the army to the less well-supplied side of the city. If, as the western writers claimed, the crusaders were on the verge of success, why did they move? Muslim sources provide some answers. Ibn al-Qalanisi, who was in Damascus at the time, confirmed that the crusaders enjoyed great success in the opening days of the siege and noted also the death of two important local holy men. But he also brings to our attention the resolution of the defenders – Damascus was a city of great spiritual importance to Islam: tradition described it as the location of the coming of the Messiah before the Day of Judgement, while Mount Kaisoun (overlooking the city) was the birthplace of Abraham and the city itself was the burial place of many other important religious figures. Prayers in the Great Umayyad mosque and a display of the revered Koran of the Caliph 'Uthman (644–56) fortified the inhabitants. Thus, while we talk about the religious zeal of the crusaders, we must also remember that of their opponents too, and in the case of Damascus, the Muslims' deep attachment to a place of such spiritual resonance. Ibn al-Qalanisi also noted that the Damascenes had, unsurprisingly, appealed for help and a steady stream of reinforcements began to arrive. Most importantly of all, it seems that Nur ad-Din had reached Homs (150 kilometres) north where he was joined by troops from Mosul. Ibn al-Athir, who wrote in Mosul in the early thirteenth century, reveals that Unur, the ruler of Damascus, told the nobles of Jerusalem that he would hand over the city to these forces unless they retreated; he offered control of Banyas as a sweetener. News of the approach of such formidable relief forces meant the crusaders needed to try for a quick victory on the other side of the city and when this proved unfeasible, they decided to retreat rather than face being trapped outside Damascus by the northern Syrian armies. At this point the Muslims may have handed over money to encourage the Franks to leave and this payment was the basis for the allegations of duplicity. Perhaps we should remember the immense hopes invested in this campaign. Bernard had practically promised the crusaders that they would be successful; with the astounding success of their forefathers in 1099 driving them onwards, the present generation had a lot to live up to. This was also the first time that kings had gone on a crusade and their prestige would have been badly tarnished by the experience. It was not, after all, as if they had been defeated in some epic engagement,

9. The Great Ummayad mosque, Damascus

but rather forced to make a humiliating withdrawal; in such circumstances, scapegoats had to be found.

It was Bernard who had the most awkward task: he had raised expectations to such a fever pitch that it was difficult to explain why God had not rewarded the efforts of the faithful. The abbot argued that the crusaders did not travel with the right intent – had their hearts been pure they would have triumphed. One writer contrasted the victory of the humble, lesser people at Lisbon with the defeat of the glory-seeking rulers at Damascus.

In essence, the Second Crusade was damaging to the settlers and the papacy. Progress was made in the Iberian peninsula, but the lack of success in the Baltic and the despair and anger engendered by the defeat of the main armies cast a shadow over crusading for many years. The settlers would need to be both resourceful and wide-ranging in their attempts to secure outside help against the emerging strength of Muslim Syria.

7

Warfare, strategy and castles in the Levant

The Frankish tenure of the Holy Land moved through phases of conquest, consolidation, expansion, defence, defeat and recovery. Each of these episodes required a range of military skills, techniques and approaches to warfare, albeit with different emphases according to circumstance. Many aspects of military engagement were familiar to the Franks; for example, warfare in eleventh-century Europe was dominated by raids and battles and these forms of conflict played a prominent role in the history of the Latin East. Other types of warfare, however, were new to the westerners, especially the tactics of their Muslim enemies and the intensive level of siege warfare, notably against urban settlements. The settlers' lack of manpower also influenced their approach to military issues in terms of battle tactics and castle-building.

RAIDS, STRATEGY AND BATTLES

Raiding was an integral part of life in the Levant and, aside from periods of truce, both sides engaged in this practice as a matter of course. The purposes of such raids were varied; they could be a prelude to a later invasion, they might be a decoy to lure opponents away from more serious military activity, but usually they were aimed at destroying or stealing crops and livestock. Document 17 ii clearly indicates the effect of a Muslim raid. One should not underestimate the psychological damage of these episodes and the worry that they might recur. William of Tyre noted the fear engendered by the raid and in some border regions the threat must have been considerable. This, in turn, impacted upon settlement patterns because the majority of Frankish farmers in the kingdom of Jerusalem located themselves away from the vulnerable borders if possible. Document 17 ii also reveals that Saladin timed his incursion for maximum effect – to coincide with the gathering of the autumn harvest. This might mean serious damage to the economy and, on top of the natural disasters such as earthquakes and droughts so prevalent in the East, a series of raids could, and did, financially break many farmers and lesser nobles. It is noticeable that from the 1160s onwards appeals to the West called for money to help cushion the damage caused by these increasingly heavy Muslim incursions, especially in northern Syria. It must be remembered that the Franks could raid Muslim territory too, and they might secure equally profitable rewards. But why did the settlers not choose to defend their lands in a more proactive fashion? If, as shown in Document 17 ii, the Franks had troops in the vicinity of their enemy, why did they elect to retreat? William of Tyre reported that the settlers made no attempt to engage their opponents, but returned to their strongholds to wait for the Muslims to leave. William's explanation for this approach was simple – the Franks wished to avoid risk and by holding to the fortified places, they had, as they saw it, done an effective job. Stating the obvious, battles were dangerous, unpredictable events. They might spread out over a large area of land which rendered communication impossible, they could change in fortune very quickly and, most seriously for the loser, their outcome could be decisive: the death of a leader or a heavy loss of manpower might precipitate irreversible consequences and events such as the demise of King Harold at the Battle of Hastings in 1066 were a lesson evident to all. By avoiding battle and its attendant dangers, the Franks lived to fight another day and the Muslims would retreat without taking the castles that were needed to conquer the land; in other words, in spite of the material damage incurred, the settlers' military capabilities remained essentially intact.

The rationale underlying this policy was dictated by the Franks' perpetual problem: a lack of manpower. The dangers of a major setback became starker as the strength of their enemies grew. Heavy defeats at the Battles of Harran (1104) and The Field of Blood (1119) saw substantial losses of Frankish troops yet the Latin settlements survived, in part because the Muslims could not, at those points, follow up their victories with permanent large-scale conquests. By the 1160s, however, the situation was beginning to change, especially in northern Syria. At the Battle of Harim in 1164 Prince Bohemond III of Antioch and Count Raymond of Tripoli were captured and most of their knights killed. Nur ad-Din rampaged through the principality, destroying crops and capturing towns and castles in the border region, but the Muslim leader judged himself as lacking the capacity to take Antioch itself. As Nur ad-Din increased in power, the Franks' limited number of fighting men became even more critical and a contemporary appeal to the West after Harim observed that the sole remaining Frankish leader, King Amalric (1163–74), was reluctant to engage in serious military activity because he had responsibilities to defend Antioch, Tripoli, Jerusalem and his interests in Egypt. Nur ad-Din, however, had 'a superabundance of troops' and could mount two campaigns simultaneously or sustain a defeat and still remain a threat.

The principle of avoiding battle followed the ideas of Vegetius, a late fourth-century writer, whose *De re militari* was familiar to many military leaders in the medieval West. Such an approach also ties in with William of Tyre's comments in Document 17 ii and was encapsulated in the famous lines of the twelfth-century Muslim writer Usama Ibn-Munqidh: 'Of all men the Franks are most cautious in warfare' (Usama Ibn-Munqidh, tr. Cobb, 2008: 25). Yet this picture is perhaps too beguiling; it did not, of course, preclude raids and incursions, and there is no doubt that the settlers did take positive action when the circumstances suited them. In 1115, Prince Roger of Antioch caught the Muslims unprepared for battle at Tell Danith and duly attacked, shattering the army of Bursuq of Mosul. In 1126, a raid on Damascus saw the Franks employ their feared cavalry charge to destroy a Muslim defence force and they won the day. Most overtly, in 1182–83, Reynald of Châtillon's raid into the Red Sea (see pp. 155–6) is evidence of Frankish aggression. One calamitous example of the Franks mistakenly choosing to fight a battle was at Cresson on 1 May 1187 when 130 Templar and Hospitaller knights attacked a far larger force of Muslims (maybe 7,000 men). When the enemy was sighted, Gerard of Ridefort, the master of the Templars, thought it cowardly to retreat (as some advised) and led the Christian charge. A Frankish chronicler wrote: 'The Saracens withstood them joyously and closed in on them so the Christians could not pass through' (The Old French Continuation of William of Tyre, in *The Conquest of Jerusalem and the Third Crusade*, tr. Edbury, 1996: 32). Only four knights, including ironically Gerard, escaped and all the others, among whom numbered the master of the Hospitallers, were captured or killed. While it is true that the Franks often chose not to fight and that some battles were hard to avoid because they had been lured into a trap, or caught by surprise, the comments of Usama and William of Tyre should not be distorted and taken to mean a complete lack of aggression on the part of the settlers. These few examples – and many others could be cited – are testimony to Frankish combativeness.

Battles were relatively common in eleventh-century Europe (less so in the twelfth), but the tactics encountered in the Levant would have been different to anything that the Franks had experienced in the West. A typical Frankish army in the East was formed as follows: the core of the army was the knights (secular knights and those of the military orders), well protected by their chain mail, helmets and kite-shaped shields, and whose most effective tactic was the charge. The impact of a mass of heavily armoured knights and their warhorses could be devastating, as Richard proved at the Battle of Arsuf in 1191 (see below, pp. 175–6). The problem for the Franks was that the charge required two essential conditions – a reasonably fixed target and relatively flat ground – that were rarely present. Given the strength of the charge, the

Muslims did everything in their power to avoid facing it and their tactics did much to neutralise this threat.

Muslim armies were also based around cavalry, the majority of whom were lightly armoured and highly skilled archers who would repeatedly ride to within 50–80 metres of the Franks, release their arrows and retreat. At the Battle of Dorylaeum (July 1097), in the early stages of the First Crusade, the Franks were unfamiliar with Muslim tactics. Fulcher of Chartres commented, 'The Turks were howling like wolves and furiously shooting a cloud of arrows. We were stunned by this . . . to all of us such warfare was unknown' (Fulcher of Chartres, tr. Ryan, 1969: 85). The purpose of this constant harassment was to break up the Frankish formation and to clear the way for an attack by their own heavy cavalry. The temptation for the Franks to respond was enormous and Document 17 i shows how difficult it was to resist this provocation. It also indicates how often the Franks reacted to such goading, the measures needed to try to prevent such a response and, in the allegations of cowardice, a common retort to the order to hold fast. In the face of these tactics the only real option for the Christians was to stay in tight formation and hope that the enemy would come close enough to them, and in sufficient numbers, that they presented a target that could be hit. Timing and close formation were essential for the charge to work effectively. Even once it had struck home, it was vital to preserve discipline and not to pursue a defeated – or apparently defeated – enemy. The feigned retreat was a favourite tactic of the Muslims and if performed properly it could lure the most experienced Franks to their doom. Confronted by a Christian charge the Muslims would fall back and spread out far enough for the knights to begin to lose formation and then, possibly in conjunction with a force prepared for ambush, they would suddenly wheel to outflank the Franks and trap small groups of them. A participant in the Third Crusade expressed his frustration at this: 'It is the Turks' habit, when they realise that their pursuit has stopped following them, to stop running away themselves – like an infuriating fly which flies away if you drive it off and returns when you stop. As long as you chase it, it flees; as soon as you stop pursuing and turn back, then the Turk follows you; if you pursue, the Turk flees.' (*Chronicle of the Third Crusade*, tr. Nicholson, 1997: 234–35).

Acquiring the control not to respond to the Muslim archers was one lesson that the Christians needed to learn. It is known that the Byzantines had evolved such tactics prior to the crusades and they must have passed on this information to the First Crusaders. But the Franks also learned through their own experiences and, as France has so convincingly shown, in the course of the First Crusade, they formed a tough and cohesive force, drawing themselves up in increasingly familiar formations and proving capable of dealing with the challenges that they faced (France, 1994). The provocation from Muslim attacks was immense and there are reports of Frankish knights looking like porcupines on account of the arrows stuck in their chain mail (although the wearer was rarely harmed seriously); the horses fared less well and were often the main casualties which would slow down the Frankish march. Another tactic preferred by the Muslims was also facilitated by their speed and manoeuvrability. As Raymond of Aguilers reported of an engagement near Antioch in 1098 'The Turks have a customary method of fighting, even when outnumbered, of attempting to surround their enemies' (Raymond of Aguilers, tr. Hill and Hill, 1968: 34). On this occasion the crusaders forestalled the move, but it was used on other occasions and to its greatest effect at the Battle of Hattin in 1187 (see below, pp. 162–3). Settler armies featured their own lightly armed archers known as Turcopoles – men who were the result of mixed-race marriages in the Levant. There was also a large proportion of infantrymen – archers who tried to protect the Christians' cavalry by keeping the Muslim horsemen at a distance, as well as spearmen whose task was to cover the archers. Muslim forces also had footmen whose roles were similar. Both armies contained religious men to tend to the warriors' spiritual well-being and to provide inspiration for the holy war: bishops and priests could often be found in the Frankish forces, while Sufi mystics and Qu'aranic readers were present in Muslim armies. Likewise, each side had people to tend to their sick and wounded. The Hospitallers fulfilled this function for the Franks and we know of doctors, surgeons and pharmacists in the Muslim ranks.

It is difficult to gauge the size of medieval armies because the sources often quote improbably high numbers (the army of the Second Crusade was not the 9,876,543 quoted by the Byzantine writer Niketas Choniates), but more realistic figures can be found. A letter written after the Battle of Harim (1164) noted that the prince of Antioch and the count of Tripoli put 600 knights into the field. The *Assizes* of the kingdom of Jerusalem (based on a legal document written in the mid-1180s) recorded that feudal service was owed for 675 knights (see Document 18). The Templars and Hospitallers could put forward about 300 knights each, which meant that at Hattin the forces of Jerusalem and the military orders were based around a core of 1,300 knights maximum. Estimates of foot soldiers indicate a further 15,000. To put this in perspective, Saladin's forces were numbered about 20,000. The Franks, therefore, had little safety net, but Saladin could call upon the resources of Egypt, Syria and the Jazira (northern Iraq) to replace or supplement his army. The creation of the military orders was one answer to the lack of manpower and it was often possible to augment the settlers' forces with the services of knights from the annual pilgrim traffic. William of Tyre noted that during the siege of Ascalon in 1153 such was the need for extra troops that King Baldwin III compelled the western pilgrims present in the Holy

Land to stay and fight for him in return for payment. There was also a small stream of westerners who came to the Holy Land to serve in its defence for a year or so as an act of piety. The future Count Charles the Good of Flanders did this in *c.* 1108, Count Fulk V of Anjou (later King Fulk of Jerusalem) in 1120, and Conrad (later King Conrad III of Germany) in 1124. In short, however, the Franks never solved the issue of limited military resources during the twelfth century.

CASTLES

While battles could exert a decisive influence on Frankish power, the key to holding on to territory was the control of castles and fortified sites, which included towns and rural manor houses. The armies of the First Crusade, while possessed of some experience of sieges in the West, had to learn how to invest and subdue such formidable sites as Antioch and Jerusalem and the duration of these struggles (ten months in the case of the former) and the strength of the defences they faced were of a new order of difficulty. The knowledge gained during the course of the crusade proved invaluable in taking the other castles and fortifications of the Levant, as the Franks established their rule. The use of siege artillery, towers and ladders was described frequently by chroniclers as was the expertise of specialist engineers, usually from the Italian fleets. The Muslims did have some artillery of their own, mainly mangonels, to resist the Christians.

After the initial phase of conquest it was then the settlers who had to refortify, develop and construct their own defences in order to preserve their hold on the Holy Land and to provide centres of authority. Castles, as in the West, were multi-functional buildings and their roles might be defensive, offensive (threatening the enemy), administrative, judicial, for accommodation, to demonstrate power, and to act as a place of refuge. The diversity of shapes and styles of Frankish castles bear testimony to the variety of functions they needed to perform, yet they all shared the same basic process during construction. In other words, a site had to be chosen to reflect a balance of defence and practicality. Water supplies had to be secured; money spent to hire workmen, masons and tools; stone quarried, oxen procured to move the stones, building cranes and scaffolding had to be made and the protection of the site ensured. Such problems were less acute where existing fortifications stood, but the complex and expensive process of building a castle should not be forgotten when we look at the results of these labours.

As the overall strategic situation evolved, the emphasis on the function of a fortified place might change too. Ellenblum (2007) has identified three phases of castle-building by the Franks in the kingdom of Jerusalem, stages apparent according to their strategic needs and the wider political situation (note that his study does not cover the principality of Antioch where the settlers often found themselves under greater military pressure from the 1130s onwards). In the first phase, that of conquest (1099–1114), the Christians took and fortified at least twenty-nine castles or settlements in the kingdom of Jerusalem, although only a small number of these were new foundations, with most based on existing sites which could include major cities such as Jerusalem and Caesarea – a natural enough course of events during the process of conquest and consolidation. Ellenblum then shows that from c.1115 to 1167 the Franks constructed a lot more castles, many of which were new and tended to be found in rural regions. Most were not, however, located on the kingdom's borders but in centres of agriculture that were usually peaceful. This indicates a period of relative calm in the kingdom and suggests that these structures were primarily concerned with administration, rather than defence. The extract from William of Tyre in Document 19 covers the group of fortresses built in the south of the kingdom near Ascalon. As perhaps the area most vulnerable to Muslim incursions it seems reasonable to ascribe a more overtly defensive function to this group of castles, namely: Castrum Arnaldi, 1132–33; Bethgibelin, 1136; Ibelin, 1141; Blanchegarde, 1142 and Gaza, 1150. Yet they were clearly designed to have an offensive capability too and succeeded in putting considerable pressure on the Egyptian-ruled city and its hinterland, preventing the cultivation of the land, for example. In the third phase (1168–87), however, the situation changed. Nur ad-Din began to capture sites on the edge of the kingdom, such as Banyas in 1164 and Hunin in 1167, while King Amalric's efforts to conquer Egypt (see below, pp. 114–19) drew resources away. That said, the Franks were still capable of highly aggressive moves themselves and the new castles of Hunin and especially Jacob's Ford, certainly had offensive capabilities too. The settlers remained formidable opponents in battle as well, as their victory at Mont Gisard (1177) illustrated. In light of this changing strategic situation, therefore, castles constructed or substantially enlarged during this period were located on the frontier areas of the north-east, the east and the southwest of the kingdom. Thus the existing sites of Safad, Belvoir, Kerak and Montreal were rebuilt and the new fortifications at Hunin and Jacob's Ford created.

The sites developed during this period were on a far greater scale than their predecessors which, in part, was a reflection of evermore sophisticated Muslim siege and artillery techniques. The rise of Nur ad-Din and Saladin meant that Muslim field armies became stronger and thus their ability to prolong sieges grew too. From the Frankish perspective their castles needed to survive longer sieges which required improved defences and a better capability to store food and water. In combination with the damaging effects of Muslim raids, this meant that the ownership and enhancement of castles became a far more expensive process, something that increasingly could only be borne by the military orders. Hence, King Baldwin IV built Jacob's Ford in 1178 but within months he handed it over to the Templars.

For the first few decades of conquest and settlement Frankish siege tactics were based around the use of artillery and siege engines, coupled with their usual superiority in ground troops. While the Muslims had artillery of their own, during the early decades of the century they favoured rapid assaults on castles, or a particular skill of theirs – tunnelling, by which means they entered Kharput in 1123 (thus capturing King Baldwin II of Jerusalem) and Edessa in 1144; their efforts were not, therefore, based on siege engines or towers. An increasing use of heavy artillery under Nur ad-Din changed the dynamics of sieges. The balance of power between the two sides became even and then tipped towards the Muslims. It was out of these circumstances that the concentric castle was born; that is, the need to survive longer sieges, to endure bombardment from heavier artillery and, with wider and deeper moats, the ability to keep catapults at a greater distance and to protect better against mines. The new castles had higher and thicker walls and with their double line of defences, offered the defenders further opportunities to fire back at their enemies. The change in the thickness of walls was dramatic: most of the early generation fortifications had walls around 2.8 to 3 metres thick, but from the late 1160s we see them growing to around 4 metres. Towers also became taller and had a greater area on their top level to enable

10. The Castle of Belvoir in the Kingdom of Jerusalem. © Sonia Halliday Photographs, photo by Bryan Knox

a larger surface on which to place archers or artillery. The fact that the concentric castles of Belvoir, Kerak and Montreal resisted Saladin for many months after his success at the Battle of Hattin is an indication of their strength because the majority of Frankish defences fell to him within days.

The forms of Frankish fortifications varied according to their position and needs and the following categorisation compiled by Boas (Boas, 1999: 93–118) outlines the main types, with the proviso that some castles could fall into more than one category.

Fortified towers: The most simple form of defensive structure was the tower, a common sight in rural areas (over seventy-five have been identified in the kingdom of Jerusalem alone). Most were two floors of vaulted rooms that could act as administrative centres for rural estates, storehouses and places of safety during enemy raids.

Enclosure castles: These were simple walled compounds with towers on each corner and sometimes along the walls. These forms were familiar from the Roman, Byzantine and Ummayad periods and could be constructed swiftly and easily. Examples can be found at Blanchegarde and Darum.

Enclosure and keep: This was a tower within an enclosure, or a development of one of the corner towers into a larger building with bigger defences and more complex entrances, such as Jubayl (Byblos) in the county of Tripoli.

Concentric enclosures: These comprised two enclosures, one within the other, with towers on all corners and along some walls. The higher inner wall provided a second line of fire as well as defence. The only surviving example – albeit the earliest known model – is at Belvoir on the borders of the kingdom of Jerusalem overlooking the Jordan valley and the important road between Jerusalem and Damascus. Boas comments that it 'represents a landmark in castle design and became the prototype of some of the finest castles built in the West' (Boas, 1999: 106). It was constructed by the Hospitallers after they purchased the site in 1168 and, as well as its concentric walls, it featured a ditch on three sides (the fourth looked out over the Jordan valley). Kennedy has described the inner court as cloister-like, reminding us of the monastic vocation of the Hospitallers (Kennedy, 1994: 61). A bathhouse, two large cisterns, a forge and a smithy indicate the accommodation functions of a castle. Such was Belvoir's strength that it held out for over a year against Saladin's forces after the defeat at Hattin until the Muslims mined the barbican.

Spur castles: These fortresses often offer the most spectacular examples of Frankish military architecture. They were built on ridges of land with (usually) steep cliffs on three sides and a strong line of defences facing the tongue of land that connected the spur to the main body of land. The most striking of these is at Saone in northern Syria. It was based on a tenth-century Byzantine castle and was developed by the Franks during the second quarter of the twelfth century. It features a rock-cut ditch of 128 metres in length, 26 metres deep and 18 metres wide, with a pinnacle of rock left standing to help carry a bridge across the chasm. With rising land overlooking the ditch, the Franks had to construct extremely powerful defences (featuring towers and a huge keep) on this side. Saone stretched out for 700 metres behind these walls and included enormous cisterns and, half-way along, a second ditch to separate off a lower bailey which was, essentially, a walled village complete with churches. In spite of the great ditch the castle succumbed to Saladin in only three days. An intense bombardment with enormous stones (up to 300 kilogrammes each) and the exploitation of the weaker defences at the second ditch enabled the Muslims to break into the upper bailey and to compel the garrison to surrender. Two other spur castles of note are Kerak in Transjordan and Krak des Chevaliers in southern Syria. The former was crucial in supervising the pilgrim and trade routes between Damascus and Egypt, while the latter overlooked the Homs valley and guarded against incursions from the Muslim lands into the Frankish-controlled coastal plain.

Hilltop castles: These could vary in form and included the formidable Montreal in Transjordan (again, constructed to monitor trade routes) which, by the 1170s, featured concentric walls and was strong enough to resist Saladin for a year and a half before capitulating.

Towns: Of course, towns were also walled and the Franks inherited most of these from their existing inhabitants although this did not prevent them from augmenting and extending the walls and gatehouses. The walls of Jerusalem, for example, were strengthened in 1116 and 1177.

Muslim fortifications tended to be urban in form and featured impressive walls and gatehouses. Saladin's new citadel at Cairo, constructed in the 1170s, was the most dramatic of these, while those at Aleppo and Damascus were also developed. The main castle-builders in the Muslim world were the Assassins whose enclave in northern Tripoli was based around a series of fortifications, the largest of which was Masyaf, a keep and enclosure castle of some complexity.

SIEGE WARFARE

All of the developments in castle-building meant that it became increasingly difficult to subdue enemy fortifications. One reason behind the growing complexity of castles was, as noted above, advances in siege technology, an area in which the urbanised Muslim world led the way. The basic weapons were mangonels – a sort of large-scale crossbow – and the trebuchet – a counterweight machine that could hurl large stones up to 200 metres (well beyond the range of archers) and inflict serious damage on walls and towers.

The bombardment from such machinery could be relentless; the Franks fired *c.* 500 stones an hour at the siege of Lisbon in 1147. Defenders could, of course, construct their own siege machinery to help resist attack. Such was the importance of these machines that armies often kept them in kit form so that they could be transported and used repeatedly. Particularly large engines were even named: the armies of the Third Crusade used 'Bad Neighbour' and 'God's Stonethrower' to great effect at the siege of Acre in 1191.

Greek fire was a favourite weapon of the Muslims, although it seems to have been little used by the Franks. Ceramic vessels containing a highly flammable mixture of boiled sulphur, pitch, nitre and petroleum were fired at the Christians, who employed hides soaked in vinegar as a method of trying to prevent the fire taking hold.

Once the walls were reached, mines, siege towers and battering rams might be employed to gain access to the site. The construction and deployment of these devices was a matter of great skill and specialist siege engineers were often employed. In the course of the attack on Lisbon during the Second Crusade, sources make a point of identifying a Pisan brought in purposely to direct operations. Some siege towers seem to have been extremely precarious devices (one at Lisbon was 28 metres high while those on the Venetian ships at Constantinople in 1203 and 1204 were even more startling, see below, p. 197) and they were always subject to intense enemy harassment, usually in the form of fire. Many siege engines (including battering rams, or 'cats' as they were sometimes known) were destroyed in this way, sometimes with their unfortunate operatives inside. Wider and deeper moats were one way of resisting siege towers, although the attackers would, if possible, try to fill the moat with rubble and debris to enable them to bring ladders and towers up to the wall. Mining skills were evident on both sides, with Zengi's successful operation at Edessa in 1144 being one outstanding example and the 200-metre long shaft dug at Lisbon in 1147 being also worthy of note. Mines were probably the most difficult form of siege warfare to resist. The *talus* of a castle (a sloping section of wall) offered some defence and if the line of the opponents' dig was known, then a counter-mine might be an option. Nonetheless, topography and time permitting, a mine was the most effective form of siege warfare.

The full range of these techniques was employed by Saladin during his campaigns after Hattin in 1187–88 and he utilised numerous siege engines at castles such as Saone in July 1188 and mines at Belvoir in January 1189. Once a city or a castle fell the fate of its defenders could vary according to circumstance: an offer of freedom was often an opening gambit to try to persuade a place to surrender quickly, but as a siege became longer and if the attackers held a strong hand, the consequences for the defenders grew evermore serious. Loss of freedom and ransom demands were likely, hostages might be handed over, or, if the siege was particularly arduous or the tension especially high, then a sack and massacre might occur. The fall of Jerusalem in 1099 is the obvious example of this and is usually contrasted with Saladin's relatively bloodless taking of the city in 1187 when he ransomed many inhabitants and allowed some of the others to leave freely. The threat of a massacre might inspire terror in places contemplating resistance, although equally it might stiffen resolve. It was a convention of medieval warfare that terms of surrender, once agreed, were adhered to. In 1139, when fighting Muslim opponents at Baalbek, Zengi attracted heavy criticism when he slaughtered his enemies after promising to release all prisoners if the citadel capitulated. All military forces, whether armies on the move, besiegers or besieged, needed supplies of food and water and it was the maintenance of these, rather than any overt military activity, that often decided the outcome of a military engagement. The Frankish predicament at Hattin is the most obvious example for an army in the field. With regard to a castle, if, as at Montreal in Transjordan in 1187–88, the attackers (in this case the Muslims) could keep their troops in place, then starving out this isolated garrison was the surest, if the slowest, way to achieve success; the defenders were eventually reputed to have gone blind through lack of salt and were compelled to surrender.

NAVAL WARFARE

Control of the sea was one respect in which the Franks established a clear superiority over their Muslim opponents and during the capture of the many coastal towns of the Levant, seapower was vital in preventing the defenders from receiving supplies and reinforcements. Given the crucial role of the sea as a lifeline to the West for trade, pilgrim traffic and crusades, it is perhaps strange that the settlers never built up a fleet of their own. There is evidence for a small fleet for the kingdom of Jerusalem in the 1160s, but generally the Franks approached outside sources for naval support. At times, such as the invasions of Egypt in 1169 and 1177, this was supplied by the Byzantine Empire, or in 1174, by Sicily, but usually it was the Italian trading cities of Pisa, Genoa and Venice who provided a fleet. As we have seen (Document 8), the Italians extracted a high price for their support, but it was a crucial economic and strategic investment for the settlers and one that paid substantial dividends. The Egyptians were the major Muslim seapower in the region and during the eleventh century the Fatimids had possessed a very strong navy, but by the period of the crusades this was in decline. Nonetheless, as long as the Egyptians held a base on the Levantine coast their shipping could harass the pilgrim and trading fleets of the West. The capture of Tyre (1124) and Ascalon (1153) were essential to ensure a safer passage for Christian shipping because the need to have a base for water supplies limited the range of the Egyptian boats, and with no port open on the coast the security of Christian shipping was much improved. The Syrian Muslims were little interested in naval matters. As Hillenbrand indicates, most were from a land-locked equestrian culture in which seafaring was regarded as a dangerous activity best undertaken by common criminals. The Arab proverb, 'It is preferable to hear the flatulence of camels than the prayers of fishes', expresses this attitude concisely (Hillenbrand, 1999: 557). Saladin, however, appreciated that a strong navy might still have an effect on Frankish strategy and he tried hard to revitalise the Egyptian navy, although lack of resources and poor seamanship rendered his plan largely useless.

CONCLUSION

During the twelfth century the Franks learned much about military tactics, siege warfare and castle-building, and at times showed themselves to be thoughtful and skilful warriors. Innovations such as the concentric castle were observed by visiting crusaders and copied back in the West; Richard the Lionheart's fortress at Château Gaillard in northern France is one such example. The perpetual problem of limited manpower, coupled with some calamitous errors of judgement and the military skills of their Muslim opponents, proved to be insurmountable in the struggle to hold on to the holy city of Jerusalem. The military orders emerged as a partial solution to the question of military resources, but large-scale crusades and even stronger castles would be required to sustain, let alone expand, the Latin East in future.

8

The aftermath of the Second Crusade: recovery and expansion, 1149–1174

THE START OF CLOSER RELATIONS WITH BYZANTIUM AND ADVANCES FOR BOTH THE CHRISTIANS AND THE MUSLIMS

The failure of the Second Crusade in 1148 was an enormous blow to the morale of the Franks in the Levant. Equally, of course, it was a boost to the Muslims because it consolidated the conquest of Edessa and, more importantly, it proved that the might of Christian Europe could be humbled. For Prince Raymond of Antioch the crusade had represented an opportunity to expand his lands in northern Syria and to challenge the power of Aleppo. After the departure of the westerners, however, he was exposed to even greater pressure from Nur ad-Din and in June 1149 at the Battle of Inab, the prince was defeated and killed. His head was cut off and sent to the caliph of Baghdad (the spiritual leader of the Sunni Muslims) to emphasise Nur ad-Din's achievement.

Raymond's death left the Franks of northern Syria deeply vulnerable and King Baldwin III marched north, as kings of Jerusalem had done in the past (1119, 1130), to restore order. The disaster at Inab prompted appeals to the West for a new crusade and senior ecclesiastical figures, including Abbot Suger of Saint Denis, Bernard of Clairvaux and Pope Eugenius set up a series of meetings to plan a new expedition. The prospects of Louis of France or Conrad of Germany leaving their lands again so quickly were remote, and in the atmosphere of bitterness and despondency generated by the defeat at Damascus – not to mention the exhaustion of men and resources – no response was forthcoming. One consequence of this lack of reaction in the West may have been Baldwin's decision in 1150 to sell the remaining Frankish castles in the county of Edessa to the Byzantines. Given the poor relations between the Greeks and Latins over recent decades this may seem strange. But, it is important to indicate that this tension had *not* involved the kingdom of Jerusalem; rather, it had formed between the Byzantines and the western crusaders and the Byzantines and Antioch. In any case, Baldwin probably felt he could not defend the isolated Edessan castles and, in light of the lack of help from western Europe, it was worth trying to build a more positive relationship with Manuel Komnenos. This move, however small, can be seen to signal the early stages of closer collaboration between the Greeks and the Latin settlers. As a fellow-Christian possessed of both substantial resources and a strategic interest in northern Syria, Manuel was an appropriate ally to work with against the Muslims. As we shall see, a better relationship with the Greeks became a key aim of the rulers of Jerusalem over the next thirty years.

The next decade was to see important advances for both the Christians and the Muslims. In late 1149 Baldwin managed to steady the situation in northern Syria and then he returned south. His attention was focused on Ascalon, the only port on the Eastern Mediterranean coast still under Muslim control; in this case, the authority of the Fatimids of Egypt. In January 1153 Baldwin started to besiege the city and after eight months the Christians captured it. This was a significant achievement for the Franks because it enhanced the southern security of the kingdom of Jerusalem, gave them a potential springboard into Egypt and, more importantly, it denied the Egyptians a port on the Eastern Mediterranean coast. The need for fresh water supplies and the limited nature of naval technology at the time meant that the operating range of ships was severely restricted. Without Ascalon, Egyptian ships were much less able to threaten the Frankish ports or intercept valuable pilgrim or commercial traffic arriving from western Europe.

The capture of Ascalon was soon offset by events at Damascus. By portraying himself as the leader of the *jihad* and contrasting himself to the pro-Frankish stance of the existing rulers, Nur ad-Din convinced a majority of the people of Damascus to let him take over the city in April 1154. For the first time in the Frankish occupation of the Levant the two key cities of Damascus and Aleppo were ruled by the same man. William of Tyre noted that 'this change was decidedly disastrous to the interests of the kingdom' (William of Tyre, tr. Babcock and Krey, 1943: 2.225). Nur ad-Din married the daughter of the previous ruler to align himself with the area even more closely and set about consolidating his power. But the Franks were not cowed by this development and quickly took the fight to the Muslims, only to suffer a heavy defeat at Jacob's Ford in June 1157. This loss, combined with the damage inflicted by an enormous earthquake, induced an appeal to Pope Adrian IV asking for help – the first such request since 1150 and the start of a series of calls that would prove the dominant feature of relations between the Latin East and the West in future decades. Adrian issued a bull for a new crusade, although it provoked a negligible reaction. On this occasion it mattered little because in the same summer Count Thierry of Flanders arrived in the Holy Land. His appearance was far too quick to have been a response to Adrian's appeal (it usually took a crusader over a year to put his affairs in order before he could set out for the Levant), but was a considerable boost to the settlers nonetheless. Thierry was an experienced crusader who had been to the Levant in 1139 and on the Second Crusade; he was from a prestigious and wealthy family; he was closely related to the ruling house of Jerusalem (his wife, Sibylla, was the half-sister of Baldwin III); and he was an extremely pious man, committed to the defence of the Holy Land; in short, the ideal crusader.

In the autumn of 1157 the Franks besieged the important castle and town at Shaizar, a crossing point of the River Orontes that dominated the fertile floodplain in the adjacent river valley. The king intended that Count Thierry should take control of Shaizar and establish a lordship there. Nur ad-Din was seriously ill at the time and with Thierry's presence, the Franks were poised to strengthen their position considerably. Yet at this moment, two of the settlers' fatal weaknesses emerged: first, the effect of rivalry between Antioch and Jerusalem; and second, resentment of newcomers arriving and securing substantial territorial benefits. Reynald of Châtillon, prince of Antioch, who had become ruler of the principality in 1153, objected to the plan. Traditionally, Shaizar had been connected with Antioch and Reynald argued that Thierry should, therefore, swear homage to him. The count refused, saying that he swore homage only to kings, not mere princes, and the siege broke down. From our perspective and knowing of the eventual demise of the Latin East, such dissensions seem baffling. Surely the settlers could have put aside their differences for what might be perceived as the greater good of the Christians? In fact, from a contemporary viewpoint the position was far more complex. Given Thierry's close ties with Baldwin, Reynald may well have feared the extension of Jerusalem's influence into northern Syria. Reynald was an outsider and, as such, had faced some opposition to his marriage to Princess Constance, the heiress to Antioch. Clearly Reynald felt threatened and was determined to establish his own authority. In these circumstances such a priority was understandable and probably explains the prince's actions. Any momentum that the Franks might have attained was further reduced when, in the winter of 1157, Nur ad-Din recovered and began to reassert his old dominance over Muslim Syria.

The spotlight continued to fall on Prince Reynald. His marriage to Constance had not been welcomed by everyone in Antioch, particularly Patriarch Aimery, who wanted to maintain the regency he was entitled to as long as the princess remained unmarried. Reynald's response to Aimery's opposition was brutal. The patriarch – an ageing man – was tied up on top of the citadel, his head was smeared with honey and the prince released a hive of bees on to him. Reynald's heavy-handed touch extended to international diplomacy. In 1156 he launched a savage raid on Cyprus, killed the Byzantine governor and sent the Antiochene troops to ravage the island. We might recall that in 1145 Prince Raymond of Antioch had travelled to Constantinople to pay homage to Manuel. Reynald's attack on the lands of his overlord was foolish in the extreme and in 1158–59 the emperor marched to northern Syria to punish him. Reynald's actions on Cyprus had also horrified King Baldwin who, as we saw earlier, had decided that closer ties with Byzantium would be to the long-term benefit of all the Latin settlers. Furthermore, in 1157 he had become betrothed to Manuel's niece, Theodora, and they married in September 1158. As Manuel reached northern Syria, Baldwin hurried to Antioch determined to try to mollify the Byzantine ruler and to bring Reynald into line. The emperor arrived in the area first and Reynald had to prostrate himself in the dust at Manuel's feet, groveling to apologise for his actions. Baldwin's presence improved the atmosphere considerably and the emperor showed his interest in developing relations with the Latin East by taking Maria, one of Reynald's step-daughters, as his bride. It seems that Baldwin and Manuel formed a close personal bond and when the king of Jerusalem broke his arm in a hunting accident it was the emperor who set it for him.

Plainly, though, a strategic purpose lay behind such diplomatic niceties and in 1159 the armies of Antioch, Jerusalem and Byzantium marched towards Aleppo. Nur ad-Din saw the gravity of this threat and offered a truce and to release the Christian prisoners he held, many of whom were Germans captured eleven years previously during the Second Crusade. The terms of this deal evidently satisfied the emperor, although one might have expected him to have capitalised on the size of the Christian armies and attacked Nur ad-Din. Perhaps Manuel still regarded the settlers as untrustworthy, and felt that if the Muslims were defeated the Antiochenes would be in a sufficiently strong position to try, yet again, to break free from Byzantine overlordship. On the other hand, a campaign of the sort mounted in 1159 would make the point to Nur ad-Din that he should not menace the Christians too seriously or else he risked facing the full might of Byzantium. From Manuel's point of view, the expedition preserved the *status quo* and he was able to enforce a long-held wish to install an Orthodox patriarch in Antioch. The office had been preserved in exile in Constantinople since the armies of the First Crusade had forced the patriarch to flee, but in 1165 Athanasius entered the city to re-establish Orthodox tenure of the patriarchal seat. From the Frankish perspective, Baldwin III had, as he had hoped, formed strong ties with the Greeks and, while Nur ad-Din had not been defeated, at the very least his ambitions had been checked.

THE RISE OF NUR AD-DIN

The danger from Nur ad-Din and the Muslims of Syria gathered real momentum during the 1160s, although before exploring this it is worth assessing the nature of his power and authority. The ruler of Aleppo and Damascus was, undoubtedly, an extremely pious man and a shrewd political operator. After his victory over Prince Raymond of Antioch at Inab in 1149 he spent considerable energy consolidating his standing in the Islamic Near East; so much so, in fact, that in 1157 the caliph of Baghdad chided him for fighting his own people rather than the Christians. The complex and fragmented nature of the Muslim Near East meant that Nur ad-Din had to bring together many rival and independent rulers to ensure the stability of his position before he could confront the Franks. Whether the *jihad* against the Christians was his overriding aim at this stage is not clear, but the sources describe a significant change of attitude in the early 1160s and a far greater devotion to the prosecution of the holy war. After his recovery from serious illness in 1157–58 he made the pilgrimage to Mecca and in 1163 he suffered a heavy defeat by the Franks at al-Buqay'a. The last event seems to have had a profound effect on him and from this time onwards he adopted a more austere style of clothing and his focus on the *jihad* assumed real prominence.

As we saw earlier (above, pp. 39–40), there are two elements to the *jihad*. The first, higher, form concerns the purification of one's soul and Nur ad-Din's personal bearing and his close association with men of religion indicate that he was determined to follow this part of the struggle, as well as to engage in the second, worldly, aspect of the fight. He also sought to bring the virtues of faith and justice to his people. Many writers describe him as a law-giver and Nur ad-Din held weekly courts to dispense justice himself and to ensure fairness to all. He encouraged teaching and learning and sponsored the construction of many mosques and *madrasas* (teaching colleges) for Sufi mystics as well as a school for the study of *hadith* (the sayings of the Prophet). He also developed civic amenities such as bath-houses, hospitals (examples of both survive in Damascus today), orphanages and caravanserai. Under Nur ad-Din the propaganda of *jihad* developed apace and it described the sufferings inflicted upon Islam by the Franks. He also laid great emphasis on the spiritual importance of Jerusalem as a place of pilgrimage for Muslims and as a city that should be brought back under Islamic control. Poetry, writings and inscriptions encouraged this message to take root in the consciousness of his subjects and, in conjunction with his own piety and the increasing role of the religious classes, this gave the *jihad* an institutional and political authority that it had thus far lacked in the conflict with the Franks.

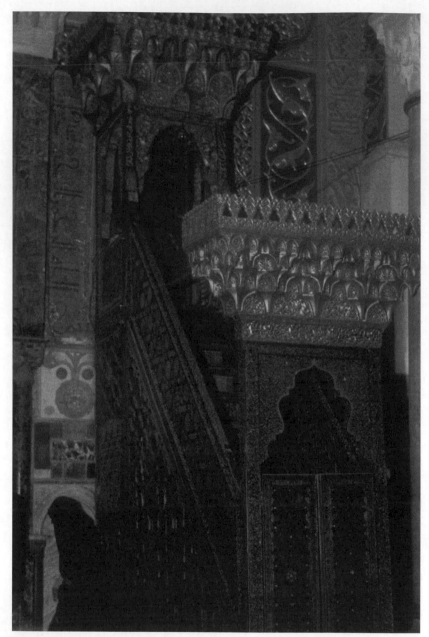

11. Nur ad-Din's pulpit in the al-Aqsa mosque, Jerusalem. Created in
Aleppo with the intention of taking its place in the al-Aqsa Mosque, it was
installed in Jerusalem in 1187 by Saladin after his capture of the city.
It was destroyed by an arsonist in 1967.

THE STRUGGLE FOR EGYPT

Nur ad-Din's main rival was not to be Baldwin III, but his brother Amalric, who ruled the kingdom of Jerusalem between 1163 and 1174. Baldwin died suddenly in 1163, aged only 33 years; once he had broken free of his mother he proved a capable and energetic ruler who showed a real awareness of the broader strategic picture through his creation of ties with Byzantium and, in the last years of his life, with his concern over Egypt. When Amalric succeeded to the throne Alexandria, Cairo and the Nile became the prime battleground between the settlers and Nur ad-Din.

What was the attraction of Egypt for the two powers? We saw earlier that it was ruled by the Shiite Fatimid dynasty. On account of the fundamental split in the Islamic faith between the Sunnis and Shiites a permanent *rapprochement* between Egypt and the Syrian Muslims was unlikely, particularly in light of Nur ad-Din's stance as the champion of Sunni orthodoxy. But the Fatimid dynasty of Egypt was in decline. Egyptian forces were defeated at Jerusalem and Ascalon in 1099, although the latter remained in Egyptian hands until 1153 and posed some threat to the southern borders of the kingdom of Jerusalem. The settlers' ambitions towards Egypt had a long history. In 1118 King Baldwin I had died *en route* home from a campaign in Egypt and his successor Baldwin II attacked the country in 1125. It seems that six years later the Franks were perceived as a sufficient threat for their ruler to try to make peace with King Fulk, although the proposal was rejected. Over the next twenty years the settlers focused on the gradual reduction of Ascalon and then, in the early 1160s, Baldwin III demanded and received an annual tribute from Egypt which demonstrated the relative strength of the two powers at this time. Further reasons existed for Baldwin's interest in Egypt. First, if the Franks did not assume some kind of lordship or take control of the land, then Nur ad-Din probably would. This would have profound strategic implications because, for the first time, the settlers would face the same enemy to the south (Egypt) as well as the east (Syria). Second, there was the question of money because Egypt was enormously wealthy. The fertility of the Nile Delta and the importance of Alexandria as the prime port of the Eastern Mediterranean meant that whoever controlled Egypt's resources would have a considerable advantage over their opponent. Both Amalric and Nur ad-Din needed to pay for their campaigns and the fact that the Franks made many requests for monetary support to the West at this time indicates their financial difficulties.

Between 1163 and 1169 Amalric launched no less than five campaigns into Egypt. Ultimately he was to fail in his bid to conquer Babylon (as the Franks referred to it), but one of the most striking features of this period was Amalric's determination in, first, trying to secure backing for his bid to conquer Egypt, and then, once Nur ad-Din had taken the country in 1169, his attempts to rally the Christians in the face of increased enemy power. In the course of these years he made diplomatic contacts with most of the senior rulers of western Europe, the emperor of Byzantium, the Pisans and the Muslim Assassins; in all, a remarkably diverse group. The mid-1160s saw the launch of an intensive diplomatic effort to persuade the West to help the settlers. Between 1163 and 1165 a series of letters (of which eleven survive) was sent to King Louis VII of France to try to induce him to launch a new crusade. The Franks stressed the spiritual and strategic importance of one of their recent losses, the city and fortress of Banyas (Caesarea Philippi in the Bible) in the north-east of the kingdom, now close to the Israeli–Lebanese border. It was described as 'the gate and the shield of the whole kingdom' and it was the place where Christ had said to Peter 'Thou art Peter and on this rock I will build my Church' (Matthew 16:18–19), the so-called Petrine Commission and the basis of papal authority down the centuries. Yet in 1164 the enemies of Christ had almost destroyed the place and the city was 'nothing more than an empty name', a point brought home by the fact that John, the recently enthroned bishop of Banyas, travelled to the West in person, thereby providing a vivid demonstration of his destitution and emphasising the need to restore the proper order of things (for the text, see *Letters from the East*, tr. Barber and Bate, 2010: 51–52). The settlers appealed to Louis, as a fellow-Christian, to protect his brothers in the East, but the failure of the Second Crusade, as well as tensions between the Anglo–Norman realm and France, meant that he was unwilling to act.

In 1163 and 1164 Amalric mounted attacks on the Egyptian fortress at Bilbais, about 50 kilometres north-east of Cairo, but these failed. One reason for this was that Nur ad-Din had exploited the king's absence in Egypt to enter Frankish lands and in the autumn of 1164 he took the important town of Harim in the principality of Antioch as well as Banyas in the kingdom of Jerusalem. A further disaster affected both Muslims and Franks alike because an enormous earthquake hit northern Syria and destroyed castles, towns, villages and crops. As usual following such a calamity, a truce was established to allow both sides to recover.

DIPLOMATIC CONTACT WITH THE WEST AND BYZANTIUM

The next decade saw an intensification in the struggle for Egypt and Amalric had to mount an unprecedented effort to secure outside support. In the aftermath of the 1164 earthquake, the years 1165 and 1166 were relatively peaceful, although Amalric's approaches to the West bore fruit in a number of ways. Pope Alexander III issued two papal bulls calling for a new crusade. The second of these was prompted by a legation led by Gilbert d'Assailly, master of the Hospitallers and the highest-ranking envoy used by the settlers for many decades. He carried the bull to northern Europe where he tried to use it to persuade the rulers of England and France to help the Holy Land. Mutual suspicion of each others' territorial ambitions continued to prevent Henry II and Louis from taking the cross, although the Angevin did institute a general tax on behalf of the settlers and, not to be outdone, Louis followed suit. These appeals also resulted in a number of French nobles taking the cross. For example, Count William IV of Nevers (in Burgundy), a man with crusading ancestors from 1099 and 1148, took a body of knights with him to Acre in 1168 only to die of sickness, a common fate for a crusader. Yet, welcome as such contingents were, they did not constitute the large force that Amalric needed. It required the participation of a king to generate the momentum for an expedition of sufficient size to threaten the Muslims; failing this, alternative sources of help had to found.

In the autumn of 1166 it seems that the king was aware of a renewed Muslim offensive, led by Nur ad-Din's general, Shirkuh, in Egypt. To counter this he gathered money from the lands of Jerusalem by instituting a tax (of one-tenth on all moveable property) approved at a special assembly of all the kingdom's nobles at Nablus. This meeting also made arrangements for the military strength of Jerusalem to gather at Ascalon in January 1167 to march south. In light of the limited response of the rulers of northern Europe and, on account of the military requirements of a campaign in Egypt (in essence, the navigability of the Nile Delta and the presence of Alexandria and Damietta, two of the country's key towns on the northern coastline), he had made an agreement for a Pisan fleet to join him. The kingdom of Jerusalem had a weak navy and, as we saw in 1124 at Tyre, when naval expertise was required, the settlers often looked to the Italian city states. Alongside their religious motivation as fellow-Christians concerned for the salvation of their souls and the defence of the holy places, strong commercial reasons must have encouraged Pisan involvement. They had existing interests in both Egypt and the Latin East and hoped to cement their position ahead of Genoa (their most bitter rivals) and Venice as the dominant western traders in the region.

Setting aside their religious differences, the threat from Shirkuh was sufficient to convince Sultan Shawar of Egypt to ally with the Franks. On payment of 400,000 dinars the Christians agreed not to leave Egypt until Shirkuh had also departed and to seal the Frankish–Egyptian alliance they established a perpetual and inviolable peace between the two powers. Count Hugh of Caesarea led the Jerusalem delegation and William of Tyre secured much eye-witness information from him, including a vivid account of the splendour of the caliph's palace:

> There, supported by columns of marble covered with designs in relief were promenades with fretted and gilded ceilings and pavements of various coloured stones. Throughout the entire circuit royal magnificence prevailed. So elegant

was both material and workmanship that involuntarily the eyes of all who saw it were ravished by the rare beauty and never wearied of the sight.

(William of Tyre, tr. Babcock and Krey, 1943: 2.319)

Contrary to all usual etiquette, Hugh insisted on the treaty being ratified by shaking the caliph's uncovered hand. This was a remarkable moment: aside from this possible breach of the caliph's dignity, strict Islamic law dictates that the *jihad* only ends when all the world has submitted to Islam. Truces were permissible in the course of this struggle, but a permanent peace of the form set out here was contrary to holy law. For the caliph to break this showed how desperate he was to fend off the threat from Sunni Islam – a deal with the Franks may have been undesired, but it gave the Shiite caliphate a chance to preserve its power in Cairo.

THE CAPTURE OF ALEXANDRIA

Shirkuh marched towards Cairo, but in March 1167 he moved south and was followed by the Franks. On 18 March the two armies met in battle at al-Babayn, well south of Cairo, and both sides inflicted losses on the other, although Shirkuh recovered quicker and regrouped to head north to Alexandria. The city surrendered to him immediately which compelled Amalric to follow him northwards and to begin a siege. Shirkuh soon withdrew and left his young nephew, Saladin, in charge of the defence of the city. Meanwhile a Pisan fleet joined the Franks. Ten galleys, a siege tower and various catapults intensified the blockade and the defenders seemed ready to capitulate. Shirkuh reappeared with a relief force and the two sides began to negotiate a truce. In August Amalric and Shirkuh both agreed to withdraw from Egypt (thus the Franks fulfilled their arrangement with Shawar), with the treaty being triggered by the surrender of Alexandria to the Franks: Amalric's standard flew from the Pharos lighthouse. Although, in accordance with the treaty, the Christians soon returned to Jerusalem, the very fact that Amalric – however briefly – had held one of the great cities of the Islamic world testified to the Franks' military abilities and the feasibility of their aim to exert some sort of power over Egypt. Such an episode would seem to indicate a full recovery from the disaster of the Second Crusade and showed that, regardless of the growing strength of his opponents, Amalric was an imaginative and resourceful leader. As the Franks left Egypt in the early autumn of 1167 it must also be remembered that there was still the possibility of a new crusade from the West and, as we will see now, the prospect of even closer relations with the Greeks.

On 29 August 1167 Amalric married Maria, a niece of Emperor Manuel, in a splendid ceremony at Tyre cathedral. It is likely that the envoys who arranged this union had raised the possibility of Byzantine support for another invasion of Egypt. The Greeks saw how vulnerable Egypt had become and the two Christian powers contemplated sharing the kingdom if it were conquered. This solution would have guaranteed the military backing that Amalric needed and, with Greek input to bolster his own limited resources, it became plausible for the king to consider exercising authority of a more permanent nature there. For the Byzantines there emerged the possibility of greater wealth and also the chance to reclaim a part of their former empire. But as the Frankish envoys (who included William of Tyre) finalised this agreement with Manuel, Amalric invaded Egypt again. This appears a perplexing move. Some said that he had responded to allegations that Shawar was attempting to escape the previous year's treaty with the Franks by allying with Nur ad-Din, others asserted that the Hospitallers lay behind this sudden aggression on account of their financial troubles (see above, p. 74).

In October 1168, again with Pisan support, Amalric set out for Egypt. On 3 November he brutally sacked the northern city of Bilbais and, as promised, gave it to the Hospitallers. The atrocities at Bilbais alienated Shawar who (whether or not he had been negotiating with them earlier) sent to Nur ad-Din and Shirkuh for help. In the meantime the Franks advanced to Cairo where an offer by Shawar to pay them huge sums of money caused their invasion to stall outside the city. As the Franks awaited payment, Shirkuh approached. Amalric marched northwards in a vain attempt to intercept him, but when this failed Shirkuh was free to take up a position outside Cairo. Amalric saw the futility of remaining in Egypt and, on 2 January 1169, withdrew to his own lands. Within a month Shawar was assassinated and Shirkuh seized Egypt. The Franks now faced a vastly more serious threat from the south, exacerbated by the loss of the immense resources of Egypt, resources that were now all in the hands of their enemies. William of Tyre noted that Nur ad-Din 'could effectively shut in the realm and blockade all coastal cities by land and sea. . . . Still more to be dreaded was the fact that he could hinder the passage of pilgrims on their way to us' (William of Tyre, tr. Babcock and Krey, 1943: 2.360).

THE MISSION OF ARCHBISHOP FREDERICK OF TYRE

In light of this new crisis in the Holy Land a further embassy was dispatched to the West. It was led by Archbishop Frederick of Tyre, the most senior churchman yet sent on such a mission. Thus, as the situation in the Levant worsened, the settlers used envoys of increasing status to present their case. Letters were addressed to all the leaders of western Europe and Frederick visited the pope in the summer of 1169. These appeals emphasised the danger to pilgrims – something of concern to all in the West – and highlighted the threat to the holy places and the suffering of the Christians in the East. Amalric noted the family ties between the settlers and their co-religionists in the West and stressed his personal concern for the welfare of pilgrims. In response to Frederick's appearance and the letters that he carried, Pope Alexander issued a new crusade bull, *Inter omnia*, on 29 July 1169. The bull called upon people to crusade in person, rather than simply sending money. Alexander observed that with the union of Egypt and Syria the fate of the Latin East lay in the balance and he urged immediate action.

The main targets of Frederick of Tyre's mission were Louis VII of France and Henry II of England. The reasons why the French monarch was approached have been discussed earlier (see p. 116), although on this occasion they resorted to a particularly sophisticated device to try to induce him to respond. Frederick offered the king the keys to the walled city of Jerusalem. The symbolism of this act would have been plain to Louis: the last time that a similar presentation took place was in 800 when a delegation from Jerusalem gave the keys of the city to the Emperor Charlemagne, the ruler of much of (the area now covered by) France, northern Italy and the western Germany; he was also a man famed for his piety. The Christians of the time looked to Charlemagne as the protector of Jerusalem and in 1169 Amalric was hoping that Louis would take on a similar role. The king and his advisors had chosen to replicate the offer from 800 because Louis and his Capetian court were known to hark back to the heritage of Charlemagne as the greatest Christian ruler in European history and were keen to associate themselves with his image in order to boost their own standing. For example, Charlemagne's banner, the oriflamme, was kept in the abbey of Saint Denis, a church intimately linked with the Capetians and a place where the Carolingian tradition was preserved and nurtured. We also saw earlier that the crusading window of 1147 included an image of Charlemagne. The offer made by the Frankish embassy in 1169 gave Louis the chance to emphasise further his ties with the Carolingians while the settlers would gain an important lever in their attempts to secure outside help. In the event, Louis declined the proposal although he professed a willingness to act if the dissension between England and France could be resolved.

Henry II ruled England and much of France. His crusading pedigree was impressive too: his ancestors included Robert Curthose, duke of Normandy, one of the heroes of the First Crusade, and his grandfather, Count Fulk V of Anjou had become king of Jerusalem in 1131. Amalric was, therefore, Henry II's uncle. There had been rumours of Henry's interest in the crusade prior to 1169, but the ferocity of his dispute with Thomas Becket, as well as simmering tensions with France, barred any progress. In the months before

Frederick reached the West there had been a serious effort to resolve these issues and the need to help defend the Holy Land was often advanced as a prime reason to do this. A contemporary lamented, 'What will the expedition to Jerusalem profit if peace is not first restored to the Church?' (John of Salisbury, 1979: 2.632–3). Might not Archbishop Frederick's news of Nur ad-Din's capture of Egypt provide further impetus to this process?

Frederick became closely involved in the diplomacy of the time and in July 1170 he was present when Henry and Louis settled some of their differences and also when the king of England and Archbishop Thomas made their peace. Contemporaries record the crusade as being a central part of these discussions; Frederick seemed on the verge of a major success and the settlers appeared poised to get the crusade they had so hoped for over recent years. Unfortunately for the Franks, and for reasons outside Frederick's control, the political situation in the West turned against them. The problems between Henry and Thomas resurfaced and culminated in the archbishop's murder at Canterbury Cathedral on 29 December 1170 by knights who acted at the king's behest. Condemnation of Henry was universal and any hopes of a crusade evaporated. 'There is a case for adding a lost crusade to the legacy of the archbishop's murder' (Phillips, 1996: 204), and Frederick was forced to return to the East, discontented and with nothing to show for his efforts.

KING AMALRIC'S EMBASSY TO CONSTANTINOPLE (1171)

In early October 1169 a Byzantine fleet of 150 galleys, sixty horse transports and twelve large supply ships reached Acre. The Franks and the Greeks besieged Damietta on the northern Egyptian coastline, but the Christians had to withdraw. The promise of a Frankish–Byzantine alliance had accomplished little, although the relationship between the two powers was soon to develop further. After a year of relative peace, once more occasioned by a series of massive earthquakes, the Franks decided, yet again, to renew their quest for outside support. William of Tyre described a dramatic scene at the High Court in Jerusalem (see Document 16 i). Many of the nobles advocated the customary mission to the West. Others, including Amalric himself, observed that this had yielded little of worth, while, on the contrary, events at Damietta demonstrated that the Byzantines were prepared to commit substantial military resources to the Eastern Mediterranean. The pro-Byzantinists noted that Manuel 'was much nearer to us [than the western Europeans], and besides far richer than the others and he could [thus] furnish the desired aid'. As the court debated who should be sent to the emperor, Amalric took the initiative and made a startling and controversial move. He claimed that no one other than he could undertake a mission of such gravity. In spite of protests the king was unmoved: 'I am determined to go; no one can induce me to recall that decision' (William of Tyre, tr. Babcock and Krey, 1943: 2.377–8). We have seen how, in the aftermath of the Second Crusade, King Baldwin III had edged closer to the Greeks via a series of marriage ties, diplomatic manoeuvres and military co-operation. But through his willingness to travel to Constantinople in person Amalric proposed a journey that no previous king of Jerusalem had ever set out on. His purpose was plainly of the highest importance, yet, intriguingly, our main source for these events, William of Tyre, was silent on the nature of any agreements made between Amalric and Manuel. He provides a wonderfully vivid description of the splendours of Constantinople and the etiquette of the imperial court, but little more. A contemporary Greek source, John Kinnamos, offers the most likely explanation for William's reticence. John wrote that Amalric obtained many things that he sought, 'including his subjection to the emperor' (John Kinnamos, tr. Brand, 1976: 209). In other words, Amalric had acknowledged the overlordship of the Byzantine ruler – a reflection of the failure of the West to provide adequate support and the king's desperate need to confront Nur ad-Din. William was probably reluctant to reveal this directly because his principal purpose in writing was to convince the people of the West that the settlers were worthy of help, but at the time he was doing the bulk of his writing (the 1180s), relations with the Greeks had become very hostile and, notwithstanding the earlier warmth between Manuel and the settlers, William regarded it as imprudent to draw attention to Amalric's subjection to the emperor.

Alongside this dramatic development the king made two further attempts to secure support. First, he sent another embassy to the West in 1171, although this appeared to make little impact. Second, and in another example of Amalric's breadth of vision in seeking assistance, he tried to establish a *rapprochement* with the Muslim sect known (even in the twelfth century) as the Assassins. This group lived in fortresses in the mountains to the west of the Orontes valley in Syria. Their fearsome reputation rested upon their ability to murder those who crossed their path, be they Muslim or Christian. The Assassins were Shiite Muslims which set them apart from the majority in Syria who were Sunnis. Even amongst the Shiites the Assassins were a splinter group who believed that the true *Imam* (head of the Islamic community) included the seventh *Imam*, Ismail, who had been disinherited from the line in the eighth century. In the 1090s supporters of his claim returned to prominence in the Alamut mountains of Persia and a group of these believers settled in the Levant, led by the charismatic 'Old Man of the Mountains', a near-legendary figure shrouded in tales of intrigue and death. The Assassins' status as Shiite left them open to persecution by Sunnis such as Nur ad-Din, who sought to uphold orthodoxy. But the Assassins, whose name probably derived from the hashish (marijuana) they were said to use, had sufficient numbers to survive in communities based around the castles of Masyaf and Qadmus. They were also strong enough to resist the Franks, who soon learned to tolerate them if they paid regular tribute to the local lords and landowners, including the military orders. It seems that in 1173, with Nur ad-Din posing an increasing threat to their safety, the Assassins felt the need to secure closer relations with the Franks. One report mentioned that The Old Man of the Mountains indicated his sect would convert to Christianity if the Templars remitted the payment owed to them, but the order ruined this plan by killing the Assassin envoys. Nevertheless, the fact that Amalric was interested to pursue this project shows his flexibility in seeking outside assistance.

Meanwhile, back in western Europe, there emerged the possibility of Henry II taking the cross after all. His absolution for the murder of Thomas Becket required him to provide 200 knights a year to serve with the Templars and a stipulation that he should take the cross for three years departing before Easter 1173. Henry sent 2,000 silver marks per annum to the Levant (further reference to this money will be made later, see below, p. 162) and it appears that he had finally made a binding commitment to travel to the East. The king also enacted various political and diplomatic moves to indicate that he was placing his affairs in order prior to departure for the Holy Land. Yet again, however, events in the West would break the settlers' hopes. A rebellion by Henry's heir, Henry the Younger, was supported by his brothers and encouraged by Louis VII of France. An uprising of this seriousness meant that there was no question of Henry leaving Europe and so the planned crusade collapsed. The king felt obliged to write to Amalric to explain the situation himself. For Henry to feel that he had to write such a letter shows clearly that Amalric expected him to arrive in the near future and demonstrated the seriousness of Henry's intentions. This point may be reinforced by noting the king's remorse at Thomas Becket's murder and the fact that the crusade formed part of his penance. Although some contemporaries had expressed scepticism about his earlier commitment to the crusade, the king would have been playing an extraordinarily dangerous game in 1173 had he raised expectations so high in Jerusalem and only a turn of events of the magnitude of a revolt could justify Henry not fulfilling his penance. A further mission from Jerusalem arrived in late 1173 to try to secure peace in the West. Pope Alexander granted the bishop of Lydda the status of papal legate (another new development in the settlers' diplomacy) and issued letters to try to facilitate peace between Henry and Louis, but to little avail.

The year 1174 saw the death of both Amalric and Nur ad-Din. The Muslim leadership had recently experienced some serious divisions and the king was determined to exploit them. Saladin had grown increasingly auto-nomous in his government of Egypt (he had taken over after the death of Shirkuh in 1169), and had declined to join Nur ad-Din in an attack on Kerak in 1173. Two years previously Saladin had deposed the Shiite caliph and had the name of the Sunni caliph of Baghdad inserted into public prayers. This was a major advance for Nur ad-Din as the champion of Sunni orthodoxy, although, unsurprisingly, it provoked some opposition and plotting against Saladin's rule from discontented Shiite factions. In light of these circumstances Amalric decided to plan another attack on Egypt and this time he secured help from the Sicilians. King William II had been amongst the targets of the embassies of 1169 and 1171 and, like the Italian seafaring cities, he could offer naval support. The Franks' prospects increased further in May 1174 when Nur ad-Din suffered a heart attack and died. William of Tyre described him as 'a just prince, valiant, wise . . . and far seeing' (William of Tyre, tr. Babcock and Krey, 1943: 2.394). Muslim sources lamented the passing of their great leader. Ibn al-Athir, an Aleppan writer of the early thirteenth century, praised his military skills, his public works, his honour for men of religion, and his great personal humility. Justice and piety were the hallmarks of Nur ad-Din's rule, but his greatest achievements were to draw together Muslim Syria and Egypt and to provide the *jihad* with a real momentum which posed the settlers by far their greatest test to date.

With the Muslim empire leaderless in Syria, with Egypt seemingly unstable and a Sicilian fleet at sea, Amalric's prospects appeared bright. Fate was not to favour the settlers, however. On 11 July, aged only 38, the king suc-cumbed to a violent attack of dysentery. William of Tyre described him as 'a man of wisdom and discretion, fully competent to hold the reins of govern-ment in the kingdom' (William of Tyre, tr. Babcock and Krey, 1943: 2.396). Amalric had proven an energetic ruler who developed a strong hold over his nobles and had done much to counter the menace posed by Nur ad-Din. His successor was Baldwin IV, a 13 year-old afflicted with leprosy, and his need for a regent and the search for a successor created many of the tensions that eventually made the kingdom so vulnerable to Saladin.

9

The Frankish rulers of the Levant: power and succession, *c.* 1100–74

Two of the most important issues that faced the rulers of the Latin states were to establish their dynastic line and to maintain authority over the nobility. These matters were familiar to other contemporary rulers, but the turbulent military situation in the Latin East and the settlers' position as a minority of the Levantine population added significant pressures to the equation. The need to integrate newcomers (and their entourages) to the political life of the Frankish East was a further challenge. Most of the evidence concerning succession and authority pertains to the royal house of Jerusalem, but reference will be made to the circumstances in Antioch, Tripoli and Edessa as well.

SUCCESSION AND CIVIL WAR: THE PROBLEM OF NEWCOMERS

The problem of succession troubled all ruling houses in the medieval period. The Capetian dynasty of France, which had just six kings between 1060 and 1270, often operated ruthless divorce policies to ensure that a male heir could be designated to succeed to the throne. Challenges to an incoming king were much rarer than in lands where the succession was unclear – the civil war that ravaged England between 1135 and 1153 was caused by the competing claims of Stephen of Blois and Henry I's daughter, Mathilda. The rulers of Jerusalem found it particularly difficult to engineer smooth successions – partly as a consequence of genetics (the birth of female rather than male offspring), partly through personal ambition and partly because of sheer ill-fortune.

The succession to Baldwin I opened up issues of relations with an outside power (Sicily) and the comparative strength of king and nobility. On Baldwin's death in 1118, the throne should, in theory, have passed to his nearest male relative, his elder brother, Count Eustace of Boulogne. Eustace had returned home after the First Crusade to rule Boulogne and his presence back in western Europe provided an opportunity for another relative of the dead king, Count Baldwin of Edessa, to take the throne. William of Tyre was not entirely comfortable with this turn of events and he felt that this was 'contrary to law, both human and divine', but he also recognised the practical side of the situation and advanced the argument of the nobles of Jerusalem:

> The affairs of the realm and the exigencies constantly arising do not allow these delays or enable us to indulge in interregnums of this kind . . . haste is imperative . . . may measures for the good of the land be speedily taken. . . . If an emergency should arise there would be no one to lead the troops. . . . Thus, for lack of a leader the welfare of the kingdom would be endangered.
>
> (William of Tyre, tr. Babcock and Krey, 1943: 1.519)

Practicality triumphed and Baldwin was crowned as King Baldwin II, but a faction among the nobility resented his accession. When, after the death of Prince Roger of Antioch in 1119, he was forced to act as regent of the principality some nobles felt that Baldwin was ignoring his responsibilities in Jerusalem and in 1123 they petitioned Count Charles the Good of Flanders to accept the throne. Charles declined the offer, but such an extraordinary move shows that the dynastic line of the ruling house of Jerusalem was far from settled.

The succession to Baldwin II was also a matter of debate because all four of his children were girls. The king and his nobles decided to ask Count Fulk V of Anjou to marry the eldest, Melisende and, as we saw above (p. 46), Fulk agreed. The actual terms of this succession arrangement, and their possible modification, provide us with a fascinating insight into both the internal politics of the Frankish East and the writings of its most important historian, William of Tyre.

It is clear that in 1134 there was a serious crisis in the kingdom of Jerusalem and a dispute between Fulk and Count Hugh of Jaffa resulted in civil war (Document 9). Hugh and his supporters made a treaty with the Muslims of Ascalon (who were only too happy to encourage such discord among the Franks) and by way of response the king marched south and besieged Jaffa. While not an unprecedented move, as we saw earlier, the agreement with a Muslim power made some of Hugh's Frankish supporters uneasy and he was forced to come to terms. He was required to forfeit his lands and to go into exile for three years. As Hugh waited for a ship to take him abroad he was stabbed and badly wounded, an attack blamed squarely upon Fulk and an episode that caused the bad feeling created by the incident to linger on. Once Hugh had recovered he went into exile in Apulia where he later died. Several questions arise from this series of events. What had provoked the revolt? Why did Hugh escape with a sentence of exile for what was so clearly an act of treason? Why was Fulk so determined to kill Hugh? The most comprehensive source for these events is William of Tyre. He blamed Hugh – a handsome young man – for being on overly familiar terms with Queen Melisende. Tension between the count and the king grew and Hugh was accused of treason and conspiring against Fulk's life. The matter was to be resolved through trial by combat, but Hugh ran away and, as we saw earlier, secured the support of the Ascalonites. The good work of the patriarch of Jerusalem resulted in an agreement that Hugh should be exiled, but after being stabbed the count gained much sympathy. William of Tyre wrote, 'it was felt that the accusations made against him, of whatever nature, had proceeded entirely from malice' (William of Tyre, tr. Babcock and Krey, 1943: 2.75). Fulk experienced great hostility, particularly from Queen Melisende who felt her reputation had been besmirched. It took considerable mediation to reconcile the two and, William wrote, from that time on 'the king became so uxorious that . . . not even in unimportant cases did he take any measures without her knowledge and assistance' (William of Tyre, tr. Babcock and Krey, 1943: 2.76). On the surface, this account of events seems reasonable enough, although it should be noted that it took place before William was born and at a time when he does not appear to have been relying on any existing written source for his information. The evidence of a more contemporary author tells a different story (see Document 9 ii). Orderic Vitalis was an Anglo–Norman monk who compiled this section of his *Ecclesiastical History* between 1123 and 1137. Admittedly he did not travel to the Latin East, but he gathered a wealth of information by talking to returning pilgrims and crusaders. He argued that Fulk generated serious antagonism among the Jerusalem nobility through trying to promote his own men too quickly and discarding the locals. This explanation has a more substantial feel to it than William of Tyre's story of rumoured romance. Hugh was a close relative of the queen and it seems that he was the leader of a group of Levantine nobles who felt – as Orderic shows us – that Fulk was trying to usurp their power by bringing in newcomers who had not earned the right to such authority. The contemporary Damascene chronicler, Ibn al-Qalanisi, wrote: 'Fulk was not sound in his judgement, nor was he successful in his administration' (Ibn al-Qalanisi, tr. Gibb, 1932: 208). The sense that Fulk may have overstepped the mark is reinforced by the comparatively light punishment dealt out to Hugh, the fury that the king faced from Melisende and her partisans, and the way in which she – and by implication her followers – saw an increase in their influence in the aftermath of the attempted murder. Two final questions occur: Why had Fulk tried so crudely to advance his own men? And why did William of Tyre conceal the true reasons behind the conflict?

When Fulk agreed to marry Melisende he did so on the understanding that he would be the sole heir to the throne once King Baldwin died. On his deathbed, however, Baldwin altered these terms and gave the kingdom over to a triumvirate consisting of Fulk, Melisende and their infant son Baldwin (later Baldwin III). Thus, Fulk's expectations and aspirations were badly dented; he had, after all, abandoned his life in the West to come over to Jerusalem. He tried to get around this restriction on his power by bringing his own men into positions of influence at the expense of the native nobility. It was, therefore, a clash between the interests of the Levantine nobles and those of the newcomers. But this created a paradox because while the westerners' extra military strength was essential to the continued existence of the Latin East, the need to reward their territorial and political aspirations might damage the interests of the settlers themselves. If, as in this case, the assimilation of outsiders was handled poorly, then the tensions inherent within the situation could surface. William of Tyre probably chose to cover up the episode because part of his purpose in writing was to show the royal house of Jerusalem in a positive light. This might persuade the people of the West to support the settlers and a detailed description of such internal dissent would do little to encourage this. Furthermore, a rebellion caused by native nobles resenting the arrival of westerners was hardly the appropriate message to send out as part of an effort to induce help from Europe. It is important to indicate that the vast majority of William of Tyre's narrative is accurate, but we should always be aware of his agenda as a historian of, and *for*, the Latin East.

In 1143 King Fulk died from serious head injuries sustained in a fall from a horse and the details of the succession are discussed earlier (pp. 48–9). When Baldwin III died childless in 1163, yet another dispute took place. The powerful Ibelin clan led the opposition to the succession of Baldwin's brother, Amalric. Their hostility was based upon Amalric's long-running relationship with, and then marriage to, Agnes of Courtenay, a noblewoman who was already married to their family member, Hugh of Ibelin. In the week after King Baldwin's death there was serious tension, but a face-saving formula allowed the union between Amalric and Agnes to be dissolved on the grounds of consanguinity (they were very distantly related) rather than bigamy. The children of the marriage, Baldwin (IV to be) and Sibylla were declared legitimate because their parents were allegedly unaware of their blood-relation, and the more damaging issue of Amalric's earlier marriage was swept under the carpet. Amalric died in 1174 and it is ironic that this was followed by the first smooth accession in the history of the kingdom of Jerusalem – that of the boy-leper, Baldwin IV, under whom broke out the most serious internal discord to date in the Latin kingdom of Jerusalem.

Succession in the ruling houses of Edessa and Tripoli was reasonably trouble-free, but the principality of Antioch saw considerable unrest. In part this was because it faced the greatest and most sustained Muslim threat over the course of the twelfth century. In consequence, its leaders were often killed in battle (Roger in 1119, Bohemond II in 1130, Raymond in 1149), or held captive by the enemy (Bohemond I in 1100–1103, Reynald in 1161–76). This meant that there was little chance to produce mature male heirs which in turn created ample scope for succession disputes. Regencies were commonplace and often led to unrest. The accession of Raymond in 1135 was particularly complicated and is an episode that also highlights the sometimes difficult relationship between the four Latin states. When Bohemond II died in 1130 he left his infant daughter, Constance, as heiress, but his widow Alice tried to usurp control for herself and attempted to prevent Baldwin II of Jerusalem, who had come north to help against the Muslims, from entering the city. In 1131–32 she repeated her defiance and this time gathered support from the counts of Edessa and Tripoli so three of the four Latin states stood ranged against King Fulk (Baldwin II had died in the interim). In 1132 and 1134 Fulk was forced to travel north to try to uphold Constance's rights and to bring her mother to heel. Alice had a core of loyal supporters who were content for her to rule, but she was opposed by another faction who disliked the unrest that she brought. In 1134 the nobles prevailed upon Fulk to choose a husband for Constance and, ignoring possible Sicilian claims (through Bohemond II's family) and Byzantine interests (the Greeks claimed overlordship of Antioch) he chose Raymond of Poitiers, son of the duke of Aquitaine.

Raymond was of a distinguished background and had a crusading pedigree through his father, Duke William IX, who had taken part in the expedition of 1101. Fear of the Sicilians caused him to travel to the Levant in disguise, and once there he had two further obstacles to overcome. First was the opposition of Princess Alice. It seems, however, that a proposal to marry Constance to Manuel, a son of Emperor John Komnenos of Byzantium, alienated some of Alice's adherents, particularly the patriarch, Ralph, whose position of religious pre-eminence would be damaged by any level of Greek involvement in the region. Ralph's help would also surmount the second obstacle that faced Raymond, namely Constance's age. She was only eight years old and according to canon law the minimum age of marriage was twelve. In light of the increasingly urgent military situation – in 1135 Zengi had taken five more important Frankish settlements in the north – the need for strong leadership was evermore apparent and the patriarch married Raymond to Constance in spite of the clear contravention of canon law, let alone basic morality. Pragmatism had triumphed over theoretical niceties, and political expediency dictated that the settlers should try to resolve their succession disputes as effectively as possible.

THE MAINTENANCE OF AUTHORITY OVER THE FRANKISH NOBILITY

The relationship between the rulers and the nobility of Jerusalem has attracted much attention from historians over the years. In essence three views have evolved. First, in the 1930s the American scholar La Monte argued that the kings were very weak and the nobles dominated a submissive monarchy (La Monte, 1932). In the 1950s Richard and Prawer posited the opposite view and stressed the power of the monarchy (Richard, 1955, trans. 1979; see collected works in Prawer, 1980), although Riley-Smith later modified this to present a slightly less weak nobility (Riley-Smith, 1973). In subsequent years Tibble looked at the subject again (Tibble, 1989). He used charter evidence to augment the narrative and legal sources employed by earlier historians to reveal a strong and vigorous monarchy determined to dominate the nobility.

The principal source for the notion of a powerful nobility is in the writings of the thirteenth-century lawyer, John of Ibelin. Tibble argued that this information distorted the picture by representing a fixed relationship between crown and nobility (in favour of the nobles), when in fact there was a fluid framework within which the kings manipulated the feudal structure to their advantage. In essence, the system provided for grants of lands or rights in return for military service; the size and form of these grants dictated the power and standing of a particular noble. Tibble suggested that the content of these grants was managed consistently enough to constitute a deliberate policy on the part of the crown. The process evolved as follows. The early years of the kingdom were marked by the formation of large lordships. Through this, the nobility could have had considerable power, but over the second and third decades of settlement this changed and it is possible to see how the monarchy began to assert itself. High mortality rates among the nobles and the financial drain caused by endless enemy raids gave the crown its opportunity because when a noble family died out, went bankrupt or rebelled, their lands would revert to the king. This enabled the monarch to reward his own supporters or to reorganise the shape and size of the fief. The principality of Galilee and the county of Jaffa were two of the larger lordships created in the early years of the kingdom. The revolt of Hugh of Jaffa (1134) revealed that these big territories could pose a threat to the crown. This could be dealt with in a number of ways. First, the lordship might be split into smaller holdings, thus producing a new tier of nobles who, because of their relatively limited resources, would be of little threat to the monarchy. Galilee was an example of this where the holdings at Toron (1115), Nazareth (c. 1121) and Banyas (1128) were separated from the principality. A second way to curtail the danger from larger lordships was to follow Fulk's policy after the revolt of Hugh of Jaffa when the land confiscated by the crown was retained by the royal house and not redistributed to other nobles. A third method of asserting royal control over the nobility was to give a lord a collection of fiefs dispersed over a broad geographical area which might help to curtail independent political action. An alternative was to offer land, but to retain some royal property within the territory, as in Transjordan where the castles at Wadi Musa (Petra) remained under crown control. Finally, a fief could be created within the larger royal domain, as in the case of Blanchegarde which lay between the royal holdings of Jaffa and Jerusalem. In the course of the twelfth century the strength of many nobles within their own lands declined, often because of the growing financial burdens brought about by even heavier enemy raids and the series of earthquakes that afflicted the Latin East. Properties needed to be sold off and increasing proportions of lordships came to be owned by the great churches of the Holy Land and the military orders. The rise of the military orders as powerful, well-financed institutions meant that they could purchase castles whose owners were in financial trouble. For example, in 1168, the French noble, Ivo of Velos, sold Belvoir to the Hospitallers for the substantial sum of 1,400 gold bezants.

The manipulation of lordships was not the only way that a king could assert his rights over the nobility. Legal measures might have a similar effect and the most prominent among these was the *assise sur la ligece*, promulgated by King Amalric in *c.* 1166. This legislated that all vassals (known as rear-vassals) of the major lords should also pay liege homage (a personal bond) to the king as well. This established a direct link between the monarch and most fief-holders, thus bypassing the higher nobility. It meant that the king could turn to the rear-vassals for support if their lord was in conflict with him. The rear-vassals benefited because they could take complaints about their lord to the king, whereas previously the strength of the great nobles had enabled them to treat the rear-vassals as they had wished. The very fact that Amalric could implement such a measure indicates a position of some authority. One further manifestation of a confident monarchy was through the issue of new coinage. We have seen how the early princes of Antioch chose to engage with the indigenous population through the designs on their money. In the first decades of the conquest it seems that an influx of coinage from western Europe was the principal currency in (especially) the kingdom of Jerusalem. During the rule of Baldwin III (1143–63), however, the opportunity was taken to make a clearer statement about Frankish identity, royal power and its tie to Jerusalem. Thus, silver deniers depicted the Tower of David, a symbol of strength and religious legacy. Under Amalric (1163–74) the coins showed the Holy Sepulchre itself to emphasise the crown's role as the guardian of the spiritual heart of the Christian faith.

In conclusion, the kings of Jerusalem seem to have developed in power down to the end of Amalric's reign. The instability of Baldwin IV's reign was brought about by the king's illness and external threats, rather than an inherent weakness in royal authority. It was the issue of Baldwin's succession that caused such trouble: had a mature, healthy ruler taken over in 1174 then, at least in terms of his relations with the nobility, he would have inherited a position of some strength.

(a)   (b)

12. Copper denier of King Baldwin III of Jerusalem showing the Tower of David (a) and Denier of King Amalric of Jerusalem (b)

10

Religious life and pilgrimage in the Levant

As a region of central importance to Christianity, Islam and Judaism there was an inherent richness and variety to religious life in the Levant. From the late eleventh century, the Frankish settlers, the hierarchy and institutions of the Catholic Church, and a huge seasonal influx of western pilgrims, imposed themselves on to this complex web. People of other denominations and faiths continued to live in, and to visit, the Holy Land, but obviously the number and influence of the westerners were far greater than before the First Crusade. This chapter will demonstrate how the Franks established and maintained the Latin Church in the Levant and, by highlighting the popularity of pilgrimage and the role of relics such as the True Cross, it will reveal some key aspects of religious life in the Frankish East.

THE ESTABLISHMENT OF THE FRANKISH CHURCH IN THE LEVANT

Once the Franks had assumed political control of the Holy Land it was inevitable that they should direct religious life. In the immediate aftermath of the capture of Jerusalem (1099) the conquerors purged non-Christians from the city, although this would be relaxed in later years to allow Muslim pilgrims to visit. Prior to the First Crusade the Holy Sepulchre had been under the custody of the Greek Orthodox community and although the Catholics assumed guardianship of the site, the Eastern Christians were permitted to remain and have freedom of worship. The Church of the Holy Sepulchre itself was a rather unimpressive collection of buildings that had grown up on the site since the time of Constantine in the fourth century. In the early 1130s the Franks decided to erect a new church complex that incorporated sites such as the Holy Sepulchre itself, Calvary and the Hill of Golgotha and they built the much larger and more splendid structure that remains to this day. On 15 July 1149 the new church of the Holy Sepulchre was inaugurated. It brought many key locations under one roof to enable pilgrims to process around the site and in doing so it followed the trend found in the principal shrine churches of the West, such as St James of Compostela (north-western Spain) and Saint Denis near Paris. The main apse was decorated with a depiction of Christ's descent into hell (the Anastasis) and, as Kühnel has observed, quoting the *Gesta Francorum*, 'The scene expressed the most ambitious of the crusaders who considered themselves "the followers of Christ by whom they had been redeemed from the power

13. Church of the Holy Sepulchre

of hell"' (Kühnel, 1994: 50). Elsewhere in Jerusalem, Muslim religious buildings, such as the Dome of the Rock, were re-dedicated as the *Templum Domini* and many other churches and institutions were founded by the Franks, including religious houses (the Orthodox church of St Lazarus in Bethany became a convent for Benedictine nuns during Melisende's reign), hospitals for pilgrims and, as we saw earlier, the military orders.

The thirteenth-century writer Jacques de Vitry summarised the establishment of the Latin Church:

> From diverse parts of the world, from every race and language, and from every nation under heaven, pilgrims full of zeal for God and religious men flocked into the Holy Land, attracted by the sweet savour of the holy and venerable places. Old churches were repaired and new ones were built; by the generosity of the princes and the alms of the faithful monasteries of regular monks were built in fitting places; parish priests and all things appertaining to the service and worship of God were properly established everywhere. Holy men renounced the world and according to their religious fervour chose places to dwell in suitable to their object and their devotion.
>
> (Jacques de Vitry, tr. Stewart, 1896: 26–27)

An issue that needed to be resolved quickly was the staffing and maintenance of the holy sites. Some clergy had taken part in the First Crusade – Godfrey of Bouillon is known to have brought monks from his own lands – but others must have joined them. Western churchmen such as Peter the Venerable (abbot of Cluny, 1122–56) and Bernard of Clairvaux (abbot of Clairvaux and the leading Cistercian monk) strongly supported the worth of pilgrimage for the layman, but railed against monks leaving their orders in Europe and claimed that they were being distracted by their quest for the earthly Jerusalem at the expense of the real work of seeking the heavenly Jerusalem in the cloister. Nevertheless the immense spiritual charge of the holy places would have drawn people to the East and also persuaded some to take up the religious life once they had reached the Levant. In fact, it was not until after the deaths of Peter and Bernard that the Cluniacs and the Cistercians founded houses in the Levant, with the former at Palmarea, near Acre (1170) and the latter at Belmont, near Tripoli (1157).

The great institutions of Frankish religious life included the Holy Sepulchre, the *Templum Domini*, the cathedral of Nazareth and the church of the Holy Nativity in Bethlehem. Religious houses needed income to survive and this came from gifts of land, privileges – in either the Levant or the West – and money from pilgrims and pious benefactors. Such important shrines naturally exerted a powerful pull on the imaginations of visiting pilgrims and crusaders. For example, in 1167 Count William IV of Nevers reached the Holy Land on crusade, but the following year he died of fever in Acre. During his visit he must have formed a strong attachment to the church of the Holy Nativity in Bethlehem because in his will he bequeathed a hospital at Clemency (near Auxerre in central France) to the house and by way of recognition for this gift he was buried in the church at Bethlehem. Such acts would have helped to strengthen the emotional bridge between the settlers in the East and their co-religionists in the West. To have local sites in Europe owned by such evocative institutions must have made the Holy Land more tangible to the people of the West and encouraged them to visit as pilgrims or to support its defence.

In the contemporary West the Cistercians led a trend for the isolation of religious houses based in rural rather than urban settings, but for reasons of scriptural association most major shrines in the Holy Land were in cities. Security considerations also dictated that more isolated institutions were rare, although they did exist, such as the monastery at Mount Tabor in eastern Galilee (the site of the Transfiguration) and a great many hermits emulated the lives of early Christian ascetics from the fourth and fifth centuries by living in remote and inaccessible sites. We tend to think of hermits as solitary figures, but the reality was rather more flexible and they often formed loose communities coming together for prayers or to eat, and there are also examples of ascetics moving between an eremitical and a coenobitic (monastic) existence. An interesting feature of these hermit communities was that they were often – as at Mount Carmel near Acre, or the Black Mountain near Antioch – places where Greek Orthodox and Latin religious men lived alongside one another, although the issue of liturgical 'contamination' was one of which the church authorities were always wary. While we must always remember that it was the Catholic hierarchy that was in ultimate control, it must have been noticeable – and perhaps surprising – to western visitors that other Christians were present in large numbers. Research indicates that of the eighty-five churches within the walls of Jerusalem, twenty-nine were administered by the Franks, three were in joint custody (including the Holy Sepulchre), and forty-six were in the possession of Greek Orthodox, Armenians, Georgians or Syrians; control of the remaining seven is unclear. There were also Coptic and Ethiopian Christians in the Holy Land, as well as Georgians, Maronites and Nestorians. The Greek Orthodox had the greatest profile, however, boasting at least seventeen monasteries in crusader Palestine and the great house of St Catherine on Mount Sinai.

There was considerable interaction between these groups, particularly at sites of religious importance. The Georgians held the Monastery of the Holy Cross, located just to the south-west of Jerusalem and venerated as the place where the wood of the Lord's Cross had grown (Tsurtsumia, 2012). It became a popular pilgrimage site that also received donations (presumably in return for prayers and commemorations by the monks) from Georgians living in the area and from Frankish settlers. Amongst the latter were Knights' Templar such as Geoffrey Fulcher, a prominent figure in the Order who, as we have seen earlier, was often used to convey appeals to the West, most notably to King Louis VII in 1163–64. Other important donors included William of Mirabel, viscount of the castle for the Ibelins; Philip of Nablus and his wife, his daughters and parents-in-law – Philip was a leading noble during the reigns of Baldwin III and Amalric who joined the Templars in 1166 and became its Master from 1169 to his death in 1171; or Rodrigo Alvarez, the founder of the Spanish Order of Mountjoy who was in the kingdom of Jerusalem between 1176 and 1180. The fact that Frankish settlers and members of the military orders were prepared to support a Georgian monastery and look to it for their spiritual wellbeing is another example of the complex interaction between Christians of the East and the West. Similarly, Queen Melisende's maternal ancestry encouraged her patronage of the Armenian Church of St James in Jerusalem.

There was also a revival in Orthodox monasticism during the twelfth century: at Mount Tabor, for example, in 1106 the pilgrim Daniel reported no Orthodox house, but by 1185 the site had both Latin and Orthodox communities. In part, this revival can be explained by the political situation. As Emperor Manuel Komnenos became more important as an ally for the Frankish settlers, it became politic to allow him to demonstrate imperial support for the Orthodox Church in the Levant. Various sites received his backing, most notably the church of the Holy Nativity in Bethlehem which was redecorated in 1169 to include mosaics which depicted events such as the seven ecumenical councils of the Church but, intriguingly, omitted the *filioque* clause, which was a prime element in the split between the two Churches. The inscriptions on the walls (in Greek) inform us that Manuel and King Amalric of Jerusalem were responsible for the work, which shows how the close military and diplomatic co-operation between the two monarchs extended into the ecclesiastical sphere. Orthodox clergy were also present on the site. We can glimpse from such examples, therefore, the cultural and religious diversity that is one element to reconstructing life in the Levant during the twelfth century.

PILGRIMAGE TO THE HOLY LAND

The majority of pilgrimages at this time entailed visiting local shrines in the West, but it was logical that the Frankish hold on the Holy Land would mean more visitors to the Levant. The German pilgrim Theoderic (*c.* 1169–74) related why Christians would want to journey to the Holy Land: 'It is holier because it is illuminated by the presence there of our God and Lord Jesus Christ and of his good Mother, and the fact that all the Patriarchs, Prophets and Apostles have lived and taught and preached and suffered martyrdom there' (*Jerusalem Pilgrimage*, tr. Wilkinson, 1988: 276).

It is not possible to give the numbers involved in pilgrimage from the West, but it must have been many thousand each year. The Order of St John's Hospital in Jerusalem was reported as having beds for 2,000 sick or destitute pilgrims in 1185. Several more hospices existed, usually with regional affinities. As well as the Latin pilgrims we must note that there were houses for the Armenian, Greek, Russian and Jacobite pilgrims too.

Most visitors from the West would have arrived by sea, but the timeframe to visit the Levant was restricted. To avoid the worst of the winter weather a ship would leave the West no earlier than late March or early April. The journey to the Levant took on average four to six weeks. Late October was the last safe time to set out for home, although this was a longer journey because it meant sailing into prevailing winds and took over two months. The flow of commercial shipping from southern France and Italy provided transport for the pilgrims. Many would have been familiar with water transport from the extensive network of river systems in medieval Europe, but to sail in the open seas was an entirely different matter and one that many people found utterly terrifying. The experience of William III of Nevers is not untypical and shows the reaction of a pious layman in such a situation: when faced with imminent shipwreck on his return voyage from Jerusalem in 1148 he acknowledged that his father had unfairly oppressed the church of St Mary Magdalene at Vézelay and swore on oath that he would give up these demands. Thus, as William's charter recorded, by God's virtue and the intervention of the saint, the ship passed out of the storm and into quiet seas.

Most pilgrims arrived at Acre, either for Easter or, as William of Tyre noted, in the late summer or early autumn, which meant that they would stay over the Christmas season. There was a whole support industry geared towards providing for, and profiting from, these pilgrims. As well as medical care and a need for accommodation, there was money to be made from the sale of souvenirs, money-changing and the supply of food. Jerusalem's notorious 'Street of Bad Cooking' is a reminder of the gastronomic hazards pilgrims might encounter and there must have been numerous beggars and guides who hoped to extract income from the visitors.

The numbers of pilgrims to the Holy Land meant it was not just the Holy Sepulchre that needed to be enlarged and modified. The church at Nazareth was another particularly important site and the earthquake of 1170 offered an opportunity to rebuild it. Archbishop Lethard II (1158–90) oversaw a spectacular construction (at around 70 metres long, only a little shorter than the Holy Sepulchre) to house the shrine grotto where the Virgin Mary was visited by the Angel Gabriel and given the message that she was to be the Mother of Jesus; this was also where Jesus grew up and where Joseph was buried. The grotto was contained within a two-storey chapel intended to be embellished with a number of beautifully carved stone capitals – a contrast to the mosaics seen at, for example, the Church of the Holy Nativity in Bethlehem. The West front of the building was also richly decorated and in an interesting example of cultural transference, these pieces have a clear stylistic connection with contemporary works in Burgundy and Provence in France. Presumably European sculptors came out to the Levant although it seems likely that most of the actual craftsmen at Nazareth were locals. While the church itself was destroyed by the Mamluk Sultan Baibars in 1263 a number of the capitals survived, some of which were discovered by workmen in 1908, the remainder in the 1950s. The extraordinary condition of these objects is thought to result from their being hidden as a precaution in the run-up to the Battle of Hattin which took place only 15 miles away in July 1187. One capital (see illustration below) shows the Virgin leading an apostle through the perils of Hell where they are assaulted by terrible demons – a likely reflection of the huge popularity of the Cult of the Virgin in this period. Others show Christ and the Apostle Thomas, St Matthew and St James.

The guardianship of pilgrim sites was of great concern to the secular authorities. The kings of Jerusalem were responsible for the defence of the

14. Capital from Cathedral Church of Nazareth

holy places and they used this as an argument to justify appealing for support from the West. They also made a point of highlighting the needs of pilgrims. When Nur ad-Din captured Egypt in 1169 a crisis meeting in the kingdom of Jerusalem cited concern for pilgrims as a main reason to send for help. King Amalric wrote that the Muslims could now blockade the coastal cities which hindered the flow of pilgrim traffic and denied westerners the opportunity to visit the holy shrines. Pope Alexander III's subsequent crusade appeal to the people of Christian Europe ascribed one reason for the fame of the Holy Sepulchre as the fact that it was 'much visited'. Interestingly, in 1175, when Manuel Komnenos addressed a request for military help to the West, he chose to describe the aim of his project as being 'to secure the road to the Holy Sepulchre', and he depicted this as a task of importance for all Christians, both Catholic and Orthodox, because *de facto* it would facilitate pilgrimage.

One of the most tangible reminders of pilgrimage is the number of accounts of such journeys that survive (*Jerusalem Pilgrimage*, tr. Wilkinson, 1988). In 1106 the Russian Abbot Daniel wrote that he had given all of his meagre wealth to guides that they might show and explain the holy sites to him and now he wanted to instruct others. Much of the material in these works is repetitive and derived or copied from two or three core guides which themselves borrowed from previous authorities rather than relying exclusively on their own observations. The authorship of these guides reveals the geographical and denominational diversity of those visiting the holy sites and the Levant. They include the writings of Saewulf (1101–3) from Britain, Abbot Daniel (1106–8) from Russia, Nikulas of Pvera (*c*. 1140) from Iceland, an account of the life of St Theotinius from Portugal (who visited the Levant in *c*. 1100), and the Germans, John of Wurzburg (*c*. 1170) and Theoderic (*c*. 1169–74). From non-Latins we have the accounts of Benjamin of Tudela (*c*. 1166–71), a Spanish Jew; Ibn Jubayr (*c*. 1184), a Spanish Muslim; and John Phocas (1185), an Orthodox pilgrim from Crete. These works describe various pilgrimage routes. Many focused on Jerusalem, but others included a range of itineraries such as the journey from the East Gate of the holy city to the place of Christ's baptism on the River Jordan. This passed through places such as Bethany (the site of the resurrection of Lazarus and where Christ's feet were washed and his head anointed), the Red Cistern (a Templar fort to protect pilgrims and also associated with the site of the story of the Good Samaritan), on through the Judean desert to Mount Quarantana (the place of Christ's Temptation and the site of a fortified monastery and a Templar arsenal), and thence on to the River Jordan itself.

Pilgrims gathered in Jerusalem in huge numbers over Easter week. Many of the visitors had come to witness the miracle of the Easter fire, the climax of Holy Week and a series of processions, blessings and absolutions around the holy sites. On Saturday worshippers of all denominations filled the Church of the Holy Sepulchre and after a lengthy service the Holy Cross was placed on the shrine of the Holy Sepulchre. Then, following an Orthodox tradition that was taken on by the Latins, all the lights in the building were extinguished and the faithful waited expectantly for one of the lamps in front of the Holy Sepulchre to re-ignite spontaneously, as a fire was believed to descend from Heaven upon the tomb of Christ; in other words, a miracle that symbolised the resurrection. The fire did not always reappear at first and sometimes repeated processions were needed to induce the flame to spark – a process that could take many hours. The year 1101 was a particularly difficult one as Caffaro of Genoa, an eyewitness vividly described (Caffaro, tr. Hall and Phillips, 2013: 51–53).

The fire would then be taken to the patriarch who lit his candle from the fire and the flame was passed from person to person. Slowly the light would spread through the choir, up to the gallery and around the whole building in an extraordinarily moving ceremony at the heart of a Christian festival in the centre of the Christian faith.

Several sites attracted worshippers from different faiths. Thus Muslims were permitted access to the Church of the Holy Nativity in Bethlehem, a Marian shrine, because Mary, as the mother of the prophet Jesus, was much revered in Islam. Or, in the case of the Dome of the Rock (to the Franks the *Templum Domini*, the Temple of the Old Testament) and the al-Aqsa mosque, they were allowed to pray; in the early 1140s, Unur, the ruler of Damascus and his key diplomat, Usama ibn Munqidh, made such visits. The most remarkable of all these multi-faith sites was undoubtedly Saidnaya, *c.* 30 kilometres north of Damascus, an Orthodox institution and located in lands always under Muslim control. Burchard of Strasbourg visited the site around 1175 and reported:

In this church I saw a wooden panel . . . placed behind the altar in an embrasure in the wall of the sanctuary guarded by an iron grille. On this panel a likeness of the blessed Virgin had once been painted, but now, wondrous to relate, the picture on the wood had become incarnate [i.e. is made flesh] and oil, smelling sweeter than any balsam, unceasingly flows from it. By which oil, many Christians, Saracens and Jews are often cured of diverse ailments [and] are restored to health and the oil never diminishes no matter how much one takes of it. . . . To this place on the Feast of the Assumption [15 August] of the glorious Virgin and on that of her Nativity [8 September], all the Saracens of that province flock to pray together with the Christians and the Saracens perform their devotions there with great reverence.

(Hamilton, 2000b: 207)

Muslim and Eastern Christian authors confirm Burchard's description of the presence of a range of worshippers. Intriguingly, amongst the Latin visitors were often Knights Templar, warriors sworn to defend the Holy Land against the Muslims but also, of course, men of religion. They carried away vials of the liquid to pass on to visitors to their own properties. A few vials of the liquid made their way back to the West and are known to have been at the monastery of Cluny, for example; thus an eastern cult was transported to the West during the medieval period. Once again, the simple perception of the crusading age being nothing more than Christian against Muslim reveals itself to be more complicated. The site remains active today with Christians and Muslims still coming to the shrine, often seeking to ensure fertility. Saidnaya was even visited by Muslim Syrian cosmonauts in the 1990s as they prayed for good fortune for their space mission; on their safe return they sacrificed a sheep to the Virgin to thank her.

THE TRUE CROSS

Relics were an integral part of medieval religious life. Most were associated with the person or possessions of a holy figure and were believed to offer an undiminished part of that saint's power which, if venerated, would enable him or her to intercede with God on the petitioner's behalf. Saints were commonly asked to assist in cases of healing, protection and good fortune. Because Christ was assumed into Heaven his relics were limited to sheddings such as blood (rather than say the preserved limbs of other saints) and objects associated with his time on Earth. Among the most venerated of all these objects was the True Cross, the wood upon which Christ was crucified. Originally discovered in the fourth century by St Helena, the mother of Constantine, the first Christian emperor, the relic was split into two pieces: one part was sent to Constantinople, the other remained in Jerusalem. The piece at Jerusalem was taken by the Persians, but rediscovered by the Patriarch Heraclius in the seventh century. After the Arab invasions later that century it was divided again and one of these fragments was found by the crusaders soon after the capture of Jerusalem in 1099. Notwithstanding its complicated history, the authenticity of the relic is, in a sense, irrelevant, because contemporaries believed in its veracity and it therefore carried an important spiritual charge. It was known that numerous other pieces of the True Cross existed in both Europe and the Levant, but the piece in Jerusalem was certainly the most important of these and it was placed in a large metal cross and decorated with gold and silver. Usually the Cross was kept in its own chapel in the Church of the Holy Sepulchre, where pilgrims offered donations, and while it played an important part in the liturgical life of the church, it had other uses too. As an item of such centrality to the Christian faith it is not surprising that the settlers in the kingdom of Jerusalem used it as an object of protection and good fortune in battle (Murray, 1998). The True Cross became regarded as an essential element in the defence of the holy places and it was taken into battle on no fewer than thirty-one occasions between its discovery in 1099 and its loss at Hattin in 1187. Fulcher of Chartres noted that it was the relic itself that was responsible for a Christian victory at the Battle of Jaffa in 1102: 'Truly it was right and just that they who were protected by the wood of the Lord's Cross should emerge as victors over the enemies of that Cross. If indeed this benevolent Cross had been carried with the king in the previous battle [Ramla], it cannot be doubted that the Lord would have favoured his people' (Fulcher of Chartres, tr. Ryan, 1969: 173). Most of these engagements took place when the Franks were defending their own lands (i.e. the function of protection noted for relics above), but the Cross might also be used in offensive engagements as well. Obviously the presence of the True Cross boosted Frankish morale and helped to convince the troops that God was on their side. In consequence, its loss at Hattin was regarded as a major disaster (note Pope Gregory VIII's comments in the papal bull *Audita tremendi*, see Document 20). The settlers' attachment to the relic, or indeed the attachment of the wider Latin world to it, can be demonstrated by the fact that its recovery was a prominent aim of all subsequent crusading expeditions to the Levant, and by reason that its return loomed large in any negotiations with Muslim powers seeking to neutralise such campaigns. It is known that other fragments of the True Cross existed in the Latin East. The rulers of Antioch, for example, carried a similar object on campaign, but this was lost at the Battle of the Field of Blood in 1119.

Another use of the True Cross was in a diplomatic context. Shavings or fragments of the relic were given to important visitors to the Holy Land or sent to churches and leading figures in the West. Thus, when William of Bures, lord of Tiberias, was dispatched to France in 1127 to try to persuade Count Fulk V of Anjou to marry Melisende, heiress to the throne of Jerusalem, he carried with him a relic of the True Cross to be presented to the church of St Julian at Le Mans. Presumably the offering of such a prestigious gift was intended to enhance the status of the embassy and to help convince Fulk to accept the offer (which he did). Fulk himself provides evidence of the gift of a relic in a more devotional context when, having become king himself, he dispatched a fragment of the True Cross back to the church of St Laud at Angers. As a church in the heart of his former homeland, Fulk was showing his ongoing devotion to the site and this again reveals how the links between the settlers and the West continued to be maintained.

THE ECCLESIASTICAL HIERARCHY

As the armies of the First Crusade established Latin control over northern Syria they allowed the existing Orthodox clergy to remain in place, thereby reflecting the planned co-operation between Byzantium and the crusaders envisaged by Pope Urban II and Emperor Alexios. Soon, however, the hostile relationship between Prince Bohemond and Alexios brought this to an end and the Orthodox patriarch of Antioch was replaced by a Latin patriarch. The conquerors could not subordinate themselves to a schismatic clergy and the imposition of the settlers' religious hierarchy was a natural reflection of their political dominance. As the twelfth century progressed Greek claims to the overlordship of Antioch were backed up by military force and by 1165 Manuel was able to accomplish a long-cherished aim by restoring an Orthodox patriarch (alongside the Latin one) in Antioch. This was a short-lived success because within five years Athanasius was crushed to death in an earthquake, a fate that the Franks viewed rather smugly as God's judgement, and after this the Latin patriarch remained as the unchallenged head of the ecclesiastical hierarchy in the north.

In the south most of the Orthodox clergy had fled the Holy Land before the First Crusade and so it was easy to appoint Latin bishops to existing (but vacant) episcopal thrones or, in the case of places such as Ramla, to set up new sees. The patriarchate of Jerusalem was obviously a position of huge prestige, but given the role of the papacy in creating the crusade movement, it, like Antioch, was kept subordinate to Rome. Many of the administrative practices of the Latin Church in the Levant were similar to those found in the West. The Church had its own courts to deal with heresy, marriage and the punishment of criminous clerks, except in the cases of murder and treason which were dealt with by the secular courts. Bishops were also responsible for licensing doctors. Income for the Church came from substantial landholdings although the money from tithes was limited by the fact that the Latin population was relatively small anyway and that tithes were not paid by the non-Latin majority.

In the West the Reform Papacy had managed to reduce, but by no means remove, the influence of secular monarchs over the election of senior clergy, and in Jerusalem the royal house certainly steered its preferred candidate to the patriarchal chair on two occasions (1157 and 1180). When bishoprics fell empty the king of Jerusalem had the right to profit from the vacant see until a replacement was appointed, although at the Council of Nablus in 1120 the notably pious King Baldwin II had released ecclesiastical tithes from secular control, a move in step with the broader Papal Reform Movement. In general, apart from some controversial elections to senior church positions, relations between crown and Church can be characterised as good and there were none of the terrible schisms that afflicted contemporary Germany, probably because the Latin East owed its very existence and continued survival to the papacy.

11

The reign of Baldwin IV, the Leper-King, the rise of Saladin and the Battle of Hattin (1187)

Historians' assessments of the period 1174 to 1187 are often coloured by their knowledge of events at the Battle of Hattin on 4 July 1187 when the army of Saladin crushed the forces of King Guy of Jerusalem and precipitated the fall of the holy city to Islam. The Franks' defeat at Hattin has been viewed as an inevitability: the vigorous rule of King Amalric and the obvious incapacity of his young son, the leper-king Baldwin IV, combined with the ceaseless in-fighting of the nobility is contrasted with the remorseless rise of Saladin and the triumph of Islam (Runciman, 1952: 2.400). This is an attractive and easily assimilated picture, but on closer inspection, a false one. First, simply because Baldwin IV (1174–85) was a leper does not mean that he, or his commanders, were incapable of effective action. While it is true that, at times, the Franks revealed an extraordinary tendency to contribute to their own downfall through political conflict and personal jealousies, they also attracted – from their perspective at least – the most wretched and unpredictable ill-luck. On Saladin's part, it should be remembered that he required thirteen years of hard struggle to establish his power and to create the conditions necessary to confront and defeat the Franks in battle. The political narrative of the period is, at times, complex and confusing, but following this thread is essential in understanding just how finely balanced the contest was, the danger that the Franks posed to Saladin and the challenges that he faced against both his Christian and Muslim opponents; this in turn, enables a proper assessment of the emir's own considerable achievements.

THE FIRST REGENCY OF COUNT RAYMOND III OF TRIPOLI

Baldwin IV was crowned king of Jerusalem on 15 July 1174, the seventy-fifth anniversary of the capture of the holy city. As a minor, aged thirteen, he would need a regent during the early years of his reign and for a brief inter-lude his father's seneschal, Miles of Plancy, controlled the land, but he was unpopular and within a few months he was murdered. He was succeeded by Count Raymond III of Tripoli, who was Baldwin's closest male relative in the East. Raymond was an intelligent, energetic man of a rather austere nature. He had spent a decade in Muslim captivity from 1164 to 1174 so in one sense, he was an outsider to the contemporary politics of Jerusalem. Alongside his existing holdings as the count of Tripoli, he had married the wealthy heiress, Eschiva of Galilee, to secure for himself one of the most important lordships in the kingdom of Jerusalem. We have a good picture of Raymond and his followers because William of Tyre, the great chronicler of the Latin East, was an ardent admirer of his (Raymond made him chancellor and archbishop of Tyre) and viewed him, by 1184, as 'the best hope for the kingdom – a man of wisdom and magnanimity' and assessed his standing thus: 'it was plain to all that the only safety lay in placing the affairs of the kingdom in his hands' (William of Tyre, tr. Babcock and Krey, 1943: 2.509). Interestingly, Ibn Jubayr, a Spanish Muslim pilgrim who was in the Levant at the same time, echoed this sentiment: 'The most considerable among the accursed Franks is the accursed count. . . . He has authority and position among them. He is qualified to be king and indeed is a candidate for the office' (Ibn Jubayr, tr. Broadhurst, 1952: 324). While Raymond had his sup-porters, the fact that he never took the throne indicates that he had many enemies too. The development of faction is a key feature of this period, although because Raymond's opponents left no equivalent voice to counter the bias of William of Tyre it has been more awkward for historians to form a balanced assessment of this group.

As Baldwin approached puberty his leprosy began to worsen. The disease is bacterial and it probably spreads through air or sustained direct contact. The bacteria can cause inflammation and damage to nerves and skin. This leads to muscle weakness, loss of feeling (symptoms noted by William of Tyre, Baldwin's tutor) and an inability to sweat. Wounds are suffered and ulcers form; subsequent infections can destroy bones, usually in the hands and feet, and result in deformity. As Baldwin grew older the form of leprosy he had became more severe; he lost his sight and the bacteria multiplied further to destroy his nose. With such a terrible illness the need to find a husband for his sister, Sibylla, intensified. As in the past, it was essential to select an individual who fulfilled the settlers' requirements of wealth, experience and, if possible, the ability to encourage a new crusade, as Fulk of Anjou had done in 1129.

In 1176 Raymond and the leading men of Jerusalem identified an ideal candidate, probably the most distinguished figure so far asked to marry an heiress in the Levant. William Longsword, son of the count of Montferrat (near Turin in north-western Italy) was from a crusading family and also a first cousin to the Capetian royal house and related to the German imperial line. He reached the Levant in October 1176 and soon married Sibylla. Thus it seemed that when Baldwin IV died or became incapacitated, a ready-made regent was in place.

In July 1176, aged fifteen, Baldwin IV came of age, Raymond's regency ended and he returned to Tripoli. The king renewed ties with Manuel Komnenos to set in train yet another attack on Egypt, a strategy that William of Tyre described as the most effective way to destroy the enemies of Christ. While the Byzantines had recently suffered a heavy defeat at the hands of the Seljuk Turks at the Battle of Myriocephalum in Asia Minor (September 1176), their navy remained intact and they were determined to enhance their trading interests in Alexandria.

THE RISE OF SALADIN

At this point we must consider the situation in the Muslim world, remembering that, in parallel to the settlers' loss of King Amalric, the Muslims had suffered the demise of their great leader, Nur ad-Din. His death fragmented the Muslim Near East and broke down the coalition of Egypt, Syria and the Jazira that he had assembled. Abu Shama, who wrote in the 1240s but used twelfth-century sources, commented that 'confusion, discord and anarchy reigned everywhere'; at this point, 'we were convinced', Jerusalem could not be taken (Abu Shama, in Barber, 1998: 16). Yet thirteen years later the holy city fell. The man who would accomplish this was born in 1137 of Kurdish stock at the castle of Takrit on the River Tigris, north of Baghdad. Saladin's early years were marked by his skill as a horseman and his reputation as a polo player. He showed sufficient military prowess to rise through the ranks of the Muslim soldiery to join his uncle Shirkuh in the conquest of Egypt in 1169 and then established his power there. In the aftermath of Nur ad-Din's death in May 1174, his son as-Salih held Aleppo, his nephew Saif ad-Din took Mosul, the Damascenes made a truce with their old Frankish allies, while Saladin, who proclaimed himself as the true heir to Nur ad-Din's legacy, consolidated his hold on Egypt and began the long task of trying to assemble a force to unseat the Franks. In order to achieve this he would need

15. Aerial photograph from the 1930s showing the Dome of the Rock and the al-Aqsa mosque picture courtesy of B. Z. Kedar

huge resources, diplomatic successes, the endorsement of the Sunni religious hierarchy, military might and good fortune. Saladin's persistence, determination and acute political judgement are key features of his career. On occasion, as we will see, he would test the Franks' strength (as in 1177 and 1183) and when it was apparent that his resources were insufficient to defeat the settlers, he would retrench and develop his position further.

In October 1174 he took control of Damascus, proclaiming himself the champion of Sunni Orthodoxy. His role in the removal of the Shiite caliph for Cairo (in 1171) gave this claim some respectability and he began to organise his government according to strict Islamic law. He soon came into conflict with his rivals in the Muslim world and in the spring of 1175 he defeated an Aleppan force at Hama. In consequence of this show of power, the head of the Sunni Orthodox faith, the caliph of Baghdad, formally invested Saladin with the government of Egypt, Yemen and Syria. Much to Saladin's frustration the mandate excluded the city of Aleppo which remained under the control of Nur ad-Din's son and representatives and this was a serious stumbling block to the sultan's authority in the Islamic Near East. William of Tyre, writing without knowledge of the defeat of Hattin, commented astutely: 'Any rise in Saladin's power was a cause for suspicion in our eyes. . . . For he was a man wise in counsel, valiant in war and generous beyond measure' (William of Tyre, tr. Babcock and Krey, 1943: 2.405). It was at this time that Saladin survived two murder attempts by the Assassins. Their Shiite faith made them an obvious objective for Saladin's claims as the guardian of Sunni Orthodoxy. The Assassins, in turn, viewed him as a prime target. One attack saw the emir's cheek slashed and his cuirass (leather chest armour) pierced, but he survived. When the attempts to kill him failed Saladin marched to the Assassins' castle at Masyaf and ravaged the region, sending a message strong enough to deter further attempts on his life in the near future. Such was his fear of assassination, however, that from this time onwards Saladin slept in a special wooden tower rather than his normal tent. In late 1176 he returned to Damascus and reinforced his position as Nur ad-Din's spiritual successor by marrying his widow. Over the next couple of years he moved to gather his strength in Egypt and Syria to confront the Franks and his Muslim opponents in the north.

Unlike Nur ad-Din, Saladin possessed two contemporary biographers who were determined to extol his virtues and to proclaim him as the hero of Sunni Islam, namely Beha ad-Din (see Who's Who, below, p. 255) and Imad ad-Din al-Isfahani. While this provides us with a wealth of information about the sultan, it has the potential to cloud the picture because at times he seems dangerously close to conforming to a model prince, a figure with a longstanding literary tradition in the Muslim world. That said, there is a large volume of evidence from other sources, other Muslim writers and Christians, as well as from epigraphy and architecture, to formulate a reasonably consistent picture. Saladin was certainly a religious man, perhaps not as entirely devout as his former master, Nur ad-Din, and he never made the *haj* to Mecca as all Muslims should. He did, however, provide substantial levels of support for *madrasas* (teaching schools) and charitable foundations. These institutions did much to provide the spiritual drive to Saladin's cause, extolling the virtues of Jerusalem (a distinct genre, known as *al-Quds* poetry), praising their patron and calling upon the populace to join him in driving out the unbelievers.

Saladin also took a keen interest in, for example, the study of *hadith*, the sayings of the Prophet. He was also known as a man of justice and generosity, doing little to enrich himself. It is true that he placed members of his family in positions of power, such as his father as the treasurer of Cairo and his brother as the ruler of Arabia. This might look like he was advancing the position of his own clan – and, of course, this is correct. But he was simply following what other rulers of the Near East had been doing for generations and given his need to develop his power in potentially hostile lands, it was prudent to use people whom he could trust. Saladin is also famous for his magnanimity and while his actions at Jerusalem in 1187 are well known, when one looks at his career before that date it is apparent that he frequently chose to spare defeated (often Muslim) opponents in order to allow for continuity of government and to prevent subsequent hostility. His aim was, after all, to draw support to himself, which, as we will see, proved a slow and difficult process.

THE INVASION OF EGYPT AND THE CASTLE AT JACOB'S FORD

As the settlers prepared to invade Egypt in the summer of 1177 they suffered a body blow when William Longsword died, leaving his wife Sibylla pregnant. When the young King Baldwin IV fell ill again, a new regent was needed and this provided the cue for another important figure to move centre stage – Reynald of Châtillon, the former prince of Antioch, who by this time was also ruler of the lordships of Hebron and, through marriage, the strategically crucial area of Transjordan, the land that bisected the Muslim territories of Damascus and Egypt. Reynald was a remarkable man; as we saw earlier, he was capable of great cruelty, but he was now hardened after surviving fifteen years as a prisoner of the Muslims and he was also on close terms with Emperor Manuel Komnenos who helped to pay his ransom. The invasion of Egypt would be bolstered by the crusade of Count Philip of Flanders, a member of the most active crusading family in twelfth-century Europe, who reached the Levant in September 1177.

Ultimately the planned attack on Egypt broke down over a disagreement as to who should rule the land if it was conquered. The settlers believed that it should be part of the kingdom of Jerusalem; Philip of Flanders wanted at least some of the land for himself; while the Byzantines probably required recognition of their overlordship as earlier agreements with the settlers had stipulated (1168). They would also take a part of the territory for themselves, gaining commercial advantages and sharing the burden of rule with the Franks. This lack of strong leadership in the Latin East meant that a real opportunity had been wasted. Saladin was still building up his power and even with the presence of two formidable sources of outside assistance nothing had been achieved. The Greeks were angered at the collapse of the expedition and returned home while Philip and a large force from Jerusalem fought a largely unprofitable campaign in northern Syria. Saladin exploited this by invading the kingdom. His forces moved confidently past Ascalon and devastated Ramla and Lydda, but at Mont Gisard, near Ibelin, he was caught unawares by a small Frankish army led by Prince Reynald and, in spite of his illness, King Baldwin IV. The Muslim army was routed and Saladin himself only just escaped. Many of his men were captured or killed, although the Franks suffered terrible casualties too with reports of 750 wounded being taken to the hospital of Jerusalem. In spite of this, the victory at Mont Gisard represented a significant achievement for the young king. It was also widely reported back in Europe which, ironically, may have caused some to regard the settlers' position as stronger than it really was, and to view their subsequent appeals for help with less concern.

On Saladin's part, events at Mont Gisard were a severe blow. It is too easy for our mental image of Saladin to think simply of him as the victor at Hattin and the conqueror of Jerusalem. History tends to ignore, or blur over, the troubles that he had reaching those points. News of this defeat was, at first, concealed from the people of Egypt, so damaging was the loss and it certainly put him on the back foot. The battle also made plain to him that the forces of Damascus and Egypt were insufficient to defeat the Franks. He would need to quell the danger from Aleppo and Mosul and, preferably, to bring them along with him. To achieve this he used a combination of force, political skill and his claims to be the defender of Sunni Orthodoxy and the only man capable of removing the infidel.

Encouraged by their success at Mont Gisard, in the autumn of 1178 the Franks made a highly aggressive move. They started to build a castle at Jacob's Ford on the River Jordan. The construction of this fortress, about 55 kilometres from Damascus, signalled a genuine challenge to the Muslims and again showed Saladin the scale of the task he faced to overcome the Franks. The fortress – currently the subject of intensive archaeological work – was planned on a grand scale and absorbed much of the settlers' financial resources. The remaining walls show large, expensively finished stonework and reveal a substantial ground plan. Baldwin himself spent several months there in the autumn of 1178 and the spring of 1179. It was intended that the Templars should garrison the castle with eighty knights (a large figure) and have up to 900 other fighting men in support. To counter this, on several occasions, Saladin tried to buy off the Franks and offered to reimburse their full expenses and more (up to 100,000 dinars), but his suggestions were declined. It is clear that, following on from the humiliation of Mont Gisard, Saladin felt extremely threatened. Force was the only other option. In June 1179 he defeated a Latin army at Marj Ayyun, in August he launched a full-scale assault on the fortress and within five days – before Baldwin could bring up a relief army – the castle fell. The defenders were captured and the Templars and archers were executed. The remains of five crusaders have been discovered in the castle (Mitchell et al., 2006). Some have multiple arrow-heads lodged in their bones; one man had his arm severed just above the elbow – at the point that his chainmail sleeve would have stopped; he had his left lower jawbone severed, three arrow wounds to his neck and one final wound that split his skull. Another has an arrow wound in his pelvis that may well have bisected his large blood vessels and caused him to bleed rapidly to death. Such horrific forensic details reveal the extraordinary brutality of warfare in a way that literary descriptions fall short, although this is not to pretend that similar horrors would fail to emerge from examining the consequences of modern combat.

Contemporary sources inform us that the dead were thrown into a cistern and archaeologists have high hopes of discovering its location, potentially revealing the skeletons of large numbers of twelfth-century crusaders. Such a find would allow us to learn much about diet, health and warfare in the Latin East. Back in 1179, however, Saladin could not take advantage of his success because of an epidemic in his army and a drought in Syria.

THE MARRIAGE OF GUY AND SIBYLLA

In the spring of 1180 the kingdom of Jerusalem was plunged into turmoil. Two years earlier Sibylla had given birth to William Longsword's son, Baldwin. Once her period of mourning had ended it was necessary to choose another husband for her. The settlers selected Duke Hugh III of Burgundy, a nephew of the queen of France and, in 1171, a visitor to the kingdom of Jerusalem. By early 1180, however, he had not set out for the Levant. In the meantime Raymond of Tripoli and Bohemond III of Antioch suddenly appeared in the kingdom of Jerusalem. King Baldwin was suffering a particularly bad phase of his illness and he feared his own deposition and the marriage of Sibylla to one of Raymond's supporters, Balian of Ibelin. Encouraged by his mother, Agnes of Courtenay, and his uncle, Joscelin (formerly count of Edessa), the king moved swiftly to try to preserve his authority. Sibylla married Guy of Lusignan, a relative newcomer to the Levant, although his brother, Aimery, was the royal constable. Guy was a Poitevin and a vassal of King Henry II of England who, as we have seen, was one of the settlers' principal targets in their approaches to the West. Perhaps it was hoped that this link might encourage Henry's support. Guy and Sibylla were married in Holy Week of 1180, a highly irregular state of affairs. The key issue here, however, is the rejection of Count Raymond's candidate – this was the moment that sparked real division among the ruling families of the Latin East.

Earlier historians (Runciman, Vol. 2, 1952; Setton, Vol. 1, 1969; Mayer, 1988) have tended to treat the struggle as one between 'hawks' and 'doves'.

16. Marriage of Guy of Lusignan and Sibylla. © Bibliothèque Municipale, Boulogne-sur-Mer

The 'doves' were said to be native barons who favoured peace with the Muslims and included Raymond of Tripoli, the Ibelins and William of Tyre. The 'hawks' (sometimes known as the 'court' party) were identified as aggressive newcomers and numbered Guy, Reynald of Châtillon, Baldwin's mother Agnes, and Gerard of Ridefort, the master of the Templars. Edbury (1993) has shown the fixed groups, and the enmities and characteristics of aggression and peacemaking attached to these parties, to be unrealistic. For example, at times, the 'doves' made aggressive moves and the 'hawks' negotiated truces. The party of newcomers included people such as Agnes and Joscelin, who were from a family settled in the Levant since the First Crusade. In reality, the division should be drawn between Baldwin's maternal line (Agnes) and his paternal line (his cousins, Raymond and Bohemond III).

In November 1180 Sibylla's younger sister, Isabella, was married to Humphrey IV of Toron. For the time being, therefore, there was no possibility of a planned western marriage into the royal house of Jerusalem, which removed one of the settlers' prime diplomatic cards. In May 1180 a two-year peace deal was agreed with Saladin because both sides had to attend to internal political matters. William of Tyre provides an indication of the slowly changing balance of power at this point: 'A truce on both land and sea, for foreigners and locals alike, was accordingly arranged and confirmed by an exchange of oaths between the two parties. The conditions were somewhat humiliating to us, for the truce was concluded on equal terms, with no reservations of importance on our part, a thing which is said never to have happened before' (William of Tyre, tr. Babcock and Krey, 1943: 2.447). In other words, the Franks had previously held the upper hand in such negotiations but now they were reduced (as William saw it) to mere equality – a decline in their relative strength, although still a long way from being inferior, of course. In the meantime, on 24 September 1180, Emperor Manuel Komnenos died, marking the demise of one of the settlers' most important supporters. His widow, Maria of Antioch, was regent for their eleven-year-old son, Alexios II. In light of Maria's origins, for the time being at least, a pro-Frankish line would continue to be followed in Constantinople and envoys from Byzantium travelled to Antioch and Jerusalem to secure backing and allegiance (as vassals) for the young emperor.

THE 1181 CRUSADE APPEAL OF POPE ALEXANDER III

The recent defeat at Jacob's Ford and King Baldwin IV's continued incapacity prompted another embassy to Europe. Templar envoys were sent to Pope Alexander III who, in January 1181, issued crusade appeals to the churchmen of the West and to Philip II of France and Henry II of England. This was Alexander's first formal crusade appeal since 1173, and the death of Manuel Komnenos, as well as events in the Levant, caused him to act. Alexander wrote that the Holy Land was 'trodden down under the incursions of the infidels'. More seriously, however, he mentioned a lack of leadership in the East and explicitly criticised King Baldwin. He equated the king's leprosy to God's judgement on the sins of the settlers – a remarkable observation in the context of an appeal for help and a perspective hardly guaranteed to encourage backing for the ruling house of Jerusalem. As noted earlier, such attitudes, in part, prompted William of Tyre to write his *Historia*. Alexander obviously saw Philip and Henry as bearing the main responsibility for the defence of the Latin East, but as before, while money was forthcoming, political circumstances in western Europe (this time it was tensions between France and Flanders) hampered the effort. From King Henry's perspective the changing situation in the Holy Land made a crusade increasingly unattractive. When planning to crusade in 1171 and 1173 he would have been working with King Amalric. While Henry may have been given considerable authority, he would, nonetheless, have been a temporary visitor only. By now Baldwin IV was very weak. Henry was Baldwin's nearest living relative on the male side of the family; his grandfather Fulk had ruled Jerusalem (1131–43); and the king of England had already made two clear, but unfulfilled, promises to crusade. With the death of William Longsword (the obvious choice as regent), should Henry himself need to leave the Holy Land, or if Baldwin died, the English monarch would stand accused of deserting Christ's patrimony. Combined with his own advancing years and the rising threat from his sons, the chances of Henry taking the cross seemed to be fading. Alexander's appeal may have prompted a small crusade led by Duke Henry of Lotharingia to come to the Holy Land in 1183. While expeditions of this sort were welcome, they were of relatively limited value and did not permit the Franks to strike a major blow in their conflict against Saladin.

PRINCE REYNALD'S ATTACK ON THE ARABIAN PENINSULA

Back in the kingdom of Jerusalem, tensions between Guy and Raymond continued, although some form of reconciliation was reached in the spring of 1182 in order to confront the imminent end of the truce with Saladin. In July 1182 the Franks and Muslims met in battle near La Forbelet in southern Galilee. Baldwin himself was present and the smaller Frankish army was able to win the day. Saladin was not discouraged and, using the Egyptian navy, a force that he had carefully built up from a period of decline under the Fatimids, he blockaded Beirut. The arrival of a joint Frankish and Pisan fleet drove him off and once again the settlers had demonstrated their resilience. In the winter of 1182–83, Reynald of Châtillon launched a campaign into the Arabian peninsula. This striking episode was designed to humiliate and embarrass Saladin and to disrupt trade and pilgrim traffic between Egypt and Mecca and Medina, the holy cities of Islam. Reynald constructed five warships in kit form and had them transported by camel down to the gulf of Aqaba on the Red Sea. No Frankish warship had ever been launched into these waters and the element of surprise was complete. At least seventeen merchant and pilgrim ships were attacked and on landing on the Arabian coast, the Christians hit towns and pilgrim caravans as well. An Egyptian fleet finally responded and the Franks were captured in early 1183 having abandoned their ships and fled inland to within a day's march to Medina. Saladin ordered the Christians to be executed in the towns and cities across his lands in order to demonstrate that he was the true defender of the faithful. Two captives were taken to Mecca where they were ritually slaughtered in front of the pilgrim masses as martyrs for their faith. Unsurprisingly, this episode evoked in Saladin a profound hatred of Prince Reynald. His secretary, Imad ad-Din described Reynald as 'the most perfidious and the most evil of the Franks, the most avid, the most eager to do injury and to make evil'. Saladin swore 'that he would have his life' (tr. Barber, 1998: 20–21). While this episode damaged the emir's prestige, he had nonetheless been making progress in his efforts to impose his supremacy over the Muslim Middle East. After Nur ad-Din's son, as-Salih, died in Aleppo in 1181, Saladin marched to Mosul to forestall its leading men taking over as-Salih's lands. Saladin accused those in Mosul of colluding with the Franks and (more realistically) dealing with enemies of the caliph of Baghdad in Persia. In May 1183 he forced Aleppo ('the eye of Syria' as he described it) to surrender, thereby bolstering his position considerably. Saladin argued that it was he, among all the rulers of Islam, whose extension of power was a source of grief and affliction to the Christians.

On the Frankish side, the pressure of mounting the military expeditions of 1182 had stretched the kingdom of Jerusalem's resources to the limit and in February 1183 the *curia generalis* imposed an unprecedented general levy: 1 per cent on all property of a value of 100 bezants, and 2 per cent on all incomes of over 100 bezants. Those with income below these levels were to pay 1 bezant, 'whatever their tongue, race, creed or sex'. The scale of this levy graphically demonstrates the cost of warfare and the settlers' serious financial needs.

Baldwin's health was in steep decline. He was blind and could not use his hands or feet, yet he refused to abdicate and tried to rule as best he could. By the autumn of 1183, however, the king's condition became so bad that he had to appoint a regent. He chose Guy of Lusignan, a man who had only minimal leadership experience in the Levant. Saladin was preparing to invade and in order to face the Muslim threat Guy summoned the full military strength of the kingdom, plus troops from Antioch and Tripoli. These forces numbered *c.* 1,300 cavalry and *c.* 15,000 infantry; the visiting forces of Duke Henry of Lotharingia joined in as well. The Christians shadowed Saladin's army in Galilee, but there was no battle. By mid-October, Saladin began to run low on supplies and had to withdraw. From a Frankish perspective, the campaign could be seen as a real success: the Muslims had conquered no land and the settlers had lost no men. Yet the failure to engage the enemy after gathering so many troops, the damage to wide areas of crops, and a raid on the Orthodox monastery on Mount Tabor left Guy open to charges of incompetence. His political opponents were swift to exploit this and King Baldwin was persuaded of the error in not confronting the Muslims and Guy was stripped of the regency. Both sides needed a breathing space: Saladin to deal properly with Mosul, the Franks to resolve their political differences.

As an aside, it is also worth remembering that alongside this ongoing political and military narrative, the daily business of trade continued between lands under Christian and Muslim rule. As Ibn Jubayr noted in September 1184 'It is one of the strangest things in the world that Muslim [trading] caravans go forth to Frankish lands while Frankish captives enter Muslim lands'. At the same time, Muslim farmers were 'living comfortably with the Franks' near Acre which, although a city he found offensive in many respects, was nonetheless 'the meeting place of Muslim and Christian merchants from all regions' (Ibn Jubayr, tr. Broadhurst, 1952: 313, 316, 318).

THE MISSION OF PATRIARCH HERACLIUS

It was decided that the king's five-year-old nephew, Baldwin, should be crowned co-king. Furthermore, in the summer of 1184, Baldwin IV's weakness, the rising strength of Saladin and the emergence of an anti-Latin regime in Constantinople (in other words, the end of any prospects of help from the Greeks), persuaded the settlers to ask the West for help again. This was the most high-level mission yet sent to Europe. It was led by Patriarch Heraclius of Jerusalem, who was accompanied by the masters of the Temple and the Hospital. The unprecedented decision to dispatch the senior churchman in the Levant on such a journey emphasised the need to defend Christ's patrimony and also demonstrated the seriousness of the situation. To send the masters of the military orders was to employ the leaders of two enormously popular institutions that were, with their huge landholdings in the West, the most visible reminders of the need to defend Christ's patrimony. The embassy met Pope Lucius III (1181–85) at Verona in September 1184. The pope issued a crusade bull and the envoys moved north, reaching Paris in January 1185. As in 1169, they offered the king of France the keys of Jerusalem in the hope that he would accept these symbols and travel to the East, automatically generating the sizable military expedition needed to defeat Saladin. Philip realised the scale of the commitment that he would need to make and as a young ruler still not comfortably established on the throne of France he declined.

In February and March 1185 Heraclius held meetings with Henry II. The king was moved to tears by reports of the danger to the Holy Land and he venerated the keys of Jerusalem and the Holy Sepulchre and promised to consult his barons to consider whether to accept them. Henry's nobles feared he might become ensnared in the politics of the Levant and recalled his coronation oath to preserve peace for all of his people; they recommended that he should stay in northern Europe. Heraclius berated the king and reminded him of his earlier promises to crusade. The patriarch exhorted his audience to act: he argued that sending money was no longer good enough and Henry should go to the Levant in person. The king decided to confer with Philip and while both monarchs promised financial and military assistance – the former in the shape of a substantial tax that might have raised 30,000 marks – they decided not to go to the East themselves. Heraclius was despondent and returned to Jerusalem in the summer of 1185. While a few nobles such as Roger of Mowbray and Hugh of Beauchamp took the cross, in essence the patriarch's mission had failed.

THE DEATH OF KING BALDWIN IV AND THE CORONATION OF KING GUY

Meanwhile Saladin had engaged in a lengthy siege of the vital fortress of Kerak in Transjordan. Baldwin was carried in a litter to the castle and at the sight of this relief force the Muslims withdrew. Faced with his imminent demise Baldwin wanted to annul the marriage of Guy and Sibylla to prevent them from reasserting control after his death. His ill-feeling towards Guy was now plain; William of Tyre wrote that 'rancour had now burst forth violently' (William of Tyre, tr. Babcock and Krey, 1943: 2.507). Guy refused to answer the royal summons, but in order to avert outright conflict Baldwin was compelled to allow him to hold on to his lands at Ascalon and Jaffa. In early 1185, Baldwin had to ask Raymond of Tripoli to take over as regent for him. Although the king had hitherto resisted giving Raymond any public position in the kingdom, the need for an experienced military leader to resist Saladin was paramount. Baldwin realised that he was dying and asked all his vassals to perform homage to Raymond and the child-king Baldwin V, although the regency was bound by a series of conditions that indicate the towering level of mistrust some felt towards the count's ambitions. Raymond insisted that he was not the legal guardian of the young king to avoid trouble if Baldwin (a sickly child) died. Furthermore, the royal castles were to be under the control of the military orders (in other words, out of Raymond's immediate reach), and if Baldwin V died before the age of majority a committee of western leaders (the pope and the rulers of England, France and Germany) should decide which of his sisters, Isabella or Sibylla, should succeed. For a kingdom to be prepared to hand over its destiny to outsiders, however prestigious they may have been, shows how serious the situation in the Levant had become by the mid-1180s.

Baldwin IV finally passed away in May 1185, aged 23. He had fought bravely against his debilitating illness and worked as hard as he could to leave a viable legacy. As Hamilton observes, he had been prepared to stand aside for Henry of Burgundy and William Longsword, although he made a serious mistake in the marriage of Guy and Sibylla, which lacked popular support. In spite of his sickness no one refused to serve him and both the settlers and the Muslims regarded him highly (Hamilton, 2000a).

Once Raymond assumed the regency he concluded a truce with Saladin which gave both sides a breathing space. In the summer of 1186 Baldwin V died (aged nine). Even by the standards of the Latin East, there followed an extraordinary series of political manoeuvres that resulted in Raymond of Tripoli's removal from power. On Baldwin V's death the count tried to gather his allies (principally the Ibelins) at his base in Tiberias in preparation to take control of the kingdom. In the meantime, Guy, Sibylla, Reynald of Châtillon and Joscelin of Courtenay assembled for the young king's funeral in Jerusalem; they were backed by Patriarch Heraclius and Gerard of Ridefort. Sibylla, as the eldest relative of the king, had a wide base of support, although the position of her husband Guy was less firm and many were unhappy at the idea of him becoming ruler. In the event, the nobles present agreed that Sibylla should succeed to the throne if she divorced Guy, although she reserved the right to choose a new husband for herself. She announced her divorce from Guy and Heraclius crowned her queen. The patriarch then asked her, in turn, to give a crown to her preferred choice of regent and future husband. In a brilliant piece of political theatre she named her choice: Guy. She placed a crown on his head and Heraclius anointed him as king. Through maintaining the right to select her 'new' husband, Sibylla – with the obvious connivance of Heraclius – had managed to fool her opponents. In doing so she showed her love and trust of Guy; as an early thirteenth-century writer commented, she was 'to be commended both for her virtue and courage. She so arranged matters that the kingdom obtained a ruler while she retained a husband' (Roger of Wendover, in: Hamilton, 2000a: 221). Raymond, predictably, was furious. He tried to argue that Sibylla's sister, Isabella, and her husband, Humphrey of Toron, should be king and queen, but Humphrey himself rejected the idea and went to offer his loyalty to Guy. Raymond and his main ally, Balian of Ibelin, refused to submit to the new king.

Christian and Muslim sources report that the count concluded a deal with Saladin who promised to make him the ruler of the Franks. Ibn al-Athir commented: 'Thus their unity was disrupted and their cohesion broken. This was one of the most important factors that brought about the conquest of their territories and the liberation of Jerusalem' (Ibn al-Athir, tr. Richards, 2007, 2.316). Clearly Raymond's thirst for power and his antipathy towards Guy were immense. The count felt that by engaging with Saladin he could avert an invasion and we must remember that truces between Christians and Muslims had been frequent during the history of the Latin East. That said, it remains a remarkable turn of events for – at this particular moment – the most powerful of the Frankish nobles to make an agreement with the man who posed such a threat to Christian lands. Ibn al-Athir's analysis shows Muslim awareness of these divisions, a factor that Saladin chose to play upon and which he recognised as being of hugely to his advantage.

In spite of the deal between the count and Saladin the prospect of peace seemed increasingly unlikely. With thirteen years' momentum behind him the sultan was now intent on invasion. The emir had spent much of 1185 fighting in northern Syria and eventually, in December, he was recognised as overlord of Mosul soon after he had extracted a promise from the city's leading men that it would provide troops to assist him. Saladin had also worked hard to ensure that his borders would be secure when his attention was focused on the Holy Land, and in c. 1184–85 he made an alliance with the emperor of Byzantium.

THE DESCENT INTO WAR

Saladin was unfailingly generous to his supporters and this, combined with the strict administration of justice and the mantle of the *jihad*, had helped to give him a strong position. Lyons and Jackson, in the most comprehensive biography of Saladin, observe that he used the resources of Egypt to conquer Syria, those of Syria to conquer the Jazira and those of the Jazira to launch his attack on the coast (Lyons and Jackson, 1982: 369). Beha ad-Din commented that the *jihad* 'had taken a mighty hold on his heart and all his being, so much so that . . . he thought of nothing but the means to pursue it' (Beha ad-Din, tr. Richards, 2001: 28). The emir's goading, encouragement and conflict with his fellow-Muslims had created a tension that could no longer be contained. Having campaigned so relentlessly as the leader of the *jihad*, Saladin *had* to deliver.

In the winter of 1186–87 Reynald of Châtillon attacked a Muslim caravan travelling from Cairo to Damascus. Some sources indicate that the caravan had a substantial armed escort which was a violation of the truce in itself. Regardless of this, Reynald's killing of Muslim pilgrims and traders gave Saladin – if he really needed it by this point – the *casus belli* (cause for war) to break the truce. In April 1187 he again besieged the castle of Kerak and his son, al-Afdal, was ordered to raid through Galilee towards Acre. News of this thrust reached the masters of the military orders near Nazareth. With a force of 130 knights and 300 sergeants they foolishly attacked an enemy force of 7,000 at the Springs of Cresson on 1 May. An overdeveloped sense of honour could not overcome the numerical deficit and only four knights escaped alive. This disaster, which provoked an appeal to the West in its own right, is often overlooked given the calamities that followed, but the damage to Frankish morale and the scale of the losses should not be underestimated as contributing towards the defeat at Hattin. Rumours that Raymond had allowed the Muslims through his lands forced him to renounce his agreement with Saladin and swear homage to King Guy.

In May and June Saladin gathered armies from Egypt, Aleppo, the Jazira and Syria – a truly formidable force. It would be an overstatement to say that he had 'united' the Islamic Near East because that was probably impossible, and the coalition that he had assembled was pretty fragile as the rapid disintegration of this confederacy after his death showed only too clearly. But, given the ethnic, linguistic and cultural diversity of these lands this was a truly remarkable achievement and the cornerstone of his ability to pressure the Franks into battle.

The Franks assembled their full strength and based themselves, as in 1183, at Sapphorie. The treasure sent over annually by King Henry II of England as part of his penance for the murder of Thomas Becket was released to hire mercenaries, while castles and cities were stripped of their garrisons. The settlers had about 1,300 knights and 15,000 footsoldiers. Saladin's forces numbered nearer 20,000, which gave him a useful, if not overwhelming, advantage. His thinking is revealed: 'In my view our best course is to meet with our full complement of Muslims the full force of the infidels . . . It is only fitting to disperse this host after it has done its best in the *jihad*' (Ibn al-Athir, tr. Richards, 2007: 119). On 2 July Saladin laid siege to Tiberias and trapped Eschiva, Raymond's wife, in the town. King Guy faced a dilemma. In 1183 he had shadowed the Muslims and seen them leave Christian lands, but this non-confrontational approach had cost him the regency. In 1187 it was Raymond of Tripoli, the man who had orchestrated his removal from power, who advocated the same policy again; namely, to shadow the enemy and wait for them to disperse. Ibn al-Athir demonstrated the shrewd thinking in this advice because he quoted Raymond as saying that Saladin's forces 'will be unable to endure the long time away from their homes and families, so he will be compelled to leave'. It is, of course, unlikely that the writer heard these words, but their sentiments undoubtedly reflect the feeling in the Muslim camp (Ibn al-Athir, tr. Richards, 2007: 321).

Even though it was his own wife under threat, it seems that Raymond's prudence had won the king's mind but, in what must have been an extraordinarily dramatic scene, on the night of 2 July 1187, Reynald of Châtillon and Gerard of Ridefort, the master of the Templars, went to the king's tent and convinced him to change his mind. Both Reynald and Gerard were vigorous opponents of Islam, the former's lengthy imprisonment and attack on Medina in 1183 showed that plainly. In the case of the latter, he was the leader of an organisation dedicated to the defence of the holy places against the efforts of Islam. They were also long-term supporters of Guy and opponents of Count Raymond. In Gerard's case, that enmity had a personal twist: as a young knight Gerard had been promised the hand in marriage of an important heiress in the county of Tripoli. Unfortunately for him, when Lucia, daughter of the recently deceased lord of Botron, became eligible she caught the eye of a Pisan merchant who offered Raymond, her guardian and overlord, her weight in gold if he could marry her. The count chose to accept this proposal. Lucia weighed in at c. 63 kilogrammes and for c. 10,000 bezants she married the merchant. Gerard was humiliated and stormed off to join the Templars, ending the possibility of another broken heart and nursing an implacable hatred of Raymond. As Mayer has indicated, it was Guy and Gerard who had seized Henry II's treasure, but they had done so without his permission (Mayer, 1982). The total of c. 30,000 silver deniers could be recalled by Henry when he chose. With the cash now spent Gerard had, therefore, to produce a victory to justify his actions. Against this background, the king was persuaded to change his mind and on the morning of 3 July, the order was given to march to Tiberias, 30 kilometres from Sapphorie and on a road without proper water supplies. This played straight into the hands of Saladin and, as Beha ad-Din saw it, 'the enemy could not bear to give in to their impulsive zeal' (Beha ad-Din, tr. Richards, 2001: 73).

THE BATTLE OF HATTIN

On 3 July the armies clashed. The Franks forged onwards towards Tiberias, but the ferocity of the enemy attacks grew. Time and again the Muslims' mounted archers fired, wheeled and turned away to safety, taking a grievous toll on the Christian infantry. As Imad ad-Din al-Isfahani wrote: 'The arrows plunged into them, transforming their lions into hedgehogs.' In the rear the Templars came under enormous pressure and this prevented Raymond of Tripoli in the vanguard (the front of the army) from pushing on to Tiberias. At nightfall the Christians camped, exhausted by the heat and lacking water. Beha ad-Din summarised: 'They were closely beset as in a noose, while still marching on as though being driven to a death that they could see before them, convinced of their doom and destruction and themselves aware that the following day they would be visiting their graves' (Beha ad-Din, tr. Richards, 2001: 73).

As the Frankish army struggled through poorly watered lands, in contrast – and to the Christians' visible distress – the Muslims could bring up ample supplies on camelback from Lake Tiberias. Although they were so closely surrounded that 'not even a cat could have escaped', on 4 July the Franks set out to try to break through to Lake Tiberias now only a tantalizing 10 kilometres away. To compound the Christians' misery the Muslims set fire to the grass and brush to dry the Franks' throats and kept up a terrible drumming to raise the tension even further. The infantry were suffering terribly and could not hold their formation. Under severe provocation they finally broke ranks and many scattered depriving the cavalry of vital protection.

Raymond of Tripoli and the vanguard charged the enemy and succeeded in breaking through to freedom – although, to some, it seemed that he had been permitted to escape, thereby confirming his overly close relationship with Saladin. True or not, there was no need for the Muslim troops to fight these knights, particularly because their charge took them downhill. They could hardly turn around and come back up, while the Muslims simply faced an even weaker Frankish force. The remaining Christians fell back to the slopes of the twin peaks of the Tell Hattin (the Horns of Hattin). Guy's red tent was pitched at the summit and his remaining cavalry charged at Saladin's own bodyguard in a desperate attempt to swing the battle by killing the Muslim leader. When these attacks failed, and with the surviving infantry in total disarray, the Muslims closed in. Finally, the royal tent and the Christians' most valued relic, the True Cross, were taken and the battle was over. King Guy and Reynald of Châtillon were captured, along with many other nobles (including western crusaders) and members of the military orders.

The largest field army yet assembled by the settlers had been destroyed and the kingdom now lay at Saladin's mercy. First, he had to deal with his prisoners. King Guy, as a fellow ruler, was treated with great courtesy and offered iced sherbert to drink. Reynald was not so fortunate; Saladin had sworn to kill him after the attack on the Muslim pilgrim caravan and when the prince refused to convert to Islam, Saladin struck him with his scimitar, severing his arm at the shoulder, before his bodyguards finished the job. The Templars and Hospitallers were also executed. While this episode runs counter to Saladin's usual reputation for magnanimity, such actions satisfied the leading clerics in his army as well as being a highly practical move. The knights of the military orders were never going to apostasise (renounce Christianity) or pay ransoms and Saladin used the opportunity to rid himself of his most feared opponents. They were dispatched – not particularly expertly – by Sufi holy men; most of the other Frankish prisoners were sold into slavery. Saladin memorialised his victory at Hattin by constructing a building called 'The Dome of Victory'.

THE FALL OF JERUSALEM

Saladin's armies swept through the kingdom taking town after town: Tiberias, Nazareth, Acre, Caesarea and Jaffa. Some places surrendered immediately, others capitulated after a brief siege. The Frankish farms and villages emptied as their inhabitants fled to Tyre on the coast or to the north. By September all the coastal towns of the kingdom of Jerusalem except Tyre were in Muslim hands. Tyre itself had been on the verge of falling when, entirely unaware of the disaster at Hattin, Conrad of Montferrat (brother of William Longsword) arrived from Constantinople where he had been working to support Emperor Isaac II Angelos. He had also married the emperor's sister, but political upheavals meant he needed to leave the city in a hurry and, given his family connections in the Latin East (his father was in the Levant too and had been captured at Hattin), he decided to travel to the Holy Land. Conrad quickly realized the gravity of the situation and took control of Tyre where his firm resistance forced the Muslims to break off the siege. Much of Tripoli and southern Antioch surrendered, leaving Tyre, the great frontier castles of the kingdom (such as Kerak) and the holy city itself remaining. Contemporary Muslim military practice was set out in al-Harawi's *Book of Stratagems* (the author was also one of Saladin's leading spies), and in accordance with this advice Saladin did not engage in long static sieges at this stage of the campaign (Hamblin, 1992). The scale of his victory meant that he could afford to leave these sites under loose supervision and finish them off at his leisure. According to one source, Jerusalem was left with only two knights to lead its defence. Patriarch Heraclius directed the resistance, but surrender was inevitable. Saladin negotiated the release of Muslim prisoners and accepted ransoms for as many of the Christians as could afford to pay. Of the remainder, the young men and women were enslaved and the elderly freed. This generosity contrasted with the massacres perpetrated by the First Crusade and is a fundamental element in Saladin's reputation for mercy, a trait that was widely admired in western Europe. No Latin was to remain in Jerusalem, although Eastern Christians could stay if they accepted the status of *dhimmi* or protected religious community. The Christian churches were stripped of their precious vessels and converted into mosques, teaching colleges or convents. Saladin was able to install the *minbar* (a pulpit, see p. 114) commissioned in 1169 by Nur ad-Din in the al-Aqsa mosque (known as the Temple of Solomon by the Franks, the headquarters of the Templars) and to complete the task begun by his former master. The Holy Sepulchre was spared, mainly to allow pilgrims to visit – subject to a payment – and Saladin repopulated Jerusalem with the descendants of former Muslim inhabitants. A few castles held on, but over time they slowly capitulated: Kerak (November 1188); Saphet (December 1188); Belvoir (January 1189);

Montreal (April 1189) and Beaufort (April 1190). Only Tyre survived and that would be the crucial bridgehead for the early stages of the Third Crusade and the Christian fightback.

Saladin's army was exhausted and many wanted to return home. He managed a successful campaign in Antioch in the spring and summer of 1188, but lands in northern Tripoli around the castles of Tartus, Krak des Chevaliers and Marqab resisted. The emir must have been aware of the oncoming *revanche* from the West; the Genoese were amongst the first to respond, while a Sicilian fleet attacked the Levantine coast in the summer of 1188. Saladin would need to rest his men, consolidate his conquests and prepare to face potentially his greatest challenge yet in the form of the Third Crusade. His victory had given him enormous honour because he had crushed the Franks in battle and removed the unbelievers from Jerusalem, just as he had claimed he would. The Franks' resources and morale were almost extinguished, yet the loss of the holy city would provoke western Europe to respond with the large-scale crusade the settlers had so persistently requested over previous decades.

CONCLUSION

In summary, the following issues characterised this period. First, after 1180 and the marriage of Guy and Sibylla, a serious feud broke out between two groups of the Frankish nobility. Second, as shown by their victory at Mont Gisard (1177), the construction of Jacob's Ford and the success in shadowing the Muslims in 1183, the Franks had considerable military capabilities in attack and defence. Third, Saladin had an extremely difficult task to impose his authority on the Muslim Near East and to gain the resources necessary to defeat the Franks. Fourth, the settlers' efforts to secure outside help were largely unsuccessful. Western Europe did not respond in the fashion hoped for and Byzantium became hostile, a factor that was crucial in creating the conditions whereby Saladin could confront the Franks. Fifth, by the mid-1180s, however, Saladin's rising power (he controlled both Aleppo and Mosul), coupled with ever stronger enmities amongst the Franks, meant the balance of power swung his way. Finally, the settlers made a disastrous mistake in choosing to march from Sapphorie to Tiberias. Whether they could have avoided battle again, or won a battle on more favourable terms is, of course, hypothetical; Guy's decision on 2 July, if understandable in political terms, was, from a military perspective, fatally flawed and Saladin was fully prepared to exploit such an error.

The Third Crusade and beyond

T he Third Crusade can justly lay claim to being the greatest crusading expedition ever. It lacked the vast breadth and ambition of the Second Crusade, although in light of the unsatisfactory outcome of that campaign and, more importantly, the calamity that befell Jerusalem in 1187 a simpler focus was perhaps unsurprising. No other crusade would boast the participation of the three most powerful secular rulers of the West: Emperor Frederick Barbarossa of Germany (1152–90), King Richard I of England (1189–99) and King Philip II Augustus of France (1180–1223). The ultimate goal of the Third Crusade was plainly the recapture of Jerusalem and, measured against this, it was a failure. But, as we shall see, on account of the political and strategic context in which the expedition took place, its achievements were highly significant for the longer-term future of the Latin East.

AUDITA TREMENDI: THE CRUSADE APPEAL OF POPE GREGORY VIII

News of the disasters at Hattin and Jerusalem soon reached the West and in October 1187 Pope Gregory VIII issued *Audita tremendi*, the call to preserve the holy city in Christian hands (see Document 20). In this, the most powerful and emotive crusade bull of all, he described recent events in the Holy Land, including Saladin's exploitation of the political infighting among the settlers and his victory at the Battle of Hattin. Gregory lamented the loss of the True Cross and the execution of the Templars and Hospitallers. The pope claimed that God's anger at the sins of man could be assuaged by an act of penance, namely, the recovery of Christ's patrimony. We can see, therefore, Gregory repeating Urban II's point that a crusade was a sufficiently arduous undertaking to be adequate penance for all properly confessed sins. Gregory also depicted the crusade as a test set by God and suggested that it was an opportunity to gain rewards either as a martyr or through a full indulgence.

Here Gregory followed St Bernard's approach in 1147 when the abbot portrayed the crusade in terms of a challenge. The usual practical privileges of protection of property and legal and fiscal benefits were outlined, along with strictures as to the proper dress for a penitential exercise. In fact, events in the East soon compounded matters and Saladin's capture of Jerusalem transformed a call to help defend the holy city into one of recovering Christ's patrimony.

CONRAD OF MONTFERRAT AND THE DEFENCE OF TYRE

Europe roused itself to avenge this injury, but it was not until the late spring of 1191 – over three and a half years after the Battle of Hattin – that the two most effective crusading armies arrived in the Eastern Mediterranean. What accounted for this lengthy delay and what impact did this have on the situation in the Holy Land?

First, it should be pointed out that numerous contingents reached the Levant in the years after Hattin. In fact, the first of these appeared so quickly that it could not have heard about the battle, but it was the presence of this force, led by Conrad of Montferrat, that proved crucial in the survival of the Frankish East. As we saw earlier, Conrad was a powerful and wealthy north Italian noble with family connections to the Capetians, the German imperial dynasty and, through his deceased brother William Longsword, the ruling house of Jerusalem. Conrad landed at Tyre in August 1187 just as Saladin's victorious army was sweeping through the Latin states. At Tyre, however, the Muslims were turned back: the marquis organised a vigorous defence of the city and Saladin had to withdraw. Crucially, therefore, the Christians maintained a foothold on the coast which could act as a bridgehead for the crusader armies of the West. With King Guy in captivity, Conrad took control over the remains of the kingdom of Jerusalem and began to hand out commercial privileges to the Genoese and the Pisans as a sign of his authority. His gallantry in fighting off Saladin was soon celebrated by western troubadours who used his bravery as a way of urging their own leaders (chiefly meaning the Angevins and Capetians) to make peace with each other so that 'the noble and valiant marquis should have more companions'. Conrad soon began to receive assistance from the West and in the course of the next three years a steady stream of forces arrived in the Latin East, including those of King William II of Sicily (in 1188), a Pisan fleet (spring 1188), and an English fleet (1190). But the army with the greatest potential to aid the Christian cause was that of Emperor Frederick Barbarossa.

THE CRUSADE OF FREDERICK BARBAROSSA

Frederick died before he could reach the Holy Land and, blinded as we tend to be by the famous clash between Richard and Saladin, it is easy to lose sight of how profound an impact this had on the outcome of the Third Crusade. Aside from the loss of much of his army, so many of the problems of leadership and authority faced by the Third Crusade might have been avoided through Frederick's presence in the East. As Holy Roman Emperor he held the most prestigious title of any monarch in western Europe; he had been in power for over thirty-six years when he took the cross; he had experience of the Levant from his part in the Second Crusade, and he had vast resources at his disposal.

Frederick's army is estimated to have numbered around 15,000 men, including a significant proportion of mounted knights, maybe as many as 3,000 (Murray, 2007). When one considers the numbers of Frankish knights at the Battle of Hattin (around 1,300), the potential of this force becomes clear. This was also a highly disciplined group, capable of covering around 20 kilometres a day which given the terrain, the need to convey baggage and supplies, not to mention enemy attacks, was a notable achievement. Perhaps even more significantly, he succeeded in one endeavour that the Second Crusade had not: in the course of his march to the East he managed to face down a hostile Byzantine Empire and then to cross Seljuk-controlled Asia Minor while preserving at least half of his military strength. Threats and diplomacy saw him past the Greeks and he achieved a decisive victory over the Turks near Iconium, modern Konya (17 May 1190), even briefly occupying the city before he handed it back to the sultan in exchange for supplies and assurances of peace. But just as Frederick was about to reach the Levant disaster struck. The emperor's determination to ford a river at Silifke in southern Cilicia was his downfall: contact with the icy water probably caused him to have a heart attack and he drowned on 10 June 1190. Frederick's body was buried at Silifke, although the bones were removed and later laid to rest in the cathedral at Tyre. The German crusade had possessed the capability to make serious inroads into the Muslim conquests and Saladin was saved from facing an opponent he had every reason to fear. Frederick's death did not, however, mean the end of the German Crusade. His son, Frederick of Swabia, assumed command of the troops and they carried on to Antioch, still a potent force. It was there, however, that a vicious outbreak of (probably) dysentery tore through the army and caused the deaths of thousands of crusaders from all ranks. The survivors made their way down to the ongoing siege of Acre (see below, pp. 170–4), where Frederick of Swabia died in January 1191, again of sickness. Contemporary writer Arnold of Lubeck lamented: 'And so the expedition ended, so that it seemed to have been almost completely wiped out' (*The Crusade of Frederick Barbarossa*, tr. Loud, 2010: 29). Such an outcome was a huge relief to Saladin who had been compelled to move troops north to face this imminent threat. Undeniably, however, the sting had been drawn from the German force and their influence on the crusade in the Holy Land was minimal.

THE CRUSADE PREPARATIONS OF RICHARD THE LIONHEART

As Frederick fought his way across Asia Minor preparations for the crusade continued in Europe. Preachers toured the West exhorting the people to take the cross to recapture the holy city. Conrad of Montferrat encouraged this in a particularly striking way because he sent a banner that depicted the atrocities committed by Saladin's men to be displayed at preaching meetings in the West. This mobile advertising hoarding was accompanied by refugees from the Holy Land who told the story of the Muslim invasion in all its grim detail.

An important reason why the rulers of England and France were slow to act was the ongoing Angevin–Capetian conflict and the death of King Henry II in July 1189. Once Richard was crowned king of England he began to channel the considerable resources of his lands (which also included Normandy, Poitou, Maine and Aquitaine) towards the cause of the crusade. One of the hallmarks of Richard's crusading career was his attention to detail and a determination to be as well prepared as possible. As Gillingham has shown (Gillingham, 1999), the king was an experienced military man who had been campaigning for almost two decades by the time of the crusade and he was well aware of the difficulties faced by earlier expeditions, particularly with regard to finance and the problem of non-combatants. It is a testimony to his planning that for much of the crusade Richard was adequately resourced; before setting out he harnessed the Angevin government machine – probably the most sophisticated of the day in Europe – to collect funds. He also decided to sail to the Levant; an effective barrier to the participation of the poor and non-combatants because cost and space on ships excluded most of the unarmed pilgrims. Henry II had instituted the 'Saladin tithe' to raise money for the crusade, but when Richard became ruler he wanted more. Roger of Howden, a contemporary writer, reported: 'He put up for sale all he had, offices, lordships, earldoms, sheriffdoms, castles, towns, lands, everything' (Gillingham, 1989: 133). The king imposed a taillage on the Jews in England and he levied a heavy payment on those who had not taken the cross, excepting people whose essential administrative roles required them to remain in the West. Records survive to show how Richard directed some of the funds raised. Over 100 ships were hired or purchased, their crews were paid for and equipment, food and horses were gathered. In 1190 alone, 60,000 horseshoes were purchased (most from the Forest of Dean) and 14,000 cured pig carcasses were delivered from Lincolnshire, Essex and Hampshire.

One reason why resources were needed on such a grand scale was because the reaction to the call for the crusade was so impressive. Archbishop Baldwin of Canterbury attracted a strong response when he toured Wales in early 1188 (a journey vividly described by Gerald of Wales, tr. Thorpe, 1978) and preached the crusade to the Holy Land. No evidence for an official tour of England exists, but sermons must have been delivered and papal letters read out. Once again, however, the call for a crusade would ignite violent feelings against the Jews as descendants of the killers of Christ and as a group that had the money the crusaders themselves lacked. Horrific massacres took place in towns such as Stamford and King's Lynn, while in York the oppressed Jewish community chose to take their own lives rather than face the mob. The authorities soon ended these disturbances, but such episodes showed that one particularly grim tradition of crusading was not easily put to rest.

It is estimated that Richard assembled about 17,000 troops in Sicily in April 1191 (the first such gathering of his entire army), the bulk of these coming from the nobility and their military households. A contingent of Welsh archers, churchmen and camp-followers formed the remainder of his force. King Philip's preparations had been slower, but he had gathered around 650 knights and 1,300 squires (plus footsoldiers), and made a contract with the Genoese to transport his army to the Levant by sea.

THE AIMS OF THE THIRD CRUSADE AND THE SIEGE OF ACRE

In the meantime, much had happened in the Holy Land. With the two kings poised to set out it is worth considering the aims of the expedition at this point and to assess the condition of the crusaders' opposition. The recapture of Jerusalem was the ultimate objective of the campaign, but events since the fall of the holy city had turned up two further issues that would need to be addressed once the crusade reached the East. One was political: namely, who should be the king of Jerusalem? The other was strategic – the result of the ongoing Frankish siege at Acre. Both crises had been precipitated by Saladin's release of Guy in June 1188. The king went to Tyre to restate his authority as the anointed ruler, but Conrad refused to hand over the city and ignited a conflict that would last until the marquis's death in April 1192. The arrival of the crusade and the political alignments that came with it would add a further twist. Conrad's rejection of Guy's authority prompted the latter to act and in August 1189 the king seized the initiative by marching to Acre and laying siege to the city. It was inevitable that his small army would soon be caught between Acre's garrison and Saladin's relieving force, but Guy's troops managed to dig in and could not be dislodged. Thus the Christian besiegers of Muslim Acre were, in their turn, besieged by Saladin. Guy's audacity won him considerable support and in April 1190 Conrad recognised him as king. Conditions were grim for both sides as the Muslims endlessly tried to tempt the Franks into open conflict and the Christians bombarded the city. As with any such engagement, there were periods of inactivity and Beha ad-Din noted that 'sometimes the two parties would mingle together singing and dancing . . . and afterwards would begin fighting again' (Beha ad-Din, tr. Richards, 2001: 100–101). Over the winter of 1189–90 the area became so muddy that the armies had to stop fighting until the spring. Disease was an inevitable companion to the rigours of a long campaign; both sides suffered terribly and in the autumn of 1190 Guy's wife, Queen Sibylla, and her daughters died. This tragedy reopened the succession issue because Guy was king only by right of his marriage and the blood-line of the house of Jerusalem now rested in Sibylla's younger sister, Isabella. If Conrad married her, as he was determined to do, the throne would surely be his. The fact that she was already married (to the ineffectual Humphrey of Toron), that one of Conrad's own previous wives may have been still alive, and that technically they were related to one another made little difference to the marquis. The courtship was brief: Isabella was abducted and, in spite of her husband's protests, a Pisan churchman was persuaded to annul their marriage and, on 24 November 1190, she married Conrad. Guy, of course, still claimed the crown for himself. Thus, when the crusade reached the Levant, Richard and Philip would have to arbitrate as to who should rule the kingdom of Jerusalem.

While the situation among the Franks of the Eastern Mediterranean was important to the crusaders, the circumstances of their opponents were of great interest as well. We have seen how hard it was for Saladin to assemble his coalition prior to Hattin and, as the man who had regained Jerusalem, he had accrued enormous prestige, a factor that enabled him to keep troops in the field. But his authority in the Muslim Near East was not unquestioned and the stalemate at Acre did much to take the gloss off his earlier successes. He needed to maintain a large army at the siege and it was essential to bring in reinforcements from various parts of his empire, such as Nubia (southern Egypt) and the Jazira (between the Upper Tigris and Upper Euphrates rivers), to help share the burden. It is worth remembering that from August 1189 onwards many of Saladin's resources were tied up at Acre and he had to operate there in the knowledge that western Europe was preparing to throw its full strength against him. He demanded that the Muslim Near East pull together to face this new onslaught and the increasingly strident tone of the appeals to his co-religionists showed his growing concern. Throughout these trials Saladin's efforts to lead by example, to share the privations of his troops (he was often ill) and his basic humanity shone through. Several stories related his generous treatment of Frankish captives and while one must beware the biographers' panegyric the broad consistency of the emir's style in all sources (whether Muslim or Christian) suggest that his reputation was well founded. Such episodes included his kindness in letting an ageing Frankish pilgrim captured at Acre complete his vows, or told of his determination to reunite a mother with her stolen infant (see Document 21). Back on the battlefield, however, in the autumn of 1190 and the early months of 1191, before Richard and Philip reached the East, Saladin made strenuous attempts to dislodge the Franks from Acre, but to little effect.

The two kings made slow progress on their journey to the East. At a meeting at Vézelay in July 1190 they agreed to split the spoils of conquest equally and then they marched southwards to the coast of France. Some of Richard's men sailed on to the Holy Land immediately, but the bulk of his troops went first to Messina in Sicily where the king was to remain from September 1190 until April 1191. Given the urgent situation at Acre such a delay seems incomprehensible, but Richard, as usual, had an eye to the longer term. Tancred of Lecce, the ruler of Sicily, owed the English crown a substantial sum of money from the marriage of Joan, Richard's sister, to Tancred's predecessor, William II (d. 1189). Richard wanted this money back to help ensure his crusade was properly financed and he used both force and diplomacy to get it. In another, less coercive incident, Richard again revealed his hard-headed business sense. He had brought with him the sword believed to be Excalibur, the weapon of King Arthur, hero of medieval romances. Tancred admired the sword so much that Richard suggested he could have it – in return for four ships. Perhaps the English king was sceptical as to the genuineness of the sword. In any case, his desire to provide for his crusade was paramount and Excalibur was duly exchanged. By this time it was winter and the sailing season was over which meant that the crusaders – including the French contingent – had to wait until spring to continue their voyage. Relations between Richard and Philip declined further over the matter of the English king's marriage. He had long been betrothed to Philip's sister, Alice, but it seems that a need to protect the southern borders of the Angevin Empire meant the king began to look elsewhere. After a period of negotiation a mission led by Richard's mother, Eleanor of Aquitaine, brought Berengaria of Navarre (in northern Spain) to the island of Sicily as the king's intended bride. The existing engagement to the French princess was broken off with Richard's court making the savage and destructive claim that Alice had slept with his father, Henry II. Such inflammatory actions were hardly likely to encourage any sense of co-operation between the two crusading monarchs. As Gillingham has noted 'this was the moment when their quarrels turned into bitter hostility' (Gillingham, 1999, p. 143).

In April 1191 the crusaders set out from Sicily, but as they passed Cyprus a storm blew up and scattered the fleet. Some of the boats were driven ashore where their occupants were captured and held by the island's ruler Isaac Komnenos, a renegade member of the Byzantine ruling house and an ally of Saladin. Isaac maltreated his prisoners; Richard wrote that, 'not unnaturally we were spurred to revenge', and he attacked the island and captured Limassol. On 12 May he married Berengaria and then, with Isaac still showing signs of hostility, he decided to take all of Cyprus. The king's campaign was swift and effective and by the end of May Isaac was forced to submit. Richard had no qualms about taking the lands of a fellow-Christian – Isaac was, after all, in alliance with Saladin – and by the outright conquest of Cyprus he signalled his strength and determination of purpose. In the long term his actions were of considerable importance both for the Latin East and for future crusades because Cyprus became a springboard for subsequent expeditions and a place of wealth and safety for the Latins of the Eastern Mediterranean. For Richard it was another source of money. He imposed a 50 per cent levy on all possessions and when an attempt to set up a Greek government under Angevin guidance failed, he sold the island to the Templars for 100,000 bezants. While Richard was in Cyprus he was visited by King Guy, himself a Poitevin (Richard's first title was duke of Poitou), who wanted help against his rival Conrad of Montferrat. Guy's appeal was welcomed and he swore homage to Richard, while Conrad had already secured the support of his kinsman, Philip; thus the deep political divisions of the Levant neatly mirrored those of western Europe.

THE CONCLUSION OF THE SIEGE OF ACRE

Richard arrived at the siege of Acre on 8 June 1191 where he received a rapturous welcome from the Franks. On the Muslim side, Saladin's *qadi* (the judge of the army) Beha ad-Din observed 'the news of his coming had a dread and frightening effect on the hearts of the Muslims' (Beha ad-Din, tr. Richards, 2001: 150). Philip's presence had made a positive impact and he secured some progress in the reduction of the city walls, but Richard's wealth, his numerous siege-engines and his personal vigour made a far more powerful impression. A month of intense bombardment, mining and attack and counter-attack took their toll on the desperate defenders. Saladin could not break the Christians' blockade and Acre was doomed. On 12 July it surrendered; the defenders bought their lives for a ransom of 2,000 gold dinars and the promise of the return of 1,500 Frankish prisoners and the True Cross. The Christians entered the city in triumph, although their success was marred by an incident involving Duke Leopold of Austria, who tried to fly his banner from the citadel. Although Leopold had been at the siege far longer than Richard and Philip, as a duke he was of lower standing, thus for him to display his banner alongside those of kings could not be tolerated. Richard's men tore down the banner and a furious Leopold left for home, nursing a deep grievance against the Angevin – a grudge he later redressed by holding Richard prisoner on his journey back to England.

With the siege of Acre concluded it was necessary to resolve who should rule Jerusalem. On 28 July 1191 Richard and Philip decided that Guy would remain king during his lifetime and, when he died, Conrad would succeed him; royal revenues would be divided evenly between the two men. On the surface this seemed an equitable settlement, but Conrad was dissatisfied and continued to press his case, often refusing to work with Richard and engaging in his own negotiations with Saladin. He was supported by Duke Henry of Burgundy, who took command of the French army after Philip had left for home on 3 August 1191. Philip suffered serious ill-health during the crusade and he needed to intervene in an important political dispute concerning the county of Flanders. His swift departure did little for his reputation, but his presence back in the West would exert a profound influence over the rest of the crusade.

In the meantime Richard had decided to march south to Jaffa. First, he had to deal with the Muslim captives taken at Acre. Possibly because the terms of the surrender had been agreed between the crusaders and the city's defenders, rather than with Saladin himself, the emir was slow to fulfil the deal and failed to pay the first ransom instalment. Unable to tolerate any delay Richard had the 3,000 Muslim prisoners marched out and massacred by his men. The brutality of this action shocked his enemy and has been bitterly criticised by many writers. His butchery contrasted starkly with Saladin's generous treatment of the inhabitants of Jerusalem in 1187, although it should be remembered that the Muslim leader had enthusiastically executed the knights of the military orders after Hattin. In reality, however callous his actions seemed, Richard had little choice. The prisoners needed to be fed and guarded; he could not simply release them or they would fight him again; and if, as many suspected, Saladin's tardiness was merely a delaying tactic to break the momentum of the Christian success at Acre and to allow him to organize his troops to the south, it was an issue that had to be dealt with. Pitiless as it was, Richard had to sustain the momentum of the crusaders' victory at Acre and he set out for Jaffa (a distance of about 120 kilometres) on 22 August 1191.

THE BATTLE OF ARSUF

The march required strict discipline in conditions of intense heat and relentless enemy bombardment. The crusader army marched in close formation with the Templars in the vanguard, Richard's own forces, those of the kingdom of Jerusalem and the French in the middle, and the Hospitallers at the rear. Outside the knights moved one half of the infantry and archers, while the others travelled with the baggage train that was between the knights and the shore. The fleet sailed alongside the army to keep it supplied – a remarkable feat of seamanship because the prevailing winds in the south-eastern Mediterranean run from south to north which meant the ships had to tack into the wind while keeping in reasonably close contact with the land force. Beha ad-Din witnessed the march and he was impressed at the Franks' fortitude: 'the enemy army was already in formation with the infantry surrounding it like a wall, wearing solid iron corselets and full-length well-made chain mail so that arrows were falling on them with no effect. They were shooting with crossbows and wounding the Muslims' horses, cavalry and infantry. I saw various individuals amongst the Franks with ten arrows fixed in their backs pressing on in this fashion quite unconcerned . . . their banner also proceeded in their midst on wheels like a huge beacon' (Beha ad-Din, tr. Richards, 2001, p. 170).

Saladin's army made endless attempts to provoke the crusaders into battle through their tactics of turn and feint and rained down a constant barrage of arrows and missiles on the Christians, but the crusaders continued to make progress. Saladin realised that he needed to risk a battle and so, on 7 September 1191, on the plains of Arsuf, he chose to fight. His trumpeters and drummers set up a terrible clamour as time and again the Muslims charged through the dust at their opponents. The Franks stood firm, suffering heavy losses of horses, but little else. As the day wore on their patience began to fray and finally two Hospitallers charged the enemy, followed by their fellow brothers and the French contingent. At this moment Richard's skill as a general was revealed. While he had expressly forbidden his men to break ranks he immediately recognised what had happened and knew that the attack had to be supported or the Frankish force would become divided up and defeated. He ordered the full might of the Christian cavalry to charge – one of the rare occasions when this most potent weapon was actually unleashed on the Muslims – and it hammered into the enemy. The central division of the Muslim army buckled first and then the entire force was beaten back and Saladin retreated from the field. Richard displayed immense personal valour and cut down the enemy with enormous vigour; his committed and clever leadership had dealt a second terrible blow to Saladin's prestige. The sultan had lost relatively few men, but after his failure at the siege of Acre to be driven from the field of battle demonstrated the strength of his opponents and meant he would need to hold his forces together for a long campaign to see the back of the crusaders.

THE MARCH ON JERUSALEM

Richard reached Jaffa on 10 September where he decided to pause, rest and refortify the town. The king would have preferred to march south and take Ascalon because it was the link between Syria and Egypt, but Saladin, fully aware of its importance, had just razed it to the ground. The king's interest in Ascalon reveals his appreciation of wider strategy and of the role of Egypt within this picture. In October 1191 Richard wrote to the Genoese and asked them to support a campaign in Egypt, planned for the summer of 1192, in return for the award of substantial commercial privileges in this highly desirable location. The major crusades of the thirteenth century would try to secure Jerusalem through the capture of Egypt and Richard believed that by appropriating the country's wealth he would deal Saladin a fatal blow. Unfortunately the bulk of the army did not share this long-term perspective because most of the crusaders had joined the expedition with the express purpose of capturing the holy city and their determination to accomplish this meant that Richard had to agree to march on Jerusalem first.

In parallel to these strategic considerations there ran a complex web of diplomacy. Both sides were aware of the toll that the conflict exerted on one another and each argued their case for the custody of Jerusalem. For Richard, 'Jerusalem is an object of worship that we [the Christians] could not give up if there were only one of us left'. For Saladin, 'Jerusalem is even more sacred for us than it is to you, for it is the place from which our Prophet came on his Night Journey . . . [and anyway] as for the land, it is also ours originally' (Beha ad-Din, tr. Richards, 2001: 186). Neither camp was likely to give any ground, although the internal tensions on each side gave some room for manoeuvre. The division between Richard and Conrad gave the Muslims an opening to exploit and rumours of a rift between Saladin and his brother, al-Adil (known as Saphadin to the Franks), may have led to the improbable suggestion that the latter should marry Richard's sister, Joan. The princess was deeply unamused by this (she had not been consulted in advance) and declined to marry 'an infidel'.

The march on Jerusalem began in late October. It was only 80 kilometres or so from Jaffa to the holy city yet by mid-January 1192 the crusaders were still 19 kilometres short of their target. In part this can be explained by the winter rains, in part by Richard's caution. Far from the reckless hero so often depicted in the history books, he was, in reality, a calculating strategist who left as little as possible to chance. He made sure that the castles along the road were refortified and that his supply lines were as secure as possible. But the closer the army got to Jerusalem, the more the realisation spread, as Richard had long been aware, that it would be almost impossible to hold the city once it was captured (see Document 22). After completing their vows the crusaders would, quite naturally, return home. Who, then, would defend Jerusalem? The resources of the settlers were simply insufficient. The military orders and the nobles of the Latin East emphasised the need to consolidate the coast, rather than over-extending the fragile Frankish settlements.

It is legitimate to consider why this could not have been foreseen from the start; at its most extreme, one could almost question the entire strategy of the crusade and to ask if such a point had not been thought through. One expla-nation may lie with the fate of the German crusaders. If Frederick Barbarossa (or indeed Frederick of Swabia) had managed to bring this army down to Acre it may well have weakened Saladin considerably, with the arrival of Richard and Philip completing the Christian victory. If the Muslims were defeated or brought to the negotiating table in a position of weakness then the security of Jerusalem could have been better assured. This is, however, only a hypothesis; the question itself is not discussed by the sources in such terms.

In mid-January it was decided to turn back; morale in the crusader army plummeted – the masses felt let down by their leaders and many returned to the variety of secular pleasures on offer in the city of Acre: Richard refortified Ascalon before heading north to try to settle his differences with Conrad. The need to resolve the kingship was made particularly urgent by the news that Philip menaced Normandy and Richard's brother, John, fomented discontent in England. Such threats had been on the cards ever since Philip left the Levant and they reduced Richard's options considerably. Meanwhile, Guy's position was growing weaker because the majority of the Jerusalemite nobil-ity supported Conrad; pragmatic as ever, Richard recognised this and called a council to debate the matter. They unanimously decided that Conrad should be crowned king while Guy should be given the rich consolation prize of Cyprus. The Templars had proven brutal and unpopular rulers and still owed Richard part of the purchase cost so they were easily persuaded to part with the island. Conrad was never to become king, however. On 28 April 1192 he was sensationally murdered on the streets of Tyre by two Assassins dressed as monks. Who had commissioned such an act? Was it the marquis's longstanding enemy, Richard? Was it Saladin? Or had the Assassins themselves borne a grudge against him? The truth will never be known, but the finger of blame – often to the convenience of his political enemies – pointed strongly at Richard. The fact that he had to travel back through Europe in disguise suggests that, whatever his complicity in the matter, he needed to take measures to deal with such accusations and the ill-will generated by these rumours.

A new king of Jerusalem was required too – and yet another husband for Isabella. Within a week of Conrad's death she married spouse number three, Count Henry of Champagne. Here, at last, was a candidate welcomed by all sides because Henry was a nephew of both Richard and Philip and had already spent two years in the Levant. He came with an illustrious crusading pedigree and his family had been specifically approached for help by the settlers during the 1160s. From Richard's perspective, Henry's accession meant that the forces of Jerusalem were now at his disposal and he could go on the offensive again.

THE SECOND MARCH ON JERUSALEM AND THE BATTLE OF JAFFA

The crusaders captured Darum, south of Ascalon, on 22 May 1192, but a week later came more bad tidings from the West with the news that Philip and John were conspiring together. Richard had to balance his commitment to the crusade against his responsibilities as ruler of the Angevin empire. The army decided to march on Jerusalem again and pressure was put upon Richard to fulfil his duty as leader, thus with a heavy heart he agreed to stay in the Levant until the following spring. The crusaders made rapid progress and within five days they were at Beit Nuba again. A contemporary writer reported that Richard laid eyes on the holy city, probably from the hill of Montjoie, yet the king and the nobles of the Latin East knew the folly of an attack on Jerusalem. It is true that the Muslims were terrified of his approach yet the same strategic considerations applied as in 1191: who would hold the vulnerable inland city once the crusaders had gone home? Richard tried hard to persuade the army of the wisdom of an invasion of Egypt, but the French contingent would not co-operate. It was stalemate and the Christians had no option but to withdraw to the coast. Relieved of the pressure on Jerusalem, for the first time in many months, Saladin took the initiative. He launched a lightning attack on Jaffa and soon seized the town, leaving a small Frankish garrison defending the citadel. Muslim forces prevented King Henry's army from marching overland to the city, but Richard chose to sail from Acre. When he arrived at Jaffa on 1 August the Christians were on the verge of surrender, but Richard waded ashore and led a devastating assault on the enemy. All were in awe of his ferocity. The author of the *Itinerarium* wrote:

> With no armour on his legs he threw himself into the sea first . . . and forced his way powerfully on to dry land. The Turks obstinately opposed them on the shore. . . . The outstanding king shot them down indiscriminately with a crossbow he was carrying in his hand, and his elite companions pursued the Turks as they fled across the beach, cutting them down. At the sight of the king, they had no more spirit in them; they dare not approach him.
>
> (*Chronicle of the Third Crusade*, tr. Nicholson, 1997: 355)

More pragmatically, Richard had prevented the Muslims from striking a serious blow against the Christians' recovery of the coast. Saladin tried to seize Ascalon too, but once again the king's military prowess won the day. With just ten mounted knights he charged the enemy and scattered the emir's forces:

> The king was a giant in battle and everywhere in the field, now here, now there, wherever the attacks of the Turks raged most fiercely. On that day his sword shone like lightning and many of the Turks felt its edge. Some were cloven in two from their helmet to their teeth; others lost their heads, arms and other limbs, lopped off at a single blow. He mowed down men as reapers mow down corn with their sickles. Whoever felt one of his blows had no need of a second. He was an Achilles, an Alexander, a Roland.
>
> (Gillingham, 1989: 215)

TRUCE

By this point the two sides had fought each other to a standstill. Both leaders were suffering from ill-health, their resources were dangerously low and they needed to settle political problems of their own. Richard, in particular, had to attend to domestic matters and on 2 September a three-year truce was signed. The Christians kept the coastline from Jaffa to Tyre, but they had to hand over Ascalon. Christian pilgrims were permitted to enter Jerusalem, although Richard refused to submit to such an indignity in person and did not visit the holy city. On 9 October 1192 the king set sail from Acre, but it was plain that he planned to return. The *Itinerarium* claimed that he said, 'O Holy Land I commend you to God. In his loving grace may He grant me such length of life that I may bring you help as He wills. I certainly hope some time in the future to bring you the aid that I intend' (*Chronicle of the Third*

Crusade, tr. Nicholson, 1997: 382). Richard never managed to crusade again, although, by a great irony, had he remained in the Holy Land for just a few months longer the balance of power would have been transformed because, worn out by decades of warfare, Saladin died on 4 March 1193.

CONCLUSION TO THE THIRD CRUSADE

How should we judge the Third Crusade? While it failed to achieve its ultimate aim of retaking Jerusalem, it did succeed in providing the Christians with a reasonably firm hold of much of the coastline and created a springboard for future crusades. Compared to the situation in the autumn of 1187, when only Conrad of Montferrat's arrival saved Tyre, the position was much improved. Conrad's leadership, then Guy's determination to blockade Acre, and finally, the energy and strength of Richard enabled the Franks to mount some sort of recovery.

Saladin had swept all before him after Hattin, but the defeats at Acre, Arsuf and Jaffa cumulatively damaged his reputation and morale in the Muslim Near East. From Saladin's perspective, the crusade (which was an inevitability once Jerusalem was in Muslim hands) had not recaptured Jerusalem and had gone home, which left him free, once the truce expired, to make another assault on the settlers. The sultan undoubtedly impressed the westerners with his chivalric behaviour and determination, and contemporary accounts of the crusade spoke very highly of him. Such was Saladin's reputation that he became a central figure in a popular thirteenth-century manual of chivalry – a real irony: Christian knighthood using one of Islam's finest warriors as an exemplar of chivalric behaviour. Perhaps his greatest success during the crusade was to hold together such a broad coalition of Muslim forces in the face of a series of military setbacks and a rising tide of dissent. This bears testimony to his personal charisma and high political skills, and his death caused a serious rift in the Muslim Near East. It is difficult to make an overall assessment of Saladin's career. Obviously he captured Jerusalem and, in this sense, he had achieved his primary goal. But his military record was patchy and sometimes – particularly in his flagrant disregard of Nur ad-Din's requests for help in the early 1170s – his motives can seem self-centred. There is no doubt that he was a pious man who fought hard to win the *jihad*, regardless of whether this meant engaging in conflict with his fellow-Muslims on the way. To him, this did not necessarily form a contradiction. In seeking to recover Jerusalem for Islam his cause was just and those who opposed him were neglecting their duty. Perhaps it is best to see him as a man of deep religious convictions who used the political and spiritual weapons at his disposal to draw his fellow-Muslims together in his attempt to expel the Christians from the Levant. The longevity of his fame certainly bears witness to a great career.

Saladin was said to have thought Richard too reckless in battle – 'he frequently hurls himself into danger imprudently' – but the Muslims correctly recognised there was far more to the king than a bold warrior. Ibn al-Athir described him as shrewd and patient, and claimed that he was 'the outstanding man of his time for bravery, cunning, steadfastness and endurance. In him the Muslims were tried by an unparalleled disaster' (Ibn al-Athir, tr. Richards, 2007: 387). Beha ad-Din believed that he possessed judgement, experience, audacity and astuteness and wrote: 'Just look at this guile in eliciting what one wants by soft words at one moment and by harsh ones at the next! We pray to God to keep the Muslims safe from his evil, for they had never been tried by anyone more devious or more bold' (Beha ad-Din, tr. Richards, 2001: 216). Muslim writers rarely complimented their enemies in such terms, but their admiration and fear of Richard was self-evident. The king used the full range of instruments available to him: the Angevin government machine, diplomacy and warfare. For every heroic deed at Jaffa can be matched by his caution on the march to Jerusalem, and for all his brilliant generalship at Arsuf and Ascalon it is possible to find the seeds of success being planted in his meticulous gathering of supplies in England and his ruthless acquisition of money on Sicily and Cyprus.

Contrary to popular legend the two leaders never met, but the respect with which each was viewed is neatly encapsulated in a comment by the bishop of Salisbury at the end of the crusade. He met Saladin as he visited Jerusalem under the terms of the 1192 truce and, as they discussed Richard's character, the bishop said to the emir: 'Putting your sins aside, if anyone, in my opinion, could combine your virtues with those of King Richard, and share them out between you so that both of you were furnished with the abilities of both, two such princes would not be found in the whole world' (*Chronicle of the Third Crusade*, tr. Nicholson, 1997: 378).

THE GERMAN CRUSADE OF 1197

As we saw earlier, Richard's suspected involvement in the murder of Conrad of Montferrat meant that he had to travel home in disguise, but as the king moved through Austria he was recognised and captured by Duke Leopold in December 1192. He was later handed over to Emperor Henry VI of Germany (1190–97) and the people of Richard's lands were required to pay an enormous ransom (150,000 marks) to free him (February 1194). As part of the terms of his release the king was forced to renounce his overlordship of Cyprus, which was transferred to Emperor Henry, thereby giving the

Germans a foothold in the Eastern Mediterranean. Henry was interested in mounting a crusade, probably in part to fulfil the vows of his father Frederick Barbarossa. He had a further connection with the Mediterranean region through his marriage to Constance, heiress to the throne of Sicily, in December 1194. Henry began to gather his forces in 1196; he secured support from the papacy and also compelled the Byzantines to provide some financial backing for the expedition. A group of German crusaders sailed from the North Sea and, like their predecessors in the 1147 campaign, fought in Portugal *en route* to the Holy Land. The full German army assembled at Bari in southern Italy in the summer of 1197 and included 4,000 knights and 12,000 other soldiers – an impressive force. The German chancellor stopped in Cyprus and offered Aimery of Lusignan a royal crown to be held from the Empire of Lusignan (Guyl had died in 1194). Aimery agreed, pleased to acquire such a strong patron, particularly given his fear of Byzantine attacks on the island. The German crusaders reached the Holy Land in late autumn 1197 and in September they laid siege to, and captured, Beirut, securing another foothold on the coast and helping to re-establish Frankish control of the sea.

On 10 September King Henry of Jerusalem died when his dwarfish entertainer fell out of a window and pulled the king along with him. Queen Isabella now anticipated husband number four (to follow Humphrey of Toron, Conrad of Montferrat, and Henry), and she married king Aimery of Cyprus to bring these two Frankish possessions into a much closer relationship. The Germans besieged the town of Toron, but in the early winter they received news of Emperor Henry's death (28 September 1197). Concerned at the political impact of such an event in their homeland, they soon decided to return to the West and the crusade ended. In any case, the Muslim world was still deeply divided between Saif ad-Din (Saladin's brother) and the emir's sons. A truce of five years and eight months was agreed.

While the French had represented the principal external influence on the Latin East during the twelfth century, largely because of the origins of so many of the First Crusaders and subsequent settlers, Henry VI's overlordship of Cyprus and the foundation of a new military order (St Mary of the Germans – later known as the Teutonic Knights) laid the seeds for much greater imperial involvement in the Levant – something that would develop significantly during the thirteenth century, especially during the reign of Emperor Frederick II (1220–50).

13

The Fourth Crusade and the sack of Constantinople, 1202–4

On 8 January 1198, at 38 years of age Lothario dei Conti di Segni was elected Pope Innocent III. His eighteen-year pontificate (1198–1216) saw crusading reach unprecedented levels of intensity and diversity with campaigns directed at Cathar heretics in southern France (the Albigensian Crusade, 1209–18), against political opponents of the papacy in southern Italy and as we will see, more by accident than design, against the Christian Byzantine Empire, an event that culminated in the disastrous sack of Constantinople by the Fourth Crusade in 1204. Innocent encouraged further crusading ventures in north-eastern Europe and the continuation of the reconquest of Spain. Contemporaries were so caught up in their enthusiasm for holy war that his pontificate also saw the near-legendary Children's Crusade (1212). Inspired by visionary experiences, groups of young people near Chartres and Cologne became convinced that they could recover Jerusalem. They marched through France and Germany to the port of Genoa, only to be refused passage to the East because they had no money or equipment. While some were sold into slavery most returned home to be ridiculed for their foolishness. In no sense was this a 'proper' crusade – it was certainly not endorsed by the papacy – but the naïve hopes of these young people demonstrated popular enthusiasm to liberate the holy city and reflected the passion for crusading Innocent had generated. Taken together, these campaigns show just how flexible and adaptable a concept crusading had become by the early thirteenth century.

THE ORIGINS OF THE FOURTH CRUSADE, 1198–1201

At the close of the twelfth century Christianity seemed to be on the back foot. Neither the Third Crusade nor the German Crusade of 1196–97 had managed to reclaim Jerusalem while the Christian kings of Spain had been thrashed at the Battle of Alarcos (1195) in central-southern Iberia. In the aftermath of this latter campaign, however, one interesting development took place showing how the scope of crusading continued to widen. Aside from fighting the Muslims the Spanish monarchs had also been in conflict with one another; such was the bitterness of this struggle that King Alfonso IX of León made an alliance with the Muslim Almohads. In consequence, Pope Celestine III (1191–98) excommunicated Alfonso and declared that those who fought the king would have 'the same remission of sins as we give to those who take up arms against the Saracens' (Edbury, 2008: 135). In other words, Celestine had granted crusading indulgences to those who opposed a Christian ruler allied with Muslims. As far back as the conflict between King Roger II of Sicily (1130–54) and Pope Innocent II (1130–43) a decree at the Council of Pisa (1135) had offered the latter's supporters the same remission of sins as that granted by Pope Urban at the Council of Clermont for those who had set out to Jerusalem; in other words a crusade indulgence. In a similar vein, during the early years of Pope Innocent III's pontificate a crusade was briefly and ineffectually preached in 1199 against Markward of Anweiler, a German adventurer in southern Italy. In trying to establish his power there Markward formed an alliance with Muslim colonies in Sicily which threatened the position of the papacy and that of the boy-king Frederick II for whom Innocent acted as regent. Such actions were also a potential hindrance to the prospect of bringing relief to the Holy Land; thus the pope promised a full crusade indulgence to those Sicilians who resisted the German and his Muslim allies. Such episodes show the idea of holy war against other Christians was not entirely unknown, although events at Constantinople were of a markedly different tenor and scale.

For all the variety of crusading at this time it was the desire to recapture the Holy Land that dominated Innocent III's thinking. He believed passionately that God had called the crusades and that it was the duty of all Christians, not just the warrior classes, to support them. In August 1198 Innocent issued a powerful new crusade appeal, *Post miserabile* (Document 23 i). It vividly depicted the loss of the holy places and sharply criticised the self-centred conflicts between the rulers of England, France and Germany. He urged the people of the West to trust in God, to remember the sacrifice that Christ had made for humankind and to think of the eternal treasures that their service would merit. Innocent set out practical measures too, asking churchmen to provide men or money to the enterprise, and promising that people who could not go on crusade in person, but who paid (or contributed as best they could) for suitable warriors to go in their place would receive remission of their sins too.

This was not the ideal moment to make such an appeal. The death of Richard the Lionheart in April 1199 and tensions over Philip Augustus's marital status prevented two major figures from taking the cross; recent set-backs in Spain and a bitterly disputed succession to the imperial throne of Germany barred other possible participants. But in November 1199 the elite knighthood of northern France gathered to hear the crusade preached at a tournament at Écry-sur-Aisne in the county of Champagne. Given that the Church condemned tournaments as events that incited the sins of pride, envy and murder this might seem curious. But for fighting men, tournaments were a central part of their lives and the best possible training for battle. To charge in teams of up to 200 knights in an arena that might extend across several miles, was the closest possible replica of real warfare. Tournaments were also social events and in the evenings the nobles gathered to celebrate and hear stories and songs, including epics of the heroes of the First Crusade such as the *Chanson d'Antioche*. It is no coincidence that two of the greatest crusading dynasties of the age, the counts of Flanders and Champagne, ruled over the heartlands of the tournament circuit, and their nobles were passion-ate participants in both holy war and martial competition.

On hearing the crusade appeal at Écry, Count Thibaut of Champagne and Count Louis of Blois, two men of admirable crusading lineages, took the cross. Thibaut's father, Henry of Champagne, had ruled Jerusalem between 1192 and 1197 while Louis took part in the Third Crusade. Other important nobles followed, such as Geoffrey of Villehardouin (see 'Who's Who'), a senior figure on the expedition and the author of a memoir of his experiences (Geoffrey of Villehardouin, tr. Smith, 2008). As we have seen before, most crusade texts were written in Latin by clergymen but the rising levels of lay literacy meant that vernacular accounts of the sort produced by Villehardouin became more common. Simon de Montfort, a noble from the Ile de France, was another to join the crusade at Écry and within a couple of months Count Baldwin of Flanders (see 'Who's Who') also committed himself to the expedition. Thus the nucleus of the Fourth Crusade came from the nobility of northern France.

In the spring of 1200 the leaders met at Soissons where they made a crucial – and ultimately fateful – decision. They chose to employ a Venetian fleet to sail to the Levant and in March 1201 a group of envoys – including Villehardouin – arrived in Venice to arrange the terms of passage. There they met Doge Enrico Dandolo (see 'Who's Who'), a remarkable man over 90 years of age and who had been blind for more than twenty years (Madden, 2003). The Venetians set out their terms to transport the crusaders to the East, covering the cost of horses, squires, knights and footsergeants, as well as promising to take part themselves (see Document 23 ii).

This represented a huge commitment on the part of Venice. To fulfil these conditions would require them to suspend their entire commercial opera-tions for a year and for the crusaders to become, effectively, their exclusive customers. Yet the deal also signals their wish to advance the cause of Christendom and we can observe the combination of civic pride and commercial aspiration, coupled with religiosity, evident with the Genoese in the early twelfth century. Thus far, the Venetians' most notable engagement in the Latin East had been the capture of Tyre in 1124, an event that involved Dandolo's father, grandfather and uncle. In 1203–4 the Venetians had fifty of their own battle galleys, headed by the vermilion-coloured vessel of the doge, along with around sixty-seventy large sailing boats that each carried up to 600 passengers and 100 crew. About 30,000 Venetians would be required to man the whole fleet – perhaps half the adult population and another demonstration of the scale of the city's commitment. The decision to take 4,500 horses necessitated the construction of dozens of special galleys, each equipped with slings to carry the animals, as well as low-level doors that, on landing, opened to allow mounted knights to charge directly into battle.

In the longer-term, the deal between the envoys and the Venetians came to exert an unrelenting influence on both the direction and the ultimate outcome of the Fourth Crusade, far beyond anything that could have been foreseen. The costs were comparable to those the Genoese had charged King Philip during the Third Crusade, but it was the sheer scale of the plan that created a devastating fault-line that drew the expedition to its tragic conclusion. The numbers promised by the French envoys were massive – compare them to the 12–15,000 men led by Frederick Barbarossa in 1189–90 – yet no crowned head had signed up for the new enterprise. The money required to pay the Venetians amounted to twice the annual income of the English or French crowns. Villehardouin and his colleagues must have been confident in the enthusiasm of people in northern France or else they were deeply (almost criminally) over-optimistic.

One further dimension to the campaign was a secret agreement between the leadership and the doge for the crusade to start by attacking Egypt, rather than the Holy Land; the intention was to use the former as a staging post *en route* to Jerusalem. Sound strategy and considerable financial advantages lay behind such a plan. As we saw earlier, King Amalric of Jerusalem (in the 1160s), the Sicilians (in 1174) and Richard the Lionheart had all wanted to invade the Nile. The massive resources of Egypt offered unparalleled opportunities to the Christian military while control of the coastline would assure security at sea. If Egypt came under Frankish power then the Muslim Near East – which had fragmented since Saladin's death in 1193 – would certainly struggle to fight the Christians off. The existence of a truce between the kingdom of Jerusalem and Muslim Syria provided another reason to begin the campaign on the Nile because this arrangement excluded Egypt.

From a Venetian perspective, the opportunity to become the pre-eminent trading city in Alexandria was an enormous attraction. The city was

17. Twelfth century Byzantine Emperor in full regalia

comfortably the greatest trading centre in the Mediterranean yet by this point Venetian presence lagged behind that of their Pisan and Genoese rivals. Should the crusade succeed, then it would bring huge commercial benefits to Venice and, if it led to the recovery of Jerusalem itself, the whole enterprise would form an astounding legacy to Dandolo's time as doge.

The envoys made a down-payment for the Venetians to begin work on the fleet and then headed back to France. Before they reached home, however, the crusade was dealt a heavy blow because on 24 May 1201 the charismatic young Thibaud of Champagne had died. He would have been an inspirational and unifying figure and his involvement drew others to take the cross; equally, his death may have actively deterred people from joining up. Perhaps to broaden the crusade's appeal the leaders approached Boniface, marquis of Montferrat, to replace Thibaut. We have already met Boniface's brothers: namely, William Longsword, briefly the husband of Sibylla of Jerusalem and father of Baldwin V; and Conrad, the man who saved Tyre in 1188 and would have ruled Jerusalem but for his death at the hands of the Assassins in 1192.

For the remainder of 1201 and into early 1202 preaching and preparations for the crusade gathered pace. The most intriguing – and potentially sinister – development took place at Christmas 1201 at the court of Philip of Swabia, king of Germany. There Boniface met the king's brother-in-law, Prince Alexios of Byzantium (see 'Who's Who'), a young man who came to play a central role in subsequent events. This meeting has been the subject of considerable debate over the years: some have used it to posit a hypothetical plot between the prince and Boniface, a deal that eventually led to the sack of Constantinople. Prince Alexios was in the West because, a few years earlier (1195), the prince's father, Emperor Isaac Angelos, had been deposed by his (Isaac's) brother who now ruled Byzantium as Emperor Alexios III (1195–1203). In accordance with custom, Isaac had been blinded and along with Prince Alexios, imprisoned. The young man had escaped and now sought help to restore him and his father to their rightful position. While his pleas had some emotional leverage, the fact that the Angeloi dynasty had savagely removed the Komnenos family from the imperial throne in the mid-1180s and that Isaac had earlier allied with Saladin counted against them. In any case, events on the crusade developed in such an unexpected fashion and, in several instances, so far beyond the prince's possible control, the idea of a grand plan hatched at Hagenau is not plausible. Prince Alexios also visited Innocent, but the pope showed little enthusiasm for his case.

THE CRUSADERS GATHER IN VENICE, 1202

From the late spring of 1202 onwards the northern French crusaders began to assemble in Venice where their envoys' terrible miscalculation soon became clear. By August, only about 12,000 of the required 33,500 men had turned up. The leadership pooled their resources but still fell 34,000 silver marks short of the 85,000 owed. This was a fiendishly difficult position: to default on their contractual obligations would be a humiliation for the crusaders and should they return home without even having set out the shame would be unthinkable. Dandolo, meanwhile, had staked both his own reputation and his city's finances on this enterprise.

By now it was September and no longer prudent to set sail for Egypt. By way of getting the crusade underway and to generate some income, Dandolo proposed an assault on the city of Zara (now Zadar in Croatia), 265 kilometres to the south-east. The Zarans were former Venetian subjects but had recently broken free and this was an opportunity for Dandolo to reassert his authority. The scheme was not without problems, however: the Zarans were Christians and their overlord, King Bela III of Hungary, had taken the cross. In theory, therefore, his lands were under Church protection and could not be attacked – especially by another crusading force. The leadership was well aware how controversial such a plan was, yet so great was the need to do something positive that they chose not to broadcast their intentions and simply gave the order to depart from Venice.

THE SIEGE OF ZARA AND THE ENVOYS OF PRINCE ALEXIOS

In October 1202 the Fourth Crusade set sail from Venice. Flying the winged-lion banner of St Mark, Doge Dandolo's vermillion-coloured vessel headed the fleet of almost 200 ships. The French hung brightly painted shields from the sides of their boats and all the crusaders sang hymns to invoke divine blessing for their campaign. Robert of Clari, another layman to record his experiences on the Fourth Crusade (see 'Who's Who') described the spectacle as 'the finest thing to see that has ever been since the beginning of the world' (Robert of Clari, trans. McNeal, 1936: 42).

By this time, however, Pope Innocent knew of the crusaders' aim and he ordered his legate, Peter of Capuano, to forbid the assault on Zara and to threaten them with excommunication if they disobeyed. This was a major weapon in the spiritual armoury of the Church – to mandate complete withdrawal from the community of Christians, including all church services and the sacraments, would lead to certain damnation. But Peter was with the crusading army and he fully appreciated their dilemma. Given the need for the crusade to get started he chose not to prevent the attack. Within the ranks of the crusaders themselves there were deep divisions. Simon de Montfort led a group bitterly opposed to the diversion to Zara: 'I have not come here to destroy Christians', was his blunt observation, but his views were ignored and on 13 November 1202 the siege of Zara began. The crusaders' formidable siege technology, a combination of towers, catapults and mines, soon caused the Zarans to agree terms of surrender.

Innocent was livid: 'Behold, your gold has turned into base metal and your silver has almost completely rusted since, departing from the purity of your plan and turning aside from the path onto the impassable road . . . you should have hastened to the land flowing with milk and honey, you turned away, going astray in the direction of the desert' (Innocent III, tr. Andrea, 2000: 41–45). He excommunicated the crusaders for their sinful actions. In reality this episode reveals the limits of papal control over crusading because Innocent's own legate had ignored his orders. The practicalities of an ongoing military expedition relied upon consent, but the French crusaders' contractual failure, coupled with the Venetians' threat to withdraw their shipping, meant that the need to sustain the crusade in the first instance won the day.

Over the winter of 1202 envoys sent on behalf of Prince Alexios reached the crusaders as they camped outside Zara. Their pitch was designed to engage with the needs and interests of all involved (see Document 23 iii). This clever piece of diplomacy seemed to offer advantages to everyone. For Innocent there was a prospect of the submission of the Greek Orthodox Church, something that popes had long desired. The deal also enabled the crusade to continue – an obvious attraction to all concerned. The debt to the Venetians would be settled, the Christians' military resources dramatically enhanced and the idea of a garrison force in the Holy Land could help to solve the long-running manpower shortage of the Latin East. There was only one real problem: the need to restore Prince Alexios to the throne of Constantinople, an issue that could require the crusaders to fight their way into the city and install him by force.

Once again, the prospect of attacking a Christian city aroused enormous debate amongst the crusaders. The fact that Prince Alexios's father had been illicitly dispossessed of his throne was significant because, as the Byzantine envoys observed, the idea of regaining land that had been wrongfully taken was a central element of crusading that dated back to Urban II's appeal at Clermont. Yet many in the rank and file were deeply disquieted. Some felt that Dandolo's enthusiasm for the plan stemmed from financial motives and a desire to avenge the arrest and ill-treatment of Venetians in Constantinople in 1171. Yet by the early thirteenth century relations between the two powers were mended. Other than Simon de Montfort (who went on to the Holy Land), the other major northern French crusaders, such as Baldwin of Flanders and Villehardouin, wanted to accept the plan and it was duly agreed. From this moment onwards the crusade was heading for Constantinople.

In the meantime, Pope Innocent had released the French crusaders from their excommunication on condition they performed penance for their sins; the Venetians, however, meanwhile remained unapologetic and therefore outside the Church. Innocent demanded the crusaders behaved correctly in future, although his phrasing was potentially ambiguous. The men should: 'neither invade nor violate the lands of Christians in any manner, unless, perchance, they wickedly impede your journey or another just or necessary cause should, perhaps, arise, on account of which you would be empowered to act otherwise' (Innocent III, tr. Andrea, 2000: 48). Intentionally or not, the clause a 'just and necessary cause' provided a loophole for the crusaders to justify their future actions and for some – almost certainly in error – to infer papal support for their decisions.

18. The Land Walls of Constantinople

THE FIRST SIEGE OF CONSTANTINOPLE, 1203

Alexios joined the crusaders at Corfu and in late May they set sail for Constantinople. Villehardouin conveyed their first awe-struck impressions of the place that the Greeks called the 'queen of cities' (see Document 23 iv). Only now did they realise the immensity of the challenge that lay ahead of them should Prince Alexios be rejected by his people. The crusaders camped in the area of Scutari on what is now known as the Asian side of the city. In early July a group of boats paraded the prince before the sea walls of Constantinople: 'Behold your natural lord,' they called out (Geoffrey of Villehardouin, tr. Smith, 2008: 38). As the crusaders' boats bobbed offshore a few inhabitants shouted abuse at the youth, but more disconcertingly, most simply ignored him. The prince's assurances that he would be acclaimed by a grateful crowd, desperate to have respite from the cruel tyrant Alexios III, proved groundless. The emperor had exploited over a century of tension between Byzantines and crusaders to nurture the notion that the prince and his Western allies planned to enslave the Greeks and subjugate them to the pope. The fact that Prince Alexios had never governed Constantinople, as well as his youth and his recent lengthy absence, meant he lacked a natural constituency of support. The crusaders despondently turned back to their

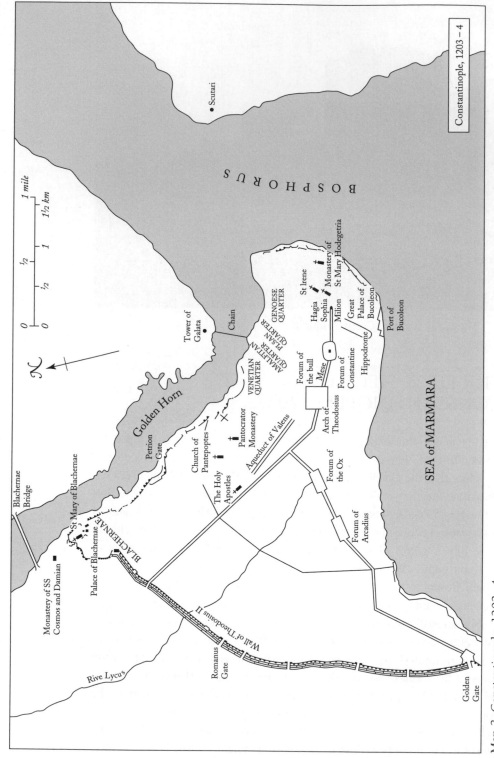

Map 3 Constantinople, 1203–4

camp and prepared to fight. For all the might of Constantinople itself, it is important to note that by the early thirteenth century the Byzantine Empire was a far cry from even the times of Manuel Komnenos three decades earlier. A startling statistic is that from 1101 to 1180 only a handful of troubles affected the political order, but between 1180 and 1204 there were fifty-eight rebellions and conspiracies, a clear degeneration of authority and strength.

Their assault began on the suburb of Galata on the northern bank of the Golden Horn. The army split into seven divisions based on regional identity, a move designed to foster the co-ordination and discipline seen on the tournament field and an element so crucial in the winning of battles. On the night of 3 July 1203 the crusaders prayed for victory as they steeled themselves to make the largest amphibious landing yet attempted by western forces in the medieval age. The fleet crossed the Bosphorus and as the boats neared the shore the crusaders' archers and crossbowmen set up a hail of covering fire. Once the ships reached the shallows the horse transports opened their doors and the mounted knights charged out. Curiously, although Emperor Alexios's troops were gathered to face the landing they retreated, missing a golden opportunity to confront the crusaders at this vulnerable moment.

The westerners soon captured the Galata Tower and then broke the huge chain that was slung across the Golden Horn to protect the harbour. Possession of the Golden Horn opened out the soft underbelly of Constantinople and after a swift rout of the moribund Byzantine fleet the Venetian ships moored just off the city walls to make clear the threat that Constantinople now faced.

The Venetians used scaling ladders on their ships to launch their next assault; the French chose to fight on land and established a fortified camp on the northern edge of the city. Alexios finally started to act and Greek raids caused the crusaders to run low on food. By mid-July they were down to only three weeks' supplies. In desperation, on 17 July, they began a twin-pronged attack. The Venetian ships bombarded the walls with arrows and stones but Doge Dandolo was infuriated by the lack of progress and commanded his galley to pull ahead. As the boat grounded Dandolo ordered himself carried ashore and, as he had anticipated, his men followed suit, desperate to avoid being shamed by a blind old man. The intensity of this thrust terrified the defenders and the Venetians gained a crucial first bridgehead. Emperor Alexios countered through a contingent of the formidable Varangian guard and although these Russian and Scandinavian mercenaries managed to halt the Venetians' momentum, the latter responded by starting a fire. Fanned by a strong westerly wind the flames quickly engulfed 120 acres of the eastern side of the city – a serious blow to the Greeks.

The sight of heavy black smoke billowing over his city prompted Alexios to take the initiative and he led out most of his army to confront the crusaders on the north-eastern edge of the city. The Byzantine forces must have out-numbered the crusaders by a large margin. The westerners (excluding the Venetians) were now only 500 knights, 500 other mounted men and around 2,000 footsoldiers: even the cooks and stable-lads donned pots and horse blankets for protection. The crusaders advanced in tight formation and Alexios, instead of choosing this moment to exploit his numerical superiority, withdrew behind the city walls. It is almost impossible to explain this tactical calamity; the popular stereotype of the effeminate and unwarlike Greek had been entirely fulfilled. The crusaders were certain that it was their martial vigour that had won the day. Hugh of St Pol proudly reported: 'When they saw that we were brave and steadfast and that we moved forward . . . in formation and that we could not be overrun or broken they rightly became terrified and confused. Retreating before us they dared not fight by day (Hugh of St Pol, tr. Andrea, 2000: 197).

This was a catastrophic blow to morale in the city. Niketas Choniates, a Byzantine eye-witness, wrote that Alexios 'returned in utter disgrace, having only made the enemy more haughty and insolent'. The crusaders had been within days of having to leave or to sue for peace because of lack of food. Choniates excoriated Alexios for his decision: 'it was as though he had laboured hard to make a miserable corpse of the city, to bring her to utter ruin in defiance of her destiny, and he hastened her along her destruction (Niketas Choniates, tr. Magoulias, 1984: 299).

On the night of 17 July the emperor fled and the following morning senior officials went to the sightless Isaac Angelos. Ignoring the custom that excluded the coronation of a blind man they offered him the throne in the hope that this would end the siege. News of overnight events in Constantinople were greeted with a huge cheer in the crusader camp: God had granted them an unlikely victory. Villehardouin led an embassy into the city where Isaac was horrified to discover the details of his son's deal with the crusaders. Reportedly he said: 'In truth, this agreement is a most burdensome one, and I do not see quite how it can be fulfilled. However, you have done both my son and myself such a service that if you had been granted the whole empire you would have well deserved it' (Geoffrey of Villehardouin, tr. Smith, 2008: 50). Villehardouin may have massaged the moral worth of Isaac's words, as well as presenting an accurate prophecy, but in sentiment at least, the first part of the phrase is likely to be accurate.

The crusaders camped across the Golden Horn in the Galata district. At first they received good supplies of food and in this positive atmosphere most chose to visit the churches of Constantinople and to see the many magnificent relic collections. A cynic might note that this also allowed them to assess the true measure of the Greeks' wealth.

What we would call today 'news management' was vital to the crusaders and they wanted to ensure that the people back home learned that their decision to go to Constantinople was of benefit to the Christian cause. They also stressed the immense advance in spiritual authority that this meant for the papacy: 'the Eastern Church (whose head is Constantinople), along with the emperor and his entire empire, reunited with its head, the Roman pontiff . . . acknowledges itself to be the daughter of the Roman Church' (Hugh of St Pol, tr. Andrea, 2000: 199–200). The reality of such a claim was, of course, rather less because no such formal submission had been made.

TENSIONS GROW BETWEEN THE CRUSADERS AND THE GREEKS

Prince Alexios thus became Emperor Alexios IV and to provide the vast sums of money that he had promised the crusaders he needed to melt down precious icons and relics, a practice bitterly resented by his own people. Choniates wrote: 'It was a sight to behold: the holy icons of Christ consigned to the flames after being hacked to pieces with axes and cast down, their adornments carelessly and unsparingly removed by force, and the revered and all-hallowed vessels seized from the churches with utter indifference and melted down and given over to the enemy troops as common silver and gold (Niketas Choniates, tr. Magoulias, 1984: 302).

By the late summer of 1203 it was too late to invade Egypt although that certainly remained the crusaders' intention. Instead they decided to help Alexios IV consolidate his authority in and around the city and to prepare for a departure in the spring of 1204. As the young emperor acknowledged, 'You should know then that the Greeks hate me on account of you. If you leave I will lose this land and they will put me to death' (Geoffrey of Villehardouin, tr. Smith, 2008: 52).

Relations between the Greeks and the remaining westerners deteriorated. A group of crusaders attacked a small mosque – probably built for Muslim traders during Isaac's earlier alliance with Saladin – but this soon turned into a broader struggle between the locals and the crusaders. The latter started a fire, a blaze that lasted for three days and ripped through large areas of wooden housing, turning more than 400 acres of the city into a smouldering wasteland. The Greeks were furious and all westerners living in Constantinople – including several thousand traders – had to flee to the crusaders' camp over the Golden Horn at Galata.

By mid-November the payments of money had stopped but the emperor knew the crusaders could not set sail for Egypt in the winter and that they relied on him for food. Tensions rose and both sides realised the need to talk. The crusaders reminded Alexios of his moral and financial duties but now added a threat: if he failed to comply, 'you should know that from this time forward they [the crusaders] will not regard you as their lord or friend. Instead they will recover what is owed to them by whatever means necessary . . . they have never acted deceitfully and it would be against the custom of their country to do so' (Geoffrey of Villehardouin, tr. Smith, 2008: 57). This warning was received with fury and the envoys barely escaped the palace alive. Yet Alexios IV was cornered – he could not deny the oath, nor could he favour the westerners.

Dandolo made a final attempt to find a peaceful solution. He urged the emperor to remember what the crusaders had done for him but the young man was so trapped by his situation that he lashed out and insulted the doge. Dandolo's response was furious: 'Wretched boy! We dragged you out of the filth and into the filth we will cast you again. And I defy you, and I give you warning that I will do you all the harm in my power from this moment forwards' (Robert of Clari, tr. McNeal, 1936: 84). Thus, as Villehardouin tersely noted, 'and so the war began' (Geoffrey of Villehardouin, tr. Smith, 2008: 58).

On the night of 1 January 1204 the Byzantines made an impressively daring move. Taking advantage of a favourable wind they dispatched seventeen vessels filled with combustible materials towards the Venetian ships. If the Greek boats became tangled with those of the Italians' then the crusaders would be in serious trouble. The Venetians' seafaring brilliance prevailed as galleys rowed out to the burning boats, threw grappling irons onto them and dragged them out into the channel, a manoeuvre of immense skill and one that undoubtedly saved the crusade.

Events of this nature only increased the likelihood of a major confrontation. A Byzantine noble known as Mourtzouphlos (a nickname meaning 'mono-eyebrow') led resistance to the crusaders. Yet another emperor, a man named Nicholas Kannavos was elected on 27 January 1204, and a desperate Alexios IV appealed to the crusaders to enter the city and help him. This proved a move too far and that night, Mourtzouphlos imprisoned him; within hours the usurper was crowned emperor (with the formal title of Alexios V). Now there were four holders of the imperial title in Constantinople (Isaac Angelos, Alexios IV, Nicholas Kannavos and Alexios V Mourtzouphlos) – a ridiculous situation for one of Christendom's greatest institutions, and a sign of just how sickly the Byzantine Empire had become.

Mourtzouphlos acted quickly to eliminate Kannavos and blind Isaac: he also started to refortify the defences of Constantinople. Three unfortunate Venetians were captured and Mourtzouphlos commanded them to be suspended from hooks in front of the city walls before he personally set them on fire to show his contempt and hatred of the westerners.

Mourtzouphlos feared that the crusaders might use Alexios IV to unseat him and so on 8 February 1204 he strangled the young man; a grim end for an individual whose efforts to recover his personal inheritance provoked terrible consequences. To the crusaders, however, the murder of Alexios IV provided a powerful justification to remove his killer. Now, camped outside an implacably hostile city, thousands of miles from home, with almost no food, and in no condition to continue to the Holy Land, their options were very limited. They could give up and face intolerable shame and criticism while their justification for going to Constantinople in the first instance also became redundant. Through a combination of all these circumstances they decided to attack the city and to remove the murderous Mourtzouphlos and those who abetted him, thereby initiating a war of conquest. The clergy also argued that the Orthodox Church was in open schism, thus: 'we tell you that this battle is right and just. If you have the right intention of conquering this land and placing it in obedience to Rome, all those of you who die here having made your confession will receive the same indulgence the pope granted you.' This verdict was, Villehardouin recorded 'a great comfort to the barons and pilgrims' (Geoffrey of Villehardouin, tr. Smith, 2008: 60). The attack on Constantinople was, in effect, a crusade. This was a very practical response to the situation by those clergy on the expedition, although it was flagrantly disobedient to the pope because by this stage Innocent had expressly forbidden an assault on the city on the basis of the schism.

THE SACK OF CONSTANTINOPLE, 1204

To execute their plan the Venetians constructed the most remarkable floating siege machines. They lashed together yard-arms to form bridges about 33 metres long, suspended high on the mast-tops and covered with hides to protect the attackers from missiles. These huge tubes would come up to the city walls and disgorge the crusader knights directly onto the battlements. Similar engines had been used the previous summer and, by way of defence, Mourtzouphlos ordered wooden towers to be placed on top of the vulnerable fortifications along the Golden Horn. These unsightly creations projected perilously outwards from the walls reaching six or seven stories in height and were covered in vinegar-soaked hides to protect them from missiles and flames.

In anticipation of victory, the crusaders planned the division of their conquest. An agreement known as the 'March Pact' stipulated that all booty was to be centrally pooled with payment of remaining debts to the Venetians taking priority. A committee of six Frenchmen and six Venetians would decide the identity of the Latin emperor and the patriarch, thus reflecting the combined efforts of both groups. A further committee was to divide up the lands of the Byzantine Empire and the Venetians were ensured a position of economic dominance. The campaign to the Holy Land was postponed until 1205, a recognition of the need to bring stability to the new states; finally, oaths were taken to try to prevent assaults on women and churchmen in the aftermath of the capture.

On 9 April 1204 the fleet – arranged in the by now familiar divisions – moved across the Golden Horn. In some places a narrow strip of land lay between the fortifications and the water and here the French put scaling ladders to the walls while siege engines began to bombard the city; in turn, the defenders fired back their own missiles and poured down boiling oil. Mourtzouphlos's bold leadership, coupled with a contrary wind that kept the Venetian ships away from the walls forced the crusaders to retreat. Morale in the crusader camp was, unsurprisingly, low. The nobles acted swiftly to encourage their troops; the clergy claimed that the day's events were simply a divine test of the crusaders' resolve. They ratcheted up their rhetoric and preached powerful sermons that sought to de-Christianise the Greeks, arguing that they were 'worse than the Jews' and that their disobedience to the papacy merited punishment. They claimed that the crusaders truly were justified in their actions and deserved divine blessing and the remission of their sins. The clergy also ordered everyone to take communion and for the camp pro-stitutes to be expelled, customary purifications before crusader battles in the East. The main body of the crusading army remained ignorant that this was in contravention to papal wishes (Queller and Madden, 1997: 181).

Four days later a second assault began: 'cries from the battle were so great that it seemed that the whole world was quaking' wrote Villehardouin (Geoffrey of Villehardouin, tr. Smith, 2008: 64). Once again they met firm resistance until a change in the wind drove the crusaders' ships up to the walls. Some of the Venetian vessels were lashed together in pairs and the ladders of the *Paradise* and the *Lady Pilgrim* embraced one of the towers. A Venetian jumped from the fortified bridges onto the walls, only to be killed but two French knights managed to get a foothold and soon the first crusader banner fluttered above the battlements of Constantinople. Serious progress, however, required an entrance at ground level.

A group of men from Amiens hacked and battered away at a small, bricked-up door down on the shoreline. One member of this group was Robert of Clari. As stones and debris thudded down onto their protective mats and shelters they managed to penetrate the makeshift barrier. Robert's brother, a cleric named Aleaumes, ignored his brother's pleas and insisted that he should go in first. He squeezed through a hole about the size of small fireplace and emerged to sustain a rain of blows. To the defenders' utter hor-ror, he stood up, stepped forwards and began to fight. The Greeks fled and

Aleaumes called back to his companions to join him. This small group of crusaders quickly found a gate which allowed mounted knights to pour into Constantinople and by nightfall they held the districts close to the Golden Horn. Overnight Mourtzouphlos fled prompting the remaining figures of authority to surrender in the vain hope that their submission would prevent any further violence.

Boniface of Montferrat took the Bucoleon Palace where he found 'such a store of precious things that it is impossible to describe' (Geoffrey of Villehardouin, tr. Smith, 2008: 66–7). While the takeover of the palaces was relatively orderly, the rank and file utterly disregarded their earlier vows to behave with restraint. Angered at months of ill-treatment by the Byzantines, bolstered by a belief in divine favour and inspired by naked greed, they despoiled churches and houses and killed and savaged without distinction. The crusaders ransacked the cathedral of Hagia Sophia, Constantinople's spiritual heart. Drunken westerners danced beneath its magnificent mosaic ceiling, a prostitute flaunted herself on the altar and then straddled the patriarch's chair, meanwhile pack animals, slipping on their own excrement, stole away the spoils of war. Even Latin churchmen joined this surge of rapacity. Abbot Martin of Pairis (a Cistercian monastery in Alsace) reached the treasury of the imperial foundation of the Church of the Christ Pantocrator. He seized the guardian, an ancient Orthodox monk and roared: 'Come, faithless old man, show me the more powerful of the relics you guard. Otherwise understand that you will be punished immediately with death' (Gunther of Pairis, tr. Andrea, 1997: 111). The petrified old monk surrendered the objects that he had so devotedly venerated for decades and the abbot departed, his robes misshapen by the booty that he concealed. Setting aside explanations of divine favour, it is hard for us – as it was for some contemporaries – to see anything meritorious in this at all. Vast numbers of relics made their way back to the churches of western Europe and while the four horses and the objects in the treasury of St Mark's in Venice are the most famous of these, many other crusaders gave precious objects to their local churches when they returned home.

The crusaders also perpetrated atrocities against the inhabitants of Constantinople. Nicholas Mesarites, a contemporary Byzantine author, wrote of 'westerners tearing children from mothers and mothers from children, treating the virgin with wanton shame in holy chapels, viewing with fear neither the wrath of God nor the vengeance of men' (Brand, 1968: 269). Choniates raged that the crusaders were simply fraudsters, sinners against Christ. He drew a sharp contrast between Saladin's generous treatment of the defenders of Jerusalem in 1187 with the savagery of the westerners against their fellow-Christians at Constantinople; the message from him was clear: even Muslims were superior to these barbaric crusaders.

On 9 May 1204 Count Baldwin of Flanders was elected the first Latin Emperor of Constantinople, one week later, dressed in the magnificent imperial robes, the Fleming was anointed and crowned. Doge Dandolo wrote to the pope and, in light of his extreme age, he requested release from his pilgrimage vow to go to Jerusalem. But Innocent had not forgiven the doge for events at Zara and responded, with some relish, that in light of the Venetian's importance to the leadership of the crusade it would endanger the expedition if he were to leave. Elegantly checkmated, the doge could argue no further and he died in the city in May 1205.

In the aftermath of the conquest the Latins fought hard to extend their power. Boniface of Montferrat seized the important city of Thessalonica, the Venetians took Crete and Corfu to set up their trading empire and the Villehardouin clan established itself in the Peloponnese peninsula. These developments prompted conflicts with neighbouring powers and at the Battle of Adrianople in April 1205, against the Christian king of Bulgaria, Louis of Blois was killed and Emperor Baldwin disappeared. This calamitous defeat prompted the first of a series of appeals for help from western Europe. Just as the early years of the Latin East were marked by a crisis in manpower, so the Latin Empire of Constantinople (as it is known) suffered from a lack of men too; in part a logical consequence of its unforeseen creation. While certain regions, such as Flanders, Montferrat and Venice, had ties to the new conquests, the thirteenth century saw many different pulls on the crusading enthusiasm of western Europe. Some were closer to home, or in the case of Jerusalem, had far more allure; thus the Latin Empire of Constantinople rarely seemed to be a top priority (Chrissis, 2013).

The most intriguing response to events on the Fourth Crusade was that of Innocent III. We saw that he tried to prevent the expedition attacking Christian lands, although as noted the phrasing of these directives proved easy to circumvent or to ignore. The pope's initial reaction to the news of the capture was very positive. In November 1204 he wrote that God had transformed the Byzantine Empire from 'the proud to the humble, from the disobedient to the obedient, from schismatic to Catholic' (Innocent III, tr. Andrea, 2000: 114). He was prepared to award full crusading privileges for the defence of the Latin Empire and into 1205 continued to speak of 'the miracle that has come to pass in these days' (Innocent III, tr. Andrea, 2000: 135). By the middle of that year, however, his tone had darkened. First, the legate on the crusade had released the men from their vows to go to the Levant – a practical move based on the vulnerability of the Latin Empire, but one that ended any prospect of the crusade going on to the Holy Land. More disturbingly, visitors to Rome began to describe the sack in detail – matters omitted by the crusaders' reports. Innocent was revolted by the sordid, grasping behaviour of the crusaders and he realised that the Orthodox

Church would never acknowledge papal primacy if it saw in the Latins 'nothing except an example of affliction and the works of Hell, so that now it rightly detests them more than dogs'. He railed at Boniface of Montferrat: 'you turned away from the purity of your vow when you took up arms not against Saracens but Christians . . . preferring earthly wealth to celestial treasures'. We sense Innocent's confusion that God had allowed this to happen: 'Who can know the mind of the Lord?' was his troubled and unsettled conclusion (Innocent III, tr. Andrea, 2000: 166, 173, 176).

The Fourth Crusade remains one of the most controversial of all crusading expeditions. Conspiracy theories place (variously) the pope, the Venetians and certain of the crusade leaders as plotting the diversion to Constantinople, yet none of these ideas are sustainable. The campaign originally planned to invade Egypt but the disastrous terms of the 1201 Treaty of Venice drew the crusaders to Zara and then laid them open to agree to the offer from Prince Alexios. It was, ironically, therefore, a Greek who drew the campaign towards Constantinople; otherwise, there is no proof that this was pre-planned by anyone. The chronic instability of the Byzantine Empire during the late twelfth and early thirteenth century, combined with – by early 1204 – the desperation and the determination of the crusaders, men whose military expertise was repeatedly honed during their experiences – created the opportunity for an improbable and tragic victory. Such events are still remembered in the Orthodox world today and when Pope John Paul II visited Athens in the summer of 2001 he was forced, most unusually, to issue an apology for the crusade.

14

Conclusion: the impact of the Crusades

THE IMPACT OF CRUSADING IN THE WEST

The crusades to the Holy Land and the settlement of the Latin East are a central part of medieval history. Through the crusading movement the power and influence of Catholic Christendom grew and the physical, cultural and intellectual horizons of the people of the West changed. With the call to the First Crusade in 1095 all of western Europe found a common cause that crossed geographical and political boundaries and brought out one of the few characteristics shared across the region, namely the Catholic faith. The crusade also reflected contemporary hopes, fears and aspirations regarding spiritual salvation and, as well as the desire for honour, financial advancement and, for some, the wish to conquer land. Four years later and the map of Christendom had changed dramatically, with Jerusalem, the heart of the Christian faith, under Catholic rule. Hitherto unthought of opportunities opened up: the papacy had created a new way of attaining salvation and had a means of exerting authority over the people of the West; many thousands of western Europeans went to settle in the Levant; large numbers of pilgrims could visit the holy sites; and the prospects for trade and the acquisition of knowledge expanded dramatically.

Along with these new opportunities came new responsibilities. There was the need to consolidate and defend these lands and there were times when crusading activity exerted a profound impact in the West. The Second and Third Crusades saw western European rulers absent from their lands for years at a time, and in the case of Emperor Frederick Barbarossa, the death of one of these men. The decision to crusade must have galvanised and absorbed a country like nothing else: households and governments had to organise themselves, to arrange regencies, to raise large sums of cash – by taxes, by voluntary contributions, loans, or mortgages – transactions which affected ecclesiastical and secular society alike. The Venetian commitment to transport the army of the Fourth Crusade was the most dramatic example of all. The practicalities of transport and supply must have commanded peoples' attention too. Smaller crusades, such as those seen in the 1160s and 1170s, would have mirrored the same effects on a lesser scale. Alongside these sudden surges of activity, other, more permanent, reminders of the fight for the Holy Land appeared in the East. Relics arrived from the Holy Land (see pp. 34, 142–3 above) to be venerated in churches across the Latin West. More prominent still were the substantial holdings of the military orders, and their presence as powerful landlords, bankers, and as ecclesiastical and medical institutions, became a factor in many peoples' lives.

THE DEVELOPMENT OF THE SCOPE OF CRUSADING

The scope of crusading evolved rapidly over the period analysed in this book. The notion of a justified holy war against the enemies of Christianity – with spiritual rewards for the participants – touched a nerve in western society that reflected contemporary military advances in Spain, Sicily and Eastern Europe, as well as the growing authority of the papacy in providing real leadership for the Catholic Church. Obviously, the crusade to the Holy Land was the most prestigious theatre of holy war, but, as Urban II recognised (see Document 2 ii), other arenas should not be neglected. Spiritual rewards were authorised for the Iberian peninsula in 1096 and full equality with the Holy Land probably emerged by 1114, or, at the latest, 1123. Crusading was to expand into other areas as well. At the time of the First Crusade there were signs that the schism between the Catholic and Orthodox Churches, which dated from 1054, was beginning to heal. However, the cordial relationship between Pope Urban and Emperor Alexios would fall foul of the tensions between the crusade leaders and the Greeks and, particularly, the territorial ambitions of Bohemond of Taranto. In 1106 Pope Paschal II extended (or tacitly accepted) a widening of the scope of crusading to include an attack on the Byzantine Empire, with a papal legate preaching full spiritual rewards for all participants. While this may be seen as an important, if neglected, forerunner of the sack of Constantinople in 1204, as we will see later, political developments in the twelfth century led to a period of positive relations between the Latin East and Byzantium. The pagans of the Baltic and Eastern Europe were not the subject of a crusade until 1147, but as early as 1108 clerics had drawn attention to the parallel of fighting the enemies of Christ and avenging the death of Christians in this region (in this case, missionaries). It was the Second Crusade that brought the Baltic into parity with the Holy Land and Spain and, as we saw earlier, the campaigns of 1147–48 represented an unprecedented and broad-ranging effort to expand the borders of Christianity in three different areas. We have also noted the award of spiritual privileges against opponents of Pope Innocent II (1130–43) during the papal schism of the 1130s and against Christians who allied with Muslims in Iberia in 1196, as well as against Markward of Anweiler in southern Italy three years later. Some popular movements associated with the First Crusade tried to extend the concept to encompass the Jews in the West, but secular rulers were unwilling to allow such disorder in their towns and churchmen did not want to disobey biblical injunctions against the killing of Jews. For these reasons the Jews were not formally targeted by the crusade authorities, which condemned such attacks. When outbreaks of anti-semitism occurred in 1146–47 Bernard of Clairvaux and King Conrad III acted quickly to stamp them out. Taking all of these theatres of war together, crusading proved to be a flexible concept, capable of serving the needs of secular and ecclesiastical powers against the enemies of Christendom, allowing both to advance their authority as well as offering the hope of salvation and material gain for the people. As noted earlier, the distinction between the secular and the spiritual should not be over-emphasised – it was perfectly possible for a pious ruler such as King Afonso Henriques of Portugal to want to extend his territory for both religious and earthly motives.

THE IMPACT OF THE CRUSADES IN THE EASTERN MEDITERRANEAN

The success of the early settlers in consolidating their tenuous hold on the Levant and then setting up four viable, yet distinct, political entities was a remarkable achievement. Edessa, Antioch, Tripoli and Jerusalem each had their own character and interacted with each other and outside forces. The Franks managed to impose or take over networks of government and administration and they held sufficient authority to keep calm a potentially threatening indigenous population. Yet the loss of Jerusalem in 1187 reveals not just the strength of their enemies, but political, diplomatic and military weaknesses. At times, for example, the Frankish states, or particular factions, were unable to work together for a common good and the interests of a certain group (such as the Hospitallers and the invasion of Egypt in 1168, see pp. 74–5) might count against the bigger picture. Rivalry between noble parties, most obviously in Jerusalem during the 1180s, also caused serious problems.

In almost every aspect of their actions the settlers were constrained by their limited manpower, which meant they needed to seek outside help, most obviously from Europe. A dichotomy lies at the heart of relations between the Latin East and the West, and one that was often, although not always, unresolved. The settlers and their co-religionists in Europe shared the bond of their Catholic faith; the Franks defended Christ's patrimony and, as such, performed a valuable duty for all; they also enabled pilgrims to visit the holy places. The settlers were bound to the West – and vice versa – by family and, over time, crusading traditions, but they were politically independent. The need to develop and maintain their territories in the Levant, coupled with the rising threat from the Muslims, meant that the Franks turned to the West for husbands to marry important heiresses and for new crusades. Both of these were essential, but both brought with them a potential loss of freedom or position for some or all of the settlers, either temporarily or permanently. Count Fulk V of Anjou, Reynald of Châtillon, Guy of Lusignan, William and Conrad of Montferrat married women of the ruling houses of the Levant and in each case this caused serious problems, even though it was often deemed appropriate (especially in Fulk's case) to look to the West to find such a figure in the hope that he would encourage closer support from Europe, as well as providing leadership and heirs. On occasions, however, such a policy worked well: Raymond of Poitiers fitted in relatively comfortably at Antioch and proved a popular and effective prince.

Notwithstanding the numerous appeals for assistance to the West, when military support did reach the Levant there was often a clash between the strategic needs of the crusaders, who were highly motivated in the fight against Islam (having spent much time and money coming to the East) yet only temporary visitors to the area, and the settlers, who needed to take a longer view of the situation and to protect their own interests. At times, the balance was achieved: Richard the Lionheart agreed with the nobles of Jerusalem and the military orders on the need to consolidate the Frankish hold on the coastline, rather than take the holy city itself (as most of the rank and file wanted) and leave the settlers hopelessly overstretched once the crusaders left for home. On occasion the crusaders could not understand why alliances or truces had been made with Muslim powers. In other words, the simple idea of the Christians and Muslims desiring and engaging in a constant state of war is a picture that had to be refined in the twelfth century, and is also a misconception that has pervaded modern images of the crusader age (Köhler, 2013). Thus the treaty between Raymond of Tripoli and Saladin, let alone the everyday business of trade and settlement described by Ibn Jubayr, or pilgrimage to sites such as Saidnaya, reveal the reality of the situation. English crusaders arrived in the Holy Land in 1185 in response to the mission of Patriarch Heraclius, yet they were met by the news that there was a truce with the Muslims (arranged, for perfectly good reasons, in the patriarch's absence), and their fighting skills were not immediately required. Practical and political constraints meant that the settlers and Muslim factions (such as the Fatimids of Egypt) would, at times, and for the benefit of both parties, either join forces or make a truce. This apparent contradiction was borne out of simple practicality and is an important feature of the Latin tenure of the Levant. In contrast to the empathy shown between Richard and the settlers in 1191–92, the failure of the Second Crusade at Damascus and the collapse of the attack on Shaizar in 1157 were both (in part) caused by the tensions between the Franks and newcomers who might take authority over the captured lands.

The fallout from the Second Crusade was considerable: the defeat of the western armies was a great boost to the Muslim world, but meant that the settlers found it far harder than before to induce a new crusade on the scale needed to defeat their enemies. Baldwin III, Amalric and Baldwin IV all tried to convince Louis VII of France and Henry II of England to take the cross, but for a variety of reasons these plans did not come to fruition. Pope Alexander III worked hard on behalf of the settlers and his series of appeals attempted to create the conditions for a new crusade and did lead to a number of lesser expeditions. In light of the lack of large-scale help, however, the Franks were forced to look elsewhere and on occasion, secured some support from the Pisans and the Sicilians. Their most important backer became, ironically, the Byzantine Empire. Under Manuel Komnenos, the Greeks and Franks formed a strong relationship based on marriages between the ruling houses, military assistance and, from 1171, Byzantine overlordship of Jerusalem, as well as Antioch (secured in 1145). When the Greeks became hostile to the Latins in the 1180s the Franks were left dangerously isolated and this was a major contributory factor to the defeat at Hattin.

The emergence of closer ties with the Greek Orthodox is reflected in other aspects of life in the Frankish East. The existence of this trend has emerged – independently – in the work of Jotischky (1995) on religious life, Ellenblum (1998) on settlement, and Phillips (1996) on relations between the Latin East and outside powers. Jotischky shows how close ties grew up between some Orthodox and Catholic religious groups and ecclesiastical houses. Ellenblum reveals how Frankish settlers often lived alongside Orthodox villagers in the kingdom of Jerusalem. Phillips demonstrates how the Franks moved towards closer political ties with the Byzantine Empire after 1150 and a further consequence of this was Manuel Komnenos's sponsorship of religious buildings, some of which were used by Orthodox and Catholics alike. The death of Manuel Komnenos changed the tenor of the political relationship and Saladin's capture of much of the kingdom of Jerusalem ended Latin tenure of rural district. For the period under consideration here, however, this broad-ranging series of links (although not existing at top ecclesiastical levels) between the two groups is an important and recently recognised aspect of the history of the Latin East.

The impact of the First Crusade and subsequent Latin settlement in the Levant was considerable. A new player suddenly appeared to join the Byzantines and the Sunni and Shiite Muslims. We have seen how unprepared the Muslim world was in 1099 and how the appearance of the First Crusade emphasised the divisions and weaknesses in place at the end of the eleventh century. The slow and steady rise of the *jihad*, from the protestations of poets at the time of the First Crusade to the stirrings of holy war after the Battle of the Field of Blood (1119), and the more prominent achievement of Zengi at Edessa in 1144 are important to recognise. The role of Nur ad-Din as a pious patron of civic and religious welfare, and as a formidable general and the conqueror of Egypt should not be overshadowed by Saladin's more famous achievements. Saladin did, of course, capture the holy city and, whatever his shortcomings as a military leader, for this reason alone he is rightly held out as the hero of Islam.

The Muslim Near East slowly composed itself after Saladin's death. The Fifth Crusade (1217–21), foundered on the banks of the River Nile. In 1229 Emperor Frederick II, who had been excommunicated by the papacy for his failure to fulfil earlier promises to crusade, managed to negotiate the peaceful return of Jerusalem and the Franks held the holy city until 1244. Both the settlers and their enemies alike (and western Europe) had to face a new threat from the 1240s onwards with the emergence of the Mongols – fierce nomadic tribesmen from Asia who swept all before them to create the largest empire in history, which stretched from Hungary to China. Aside from this, political wrangles with the German Empire (Frederick II had married the heiress to Jerusalem in 1225) and, latterly, involvement with Charles of Anjou, the Capetian ruler of Sicily, clouded political life in the Levant. Two crusades from King Louis IX of France (1248–54 and 1270) failed to defeat the Muslims and the Mamluk Sultan Baibars pushed the Franks to breaking point during the 1260s. Finally, in 1291, Acre fell and the Latin East was at an end, although the Lusignan dynasty continued to rule Cyprus.

The period covered in the bulk of this book marked, in territorial terms at least, the zenith of the Frankish presence in the Levant. As we saw at the start of this work, the idea of the crusade remains potent today. This book has sought to contextualise and bring to life the motives, endeavours and contradictions underlying this compelling and important episode in history.

DOCUMENTS

Document 1   ACCOUNTS OF THE COUNCIL OF CLERMONT, 1095

There are a wealth of narrative sources for the First Crusade, but we have no extant contemporary account of Pope Urban II's speech at the Council of Clermont in November 1095. The only official document is extremely brief (see p. 18), although plain in its message. The potential problem with the narrative versions of his call to arms is that they were all composed after the capture of Jerusalem. While some of these accounts are from eye-witnesses at Clermont, they were all written up later; there is no common shared text and there is a concern that the writers may have manipulated parts of their material to reflect the actual outcome of the crusade. In spite of these drawbacks, however, certain themes do emerge, including the suffering of the Christians in the East, the mistreatment of pilgrims, the pollution of the holy places, the spiritual importance of Jerusalem and also the rewards (secular and spiritual) of taking the cross. For reasons of space the texts here are only extracts from these narratives.

(i) The account of Robert of Rheims (also known as Robert the Monk, written *c.* 1110)

Race of the French, race living beyond the Alps, race chosen and beloved by God, as is radiantly shown by your many deeds, distinguished from all other nations as much by the situation of your lands and your Catholic faith as by the honour you show to Holy Church; to you we direct our sadness and to you we send our exhortation. . . . A grave report has come from lands around Jerusalem and from the city of Constantinople . . . that a people from the kingdom of the Persians, a foreign race, a race absolutely alien to God . . . has invaded the land of those Christians, has reduced the people with sword, rapine and flame and has carried off some as captives to its own land, has cut down others by pitiable murder and has either completely razed the churches of God to the ground or enslaved them to the practice of its own rites. These men have destroyed the altars polluted by their foul practices . . . they cut open the navels of those whom they choose to torment with a loathsome death. . . . They tie some to posts and shoot at them with arrows; they order others to bare their necks and they attack them with drawn swords, trying to see whether they can cut off their heads with a single stroke. What shall I say of the appalling violation of women, of which it is more evil to speak than to keep silent? . . . On whom, therefore, does the task lie of avenging this, of redeeming the situation, if not on you, upon whom above all nations God has bestowed outstanding glory in arms, magnitude of heart, litheness of body and the strength to humble anyone who resists you to their hairy crown?

May the stories of your ancestors move you and excite your souls to strength; the worth and greatness of King Charlemagne and of Louis his son and of others of your kings, who destroyed the kingdoms of the pagans and extended into them the boundaries of Holy Church. May you be especially moved by the Holy Sepulchre of Our Lord and Saviour, which is in the hands of unclean races, and by the Holy Places, which are now treated dishonourably and are polluted irreverently by their unclean practices. Oh most strong soldiers and the offspring of unvanquished parents, do not show yourselves to be weaker than your forbears but remember their strength! . . . for this land you inhabit is everywhere shut in by the sea, is surrounded by ranges of mountains and is overcrowded by your numbers; it does not overflow with copious wealth and scarcely furnishes food for its own farmers alone. This is why you devour and fight one another, make war and even kill one another as you exchange blows. Stop these hatreds among yourselves, silence the quarrels, still the wars and let all dissensions be settled. Take the road to the Holy Sepulchre, rescue that land from a dreadful race and rule over it yourselves, for that land that, as scripture says, floweth with milk and honey was given by God as a possession to the children of Israel.

This royal city, placed at the centre of the world, is now held captive by her enemies and is enslaved to pagan rites by a people which does not acknowledge God. So she asks and prays to be liberated and calls upon you increasingly to come to her aid.

But we do not order or urge old men or the infirm or those least suited to arms to undertake this journey; nor should women go at all without their husbands or brothers or official permission: such people are more of a hindrance than a help, more of a burden than a benefit.

(ii) The account of Guibert of Nogent (written before 1108)

If, indeed, one reads in the sacred and prophetic writings that this land was the inheritance and the holy temple of God before the Lord walked and appeared there, how much more holy and worthy of reverence must we consider to be fitting for the place where the blood of the Son of God, holier than heaven or earth, poured out and where his body, dead to the fearful elements, rested in the grave? . . . Many bodies of the saints that had slept arose and came into the Holy City and appeared to many, and it was said by the prophet Isaiah, his Sepulchre shall be glorious, no subsequent evil can remove that same holiness, since it has been imparted to the city by God himself, the sanctifier, by his own action. In the same way nothing can be taken from the glory of his Sepulchre.

If you consider that you ought to take great pains to make a pilgrimage to the graves of the apostles (in Rome) or to the shrines of any other saints, what expense of spirit can you refuse in order to rescue, and make a pilgrimage to, the cross, the blood, the Sepulchre? Until now you have fought unjust wars: you have often savagely brandished your spears at each other in mutual carnage only out of greed and pride, for which you deserve eternal destruction and the certain ruin of damnation! Now we are proposing that you should fight wars which contain the glorious reward of martyrdom, in which you can gain the title of present and eternal glory.

If, therefore, you stir yourselves to the exercise of holy battles, so that you may repay Jerusalem the debt you owe her for the grace which she has lent you – it is from her that you have received the first implantations of the knowledge of God – and so that through you the Catholic name, which will resist the perfidy of Antichrist and the Antichristians, may be spread, who cannot but infer that God, who surpasses the hope of all in the super-abundance of his power, will burn up through your spark such thickets of paganism that he will spread the rudiments of his law throughout Egypt.

Dearest brethren, these times will perhaps only be fulfilled when through you, with God working with you, the powers of the pagans will be thrust back. And the end of the world is already near, although the gentiles have not been converted to the Lord: according to the apostle Paul there must be a revolt from the faith. . . . Think, I beseech you, of the hearts giving birth to such rejoicing when we see the Holy City revived by your assistance and the prophetic, nay rather divine, predictions fulfilled in our own times.

Consider those who go on pilgrimage and travel across the Mediterranean. How many payments, how much violence are the richer subjected to, being forced to pay tolls for almost every mile they go and taxes; at which city gates, entrances of churches and temples they have to pay fees; how they have to journey from one place to the next, accused of having done something; how it is the habit of the governors of the gentiles to force them savagely with blows to pay for their release when they have refused to pay a bribe!

. . . But since this pious intent [the protection of liberty] is not in the souls of everyone, and instead the desire of having [i.e. material greed] spreads through everyone's hearts, God has, in our time, instituted holy warfare in order that the arms-bearers and the wandering masses, who in the fashion of the ancient pagans were engaged in mutual slaughters, might find a new way of obtaining salvation; so that they might not be obliged to leave the world completely, as used to be the case, by adopting the monastic way of life or any form of professed calling, but might attain some measure of God's grace while enjoying their usual freedom and dress. . . .

(iii) The account of Baldric of Bourgueil (written *c.* 1105)

Christian blood, which has been redeemed by the blood of Christ, is spilled and Christian flesh, flesh of Christ's flesh, is delivered up to execrable abuses and appalling servitude.

Until now we have, as it were, disguised the fact that we have been speaking of holy Jerusalem, brethren, because we have been ashamed and embarrassed to talk about her; for that very city in which, as you know, Christ himself suffered for us, since our sins demanded it, has been overwhelmed by the filth of the pagans and, I say it to our shame, led away from the service of God. . . . To what use now is put the church of Blessed Mary, where her own body was buried in the valley of Josaphat? What of the Temple of Solomon, not to mention the fact that it is the Lord's, in which the barbaric races worship their idols, which they have placed there against the law and against religion? We will not recall the Lord's Sepulchre, because some of you have seen with your own eyes to what abomination it has been handed over. . . . Yet in that place – I am only saying what everyone knows – God was laid to rest; there he died for us; there he was buried. How precious is that place of the Lord's burial, how desirable, a place beyond compare! Indeed God does not let a year go by without performing a miracle there; when the lamps in the Sepulchre and in the church around it have been put out at Passiontide, they are relighted by divine command. Whose stony heart could remain unmoved, brethren, by so great a miracle?

What are we saying, brothers? Listen and understand. You have strapped on the belt of knighthood and strut around with pride in your eye. You butcher your brothers and create factions among yourselves. This, which scatters the sheepfold of the Redeemer, is not the knighthood of Christ. The Holy Church keeps for herself an army to come to the aid of her people, but you pervert it to knavery. . . . You oppressors of orphans, you robbers of widows, you homicides, you blasphemers, you plunderers of others' rights; you hope for the rewards of brigands for the shedding of Christian blood and just as vultures nose corpses you watch and follow wars from afar. Certainly this is the worst course to follow because it is utterly removed from God. And if you want to take counsel for your souls you must either cast off as quickly as possible the belt of this sort of knighthood or go forward boldly as knights of Christ, hurrying swiftly to defend the eastern Church.

It ought to be a beautiful ideal for you to die for Christ in that city where Christ died for you, but if it should happen that you should die here, you may be sure that it will be as if you had died on the way, provided, that is, Christ finds you in his company of knights. . . . Do not worry about the coming journey: remember that nothing is impossible for those who fear God, nor for those who truly love him. . . . Gird thy sword, each man of you, upon thy thigh, Oh thou most mighty. Gird yourselves, I say, and act like mighty sons, because it is better for you to die in battle than to tolerate the abuse of your race and your Holy Places.

Louise and Jonathan Riley-Smith, *The Crusades: Idea and Reality, 1095–1270*, Edward Arnold, London, 1981, pp. 37, 42–53, except the last section of extract ii, tr. Jonathan Phillips from: Guibert of Nogent, *Dei gesta per Francos*, ed. Robert Huygens, Corpus Christianorum Continuatio Medievalis 127A, Brepols, Turnhout, 1996, p. 87.

Document 2 LETTERS OF POPE URBAN II, 1095–99

Pope Urban wrote numerous letters to elicit support for the campaign in the East. Letters are an important source because, unlike many narratives, they are contemporary compositions by key players. Document (i) is significant because it is dated so soon after the Council of Clermont and is a statement in Urban's own words of the purpose of the crusade. Document (ii) is useful in revealing the attraction of the crusade to those fighting in Spain and Urban's willingness to offer the reward of martyrdom to those fighting the holy war in Iberia and his portrayal of the campaign there as of equal merit as the crusade to the Holy Land.

(i) Urban to all the faithful in Flanders, December 1095

We believe that you, brethren, learned long ago from many reports the deplorable news that the barbarians in their frenzy have invaded and ravaged the churches of God in the eastern regions. Worse still, they have seized the Holy City of Christ, embellished by his passion and resurrection, and – it is blasphemy to say it – they have sold her and her churches into abominable slavery.

(ii) Urban to the counts of Besalú, Empurias, Roussillon and Cerdaña and their knights, *c.* January 1096–29 July 1099

If the knights of other provinces have decided with one mind to go to the aid of the Asian Church and to liberate their brothers from the tyranny of the Saracens, so ought you with one mind and with our encouragement to work with greater endurance to help a church so near you resist the invasions of the Saracens. No one must doubt that if he dies on this expedition for the love of God and his brothers his sins will surely be forgiven and he will gain a share of eternal life through the most compassionate mercy of our God. So if any of you has made up his mind to go to Asia, it is here instead that he should try to fulfil his vow, because it is no virtue to rescue Christians from the Saracens in one place, only to expose them to the tyranny and oppression of the Saracens in another.

Louise and Jonathan Riley-Smith, *The Crusades: Idea and Reality, 1095–1270*, Edward Arnold, London, 1981, pp. 38, 40.

CHARTERS FROM THE FIRST CRUSADE   **Document 3**

Charters have emerged as a vital form of contemporary evidence in revealing the motives, financial arrangements and other practical aspects of going on crusade. This material is discussed in more detail in the Introduction, but here are extracts from several charters to show such activities.

(i) The brothers Bernard and Odo's agreement with the abbey of Cluny shows an awareness of the dangers of the crusade and also reveals the precision with which items of property are listed. Note also the malediction clause (a curse) at the end on those who try to upset the arrangement. The charter dates from 1096.

May it be known to all gathered in the bosom of the church of the holy mother, both at present and in future, that we, Bernard and Odo, brothers, for the remission of our sins, setting out with all the others on the journey to Jerusalem, have made over for 100 solidi to Artald, deacon of Lordon, a manor known as Busart, which we were holding in the county of Macon, in the village of Flagiaco, with everything that pertains to that manor, namely, the houses, the buildings, fields, woods, vines, meadows, pasture, streams and the water channels that flow around them and the cultivated and uncultivated land. We are making this arrangement on the condition that if, in the course of the pilgrimage that we are undertaking, because we are mortal and may be taken by death, the manor, in its entirety, may remain under the control of St Peter and the monastery of Cluny, which is under the reverend father Hugh. But if we may have returned and come back to the manor, we may keep it in our lifetime, but after our death this may forestall a claim by any of our heirs, and it will pass in its entirety, without objection, to St Peter and to Cluny, for our well being and that of all our relatives, living or deceased, and be the place of our burial. The boundaries of this manor are the public road and, on three sides, the land of St Peter [Cluny's land]. If, however, another lays claim to this gift, not only is it protected from that which is sought, but may he suffer every curse [malediction] and perpetual excommunication from God and the holy apostles for his sins, unless he recovers his senses. Signed by Bernard and Odo who made this donation and gift; Humbert Ungri, Ili of Craia, his brother Hugh of Merule, who has a sister, and many others.

Translated by Jonathan Phillips from: *Recueil des chartes de l'abbaye de Cluny*, eds Auguste Bernard and Alexandre Bruel, 6 vols, Paris, Imprimerie Nationale, 1876– 1903, vol. 5, pp. 51–52, 59.

(ii) Charters might express a crusader's motivation and might also reflect a general feeling across the wider society, as in this case.

(a) Be it known to the faithful of Christ, now and in the future, that I, Achard of Montmerle, knight, of the castle that is called Montmerle, and son of William who is himself called of Montmerle; I, excited by the same intention as this great and enormous upheaval of the Christian people wanting to go to fight for God against the pagans and the Saracens; and, to enable this to take place, and desiring to go there armed, have made an agreement of this kind with lord Hugh, venerable abbot of Cluny and his monks. . . . [Details of the transaction follow.] Dated 12 April 1096.

(b) We wish it be made known to those present and to those of future generations that Duke Odo of Burgundy, fired by divine zeal and love of Christianity, wishes to go to Jerusalem with all the others of the Christians, but before setting out, it should be clearly known that if, at the end of his journey, his strength does not enable him to return with the multitude, then after his death, whenever it is known, he has granted to God and St Mary the village of Marcenay, to be held in hereditary possession. Namely, the cultivated and uncultivated land and all the rights of justice over it, just as he held the same village during his life and just as his brother lord Hugh, then most invincible duke, and later a monk of Cluny, did; this is conceded to the church of Molesme, to be held freely by the brothers after his death and taken possession of for their use in perpetuity afterwards. [Details of the transaction follow, dated *c*. 1100.]

Cartulaires de l'abbaye de Molesme, ed. Jacques Laurent, 2 vols, Paris, Imprimerie Nationale, 1907–11, vol. 2, p. 18.

(iii) Spiritual, as well as practical, preparations were needed before setting out on the crusade. In another charter, Duke Odo wished to make good for the wrongs that he had committed against the monastery of St Bénigne at Dijon.

I entered the chapter of St Bénigne of Dijon and, with the monks sitting round the room and many members of their household standing by, I corrected the injuries which I had, until now, been accustomed to inflict. I recognized my fault and, having sought mercy, I asked that I should be absolved, and I promised amendment in future if I should happen to return. . . . [Dated *c*. 1101.]

Chartes et documents de Saint-Bénique de Dijon, eds Gerard Chevrier and Marcel Chaume, 2 vols, Dijon, 1943–86, vol. 2, p. 175.

THE POGROMS AGAINST THE JEWS, 1096–97   **Document 4**

The bulk of this powerful account of the attacks on the Jews of the Rhineland was written in Mainz c. 1140, with some later additions by anonymous contributors. The author's main concern was to display the glorious martyrdom of the Jewish communities and not the pain of forced conversions or the success of the First Crusade at Jerusalem. Much of the chronicle is borne out by Christian sources, although they differ in emphasis and minor details of fact compared to this text. This extract reveals the coming of the crusaders, their motivation and their attack on Worms in May 1096.

The Chronicle of Solomon bar Simson:

At this time arrogant people, a people of strange speech, a nation bitter and impetuous, Frenchmen and Germans, set out for the Holy City, which had been desecrated by barbaric nations, there to seek their house of idolatry and banish the Ismaelites and other denizens of the land and conquer the land for themselves. They decorated themselves prominently with their signs, placing a profane symbol – a horizontal line over a vertical one – on the vestments of every man and woman whose heart yearned to go on the stray path to the grave of their Messiah. Their ranks swelled until the number of men, women and children exceeded a locust horde covering the earth; of them it was said: 'The locusts have no king.' Now it came to pass that as they passed through the towns where Jews dwelled, they said to one another: 'Look now, we are going a long way to seek out the profane shrine and to avenge ourselves on the Ismaelites, when here, in our very midst, are the Jews – they whose forefathers murdered and crucified him for no reason. Let us first avenge ourselves on them from among the nations so that the name of Israel will no longer be remembered, or let them adopt our faith and acknowledge the offspring of promiscuity.'

When the Jewish communities became aware of their intentions, they resorted to the custom of our ancestors, repentance, prayer and charity. . . .

On the twenty-third day of Iyar they [the crusaders] attacked the community of Worms. The community was then divided into two groups; some remained in their homes and others fled to the local bishop seeking refuge. Those who remained in their homes were set upon by the steppe-wolves who pillaged men, women and infants, children and old people. They pulled down the stairways and destroyed the houses, looting and plundering; and they took the Torah Scroll, trampled it in the mud, and tore and burned it. The enemy devoured the children of Israel with open maw.

The Jews and the Crusaders: The Hebrew Chronicles of the First and Second Crusades, tr. and ed. Shlomo Eidelberg, University of Wisconsin Press, Madison, WI, 1977, pp. 21–23.

———————◀●▶———————

Document 5   THE MUSLIM REACTION TO THE FIRST CRUSADE

To modern-day westerners poetry is often the preserve of the classroom alone, but in the medieval Islamic world it was a common method of political comment and the ability to compose high-quality verse was greatly valued. These texts show the anger felt by some at the inaction of the Sunni Muslim leadership when the First Crusade reached the Levant and the need to respond and fight back.

Text (iii) by al-Sulami is especially noteworthy because of its early date and because of his overview of the wider Christian–Muslim conflict. Even more important are his highlighting of the Muslims' duty to fight jihad; his anger at the rulers of the Near East for their failure to confront the Franks; for his outlining of rewards – both secular and spiritual; his framing of the conflict as a test for devout Muslims; his identification of the Muslims of the Near East as chosen by God for this task – and for his appreciation of the settlers' weaknesses. In as-Sulami's lifetime, and for a few decades afterwards, however, few heeded his message.

(i) Anonymous Muslim poet concerning the First Crusade, early twelfth century.

> The unbelief of the infidels has declared it lawful to inflict harm on
> Islam, causing prolonged lamentation for the faith.
> What is right is null and void and what is forbidden is [now] made licit.
>   The sword is cutting and blood is spilt.
> How many Muslim men have become booty?
> And how many Muslim women's inviolability has been plundered?
> How many a mosque have they made into a church!
> The cross has been set up in the *mihrab*.
> The blood of the pig is suitable for it.
> Qurans have been burned under the guise of incense.
> Do you not owe an obligation to God and Islam,
> Defending thereby young men and old?
> Respond to God: woe on you! Respond!

(ii) Ibn al-Khayyat (died *c.* 1125). An ode to his patron, a commander of the city of Damascus, early twelfth century (extracts).

> The polytheists have swelled in a torrent of terrifying extent.
> How long will this continue?
> Armies like mountains, coming again and again, have raged forth
>   from the land of the Franks . . .
> The tribe of polytheism do not reject [any kind] of corruption.
> Nor do they recognise any moderation in tyranny . . .

How many young girls have begun to beat their throats and necks
   out of fear of them [the Franks]?
How many nubile girls have not known the heat [of the day] nor
   felt the cold at night [until now]?
They are almost wasting away with fear and dying of grief and
   agitation.

Carole Hillenbrand, 'The First Crusade: The Muslim Perspective', *The First Crusade: Origins and Impact*, ed. Jonathan Phillips, Manchester University Press, Manchester, 1997, pp. 137–38.

(iii) Al-Sulami, *c*. 1105, 'The Book of *Jihad*'

They [the crusaders] looked out over Syria, on separated kingdoms, dis-united hearts and differing views linked with hidden resentment, and with that their desires became stronger and extended to what they all saw. They did not stop, tireless in fighting the *jihad* against the Muslims. The Muslims were sluggish, and (we were) avoiding fighting them and were reluctant to engage in combat until they conquered more than their greatest hopes had conceived of the country, and destroyed and humiliated many times the number of people that they had wished. . . . The [crusaders'] desires are multiplying all the time because of what appears to them of the (Muslims') abstinence from (opposing) them, and their hopes are invigorated by virtue of what they see of their enemies' contentedness with being unharmed by them, until they have become convinced that the whole country will become theirs and all its people will be prisoners in their hands. May God in his generosity humble their ideas by bringing together everyone and arranging the unity of the people, for He is near, and answers (prayers) . . .

[In the past] Every Muslim (who was) free, responsible and capable of taking part in an expedition went out on one, seeking by it to exalt the word of God (who is praised), to demonstrate his religion, to suppress by it his enemies the polytheists, to achieve the reward which God (who is praised) and His Prophet promised him from (fighting) the *jihad* in His cause, and to gain their (the enemies') wealth, women and lands, until there were, of those who came to face them (the enemy), enough to fight them in it (the expedition). That is to say that the *jihad*, is an obligation of sufficiency . . .

Know that God (who is praised) only sent this enemy to you as a trial, to test your steadfastness with it. He said (God blesses and is exalted), "Let Us test you so that We will know those of you that fight hard and are steadfast, and We will test your experiences."

Know – God have mercy on you – after that, that your Prophet (God bless him) promised a group of his people victory over their enemies, and took them from the people of Syria in particular, rather than from the others. So it may be that you are those particular people rather than others of you . . .

Give precedence to *jihad* of yourselves over *jihad* against your enemies, for if yourselves are among your enemies prevent them from being disobedient to their Creator (who is praised). You will succeed in your hopes of victory over them. Make right what is between you and your Creator, and He will make right for you what is wrong in your (current) state of being, and reconcile your enmity.

From them come our hopes of hastening a victory over them (the Franks) because of what is true concerning their weakness, the paucity of their cavalry and numbers, and the (far) distance of their reinforcements and support . . .

Extracts from as-Sulami's (d. 1106) 'The Book of *Jihad*', trans. Niall Christie, 2001, available at http://www.arts.cornell.edu/prh3/447/texts/Sulami.html (accessed 5 December 2013).

Document 6   FRANKISH SETTLEMENT AND IDENTITY

(i) This extract from Fulcher of Chartres's Historia Hierosolymitana *reveals how the early generations of Frankish settlers formed a sense of identity for themselves in the Levant. Fulcher, a priest, participated in the First Crusade and accompanied his lord, Baldwin of Boulogne, in the capture of Edessa (1098) and thence south to Jerusalem when Baldwin became king in 1100. His work covers the period 1095 to 1127 and is the most valuable account of the first decades of the Latin East.*

We who were once Occidentals [westerners] have now become Orientals. He who was a Roman or a Frank has, in this land, been made into a Galilean or a Palestinian. He who was of Rheims or Chartres has now become a citizen of Tyre or Antioch. We have already forgotten the places of our birth; already these are unknown to many of us or not mentioned any more. Some already possess homes or households by inheritance. Some have taken wives not only of their own people, but Syrians, Armenians, or even Saracens who have achieved the grace of baptism. Words of different languages have become common property known to each nationality, and mutual faith unites those who are ignorant of their descent. . . . He who was born a stranger is now as one born here; he who was born an alien has become a native. Our relatives and parents join us from time to time, sacrificing, even reluctantly, all that they formerly possessed. Those who were poor in the Occident, God makes wealthy in this land. Therefore why should one return to the Occident who has found the Orient like this? God does not wish those to suffer want, those who with their crosses dedicated themselves to follow Him, even to the end.

Fulcher of Chartres, *A History of the Expedition to Jerusalem, 1095–1127*, ed. Harold Fink, tr. Frances Ryan, University of Tennessee Press, Knoxville, TN, 1969, pp. 271–72.

(ii) The Canons of the Council of Nablus were produced in January 1120 in an atmosphere of worry and fear given a series of recent natural disasters and Muslim attacks. The measures outlined below suggest that improving the settlers' morality was seen as an important way to regain divine favour and to bolster the Franks' position.

In the one thousand two hundred and twentieth year since the Incarnation of our Lord, as a consequence of our sins, the territory of Jerusalem is being ravaged by many hardships, its crops have been devoured by locusts and mice for four years now, and it is being made desolate by incessant attacks and ambushes by the Saracens, with very many pilgrims and citizens killed. This is why the Patriarch Garmund, a man of dove-like simplicity, and Baldwin, the second king of the Latin community of Jerusalem, a disciple of humility and son of good fortune, attempting through their pious prayers and just deeds to confront the danger threatening the citizenry, and driven by divine inspiration, went into conclave in Nablus, a city of Samaria, in the second year of Baldwin's reign and of Garmund's patriarchate, together with the dignitaries of the church and the leading men of the kingdom, to settle the legal basis for that church and the territory, and in face of so pressing a national crisis they established the decrees which we have set out below to discipline a people out of control. For since at that particular time the people of the aforementioned territory were indulging every form of decadent desire, and in consequence were endangered by the damaging effects of daily misfortunes, there seemed to them to be only one means of escape; to call upon God's mercy and to impose some legal curbs on the sins of this decadent population, so that with sinful behaviour coming to an end, divine retribution would [likewise] come to an end, as we read happened in the case of the Israelites, and the mercy of God, who seeks not the death but the correction of the sinner, would snatch His repentant sons from the dangerous threat posed by their enemies. The fact is that these enemies, that is to say the Saracens, had, alas, during the summer of the previous year, killed Roger, prince of Antioch and virtually all the Christians in the principality of Antioch whom they had crushed in war, and were making incursions more frequently than usual into the territory of Jerusalem. So much for these matters.

Canon 12: If anyone shall be proved to have slept with a Saracen woman with her consent, let him have his penis removed and let her nose be cut off.

Canon 13: Whichever man forcibly rapes a Saracen woman of his household, he should be castrated; she should be seized on behalf of the fisc.

Canon 14: Anybody who forcibly rapes another man's female Saracen should suffer an adulterer's punishment [that is, castration and expulsion].

Canon 15: When a Christian woman unites sexually, of her own volition, with a Saracen man, both are to be punished like adulterers. If, however, she is forcibly raped by him, she shall not be held guilty, but the Saracen will be made a eunuch.

Canon 16: If a Saracen man or a Saracen woman dresses in the Frankish fashion they are to be enslaved.

Canon 20: If a priest has carried weapons for defensive purposes, let him not be blameworthy. But if he abandons the tonsure by reason of military service or some duty of the court, let him confess this to the Church within the prescribed time and restore the tonsure and thereafter conduct himself in accordance with the patriarch's orders; but if he keeps this to himself for a longer period, let him restrict himself in line with the intentions of the king and the patriarch.

(iii) William of Malmesbury was one of the most important historians of what we call Anglo-Norman England and he wrote this History of the English Kings *during the 1120s. He made mention of the success of the First Crusade and his comments here reflect a recognition of the magnitude of that achievement, the heroic status accorded to the leaders of the expedition and the difficulties faced by the Frankish settlers in the Levant.*

Only Godfrey and Tancred remained, leaders of high renown, to whose praises posterity, if it judge aright, will assign no limits; heroes who from the cold of uttermost Europe plunged into the intolerable heat of the East, careless of their own lives, if only they could bring help to Christendom in its hour of trial. Besides the fear of barbarian attacks, exposed to constant apprehension from the rigours of an unfamiliar climate, they made light of the certainty of peace and health in their own country; few as they were, they overwhelmed so many enemy cities by the fame and operation of their prowess, setting a noteworthy example of trust in God, in that they were ready to remain without hesitation in a place where either the air they breathed would be loaded with pestilence, or they would be killed by the fury of the Saracens. Let poets with their eulogies now give place, and fabled history no longer laud the heroes of Antiquity. Nothing to be compared with their glory has ever been begotten in any age. Such valour as the Ancients had vanished after their death into dust and ashes in the grave, for it was spent on the mirage of worldly splendour rather than on the solid aim of some goodly purpose; while of these brave heroes of ours, men will enjoy benefit and tell the proud story, as long as the round world endures and the holy Church of Christ flourishes.

William of Malmesbury, *Gesta Regum Anglorum: The History of the English Kings*, ed. and tr. R.A.B. Mynors, R.M. Thomson and M. Winterbottom, 2 vols, Clarendon Press, Oxford, 1998, vol. 1, p. 655.

THE MILITARY ORDERS   **Document 7**

Such was the radical nature of the idea of a fighting monk that it was neces-
sary for Hugh of Payns, the first master of the Templars, to get the leading
churchman of western Europe, Abbot Bernard of Clairvaux, to explain
why the concept was valid. Some people presumably had reservations about
this, but the strength of Bernard's argument and the enormously positive
response to the launch of the Templars indicates that most were soon con-
vinced. The second document is a translation of a recently discovered
account of the treatment of the sick in the Hospital of St John in Jerusalem
c. 1180 and gives an indication of contemporary healthcare.

(i) A Justification of the Knights Templar, *c.* 1130. Bernard of Clairvaux, 'In
Praise of the New Knighthood'.

To Hugh, knight of Christ and master of Christ's militia, Bernard, abbot
in name only of Clairvaux, may you fight the good fight. . . . I will briefly
describe the (ideal) life and virtues of the knights of Christ. . . . First, they are
disciplined and obedient. . . . Therefore these knights come and go at the
order of their superior. . . . They live as brothers in joyful and sober company, without wives or children. So that their spiritual perfection will lack
nothing, they dwell in one family without any personal property. . . . They
never sit idly nor wander aimlessly. . . . There is no distinction (by rank)
among them: deference is shown to merit rather than to noble birth. . . . No
inappropriate word, idle deed, unrestrained laughter, not even the slightest
whisper or murmur is left uncorrected, once detected. They forswear dice
and chess. They abhor hunting, and they take no delight in the ridiculous
cruelty of falconry. . . . Indeed, seldom do they wash, and never do they set
their hair, being content to appear tousled and dusty, bearing the marks of
the sun and of their armour.

When the battle is at hand, they arm themselves inwardly with faith and
outwardly with steel rather than with decorations of gold, since their business is to strike fear in the enemy rather than to incite cupidity. They seek
out strong and fast horses rather than well-plumed ones, for they fight to win
rather than to display pomp. They think not of glory but rather seek to be
formidable. At the same time, they are not quarrelsome, rash, or unduly
hasty, but draw themselves up into orderly ranks in a sober, prudent, and
purposeful manner.

No matter how outnumbered, they are never awed by the fierce enemy
hordes. Nor do they overestimate their own strength, but trust in the Lord
to grant them victory.

I do not know if it is more appropriate to call them monks or knights;
perhaps it is better to recognize them as being both, for they lack neither

monastic meekness nor military fortitude. What can I say except that God has empowered this (new order), and it is a marvellous sight to my eyes. God chose these men whom he recruited from the ends of the earth; they are valiant men of Israel chosen to guard the tomb of Solomon, each man, sword in hand, superbly trained to conduct war.

Theodore Evergates, *Feudal Society in Medieval France: Documents from the County of Champagne*, University of Pennsylvania Press, Philadelphia, PA, 1993, pp. 98–101.

(ii) A Contemporary Account of the Treatment of the Sick in the Hospital of St John, Jerusalem (Anonymous)

It was ordained by the master of the Hospital and by the General Chapter that each patient should have each day half a soft loaf and sufficient house-bread, and the same wine as the convent. The doctors should observe closely the qualities of the sick and what illnesses they have, and should inspect their urine and give syrups and electuaries and other things which may be necessary for sick people and forbid contrary things and give them useful ones and the more ill and the more infirm are the patients they see, the more concerned yet they should be to restore their health. Foods for the sick should be thus: from Easter to Michaelmas they have the meat of chickens and other fowl, and meat of goats and lambs not yet one year old and meat of sheep one year old and more as often as the physician may instruct them to be provided. From Michaelmas to Lent, meat of chickens and the same as was said before, and pork from the male animal one year old according as the doctor shall prescribe. Sick people should never eat female flesh from an animal with four feet, nor are the brothers who serve the sick ever to give them any. In Lent fresh fish is to be given to the sick three times a week, if the patient dare to eat it for his sickness, and this is to be done on the advice of the doctor. Broth and other cooked dishes of vegetables and barley flour and other foods suitable for the sick are to be given to them on the advice of the doctor, and they are to be given to them well prepared on the days appointed. Eels and cheese and lentils and beans and cabbages and other foods which are contra-indicated for the sick, we prohibit them to be given to them.

A third part of the tree-fruits, such as pomegranates and other apples, pears, plums, figs and grapes are to be given to them as the masters who were before us laid down and ordained in the chapter of the hospital of Jerusalem both for the use of the poor and for their provision.

In each ward of sick people there are to be now and henceforth 12 ser-geants who make the beds for the sick and keep them from soiling and take them to the privies and guide them and support them closely. From proces-sion to procession – that is, from Easter to the feast of the Holy Cross – more sergeants are to be appointed according to the organisation of the brother Hospitaller. Among the wards are to be brothers who keep watch at night, that is to say two brothers who are to keep watch each night in order that nothing adverse should happen to our sick lords.

Translated by Susan Edgington, from MS Vat. Lat. 4852, ff. 89r–91r.

TRADING PRIVILEGES OF THE VENETIANS, 1123–24   **Document 8**

The Pactum Warmundi *is taken from* William *of* Tyre's Historia. *It is a formal legal agreement outlining the privileges accorded to the Venetians for their support in the attack and capture of Tyre. William was also chancellor of the kingdom of Jerusalem and it is likely that he copied this document directly from the royal archives into his history during its composition c. 1170–85.*

A copy of the treaty containing the agreement made between the Venetians and the princes of the kingdom of Jerusalem in the matter of the siege of Tyre.

In the name of the holy and indivisible trinity, Father, Son, and Holy Ghost . . . Domenigo Michieli, doge of Venice, of Dalmatia and Croatia, and prince of the empire, accompanied by a great host of knights and a mighty fleet of vessels, came as a conqueror to the much-needed defence of the Christians. He had come directly from his victory over the pagan fleet of the king of Babylon, upon which he had wrought terrible havoc as it lay before the harbourless shores of Ascalon.

Baldwin, the second king of Jerusalem, was at that time, because of our sins, held captive with many others in the toils of the pagans, a prisoner of Balak, prince of the Parthians. Therefore, we, Gormond, by the grace of God patriarch of the Holy City of Jerusalem, being assembled at the city of Acre, in the church of the Holy Cross, with the suffragan brethren of our church, with William of Bures, the constable, with Payens, the chancellor, and in conjunction with the allied forces of the whole kingdom, we, I say, have confirmed the promises of the said King Baldwin according to the propositions made in his own letters and messages which the king himself had previously sent by his own envoys to Venice to the same doge of the Venetians. This we have given by our own hand and by the hand of the bishops and the chancellor, with the kiss of peace also, as our rank required. All the barons also whose names are written below have decreed and confirmed on the holy scriptures of the blessed apostle Mark, to the aforesaid doge and his successors, and to the people of Venice, the conditions of the treaty as written below; that, without any contradiction, these promises just as they are written below, so shall they remain unalterable and inviolate in the future to him and his people forever. Amen.

In every city of the above-mentioned king, under the rule of his successors also, and in the cities of all his barons, the Venetians shall have a church and one entire street of their own; also a square and a bath and an oven to be held forever by hereditary right, free from all taxation as is the king's own property.

In the square at Jerusalem, however, they shall have for their own only as much as the king is wont to have. But if the Venetians desire to set up at Acre, in their own quarter, an oven, a mill, a bath, scales, measures and bottles for measuring wine, oil, and honey, it shall be permitted freely to each person dwelling there without contradiction to cook, mill, or bathe just as it is freely permitted on the king's property. They may use the measures, and the scales, and the measuring bottles as follows: when the Venetians trade with each other, they must use their own measures, that is the measures of Venice; and when the Venetians sell their wares to other races, they must sell with their own measures, that is, with the measures of Venice; but when the Venetians purchase and receive anything in trade from any foreign nation other that the Venetians, it is permitted them to take it by the royal measure and at a given price. For these privileges the Venetians need pay no tax whatever, whether according to custom or for any reason whatsoever, either on entering, staying, buying, selling, either while remaining there or on departing. For no reason whatever need they pay any tax excepting only when they come or go, carrying pilgrims with their own vessels. Then indeed, according to the king's custom, they must give a third part to the king himself.

Wherefore, the king of Jerusalem and all of us on behalf of the king agree to pay the doge of Venice, from the revenues of Tyre, on the feast day of the apostles Peter and Paul, three hundred Saracen besants yearly, as agreed upon.

Moreover, we promise you, doge of Venice, and your people that we will take nothing more from those nations who trade with you beyond what they are accustomed to give and as much as we receive from those who trade with other nations.

William of Tyre, *A History of Deeds Done Beyond the Sea*, ed. Emily Babcock, tr. August Krey, 2 vols, Columbia University Press, New York, 1943, vol. 1, pp. 552–55.

THE REBELLION OF COUNT HUGH OF JAFFA, 1134   **Document 9**

The rebellion of Count Hugh of Jaffa is an interesting episode for several reasons. It shows the tensions in accommodating newcomers into the political structure of the kingdom of Jerusalem and reveals the twists and turns in the legacy of King Baldwin II. Note the change in the terms of Fulk's kinship. In i(a) he married Melisende (in 1129) in the expectation of ruling in his own right. In i(b), two years later, he is made to rule alongside his wife and son. It also demonstrates the agenda of William of Tyre who, writing c. 1170–85, was concerned to justify the settlers' defence of the Holy Land to those in the West. Here, he chose to blur an episode, distant to his own time, that reflected badly on the relationship between the Franks of the East and newcomers from Europe. The account of Orderic Vitalis, an Anglo-Norman monk who composed this section of his Ecclesiastical History *in c. 1136–41, provides a complement to William of Tyre's version and probably reveals the real reason behind Hugh of Jaffa's revolt.*

(i) William of Tyre's version

(a) Baldwin was anxious . . . to provide for the succession. Accordingly, after long deliberation, by the unanimous advice of the nobles . . . he sent to invite Fulk to marry his daughter and become the heir to the throne. The count accordingly arranged his own affairs and set the county [of Anjou] in order . . . he set forth on the journey attended by a splendid retinue of nobles. Within a few days of his arrival in the kingdom, the king gave him his eldest daughter to wife [1129].

(b) The king [Baldwin II] percieved that the day of his death [21 August 1131] was at hand. . . . He then summoned to him his daughter [Melisende] and his son-in-law [Fulk] and the boy Baldwin [the future Baldwin III]. To them, in the presence of the patriarch and the prelates of the Church and some of the nobles who happened to be present, he committed the care of the kingdom with full power.

(c) On the return of the king from Antioch, a very dangerous disturbance arose. For certain reasons, some of the highest nobles of the realm: namely, Hugh, count of Jaffa, and Romain of Le Puy, lord of the region beyond the Jordan, are said to have conspired against the lord king. . . .

Some said that the king cherished a deep mistrust of the count who was rumoured to be on too familiar terms with the queen, and of this there seemed to be many proofs. Hence, spurred on by a husband's jealousy, the king is said to have conceived an inexorable hatred against the man.

Count Hugh was young, tall of stature, and of handsome countenance . . . in respect to physical beauty and nobility of birth, as well as experience in the art of war, he had no equal in the kingdom.

One day, Walter of Caesarea . . . at the instigation of the king himself, it was claimed, publicly accused Hugh of high treason and of having conspired against the life of the king. The count denied the charge, but said that although he was innocent he would submit to the judgement of the court on the accusations. . . . Single combat was decreed according to the custom of the Franks, and a suitable day was set for the combat. The count then left the court and returned to Jaffa. He did not present himself on the appointed day, however . . . and his actions brought upon himself . . . even greater suspicion of the crime imputed to him. The assembly of nobles condemned him in his absence as guilty of the charge against him.

[Hugh then sought help from the Egyptians of Ascalon – a grave error that lost him most of his important supporters among the nobility. The patriarch of Jerusalem managed to make peace between Hugh and the king and the count was to go into exile for three years. As he waited to leave he was stabbed.]

But one sentiment issued from the lips of all; namely, that not without the knowledge of the king could this crime have been committed. . . . Through the crowd ran the cry that the count had been suffering unjustly from a charge of which he was innocent. . . . Accordingly, the count grew in universal favour and good will and it was felt that the accusations made against him, of whatever nature, proceeded entirely from malice.

[Fulk managed to exonerate himself from having ordered the murder, but the issue rumbled on.]

From that time, all who had informed the count and thereby incited the king fell under the displeasure of Queen Melisende and were forced to take diligent measures for their own safety. . . . It was not safe for these informers to come into her presence. . . . Even the king found that no place was entirely safe among the kindred and partisans of the queen. At length, through the mediation of certain intimate friends, her wrath was appeased, and the king finally, after persistent efforts, succeeded in gaining a pardon for the other objects of her wrath – at least to the extent that they could be introduced into her presence with others. But from that day forward, the king became so uxorious that, whereas he had formerly aroused her wrath, he now calmed it, and not even in unimportant cases did he take any measures without her knowledge and assistance.

William of Tyre, *A History of Deeds Done Beyond the Sea*, ed. Emily Babcock, tr. August Krey, 2 vols, Columbia University Press, New York, 1943, vol. 2, pp. 50–51, 45–46, 70–76.

(ii) The version of Orderic Vitalis

To begin with he [Fulk] acted without the foresight and shrewdness he should have shown, and changed governors and other dignitaries too quickly and thoughtlessly. As a new ruler he banished from his counsels the leading magnates who from the first had fought resolutely against the Turks and helped Godfrey and the two Baldwins to bring towns and fortresses under their rule, and replaced them with Angevin strangers and other raw new-comers to whom he gave his ear; turning out the veteran defenders, he gave the chief places in the counsels of the realm and the castellanships of castles to new flatterers. Consequently great disaffection spread, and the stubbornness of the magnates was damnably roused against the man who changed officials so gauchely. For a long time, under the influence of the powers of evil, they turned their warlike skills, which they should have united to exercise against the heathen, to rend themselves. They even allied on both sides with the pagans against each other, with the result that they lost many thousands of men and a certain number of fortresses.

Orderic Vitalis, *The Ecclesiastical History*, ed. and tr. Marjorie Chibnall, 6 vols, Oxford University Press, Oxford, 1969–80, vol. 6, pp. 391–93.

THE SETTLERS' TREATMENT OF MUSLIMS IN THE FRANKISH EAST   **Document 10**

Ibn Jubayr was a Spanish Muslim from Granada who made the haj *(pilgrimage) to Mecca in the mid-1180s. He spent a short period of time (32 days) in the Latin East in 1184 and has left this important account of the treatment of his co-religionists. Document ii concerns the Hanbalis, a radical Islamic sect who farmed land around Nablus until they fled to Damascus in the 1150s. The writings of Diya al-Din reflect this radical position and were written after Saladin's conquests of 1187.*

(i) Ibn Jubayr

(a)   One of the astonishing things that is talked of is that although the fires of discord burn between the two parties, Muslim and Christian, two armies of them may meet and dispose themselves in battle array, and yet Muslim and Christian travellers will come and go between them without interference. In this connection we saw at this time, that is the month of Jumada 'l-Ula, the departure of Saladin with all the Muslims troops to lay siege to the fortress of Kerak, one of the greatest of the Christian strongholds lying astride the Hejaz road and hindering the overland pas-sage of the Muslims. Between it and Jerusalem lies a day's journey or a little more. It occupies the choicest part of the land in Palestine, and has a very wide dominion with continuous settlements, it being said that the number of villagers reaches four hundred. This Sultan invested it, and put it to sore straits, and long the siege lasted, but still the caravans passed successively from Egypt to Damascus, going through the lands of the Franks without impediment from them. In the same way the Muslims continuously journeyed from Damascus to Acre (through Frankish territory), and likewise not one of the Christian merchants was stopped or hindered (in Muslim territories).

The Christians impose a tax on the Muslims in their land which gives them full security; and likewise the Christian merchants pay a tax upon their goods in Muslim lands. Agreement exists between them, and there is equal treatment in all cases. The soldiers engage themselves in their war, while the people are at peace and the work goes to him who conquers. Such is the usage in war of the people of these lands; and in the dispute existing between the Muslim Emirs and their kings it is the same, the subjects and the merchants interfering not. Security never leaves them in any circumstance, neither in peace nor in war. The state of these countries in this regard is truly more astonishing than our story can convey. May God by His favour exalt the word of Islam.

(b) This city [Banyas] is on the frontier of the Muslim territories. It is small, but has a fortress below the walls of which winds a river that flows out from one of the gates of the city. A canal leading from it turns the mills. The city had been in the hands of the Franks, but Nur ad-Din – may God's mercy rest upon his soul – recovered it [in 1165]. It has a wide tillage in a continuous vale. It is commanded by a fortress of the Franks called Hunin three parasangs from Banyas. The cultivation of the vale is divided between the Franks and the Muslims, and in it there is a boundary known as 'The Boundary of Dividing'. They apportion the crops equally, and their animals are mingled together, yet no wrong takes place between them because of it.

(c) We moved from Tibnin – may God destroy it – at daybreak on Monday. Our way lay through continuous farms and ordered settlements, whose inhabitants were all Muslims, living comfortably with the Franks. God protect us from such temptation. They surrender half their crops to the Franks at harvest time, and pay as well a poll-tax of one dinar and five qirat [24 qirats to one dinar] for each person. Other than that, they are not interfered with, save for a light tax on the fruits of trees. Their houses and all their effects are left to their full possession. All the coastal cities occupied by the Franks are managed in this fashion, their rural districts, the villages and farms, belonging to the Muslims. But their hearts have been seduced, for they observe how unlike them in ease and comfort are their brethren in the Muslim regions under their Muslim governors. This is one of the misfortunes afflicting the Muslims. The Muslim community bewails the injustice of a landlord of its own faith, and applauds the conduct of its opponent and enemy, the Frankish landlord, and is accustomed to justice from him.

Ibn Jubayr, *The Travels of Ibn Jubayr*, tr. Ronald Broadhurst, Jonathan Cape, London, 1952, pp. 300–301, 315, 316–17.

(ii) Diya al-Din – The Account of the Hanbalis

I heard more than one of our teachers saying that the Muslims fell under the domination of the Franks in the regions of Hayt al-Maqdis and its provinces, working the land for them. They [the Franks] used to punish them [the Muslims], jail them and levy a fee which resembles jizya. The greatest of the Franks was Ahuman b. Barizan [Baldwin of Ibelin] – may God curse him. Under his rule were Jamma'il, the village of our teachers, Marda, Yasuf and other villages. It so happened that whereas the infidels used to collect one dinar from everyone under their control, he – may God curse him – levied four dinars from each of them. He used to mutilate their legs. Among the infidels there existed no one more evil or greater in violence than him – may God put a shame on him. So Ibn Barizan planned to kill Ahmad b. Qudama. One of his [Ibn Barizan's] clerks, whose name was Ibn Tasir, informed the shaykh. The shaykh came to a decision to proceed to Damascus and he went there. Ibn Tasir was an official of Baldwin and his assistant [wazir]. He believed in Muslim holy men and was benevolent towards them. This was told to me by Muhammad b. Abi' Attaf. Another person said that of those who were under the subordination of the Franks, shaykh Ahmad was the first to emigrate both out of fear for his life and because he was unable to practise his religion.

Joseph Drory, 'Hanbalis of the Nablus Region in the Eleventh and Twelfth Centuries', *Asian and African Studies* 22 (1988), pp. 93–112.

(iii) Among the Franks there are some who have become acclimatized and frequent the company of Muslims. They are much better than those recently arrived from their lands, but they are the exception and should not be considered representative. Here is an example. I sent one of my men to Antioch on an errand. At the time, Chief Tadrus ibn al-Saffi was there, and his word had great influence in Antioch; there was a mutual bond of friendship between us. One day he said to my man, 'A Frankish friend of mine has invited me to his home. You should come along so you can observe their ways.' My man told me:

I went along with him and we came to the home of one of the old knights who came out in one of the first expeditions of the Franks. He was since removed from the stipend-registry and dismissed from service but he had some property in Antioch off which he lived. He presented a very fine table with food that was extremely clean and delicious. But seeing me hold back from eating, he said, 'Eat and be of good cheer! For I don't eat Frankish food: I have Egyptian cooking-women and never eat anything except what they cook. And pork never enters my house.' So I ate, though guardedly, and we left.

After passing through the market, a Frankish woman suddenly hung on to me while babbling in their language – I didn't understand what she was saying. Then a group of Franks began to gather round me and I was certain that I was going to perish. But suddenly, who should turn up but that knight . . . [He said to that woman] . . . 'What's the matter with you and this Muslim?'

'This man killed my brother 'Urs.' This 'Urs was a knight in Apamea whom someone from the army of Hama had killed.

The knight shouted at her and said, 'This man is a merchant, who neither fights not attends battle.' And he yelled at the assembled crowd and they dispersed. He then took me by the hand and went away. This, the effect of that meal was my deliverance from death.

Usama ibn Munqidh, *The Book of Contemplation: Islam and the Crusades*, tr. Paul M. Cobb, Penguin, London, 2008, pp. 153–54.

Document 11   THE CALL TO THE SECOND CRUSADE, 1146

This is the first surviving papal bull calling a crusade to the Holy Land. It was first issued at Viterbo, near Rome, on 1 December 1145, and was reissued, with minor amendments, in the form here four months later. It was the centrepiece of the preaching campaign of 1146–47 and would be the cornerstone of papal appeals for the next three decades.

Pope Eugenius III, writing to King Louis VII of France and his subjects, proclaims the Second Crusade on God's behalf. The bull *Quantum praedecessores*, 1 March 1146.

We have learned from what men of old have said and we have found written in their histories how greatly our predecessors the Roman pontiffs have worked for the liberation of the eastern Church. Indeed our predecessor of happy memory, Pope Urban, sounding forth like a heavenly trumpet, took care to induce sons of the Holy Roman Church from several parts of the world to free it. In answer to his call men from beyond the Alps, especially the most strong and vigorous warriors of the kingdom of the French, and also those from Italy, fired with the ardour of love, assembled and once a great army had been collected together, not without much shedding of their own blood but attended by divine aid, freed from the filth of the pagans that city in which it was Our Saviour's will to suffer for us and where he left us his glorious Sepulchre as a memorial of his passion, together with many other places of which, to avoid being lengthy, we have refrained from reminding you. By the grace of God and the zeal of your fathers, who strove to defend them over the years and to spread the Christian name among the peoples in the area, these places have been held by Christians until now and other cities have courageously been taken from the infidels. But now, because our sins and those of its people demanded it, there has occurred what we cannot make known without great sadness and lamentation. The city of Edessa, in our togue known as Rohais, which also, it is said, alone under Christian rule had respect for the power of God at that time when all the land in the East was held by the pagans, has been taken by the enemies of the cross of Christ, who have also occupied many Christian castles. And the archbishop of that city and his clerics and many other Christians have been killed there, while the relics of the saints have been trampled under the infidels' feet and dispersed. We recognise how great the danger is that threatens the Church of God and all Christianity because of this and we do not believe that it is hidden from your under-standing. It will be seen as a great token of nobility and uprightness if those things acquired by the efforts of your fathers are vigorously defended by you, their good sons. But if, God forbid, it comes to pass differently, then the bravery of the fathers will have proved to be diminished in the sons.

And so in the Lord we impress upon, ask and order all of you, and we enjoin it for the remissions of sins, that those who are on God's side, and especially the more powerful and the nobles, should vigorously gird themselves to oppose the multitude of the infidels who are now rejoicing in the victory they have gained over us, to defend in this way the eastern Church, which was freed from their tyranny, as we have said before, by so much spilling of your fathers' blood, and to strive to deliver from their hands the many thousands of our captive brothers, so that the dignity of the name of Christ may be enhanced in our time and your reputation for strength, which is praised throughout the world, may be kept unimpaired and unsullied. And let the good Mattathias be an example to you. He did not hesitate for a moment to expose himself with his sons and relatives to death and to leave all he had in the world to preserve his ancestral laws; and at length with the help of divine aid and with much labour he and his offspring triumphed powerfully over their enemies.

We, providing with a father's concern for your peace of mind and the abandonment of the eastern Church, by the authority given us by God concede and confirm to those who, inspired by devotion, decide to take up and complete so holy and very necessary a work and labour that remission of sins which our aforesaid predecessor Pope Urban instituted. And we decree that their wives and children, goods and possessions should remain under the protection of the Holy Church; under our protection and that of the archbishops, bishops and other prelates of the Church of God. And by apostolic authority we forbid any legal suit to be brought thereafter concerning all the possessions they hold peacefully when they take the cross until there is absolutely certain knowledge of their return or death. Since, moreover, those who fight for the Lord ought not to care for precious clothes or elegant appearance or dogs or hawks or other things that are signs of lasciviousness, we, in the Lord, impress upon your understanding that those who decide to begin so holy a work ought to pay no attention to multi-coloured clothes or minivers or gilded or silvered arms, but should with all their strength employ care and diligence in taking such arms, horses and the rest with which they may the more ardently overcome the infidels. All those who are encumbered with debts and undertake so holy a journey with pure hearts need not pay usury on past loans; and if they or others on their behalf are bound by oath or faith to usurious contracts we absolve them by apostolic authority. And they may raise money on their lands or other possessions, having informed relatives or the lords to whose fiefs they belong, and they may freely pledge them to churches or churchmen or to others of the faithful without any counterclaim, for otherwise they will not want or have the means to go. By the authority of omnipotent God and that of Blessed Peter the Prince of the Apostles conceded to us by God, we grant remission of and absolution from sins, as instituted by our aforesaid predecessor, in such a way that whosoever devoutly begins and completes so holy a journey or dies on it will obtain absolution from all his sins of which he has made confession with a contrite and humble heart; and he will receive the fruit of everlasting recompense from the rewarder of all good people.

Louise and Jonathan Riley-Smith, *The Crusades: Idea and Reality, 1095–1270*, Edward Arnold, London, 1981, pp. 57–59.

Document 12   RECRUITMENT FOR THE SECOND CRUSADE – TROUVÈRE SONG, 1146–47

As well as official documents such as Quantum praedecessores, *unofficial forms of recruitment also existed. This song was written in Old French and would have been sung in courts and public places as the crusade gathered support. It is important as a secular source (rare at this time), although in this instance, the composer seems to have heard* Quantum praedecessores *because there are some similarities of message. In other respects, however, this is plainly a secular document appealing to the interests and sensibilities of the knightly classes.*

Troubadour Song (Anonymous)

Knights, you are in very good hands now that God has called for your help against the Turks and the Almoravids who have done Him such dishonour. They have wrongfully snatched his fiefs; our sorrow at this should indeed be great since it was there that God was first offered service and acknowledged as Lord.

Anyone who now goes with Louis need have no fear of Hell, for his soul will be in Paradise with the angels of Our Lord.

Edessa is taken, as you know, and the Christians are sorely afflicted because of it: the churches are burnt and abandoned, God is no longer sacrificed there. Knights, make your decisions, you who are esteemed for your skill in arms; make a gift of your bodies to Him who was placed on the cross for you.

Take your example from Louis, who has more to lose than you: he is rich and powerful above all other crowned kings; yet he has given up miniver and ermine, castles, towns and citadels and turned to Him who was crucified for us.

God gave up his body to the Jews that He might free us from bondage. They wounded Him in five places so that he suffered passion and death. Now He is calling upon you because the Canaanites and the troops of the cruel Sanguin [Zengi] have played many a wicked trick upon Him: the time has come to pay them back for it!

God has organised a tourney between Heaven and Hell, and so He is asking all His friends who are willing to support His cause not to fail Him. . . .

For the son of God the Creator has fixed a day for being at Edessa; there shall the sinners be saved . . . who will fight fiercely and, for love of Him, will go and help Him in this hour of need . . . to wreak the vengeance of God.

Let us go and take possession of Moses in his tomb on Mount Sinai. Let us snatch it from the hands of the Saracens as also the rod with which, at a single stroke, he opened the Red Sea and all his people came after; Pharaoh followed in pursuit and was killed with all his men.

Les chansons de croisade avec leurs mélodies, eds J. Bédier and P. Aubry, Luzac, Paris, 1909, pp. 8–11. Translated by Mike Routledge, Department of French, Royal Holloway, University of London.

THE REGULATIONS IMPOSED ON THE CRUSADERS SAILING TO   **Document 13**
LISBON, 1147

Given the diverse backgrounds of the crusading armies, discipline must have been very difficult to enforce on campaign. This is an attempt to set ground rules for conduct and may have been born out of the tensions experienced between contingents on the First Crusade. In any case, it appears to have been a success because the Second Crusade conquered Lisbon, in part because of the (relative) unity of the attacking armies.

Among these people of so many different tongues the firmest guarantees of peace and friendship were taken; and, furthermore, they sanctioned very strict laws, as, for example, a life for a life and a tooth for a tooth. They forbade all display of costly garments. Also they ordained that women should not go out in public; that the peace must be kept by all, unless they should suffer injuries recognised by the proclamation; that weekly chapters be held by the laity and the clergy separately, unless perchance some great emergency should require their meeting together; that each ship have its own priest and keep the same observances as are prescribed for parishes; that no one retain the servant or seaman of another in his employ; that everyone make weekly confession and communicate on Sunday; and so on through the rest of the obligatory articles with separate sanctions for each. Furthermore, they constituted for every thousand of the forces two elected members who were to be called judges or *coniurati*, through whom the cases of the constables were to be settled in accordance with the proclamation and by whom the distribution of moneys was to be carried out.

The Conquest of Lisbon (De expugnatione lyxbonensi), tr. Charles David, with a new foreword by Jonathan Phillips, Columbia University Press, New York, 2001, p. 57.

Document 14   THE GREEKS AND THE SECOND CRUSADE, 1147–48

The attitude of the Greeks to the Second Crusade was, generally, one of hostility. They did not want large western armies outside Constantinople and they feared the impact of the crusade on their newly imposed overlordship of the principality of Antioch. They were accused by some western writers of treachery, but here is evidence from a Byzantine source of such behaviour. Niketas Choniates was a secretary to the Byzantine emperor and wrote after the sack of Constantinople by the Fourth Crusade (1204). His style is heavily influenced by classical writers, a convention required in the elite court circles that formed his audience.

The Annals of Niketas Choniates

The passage of the king, who shortly was to be joined by his fellow Franks, was viewed with satisfaction by the Romans, like the passing of some dire portent from heaven. Once again, the emperor had the same care for his own provinces which he had formerly exercised. He did not neglect to provide them with supplies of food, and market wares were once again set out on the roadside. The Romans, following Manuel's instructions, set up ambushes in strategic places and along the defiles of mountain passes, where they slew no small number of the enemy. When the Germans approached the gates of the cities, the citizens did not display their wares but rather let ropes down from the wall so that they could first pull up the money in payment for whatever they were hawking and then let down only as much as suited them, whether it was bread or any other saleable foodstuff. By knowingly committing these unlawful acts, they incensed the All-Seeing Eye, for cheating at the scales and for taking no pity on them as strangers, and for not even setting before them, as co-religionists, any of their own household stores, instead seizing from their throats that which was necessary to sustain the body. The worst of the inhabitants, especially those motivated by inhumanity, did not let down even the tiniest morsel but, drawing up the gold and silver, deposited the coins in their bosoms and disappeared, not to be seen again on the walls between the towers. Some, mixing lime with the barley groats, concocted a fatal mixture.

Whether all this, in truth, was commanded by the emperor, as was rumored, I do not know with certainty: it was, nonetheless, an iniquitous and unholy deed. The emperor's purpose was neither in doubt nor was it cast in the shadow of the curtain of falsehood: he minted debased silver coinage which he offered to the Italian troops to pay for their needs. In short, every ill the emperor himself had contrived was present, and he commanded others to inflict such harm so that these things should be an indelible memorial for posterity, deterents against attacking the Romans.

Niketas Choniates, *O City of Byzantium, The Annals of Niketas Choniates*, tr. Harry Magoulias, Wayne State University Press, Detroit, MI, 1984, pp. 38–39.

THE *JIHAD* GATHERS MOMENTUM UNDER NUR AD-DIN AND SALADIN   **Document 15**

As noted earlier, poetry was a crucial format for the transmission of ideas in the Muslim world at this time. Skilled poets were prominent figures in the courts of the Near East and helped to convey the theoretical ideas of the anti-Frankish jihad. The first of these documents concerns Nur ad-Din, a name that means 'Pillar of Light', hence the use of such imagery in a poem that offers praise and thanks for his leadership and his virtues. The second poem is by Imad ad-Din al-Isfahani, who worked for Nur ad-Din, and later for Saladin. He writes in praise of Nur ad-Din's general, Shirkuh, on his conquest of Egypt and defeat of the Fatimid vizier, Shawar; these events are seen as a precursor to the liberation of Jerusalem. The third piece, also by Imad ad-Din al-Isfahani, is an extract from a poem that incites Saladin to advance the **jihad** *by cleansing the land of their unbelief and to take revenge on the Franks.*

(i) In praise of Nur ad-Din after his recovery from illness in 1157.

> Oh sun without eclipse and without concealment, lights request that
>   your light remains.
> The full moon is incomplete whilst you are complete. You have light
>   while it has a glow.
> Your cure is for Islam from diseases that gripped it, and your cure is
>   death for your enemies.
> What are you except a sword that does not become rusty though lack
>   of use, while you are always active in striking.
> If a loss comes to you, the eyes of your people take it far from you.
> If the earth paid a ransom that the sky does not fall, then the kingdoms
>   pay the countries' ransom for you.
> You provide for them if rain is withheld, as well as for their needs.
> And you are their best when we recount the good people.
> And in the bed of the kingdom is a kingdom for God.
> And happiness and bounty is hidden for the sake of God.
> Protect the religion in this kingdom, so that those who remain awake
>   in the night do not snatch it.
> Its buildings have risen, and they are in his hands.
> And they are fenced and a bracelet [of protection].
> Oh, Nur ad-Din, the horizons will darken if you do not illuminate them,
>   and the religion will be darkness.
> You have remained healthy because Islam, so protect the lands of Islam
>   when they are oppressed, protect them.
> You became sad and distressed, and when you did the world became
>   troubled.
> Time does not permit you to stay forever for us, and every wound of
>   yours is enormous to us.

Ibn Munir, in: Abu Shama, *The Two Gardens*, vol. 1, p. 317, trans. Osman Latiff, 2013. *Kitāb al-rawdatayn fi akhbār al-dawlatayan*, ed. Ibrahim Shams al-Din, 4 vols, Dar al-Kotob al-Ilmiyah, Beirut, 2002.

(ii) In praise of Shirkuh's victory in Egypt, 1169

> You liberated Egypt and I hope that while you are a liberator of Egypt,
>   you will be easing the way to liberate Jerusalem.
> We raised our hands to God in thankfulness, since Islam will not be
>   harmed because of you.

The people of Islam complained to you of their being orphans, so you
  stood for them in the place of a comforting father.
In every home of the Franks you will find a woman who wails; because
  of what struck them they spend their nights in grief.
You have saved the servants [worshippers] from the evil of Shawar.
So [look] how much and how much you have achieved for the party of
  God [Hizbullah].
He [Shawar] is the one who made the Franks aspire to the lands of
  Islam . . .
He [Shirkuh] returned the caliphate to the 'Abassids; leave the claimant
  [of the Fatimid caliphate] to meet the worst enemy.
Do not cut merely the tail of the snake while leaving the snake to escape.
My strong wish it that you cut the head like the tail.

Imad ad-din al-Isfahani, in: Ibn Wasil, *Mufarrij*, vol. 1, pp. 165–67, trans. Osman
Latiff, 2013. *Mufarrij al'Kurub fi akhbar Bani Ayyub*, vol. 1, ed. Jamal al-Din al-
Shayyal, Cairo, 1953.

(iii) Extracts from a poem inciting revenge upon the Franks

So rise and open Jerusalem, and cause bloodshed in it. When the blood
flows, it will cleanse the city.

And bestow death upon the *Asbatar* [the Hospitallers] and let the ceiling
collapse on the bishop.

And save those countries from unbelief, so that God will save you at the
standing [on the Day of Judgement].

Imad ad-Din al-Isfahani, in: Abu Shama, *The Two Gardens*, vol. 2, p. 296. trans.
Osman Latiff, 2013. *Kitāb al-rawdatayn fi akhbār al-dawlatayan*, ed. Ibrahim Shams
al-Din, 4 vols, Dar al-Kotob al-Ilmiyah, Beirut, 2002.

AMALRIC'S DECISION TO TRAVEL TO CONSTANTINOPLE, 1171   **Document 16**

*William of Tyre recounts Amalric's determination to lead this mission in
person, enabling us to see the king's power over his nobles. Amalric was
received with great ceremony in Constantinople. The Franks were shown
around the city and its churches and were entertained in lavish style.
Discussions concerning an attack on Egypt were held and Amalric also set
out the needs of his kingdom. William of Tyre provides a vivid description of
the visit, but of the details agreed between the two men he only noted a treaty
'agreeable to both the emperor and the king and put into writing, to which
the seals of both were affixed'. In fact William was probably concealing the full
picture from the western audience of his Historia (see above, pp. 121–2),*

and the contemporary Byzantine writer, John Kinnamos (an imperial secretary), gives a succinct insight into the reality of the arrangement: Amalric had visited Constantinople in person in order to swear homage to Manuel in return for his support.

(i) William of Tyre

The king [Amalric] summoned all his nobles to him and laid before them the needs of the realm. For he perceived that the kingdom was weighed down by many troubles, that the enemies of the Christian faith were constantly increasing not only in number and valour but in wealth and riches as well. . . .

The king therefore requested the advice of his nobles as to how these evil conditions could be remedied and the kingdom saved. They advised that aid from the princes of the West should be implored to combat these troubles; they had no other plan of relief to suggest.

Accordingly, with the common consent of all, it was resolved that a delegation consisting of men of high rank be sent to explain the difficulties of the kingdom to the princes of the West and to ask their aid. The envoys were instructed to visit the pope and those illustrious lords, the emperor of the Romans, the kings of France, England, Sicily and the Spains, and also other distinguished dukes and counts and implore their assistance in combatting the imminent perils now threatening the kingdom. It was further resolved that the precarious situation of the realm be made known to the emperor of Constantinople. Since he was much nearer to us and was besides far richer than the others, he could more easily furnish the desired aid. It was specified also that the envoy sent to the emperor should be a person so gifted with wisdom, eloquence and authority that by his tact and ability he might incline the mind of that great prince to comply with our wishes.

While they were deliberating over the selection of a suitable person to undertake this important mission, the king had been consulting with some of his more intimate counsellors. He now laid before the assembly a plan which he had conceived. He declared that a mission of such importance could be undertaken by no one but himself and added that he was prepared to undergo all perils and hardships to relieve the desperate necessity of the kingdom. The nobles of the realm, though filled with admiration, were almost overcome by this proposal and protested that the task was too arduous; moreover, without the presence of the king the realm would be desolate. Amalric answered, however, 'Let the Lord, whose minister I am, rule the kingdom; as for me, I am determined to go; no one can induce me to recall that decision.'

Accordingly, on 10 March [1171], attended by a great retinue as befitted the royal majesty, he set out on the journey.

William of Tyre, *A History of Deeds Done Beyond the Sea*, ed. Emily Babcock, tr. August Krey, 2 vols, Columbia University Press, New York, 1943, vol. 2, pp. 377–83.

(ii) John Kinnamos

In the meantime, the king of Palestine came to Byzantium to petition the emperor for what he required. Obtaining what he sought, he agreed to many things, including his subjection to the emperor on those terms.

John Kinnamos, *The Deeds of John and Manuel Comnenus*, tr. Charles Brand, Columbia University Press, New York, 1976, p. 209.

MUSLIM AND FRANKISH MILITARY TACTICS   **Document 17**

Walter the Chancellor was an eye-witness source from the Principality of Antioch who was concerned to record events for posterity. His writings covered the period 1114–22 and here he describes the temptation posed to the Franks by a Muslim incursion and the difficulties of Prince Roger of Antioch in persuading his men not to respond – as, of course, the Muslims hoped they would do, thereby drawing them out of formation and enabling the Christians to be defeated. William of Tyre outlines a more prudent approach – that of avoiding battle – which often gave the settlers their best results.

(i) Walter the Chancellor

While they [the Muslims] were doing their best to attack our men dreadfully, a rumour reached their ears announcing that the king's approach was very close. They, indeed, had confidence not in the power of the Holy Ghost, but in the great numbers of their army. . . . They shook their spears, loosed their arrows and charged almost into our camp. When he saw this, the renowned prince [Roger of Antioch], riding a swift horse, unsheathed his sword and rode around his men's encampment, declaiming: '. . . If anyone dares to ride out now, he will perish by my sword.' Indeed, on the contrary, he warned every one of them to stand before his camp, weapons in hand and mind alert, and yet not to venture in any way or to signal the start of the battle for themselves. Therefore the Persians marvelled that a race so ready for war and always intolerant of injury, who had been provoked so often by arrows, afflicted so often by jeers, was so long-suffering, because the Christians did not signal the start of battle and were already submitting as if fear had conquered them. Some of our men even considered it an act of cowardice; however some of greater perspicacity interpreted it as the purpose of the prince so that, when he was sure the time was right, they would be stronger to attack, not at the enemy's summoning, nor in anticipation of their forces, but by the prudent disposition and enormous experience of himself and the king, whose arrival was very near. For, as experience shows, a handful of warriors with boldness and ingenuity will more often prevail in war then an ill-disciplined and unreliable multitude of armed men.

Walter the Chancellor, *The Antiochene Wars*, tr. Thomas Asbridge and Susan Edgington, Ashgate, Aldershot, 1999, pp. 92–93.

(ii) William of Tyre

The count had retired with his forces to the city of Arka and was there await-ing an opportunity to engage the enemy without too much risk. The knights of the Temple who lived in the same vicinity also remained shut up in their strongholds; they expected almost hourly to be besieged and did not wish to risk an encounter with the Turks. The brothers of the Hospital had likewise retired in alarm to their fortified castle of Krak. They felt that if, in the midst of such confusion they could defend the fortress just named from injury by the enemy, their duty had been done. . . . During this time Saladin ranged here and there over the plain, especially the cultivated fields, and without opposition traversed the entire locality. He burned all the crops, those that had been gathered into the granaries, those still stacked in the fields, and the growing grain as well. He drove off cattle as booty and laid waste the whole country in every direction.

William of Tyre, *A History of Deeds Done Beyond the Sea*, ed. Emily Babcock, tr. August Krey, 2 vols, Columbia University Press, New York, 1943, vol. 2, pp. 447–48.

Document 18   KNIGHT SERVICE OWED IN THE KINGDOM OF JERUSALEM, *c.* 1185–86

This is an extract from **Le Livre des Assises** *of John of Ibelin, count of Jaffa (c. 1216–66). John was a prominent politician in the Latin East in the mid-thirteenth century who wrote a treatise on the High Court of the kingdom of Jerusalem that included a list of the military capacity of the kingdom based upon records from c. May 1185 to April 1186; in other words, just before Saladin's victory at Hattin. For reasons of space, only a segment of the text is included here (for the full account, see the reference below), but it gives some indication of the organisation and scale of the forces of the kingdom. The numbers listed in this work would be supplemented by members of noble house-holds visiting western knights and mercenaries. Note the mention of women on the lists – probably widows or wives whose husbands were in captivity. Sergeants were well-armed footsoldiers, not mounted knights.*

The barony of the county of Jaffa and Ascalon to which Ramla, Mirabel and Ibelin belong owes 100 knights:

Jaffa	25
Ascalon	25
Ramla and Mirabel	40
Ibelin	10

The barony of the principality of Galilee owes 100 knights:

Land this side of the River Jordan	60
Land the other side of the River Jordan	40

The barony of Sidon to which Beaufort, Caesarea and Bethsan belong owes 100 knights:

Sidon and Beaufort	50
Caesarea	25
Bethsan	25

The lordship of Kerak, Montreal and Saint Abraham owes 60 knights:

Kerak and Montreal	40
Saint Abraham	20

The lordship of Count Joscelin owes 24 knights:

Château du Roi	4
Saint George	10
The land of Geoffrey Le Tor	6
The land of Philip Le Rous	2
The chamberlainy	2

[John then lists the services owed by the bishops of the kingdom, which totalled 34 knights; then the services owed by the cities of the kingdom of Jerusalem. Jerusalem itself owed 41 knights, Nablus 85, Acre 80, Daron 2, Beirut 21, and, listed here in full, Tyre owed 28.]

The lordship of Tyre owes 28 knights:

The Venetians	3
Simon of Marcini	3
The wife of William Le Grand	2
The wife of Gobert Vernier	1
Fulk of Falaise	2
Anseau, the son of Charles	1
Gerard Gazel	2
Henry of Maschelin	1

Adam of Arsuf	1
Denis, the son of Geoffrey	1
Raoul Le Bouteiller	2
Roger Savari	7
Simon des Molins	1
Roger Le Gaste Bouteillier	1

The total number of knights is 677 [*sic* 675]

[John also lists the aids, in the form of sergeants, owed by the churches and the burgesses at times of great need. A few are listed below, with the grand total of sergeants from all the dues.]

The patriarch of Jerusalem owes	500
The chapter of the Holy Sepulchre	500
The Church of St Mary of the Latins	50
The city of Acre	500
The city of Caesarea	50
The bishop of Sebastea	100
The archbishop of Tyre	150
Jaffa	100
Haifa	50
Tiberias	200

The total number of sergeants [including those not listed here], 5,175.

Peter Edbury, *John of Ibelin and the Kingdom of Jerusalem*, Boydell, Woodbridge, 1997, pp. 195–200.

Document 19   THE CONSTRUCTION OF FORTRESSES AROUND ASCALON

This document reveals several aspects of Frankish military strategy. First, from the 1130s onwards there was a deliberate attempt to stifle the threat from the Muslim-held city of Ascalon. This settlement posed a serious menace to the south-west of the kingdom of Jerusalem, including the pilgrim road from Jaffa to the Holy City, and was the sole remaining Muslim-controlled port on the Levantine coast. The Franks constructed a series of castles in the vicinity of Ascalon to prevent raids on their lands and also to exert pressure on the Muslim garrison. Eventually this paid off and in 1153 the Christians took the city. Note also how the construction of the castles increased the security of the settlers and the productivity of their lands – an important and desired consequence of this policy.

The Christians perceived that the bold incursions of the enemy showed no signs of ceasing; their forces were constantly renewed and, like the hydra, they gained increased strength after the death of their citizens. Hence after long deliberation, our people resolved to erect fortresses around about [Ascalon]. These would serve as defences against this monster which ever increased by the loss of its heads and, as often as it was destroyed, was reborn to our exceeding peril. Within these strongholds forces could be easily assembled which, from their very proximity would check the enemy's forays. Such fortresses would also serve as bases to make frequent attacks upon the city itself. [The castles of Bethgibelin and Ibelin were built and, encouraged by their effect, Blanchegarde was constructed in 1142.]

As soon as it was finished the king [Fulk] took it under his own protection . . . and committed it to the care of wise men who had long experience in warfare. . . . Often by themselves, more often in company with men at arms from the other fortresses built with similar intent, these men used to issue forth to encounter and defeat the enemy when they tried to make raids from the city. Occasionally they even attacked the men of Ascalon on their own initiative, wrought great havoc on them and frequently triumphed over them. The result was that those who dwelt in the surrounding country began to place great reliance on this castle as well as on the other strongholds, and a great many suburban places grew up around it. Numerous families established themselves there, and tillers of the fields as well. The whole district became much more secure, because the locality was occupied and a more abundant supply of food for the surrounding country was made possible.

William of Tyre, *A History of Deeds Done Beyond the Sea*, ed. Emily Babcock, tr. August Krey, 2 vols, Columbia University Press, New York, 1943, vol. 2, pp. 131–32.

THE CALL FOR THE THIRD CRUSADE, 1187   **Document 20**

The news of the loss of Jerusalem is said to have caused Pope Urban III to die of a heart attack. His successor, Pope Gregory VIII, issued this lengthy appeal to the people of the West, in the bull Audita tremendi, *urging them to react to the fall of the holy city. He plainly blamed the settlers' infighting, but also the sins of all Christians. He urged people to accept God's challenge and to undertake a penitential exercise in the form of the crusade. Note, the text in italics represents quotes from the Bible, used by Gregory to give his arguments greater effect.*

On hearing with what severe and terrible judgement the land of Jerusalem has been smitten by the divine hand, we and our brothers have been confounded by such great horror and affected by such great sorrow that we could not easily decide what to do or say: over this situation the psalmist laments and says, *Oh God, the heathens are come into thine inheritance.* Taking advantage of the dissension which the malice of men at the suggestion of the devil has recently aroused in the land of the Lord, Saladin came on those regions with a host of armed men. There advanced against him the king, the bishops, the Templars, the Hospitallers and the barons with the knights and the people of the land and the relic of the Lord's cross, which used to afford a sure safeguard and desired defence against the invasion of the pagans through remembrance and faith in the passion of Christ, who hung on it and redeemed the human race on it. They were attacked and, when our side had been overpowered, the Lord's cross was taken, the bishops were slain, the king was captured and almost everyone else was either killed by the sword or seized by hostile hands, so that very few were said to have escaped in flight. The bishops, moreover, and the Templars and the Hospitallers were beheaded in Saladin's sight. We do not think that we ought to describe the events in letters until somebody comes to us from those parts who can explain more fully what really happened: how, once the army had been overcome, the infidels invaded and ravaged everything so that it is said that there are very few places left which have not fallen into their hands. But, although we have to say with the prophet *Who will give water to my head and a fountain of tears to my eyes, and I will weep day and night for the slain of my people,* we ought not to be so downhearted that we fall into want of faith and believe that God, angered by his people in such a way as to allow himself to become infuriated by the manifold actions of a host of common sinners, will not through his mercy be quickly placated by penance, that he will not console us and that after tears he will not bring rejoicing. For anyone of sane mind who does not weep at such a cause for weeping, if not in body, at least in his heart, would seem to have forgotten not only his Christian faith, which teaches that one ought to mourn with all those who mourn, but even his very humanity, since every sensible man can surmise the details which we have left out, from the very magnitude of the peril, with those savage barbarians thirsting after Christian blood and using all their force to profane the Holy Places and banish the worship of God from the land. First the prophets and then the apostles of God might be established in that land and flow out from it to all the regions of the world. Moreover – this is the greatest and most unutterable fact – God, through whom all things were made, desiring to be made flesh, wished in his ineffable wisdom and incomprehensible mercy to bring about our salvation there through the infirmity of the flesh, which is to say, hunger, thirst, the cross and death, and through his resurrection, according to the saying, he *hath wrought salvation in the midst of the earth*; he deigned to work this through himself, which the tongue cannot speak of nor the heart of man contemplate. The Holy Land has now endured what we read that it suffered under men of old. What a great cause for mourning this ought to be for us and the whole Christian people!

We ought not to believe, however, that these things have happened through the injustice of a violent judge, but rather through the iniquity of a delinquent people, since we read that when the people turned to the Lord *one* pursued *after a thousand, and two* chased *ten thousand* and when the people itself was at peace the army of Sennacherib was consumed by an angelic hand. But on the other hand that *land* devoured *its inhabitants,* nor could it remain in a quiet state for long, nor could it keep in check transgressors against the divine law. And these instances served as lessons and examples to those who were making their way to the heavenly Jerusalem and those who may not reach it except by the exercise of good works and through many temptations. But these things could first have been feared when Edessa and other land passed into the power of the pagans and it would have been prudent if the people who were left returned to penance and pleased the Lord by turning to him whom they had offended by transgression. For his anger does not come suddenly, but he puts off revenge and gives men time to do penance; in the end truly he, who does not fail to give judgement in his mercy, exacts his punishment to penalise the transgressors and to warn those who are to be saved. Faced by such great distress concerning that land, moreover, we ought to consider not only the sins of its inhabitants but also our own and those of the whole Christian people, and we ought to fear lest what is left of that land will be lost and the power of the infidels rage in other regions, since we hear from all parts of the world about quarrels between kings and princes, cities against cities, and about scandals. We can weep with the prophet and say, *There is no truth and there is no knowledge of God in the land. Theft and lying and killing and adultery have overflowed: and blood hath touched blood.* It is, therefore, incumbent upon all of us to consider and to choose to amend our sins by voluntary chastisement and to turn to the Lord our God with penance and works of piety; and we should first amend in ourselves what we have done wrong and then turn our attention to the treachery and malice of the enemy. And let us in no way hesitate to do for God what the infidels do not fear to attempt against the Lord.

And so consider, my sons, how you came into this world and how you are going to leave it, how all things are passing and how too your life is transitory, and accept with an act of thanksgiving the opportunity for repentance and doing good, as much as it pertains to you, and give yourselves not to destruction but to the service of him from whom you have received both your existence and all the things you have; because you cannot exist of yourselves or possess anything by yourselves, you who cannot create one single gnat upon the earth. We are not saying, 'Forgo what you possess', but 'Send it ahead into the heavenly barn and deposit in his house *where neither the rust nor moth doth consume, and where thieves do not break through or steal'*, labouring for the recovery of that land in which for salvation truth arose from the earth and did not despise to suffer for us the gibbet of the cross. And do not make your way there for money or for worldly glory, but according to the will of God who taught by his own action that one ought to lay down one's life for one's brothers; and commend to his care your riches, which whether you like it or not you will leave in the end to heirs you will not know. It is nothing new for this land to be struck by divine judgement, nor is it unusual for it, once whipped and chastised, to seek mercy. The Lord, indeed, could save it by his will alone, but it is not for us to ask why he has acted thus. For perhaps the Lord has wished to find out and bring to the notice of others whether there is anyone who has knowledge of him or is seeking after him and might joyfully embrace the chance of penitence offered to him and, in laying down his life for his brothers, may be killed in a brief moment and gain eternal life. Hear how the Maccabees, on fire with zeal for the divine law, exposed themselves to every danger to liberate their brothers and taught that not only riches but also persons ought to be laid down for the salvation of their brethren, encouraging each other and saying, *Gird yourselves and be valiant men, for it is better for us to die in battle than to see the evils of our nation and of the holies*. And may you, led to the light of truth through the incarnation of Our Lord Jesus Christ and instructed by the examples of many saints, perform without any fear what the Maccabees, set only under the law [of Moses], did; and do not fear to surrender earthly and few things that will last a short time in exchange for those good things which have been promised and reserved for you, *that eye hath not seen, nor ear heard: neither* have they *entered into the heart of man*; about which Saint Paul says *that the sufferings of this time* are *not worthy to be compared with the glory to come that shall be revealed in us*.

But to those who with contrite hearts and humbled spirits undertake the journey and die in penitence for their sins and with right faith we promise full indulgence of their faults and eternal life; whether surviving or dying they shall know that, through the mercy of almighty God and the authority of the apostles Peter and Paul, and our authority, they will have relaxation of the reparation imposed for all their sins, of which they have made proper confession. And their goods and families shall stand under the protection of the Holy Roman Church and also of the archbishops and bishops and other prelates of the Church of God from the time when they take the cross. And no legal suit will be brought concerning those things they hold peacefully up to the time of their taking the cross until there is absolutely certain knowledge of their return or death; their goods are to remain in the meantime undiminished and unmolested. Also they are not to be forced to pay usurious interest if they are bound to anyone, but let them remain absolved from it and unmolested. Nor are they to go in rich clothes and with dogs or birds or other things which might seem to serve rather for delight and luxury than for necessary use; but they should go with modest provision and dress, in which they may appear rather to do penance than to affect empty pomp.

Louise and Jonathan Riley-Smith, *The Crusades: Idea and Reality, 1095–1274*, Edward Arnold, London, 1981, pp. 64–67.

SALADIN'S GENEROSITY, *c.* 1189–90

Document 21

Beha ad-Din was a close associate and admirer of Saladin and acted as the qadi al-'askar (judge of the army) from 1188 to 1193. He was, therefore, an eye-witness to many events at the time of the Third Crusade and was personally close to the sultan. The precise date of composition is difficult to ascertain but was probably before 1216. The extract here is one of the many stories concerning Saladin's generosity of a sort related by both Frankish and Muslim writers.

The Muslims had thieves who would enter the enemy's tents, steal from them, even taking individuals, and then make their way back. It came about that one night they took an unweaned infant three months old. They brought it to the sultan's tent and offered it to him. Everything they took they used to offer him and he would reward and recompense them. When the mother missed the child she spent the whole duration of the night pleading for help with loud lamentations. Her case came to the notice of their [the Franks'] princes, who said to her, 'He [Saladin] has a merciful heart. We give you permission to go to him. Go and ask him for the child and he will restore it to you.' So she went to ask the Muslim advance guard for assistance, telling them of her troubles through a *dragoman* who translated for her. They did not detain her but sent her to the sultan. She came to him when he was riding on Tell al-Kharruba with me and with a great crowd attending upon him. She wept copious tears and besmirched her face with soil. After he had asked about her case and it had been explained, he had compassion for her, and with tears in his eyes, he ordered the infant to be brought to him. People went and found that it had been sold in the market. The sultan ordered the purchase price to be paid to the purchaser and the child taken from him. He himself stayed where he had halted until the infant was produced and then handed it over to the woman who took it, wept mightily, and hugged it to her bosom, while people watched her and wept also. I was standing there among the gathering. She suckled the child for a while and then, on the orders of the sultan, she was taken on horseback and restored to their camp with the infant.

Consider this compassion which encompasses all humanity. O God, You created him merciful, show him Your ample mercy, O mighty and generous One! Consider, too, the testimony of the enemy to his gentleness, generosity, mercy and compassion.

Beha ad-Din Ibn Shaddad, *The Rare and Excellent History of Saladin*, tr. Donald Richards, Ashgate, Aldershot, 2001, pp. 147–48.

Document 22   THE THIRD CRUSADE TURNS BACK FROM JERUSALEM, 1192

As the Third Crusade approached Jerusalem the realisation that the holy city could not be held dawned upon the mass of crusaders. Having set out from the West determined to regain Jerusalem, this was a bitter blow to the army and caused morale to plummet. The text is a combination of the work of an anonymous English participant in the crusade and the thirteenth-century writer, Richard de Templo, an Augustinian based in London.

So in the year of Our Lord 1192, not many days after the Lord's Epiphany [6 January], a council was convened. The wiser people decided that they and the more discerning inhabitants of the country must have another discussion as to whether it would be more advantageous to advance and attack the city of Jerusalem or to turn elsewhere. . . . The Templars, Hospitallers and Poulains [the settlers] made a very strong case with various supporting arguments for completely abandoning the advance and instead pressing on with rebuilding the city of Ascalon. From there they could look out for Turks coming from Babylonia [Egypt] to Jerusalem, carrying foodstuffs. The leaders in general eventually gave their approval to this advice, believing at that time the most advantageous course of action was to rescue Ascalon from the Turks, rebuild it and keep watch so that the Turks would no longer have unhindered passage there.

However, when the army was actually informed about the decision to retreat, the common people pined away with indescribable grief. All sighed and groaned because their heartfelt hope of visiting the Lord's Sepulchre had suddenly been ended. Sadness hung over them, completely swallowing up their previous joy over the advance. Despair at what they now heard wiped out the earlier hope. In distress they called down evil on those who had published this decree, cursing the delay in carrying out their vow and those who caused things to go against them.

Yet of these people had been more fully informed about the poor state of those [Muslims] who were in Jerusalem, they would have been less troubled by anxiety and taken some comfort from their enemies' adversities. The Turks who had shut themselves in Jerusalem were indeed in the direst straits. . . . Without doubt, the long-desired city of Jerusalem could have been easily captured. Yet it could not have been held by our people for long, because when the pilgrimage was completed the people would have gone home and there would not have been anyone left who could defend it.

Chronicle of the Third Crusade (Itinerarium peregrinorum et Gesta Regis Ricardi), tr. Helen Nicholson, Ashgate, Aldershot, 1997, pp. 283–84. See also pp. 335–36.

THE FOURTH CRUSADE AND THE SACK OF CONSTANTINOPLE, 1204   **Document 23**

These four documents cover several of the key moments during the Fourth Crusade. The first is an extract from Pope Innocent III's powerful crusade appeal from 1198, **Post miserabile.** *The second is from the chronicle of Geoffrey of Villehardouin and contains the Treaty of Venice (1201), the fateful deal negotiated between the northern French crusaders (including Villehardouin himself) and the Venetians that did so much to draw the expedition towards its fateful outcome. The third document is also from Villehardouin, and is the offer made to the crusaders by Prince Alexios which did much to draw them towards Constantinople. The fourth is Villehardouin's own voice, vividly conveying the sense of awe felt by the crusaders as they laid eyes upon 'the Queen of Cities' and putting their decision to attack the place in some sort of perspective.*

(i) Pope Innocent calls the Fourth Crusade, 1198

Following the pitiable collapse of the territory of Jerusalem, following the lamentable massacre of the Christian people, following the deplorable invasion of that land on which the feet of Christ stood and where God, our King, had deigned before the beginning of time, to work out salvation in the midst of the Earth, following the ignominious alienation from our possession of the vivifying Cross . . . the Apostolic See, alarmed over the ill-fortune of such calamity, grieved. It cried out and wailed to such a degree that due to incessant crying out, its throat was made hoarse, and from incessant weeping its eyes almost failed. . . . Still the Apostolic See cries out, and like a trumpet it raises its voice, eager to arouse the Christian peoples to fight Christ's battle and to avenge the injury done to the Crucified One . . .'

Pope Innocent III, *Contemporary Sources for the Fourth Crusade*, trans. Andrea, 2000, pp. 10–11.

(ii) The Treaty of Venice, April 1201

We will build horse transports to carry 4500 horses and 9000 squires with 4500 knights and 20,000 foot sergeants travelling in ships. And we will agree to provide food for all these horses and people for nine months. This is the minimum we will provide in return for a payment of four marks per horse and two marks per man. All the terms we are offering you would be valid for one year from the day of our departure from the port of Venice, to do service to God and Christendom, wherever that might take us. The total cost of what has just been outlined would amount to 85,000 marks. And what's more, we will provide, for the love of God, fifty armed galleys, on condition that for as long as our association lasts we will have one half of everything we capture on land or at sea, and you will have the other.

Geoffrey of Villehardouin, 'The Conquest of Constantinople', *Joinville and Villehardouin: Chronicles of the Crusades*, tr. C. Smith, Penguin, London, 2008, p. 9.

(iii) Prince Alexios of Byzantium's representatives offer to the crusaders, Zara, January 1203

Since you have left home in the cause of God, right and justice, you should, if you are able, restore their inheritance to those who have been wrongly dispossessed. . . . If God permits you to restore Alexios to his inheritance, he will place the entire empire of Byzantium in obedience to Rome, from which it has formerly been cut off. Secondly, he understands that you have spent your own money and are now poor. Therefore, he will give you 200,000 marks of silver and provisions for the whole army, both the great men and the lesser. He will also go with you in person to the land of Egypt, accompanied by 10,000 men (or he will send them at his expense if you think that would be better). He will provide you with such service for one year. And throughout his life he will maintain 500 knights in the land overseas, supported with his own money.

Geoffrey of Villehardouin, 'The Conquest of Constantinople', *Joinville and Villehardouin: Chronicles of the Crusades*, tr. C. Smith, Penguin, London, 2008, p. 26.

(iv) The Fourth Crusaders see Constantinople for the first time, June 1203

Now you can be assured that those who had never seen Constantinople before gazed at it for a long time, barely believing that there was such a great city in all the world. They saw its high walls and mighty towers, with which the city was completely encircled, as well as the fine palaces and impressive churches, of which there were so many that none could believe it if he did not see it with his own eyes. . . . Know that there was no man there so bold that his flesh did not tremble, which should come as no surprise for never was such a great project undertaken by as many men since the creation of the world.

Geoffrey of Villehardouin, 'The Conquest of Constantinople', *Joinville and Villehardouin: Chronicles of the Crusades*, tr. C. Smith, Penguin, London, 2008, p. 34.

Who's who

Adhémar of Le Puy (d. 1098) Papal legate on the First Crusade and a key figure in preserving the strength and morale of the crusading army until the siege of Antioch. Died of illness just after the capture of the city.

Alexios Komnenos, Byzantine emperor (r. 1081–1118) His appeal sent to Pope Urban II at Piacenza in March 1095 helped to prompt the First Crusade, but he was deeply unsettled by the arrival of huge western armies at Constantinople. A subsequent dispute concerning the overlordship of Antioch soured relations between the settlers and Byzantium for decades to come.

Alexios, prince of Byzantium, Emperor Alexios IV (r. 1203–4) Prince Alexios Andronicos was the son of the blinded and deposed Isaac Angelos who lost his throne in 1195. Prince Alexios escaped from captivity and sought help in the West, but it was only when the Fourth Crusade became entangled by its failure to fulfil its obligations to the Venetians that he was able to get assistance. A generous offer of support to the crusade was predicated upon his return to power and when rejected by his people he needed the crusaders' weapons to get him the throne. Caught between paying the westerners and the anger of his people at losing their money he was murdered in early 1204 by the leader of the anti-western faction, Mourtzouphlos (who became Emperor Alexios V).

Alice, princess of Antioch After the death of her husband, Prince Bohemond II, in 1130, Alice tried hard to rule Antioch in her own right. She incited opposition to intervention from Jerusalem and intermittently held power until the arrival of Raymond of Poitiers in 1136. Her machinations enraged William of Tyre who called her a 'malicious and scheming woman'.

Amalric, king of Jerusalem (r. 1163–74) Described as a strong, sober, legally minded and clever man, always curious to learn; however, he was also fat (he had breasts that hung down to his waist), taciturn, greedy for money and, before he was king, a serial philanderer. An energetic and powerful ruler, he dominated his nobles, led five campaigns into Egypt and journeyed to Constantinople in person to swear homage to Manuel Komnenos. He died just before another invasion of Egypt, aged only 38.

As-Sulami (d. 1106) The author of a rare *Book of Jihad* from the years immediately after the First Crusade. His explanation for the success of the crusade included harsh criticism of the Muslim nobility for their indifference to the invasion and their failure to fulfil their duty to fight the invaders. He attracted only a few people to his sermons suggesting that the religious classes were, at this time, not drawn to his message.

Baldwin I, king of Jerusalem (r. 1100–18) The count of Boulogne took part in the First Crusade and founded the county of Edessa in 1098. When his brother Godfrey of Bouillon died in 1100 Baldwin became king of Jerusalem. He repelled Egyptian attacks in his early years and then extended the boundaries of the kingdom into Transjordan (1115) and led the capture of several cities on the coast. A tall man and a great warrior, he was said to have struggled against the sins of the flesh; he nonetheless died childless.

Baldwin II, king of Jerusalem (r. 1118–31) Succeeded his relative Baldwin I as count of Edessa and then as king in 1118. He was a tall man with a thin blond beard to his waist, a formidable warrior and an extremely pious individual with callouses on his knees from constant kneeling. The rival candidacy of Baldwin I's European-based brother Eustace meant a difficult start to his reign, compounded by holding the regency of Antioch and imprisonment by the Muslims in 1122–23. On his release Baldwin led numerous campaigns against Aleppo, Damascus and Egypt and he launched a crusade appeal in 1127 to attack Damascus. He married his eldest daughter Melisende to Count Fulk V of Anjou to ensure the succession of his line.

Baldwin III, king of Jerusalem (r. 1143–63) Son of King Fulk, and a minor when he came to the throne. His mother Melisende acted as regent, but she refused to hand over power until 1152, causing near civil war in the kingdom. Described as a tall, dignified and well-educated man, he was also pious, generous and abstemious. He was said to be too keen on dice and games of chance for a king. Baldwin led the move towards more positive relations with the Byzantine Empire (1150 onwards) and captured Ascalon in 1153. These successes were offset by the failure of the Second Crusade (1148) and Nur ad-Din's takeover of Damascus (1154).

Baldwin IV, king of Jerusalem (r. 1174–85) The leper-king ruled from the age of 13 and was severely afflicted by this chronic condition. By his late teens he was blind, his nose had disappeared and his limbs were badly deformed. The need for regents caused real tensions in the kingdom, although Baldwin took part in some military campaigns, notably the victory at Mont Gisard (1177). A brave, intelligent youth, he succumbed to his illness aged 23.

Baldwin V, king of Jerusalem (r. 1185–86) The son of William of Montferrat and Sibylla of Jerusalem. He succeeded his uncle, Baldwin IV, but was only eight years old and under the regency of Count Raymond of Tripoli. A sickly child, he died after barely a year on the throne.

Baldwin, count of Flanders (r. 1192–1205), Latin Emperor of Constantinople (r. 1204–5) Baldwin took the cross in early 1200 and led a substantial contingent to Venice for the Fourth Crusade. He was known for his piety and bravery and emerged as a suitable candidate to be elected the first Latin Emperor. Baldwin was then crowned in a lavish ceremony that reflected much of the traditional Byzantine splendour. He disappeared during a campaign at Adrianople in northern Greece in 1205 and was never seen again, although an imposter (who explained his lack of height relative to how people remembered Baldwin as a consequence of the harsh conditions of captivity) was briefly taken seriously in the 1220s before being exposed and executed.

Beha ad-Din (d. 1234) He worked closely with Saladin and was the *qadi al-'askar* (judge of the army) from 1188 until 1193. His account of Saladin's life is a clear, readable and personally observed portrait of a man he greatly admired and provides a valuable Muslim perspective of the events of the Third Crusade.

Bernard of Clairvaux (1090–1153) The most prominent churchman of the twelfth century. A Cistercian monk, abbot of Clairvaux, and advisor to kings and popes for much of his adult life. A man of real austerity whose devotional practices often left him physically debilitated. The author of many letters and theological tracts, he also wrote *In Praise of the New Knighthood* for the Templars and was a strong advocate for the order. His emotive and powerful preaching aroused Europe to the Second Crusade (1145–49), but when the expedition to the Holy Land failed he had to face a harsh backlash from those he had assured were 'the lucky generation'.

Bohemond of Taranto, prince of Antioch (1098–1111) The greatest warrior of the First Crusade. A Norman from southern Italy who took part in a failed invasion of the Byzantine Empire in the 1080s. A lack of prospects in Italy led him to set up the principality of Antioch during the First Crusade in contravention of oaths sworn to Alexios Komnenos. When at Constantinople, his striking appearance – he was a tall, yet slightly stooped man with a broad chest and strong arms, short brown hair and red stubble – impressed Alexios's daughter Anna who wrote admiringly of his physique, if despising his actions. Imprisoned by the Muslims of northern Syria from 1100 to 1103. He travelled to the West in 1105–7 to raise a new crusade – against the Greeks. His attack in 1108 did not succeed and he returned to southern Italy where he died.

Bohemond II, prince of Antioch (1126–30) A minor who was living in the family lands in Norman Sicily when he succeeded to the title of Antioch in 1119. After reaching his majority in 1126 he travelled to the Levant to claim his position. He married Alice, a daughter of Baldwin II of Jerusalem, and fathered Princess Constance. He died in battle in 1130.

Caffaro of Genoa (*c*. 1080–1166) Caffaro composed the first surviving accounts of the First Crusade by a layman as part of his *Annals of Genoa* (also the first civic history in the Latin West) and his *Liberation of the Cities of the East*. These were written in the 1150s but based on years of private and eye-witness records and reflect a unique blend of piety, civic pride and religious devotion. Caffaro was present in Jerusalem for Easter 1101 and the capture of Caesarea. He was a prominent diplomat and held the post of consul on multiple occasions. He also wrote an account of the capture of Almeria and Tortosa during the Second Crusade.

Conrad III, king of Germany (1138–52) Conrad led the largest contingent on the Second Crusade and proved himself a brave warrior. His forces lacked discipline, however, and many were lost in Asia Minor. He laid the blame for the failure of the Second Crusade at the door of the Franks, accusing them of being bought off by the Damascenes (1148). He died before he could be crowned emperor in Rome, hence the royal, rather than the imperial title of his predecessors and those who followed him.

Conrad of Montferrat (d. 1192) From a powerful north Italian family and the brother of William of Montferrat (d. 1177), former husband of Sibylla of Jerusalem. By chance Conrad arrived in the East just in time to lead the defence of Tyre in 1187 and subsequently he contested the kingship with Guy of Lusignan. Finally chosen to rule, he was murdered by Assassins before he could take power.

Enrico Dandolo (*c*. 1107–1205) Blind as the result of a head injury incurred during the 1170s (not inflicted by the Greeks as some sources claimed) this remarkable man ruled as doge (duke) from 1192 and led the city's contingent on the Fourth Crusade. Hugely disliked by Pope Innocent III for turning the expedition towards the recovery of Zara he was much admired by the other crusade leaders for his intelligence and judgement. He played a major role in the strategic and diplomatic aspects of the crusade as well as inspiring Venetian troops through his own bravery.

Eugenius III, pope (1145–53) The first Cistercian pope and a protégé of Bernard of Clairvaux. Along with Bernard, he organised the Second Crusade and preached in Italy and Paris to raise men. The author of *Quantum prae-decessores*, the first surviving papal crusade bull, a carefully crafted work that provided the template for such documents for decades to come.

Frederick Barbarossa, Holy Roman Emperor (1152–90) The most senior figure in western Europe, Frederick ruled over a vast territory encompassing Germany, Burgundy (south-eastern France) and northern Italy. Frederick took part in the Second Crusade (1145–49), but spent much of his reign in conflict with the papacy and the north Italian towns. He was the first major leader to set out on the Third Crusade and successfully crossed the hostile Byzantine Empire and defeated the Seljuk Turks. He died of a heart attack crossing a river at Silifke in southern Turkey.

Fulcher of Chartres (d. 1127) The chaplain of Count Baldwin of Boulogne, he was educated at the cathedral school of Chartres. He took part in the First Crusade and the conquest of Edessa, and then went to Jerusalem when his master acceded to the throne in 1100. His eye-witness history is an intelligent and balanced work and the most important account of the early decades of the Latin East.

Fulk, king of Jerusalem (1131–43) Count Fulk V of Anjou visited Jerusalem in 1120. He was chosen to marry Melisende, the heiress to the throne, and travelled East, with a crusade, in 1129. Fulk became king in 1131, but tried to rule without input from Melisende and to advance his own men ahead of the native barons which led to the revolt of Hugh of Jaffa in 1134. The king was a gentle and pious man, although said to have had an embarrassingly bad memory for names and faces. He died from severe head injuries after falling from his horse while hunting hares outside Acre in 1143.

Geoffrey of Villehardouin (*c.* 1150–*c.* 1212/18) An experienced warrior and administrator who held the post of marshal of Champagne from 1185, Villehardouin was one of the envoys who negotiated the fateful contract with the Venetians that so crippled the Fourth Crusade. He took part in the campaign and became marshal of the Latin Empire in 1207. His *Conquest of Constantinople* is probably the first example of historical writing in Old French prose.

Gerard of Ridefort Master of the Templars. An aggressive military commander, he led the unsuccessful engagement at Cresson (May 1187) and encouraged King Guy to fight at Hattin. Captured, but later released, by Saladin, he was killed outside Acre in 1189 when his forces became isolated.

Gilbert d'Assailly Master of the Hospitallers from 1163 until *c.* 1171. Gilbert led an important diplomatic mission to the West in 1166 and was responsible for a dramatic intensification of the order's military activities. He probably persuaded King Amalric to invade Egypt in late 1168, but when the expedition failed, the order faced financial crisis and Gilbert suffered a nervous breakdown.

Godfrey of Bouillon, ruler of Jerusalem (1099–1100) Duke of Lower Lotharingia since 1076. A powerful and pious warrior who took part in the First Crusade and in its later stages emerged as a figure of great authority. After the capture of Jerusalem he was chosen to rule the city and held the title 'Advocate of the Holy Sepulchre', for just over a year before his death.

Guy of Lusignan, king of Jerusalem (1186–92), king of Cyprus (1192–94) A newcomer from the West, he married Sibylla, heiress to the throne of Jerusalem, in 1180. His position provoked much opposition and he lost the regency he had held 1183–84. He became king in 1186, and it was his fatal decision to march for Tiberias and to face Saladin in battle. He was captured at Hattin, but on his release in 1189 he made partial amends by besieging Acre and giving the Third Crusade a genuine target. Still not a credible king of Jerusalem, he was handsomely compensated by Richard I with the grant of Cyprus.

Henry II, king of England (1154–89) Closely related to the ruling house of Jerusalem, Henry, as a wealthy western ruler, was often approached to help the settlers. He appeared on the verge of taking the cross in 1170 and 1173, but domestic political events prevented him from setting out for the Levant. He offered generous financial support to the Franks, in part as penance for the murder of Thomas Becket.

Heraclius, patriarch of Jerusalem (d. 1191) A key player in the factional disputes of the 1180s, Heraclius was a well-educated and worldly man who engineered the coronation of Guy and Sibylla in 1186. He also led a major embassy to the West in 1184–85 to try to elicit a new crusade. There are some suggestions that he was the lover of Agnes of Courtenay, the mother of King Baldwin IV and Sibylla.

Hugh, count of Jaffa He was a relative of Queen Melisende and led a revolt against King Fulk, probably in protest at the Angevin's imposition of his own men in positions of power at the expense of the native nobility. Hugh was exiled, but his actions did see a reduction in Fulk's influence.

Hugh of Payns The first master of the Templars. This Frenchman founded the Templars in 1119 and travelled to Europe in 1127 to secure ecclesiastical backing and to raise men and money for the order – in both he succeeded admirably. He was also responsible for recruiting men for the 1129 Damascus crusade.

Ibn al-Qalanisi (d. 1160) The author of one of the earliest surviving contemporary Muslim narratives. A native of Damascus and a well-educated career administrator, he was twice mayor of the city. His work derives from oral and written reports as well as his own observations of the First and Second Crusades and Nur ad-Din's takeover of his beloved home city.

Ibn Jubayr (1145–1217) A Spanish Muslim pilgrim who, from 1183 to 1185 travelled from Iberia, through Egypt, to Mecca and Medina, up through Baghdad and Aleppo, down to Damascus (his favourite city) and then spent about three weeks in the kingdom of Jerusalem before journeying home via a shipwreck on Sicily. His wonderful book of *rihla* (Travels) provides a vivid picture of the lands and peoples he saw and his observations on Frankish treatment of Muslims in their lands in the period just before the Battle of Hattin are vital in our assessment of relations between the Christians and the indigenous peoples of the East.

Innocent III, Pope (1198–1216) Elected pope at the age of 37, this highly trained theologian and lawyer was, along with Urban II, arguably the most important of all popes for the crusading movement. His determination to enhance the spiritual purity of western Christendom in order to gain God's support for the recovery of the Holy Land formed the framework for his pontificate. He launched numerous crusading expeditions including the Fourth and Fifth Crusades, the Albigensian Crusade against southern French Cathars, as well as encouraging campaigns against the pagans of the Baltic region, the Muslims of Iberia and enemies of the papacy in southern Italy. His papacy also saw the Fourth Lateran Council (1215) the largest gathering of churchmen (over 900 abbots, almost 500 bishops, patriarchs and archbishops) of the medieval age.

Louis VII, king of France (1137–80) A most pious king ('more monk than king', according to his wife – later ex-wife – Eleanor of Aquitaine), who was the first western ruler to take the cross for the Second Crusade. He led a large army to the Levant, although his forces were badly mauled in Asia Minor. Then, at Antioch (1148), accusations of an affair between Eleanor and her uncle, Prince Raymond, led to a swift march south. As king of France, he was the subject of many appeals from the settlers in the 1160s and 1170s, but while he gave money, his struggle with Henry II of England prevented him from taking the cross again.

Manuel Komnenos, Byzantine emperor (1143–80) A central figure in the history of the Latin East, Manuel had to balance the various threats to his borders, and his interest in regaining southern Italy, with his wishes to be overlord of Antioch and to advance the Christian position in the Levant. Strongly pro-Latin, he took an Antiochene bride and provided naval support for invasions of Egypt in 1169 and 1177. He accepted the homage of King

Amalric in 1171 and also sponsored Orthodox ecclesiastical institutions in the Levant. His death meant the loss of a valuable buttress to the Frankish East.

Melisende, queen of Jerusalem (1131–52) The eldest daughter of King Baldwin II, she married Count Fulk V of Anjou in 1129, and bore him two sons, Baldwin and Amalric. An astute political operator, she reduced the influence of Angevin newcomers and then, on Fulk's death, preserved her hold on power well into Baldwin III's majority, including the time of the Second Crusade. William of Tyre and Bernard of Clairvaux both admired her skills in government. Melisende was also a great patron of Christian churches (her mother was Armenian) and the arts. She died in 1161.

Nur ad-Din (1117–74) He was the man who advanced the *jihad* most strongly before Saladin. He was a tall man with a beard, but no moustache, and beautiful eyes. A son of Zengi, his powerbase was in northern Syria at Aleppo. He helped to head off the Second Crusade from Damascus in 1148 and then killed Prince Raymond of Antioch in 1149. A very devout and austere man, he did much to promote religious learning and the welfare of his people through the construction of hospitals and bathhouses and by the administration of justice. He was a dangerous opponent of the Franks and captured Banyas in 1165, and then, crucially, Egypt in 1169. He faced some challenge from Saladin in his final years, but always posed a serious threat to the Franks.

Philip, count of Flanders (1168–91) The son of Count Thierry of Flanders, Philip arrived with a large crusade in 1177–78, but political wrangling prevented a proper invasion of Egypt, as planned. He fought a campaign in northern Syria, late in 1177 and into 1178. The count returned to the Holy Land on the Third Crusade, but died of illness at the siege of Acre.

Raymond of Poitiers, prince of Antioch (1136–49) A member of the prestigious ducal house of Aquitaine, Raymond was selected to marry Constance, the heiress to Antioch. He proved an able and vigorous prince, who managed to see off Byzantine invasions of the principality in 1137–38 and 1142; he was, however, forced to travel to Constantinople in 1145 to swear homage to Manuel. Raymond believed that the Second Crusade would increase Antiochene power in northern Syria, but disagreements with King Louis VII of France and rumours of an affair between the prince and Queen Eleanor ended this hope. He was killed by Nur ad-Din's forces at the Battle of Inab and his head was sent to the caliph of Baghdad.

Raymond of Saint Gilles, count of Tripoli (d. 1105) The count of Toulouse was the senior leader of the First Crusade armies and a confidant of Pope Urban II. He left his homeland determined to settle in the East, although when he failed to secure the crown of Jerusalem (he had antagonised many of the other crusade leaders) he went north to found the county of Tripoli.

Burns sustained in a skirmish in 1104 contributed to his death in February 1105, four years before the city of Tripoli itself came under Frankish power.

Raymond III, count of Tripoli (d. 1187) This slightly-built, swarthy and energetic man was one of the key players in the history of the kingdom of Jerusalem. He became count of Tripoli in 1152, but was in Muslim captivity from 1164 to 1171 (where he learned to read). He married the heiress of Galilee and became a prominent player in the kingdom of Jerusalem, acting as regent for Baldwin IV between 1174 and 1176 and for Baldwin V in 1185–86. He worked closely with the Ibelin family and was regarded by many as the most capable candidate for the throne. His opponents, Guy and Sibylla, secured power and he rebelled, opening negotiations with Saladin. He fought alongside Guy at Hattin and managed to escape the field of battle. He died later that year, probably of pleurisy.

Reynald of Châtillon (d. 1187) Contrary to William of Tyre's asides, Reynald was from a noble French family, rather than the lowly stock that the writer (who disliked him strongly) suggested. He arrived in the Levant and soon caused a stir by marrying Constance, the widowed heiress of Antioch (1153). He was a brutal and undiplomatic ruler who ordered the Byzantine-controlled island of Cyprus to be ravaged in 1156. He was compelled to pay homage to Manuel in 1159 and then spent the years 1160 to 1175 as a prisoner of the Muslims, which hardened his opposition to the infidel even further. He came to play a prominent role in the political struggles in Jerusalem by his acquisition of the lordship of Transjordan. He was regent for Baldwin IV between 1178 and 1180 and devised the bold seaborne raid on Medina in late 1182. His attack on a Muslim caravan in 1187 provoked Saladin to war. Reynald's actions had aroused deep hatred in Saladin and he was executed by the emir himself after the Battle of Hattin.

Richard I, king of England (1189–99) This highly educated and strategically cautious monarch is famous as the greatest warrior of the Third Crusade and his fighting prowess and intelligence were hugely respected by his Muslim opponents. The king captured Cyprus in 1191, and freed Acre in the same year, but his attempts on Jerusalem failed. Richard planned to return to the Holy Land, but his imprisonment on the way home, the huge ransom needed to free him and the ongoing conflict with France conspired to keep him in the West until his premature death from gangrene, contracted from an arrow-wound besieging a castle in Aquitaine.

Robert of Clari (c. 1180–after 1216) A poor knight from Amiens in northern France who took part in the Fourth Crusade and brought back numerous relics for the nearby abbey of Corbie. His account of the campaign is notable for giving the view of the lesser knights and he is critical of what he judges to be the greed of the leadership. His vivid and lively prose recounts the history of Byzantium and he describes the wonderful buildings and relics that he saw. He wrote in Old French, showing how literacy was spreading through lay society by the early thirteenth century.

Roger of Salerno, prince of Antioch (1112–19) Roger was the nephew of Tancred and continued to press the Muslims of northern Syria. He won a great battle at Tell-Danith in 1115, but poor tactics led to his death (along with most of the Antiochene nobility) at the Battle of the Field of Blood in 1119.

Saladin (1137–93) Born of Kurdish stock, this highly skilled horseman rose through the ranks to take control of Egypt on behalf of Nur ad-Din in 1169. He is described as a short man, with a roundish face, a trim black beard and keen, alert black eyes. He placed members of his family in positions of power and seemed to challenge his master's authority. When Nur ad-Din died, Saladin took on the mantle of the defender of Islam and set about unifying the Muslim world through warfare and diplomacy. Famed for his austerity, generosity and justice, Saladin increased the pressure on the Franks until he defeated them at the Battle of Hattin in 1187. The subsequent capture of Jerusalem assured him of heroic status, although the successes of the Third Crusade at Acre, Arsuf and Jaffa dented this image, among contemporaries at least. He died aged 56, worn out by years of campaigning.

Sibylla, queen of Jerusalem (d. 1190) Because her brother, Baldwin IV, was a leper, Sibylla was the heiress to Jerusalem. Her first marriage to William Longsword, count of Montferrat, lasted only a few months and left her pregnant with Baldwin V. A proposed marriage to the count of Burgundy fell through and in 1180 she married Guy of Lusignan. Sibylla and Guy fought hard to hold power and successfully outmanoeuvred Raymond III of Tripoli to take the crown. Sibylla died of illness at the siege of Acre in 1190.

Tancred, prince of Antioch (d. 1112) Tancred took part in the First Crusade with his uncle, Bohemond of Taranto. He became regent of Antioch when Bohemond was in Muslim captivity and then took over the principality while his uncle was in the West. Tancred fought hard against the Muslims of northern Syria and reduced Aleppo to subservience. He also sought Muslim support in his unsuccessful efforts to take over Edessa in 1108 and thereby establish Antiochene pre-eminence in the region.

Thierry, count of Flanders (1128–68) This man was the most devoted – and hardy – crusader of all. He journeyed to the Levant and back four times in 1139, 1147–48, 1157–58 and 1164 – and lived to tell the tale. He was from a line of crusading counts and was related to the kings of Jerusalem. The stability and wealth of Flanders allowed him to indulge his piety. It was planned that he should take over the lordship of Shaizar if the Christians captured it in 1157, but the attack failed.

Urban II, Pope (1088–99) The first Cluniac monk to become pope, Urban was of a Burgundian noble family and became a strong advocate of papal reform. He worked to advance the *reconquista* in Spain, as well as launching the First Crusade at the Council of Clermont in November 1095.

Usama ibn Munqidh (1095–1188) Member of an aristocratic family from Shaizar in northern Syria, Usama made a career as a warrior, diplomat and poet across the Muslim Near East, managing through his talents, to move between Unur's Damascus in the 1140s, Fatimid Cairo and then back to serve Saladin in Damascus again. He produced many written works, including a very popular collection of poetry as well as his most famous piece, a strongly autobiographical reflection on Fate entitled *The Book of Contemplation* outlining his life experiences, including many dealings with the Frankish settlers. This latter work is the source for many examples of interaction between the Muslim and Christian inhabitants of the Near East.

Walter the Chancellor Historian and author of a first-hand narrative account of events in Antioch between 1114–15 and 1119–22, including therefore, the Battle of the Field of Blood (1119) and the regency of King Baldwin II of Jerusalem. He is by far the most detailed authority for this period. His perspective was that belief in God and right intention would be rewarded by victory and that deviation from these principles brought about defeat. The date of his death was before 1127.

William of Tyre (c. 1130–85) Historian and author of the most important history of the Latin East. William was born in the Levant and educated in Europe c. 1145 to c. 1165. On his return to the East he secured high ecclesiastical position, becoming archbishop of Tyre in 1175 and was chancellor from 1170 until Amalric's death in 1174. He led a diplomatic mission to Constantinople in 1167–68, and was a strong supporter of Count Raymond III of Tripoli's candidacy as ruler of Jerusalem. His work was intended to convince the people of the West that the settlers in the Holy Land deserved help. William died in 1185 and so his history is not clouded by the events of Hattin, although such was the value of his writing that it was soon widely circulated in Europe and added to by later writers. William also wrote a history of the Muslims of the Near East, although this is lost.

Zengi (d. 1146) The most fearsome of the Muslim leaders, Zengi terrified his own people as well as the Christians with his ruthless and cruel actions. He spent much of his career fighting his co-religionists, but his capture of Edessa in 1144 was a landmark for the advance of the *jihad* and ensured a posthumous reputation as a true defender of Islam. He was murdered in a drunken stupor by one of his servants.

Bibliography

A huge number of relevant publications have appeared since the first edition of this book. In order to reflect these advances in scholarship and for reasons of space, I have slimmed down the existing list of titles to incorporate more up-to-date studies where appropriate. The emphasis throughout this book is, for reasons of utility, on materials translated into English.

An accessible one-volume overview of the crusades from medieval to modern times is Jonathan Phillips, *Holy Warriors: A Modern History of the Crusades*, Bodley Head, London, 2009. For those seeking a more lengthy treatment of the medieval field especially, see Christopher Tyerman's *God's War: A New History of the Crusades*, Penguin, London, 2006. An interesting and original approach is taken in Norman Housley's lively *Fighting for the Cross: Crusading to the Holy Land*, Yale University Press, New Haven and London, 2008 which traces the process and experience of crusading in thematic form. A splendid and up-to-date history of the challenges faced by the Franks as they tried to establish and consolidate their power in the Levant down to 1192 is Malcolm Barber's *The Crusader States*, Yale University Press, New Haven and London, 2012. Andrew Jotischky's fluently written *Crusading and the Crusader States*, Longman, Harlow, 2005, covers this material too, as well as the major crusading expeditions themselves, and other theatres of holy war. Also worth noting are two useful essay collections, picking out themes of crusading history: Conor Kostick (ed.), *The Crusades and the Near East: Cultural Histories*, Routledge, Abingdon, 2011 and Helen Nicholson (ed.), *Palgrave Advances in the Crusades*, Palgrave Macmillan, Basingstoke, 2005. Finally there is the excellent encyclopedia edited by Alan V. Murray, *The Crusades: An Encyclopaedia*, 4 volumes, ABC-Clio, Santa Barbara, CA, 2006.

Individual original sources can be found listed in the 'Printed Primary Sources' section below. Good collections of material are:

Barber, M.C. and Bate, K., *Letters from the East: Crusaders, Pilgrims and Settlers in the 12–13th Centuries*, Ashgate, Farnham, 2010.

Bird, J., Peters, E. and Powell, J.M. (eds), *Crusade and Christendom: Annotated Documents in Translation from Innocent III to the Fall of Acre, 1187–1291*, University of Pennsylvania Press, Philadelphia, 2013.

Gabrieli, F., *Arab Historians of the Crusades*, tr. E.J. Costello, University of California Press, Berkeley, 1969.

Hallam, E.M. (ed.), *Chronicles of the Crusades*, Phoebe Phillips Editions, London, 1989.

Peters, E. (ed.), *The First Crusade: 'The Chronicle of Fulcher of Chartres' and Other Source Materials*, University of Pennsylvania Press, Philadelphia, 1998.

Riley-Smith, L. and Riley-Smith, J.S.C., *The Crusades: Idea and Reality 1095–1274*, Edward Arnold, London, 1981.

Useful discussions about source material can be found in the introductions of most texts used in the Documents section, but other important works are:

Bull, M.G., 'The Diplomatic of the First Crusade', *The First Crusade: Origins and Impact*, ed. J.P. Phillips, Manchester University Press, Manchester, 1997, pp. 35–56.

Constable, G., 'Medieval Charters as a Source for the History of the Crusades', *Crusade and Settlement*, ed. P.W. Edbury, Cardiff University Press, Cardiff, 1985, pp. 73–89.

Edbury, P.W. and Rowe, J.G., *William of Tyre: Historian of the Latin East*, Cambridge University Press, Cambridge, 1988.

The origins of the First Crusade are best treated in the work of three authors: Marcus Bull has clearly established the links between the lay nobility and the Church (a key aspect of the background to the crusade) in his *Knightly Piety and the Lay Response to the First Crusade*, Clarendon Press, Oxford, 1993. The importance of pilgrimage is emphasised in Bull's 'Pilgrimage Origins', *History Today* 47 (March 1997), pp. 37–42. The broader context of eleventh-century society is neatly illuminated in his 'Origins', *The Oxford Illustrated History of the Crusades*, ed. J.S.C. Riley-Smith, Oxford University Press, Oxford, 1995, pp. 13–33. John Cowdrey's studies have revealed the development of the crusade in papal circles: 'Pope Urban II's Preaching of the First Crusade', *History* 55 (1970), pp. 177–88; 'Pope Urban and the Idea of the Crusade', *Studi Medievali* 36 (1995), pp. 721–42. Jonathan Riley-Smith's work is fundamental in our assessment of the origins of the crusading movement and in trying to understand the motives of the First Crusade. His book, *The First Crusade and the Idea of Crusading*, Athlone Press, London, 1986, is highly recommended in this context. Much of his work on family connections between crusaders is brought together in *The First Crusaders 1095–1131*,

Cambridge University Press, Cambridge, 1997. Two further contributions to the study of the motivation are William J. Purkis, *Crusading Spirituality in the Holy Land and Iberia, c.1095–c.1187*, Boydell, Woodbridge, 2008 which uncovers the influence of contemporary devotional activities on the crusaders, as well as considering the importance of pilgrimage and the relationship between crusading in Iberia and the Near East. Jonathan Phillips, 'Caffaro of Genoa and the Motives of the Early Crusaders', *Religion as an Agent for Change*, ed. P. Ingesman, E. J. Brill, Leiden, 2014, looks at the First Crusade from the perspective of the Italian trading community.

Two lively narrative accounts of the progress of the expedition are Tom Asbridge's *The First Crusade: A New History*, The Free Press, London, 2004 and Conor Kostick's *The Siege of Jerusalem: Crusade and Conquest in 1099*, Continuum Books, London, 2009 which as its title suggests, concentrates on the capture of the holy city in particular. Jay Rubenstein's vivid *Armies of Heaven: The First Crusade and the Quest for the Apocalypse*, Basic Books, New York, 2011 lays important emphasis on the strand of apocalyptic feeling current in contemporary Europe. Peter Frankopan's *The First Crusade: The Call from the East*, Bodley Head, London, 2012 adopts the perspective of the Byzantine Empire and makes a full and convincing case for the role of the Greeks in the origins of the crusade. By far the best analysis of events at Jerusalem in 1099 is Benjamin Z. Kedar's 'The Jerusalem Massacre of July 1099 in the Western Historiography of the Crusades', *Crusades* 3 (2004), pp. 15–76.

The early years of the Frankish East are covered in a variety of works. The clearest overview is certainly contained in Barber's *Crusader States*, 2012, noted earlier. Alan V. Murray's *The Crusader Kingdom of Jerusalem, 1099–1125*, Prosopographica et Genealogica, Oxford, 2000, is the leading analysis of this period. A detailed study of the foundation of Antioch is Tom Asbridge's *The Principality of Antioch, 1098–1130*, Boydell, Woodbridge, 2000. The reigns of Fulk and Melisende have been the subject of detailed study by Hans Mayer and his magisterial article, 'Studies in the History of Queen Melisende of Jerusalem', *Dumbarton Oaks Papers* 26 (1972), pp. 93–182 is well worth examining. Melisende and her sister Alice are discussed in Bernard Hamilton's 'Women in the Crusader States: The Queens of Jerusalem (1100–90)', *Medieval Women: Studies in Church History, Subsidia 1*, ed. D. Baker, Blackwell, Oxford, 1978, pp. 143–74, and Melisende as a patron of the arts is amply illustrated in Jaroslav Folda, *The Art of the Crusaders in the Holy Land, 1095–1187*, Cambridge University Press, Cambridge, 1995. An overview of Melisende is in Phillips, *Holy Warriors*, 2009, pp. 50–74. The accession of Prince Raymond is discussed in Jonathan Phillips's *Defenders of the Holy Land: Relations between the Latin East and the West, 1119–87*, Clarendon Press, Oxford, 1996.

The Muslim reaction to the First Crusade and the rise of Zengi are the province of Carole Hillenbrand and her articles, 'The First Crusade: The Muslim Perspective', *The First Crusade: Origins and Impact*, ed. J.P. Phillips, Manchester University Press, Manchester, 1997, pp. 130–41, and 'Abominable Acts: The Career of Zengi', *The Second Crusade: Scope and Consequences*, eds J.P. Phillips and M. Hoch, Manchester University Press, Manchester, 2001, pp. 111–32, are essential reading. Hillenbrand's book, *The Crusades: Islamic Perspectives*, Edinburgh University Press, Edinburgh, 1999, opened out the impact of the crusades in the Near East to a remarkable extent and remains the starting point for this subject. Konrad Hirschler's 'The Jerusalem Conquest of 492/1099 in the Medieval Arabic Historiography of the Crusades: From Regional Plurality to Islamic Narrative', *Crusades* 13 (2014) is a highly original analysis of the ways in which accounts of the fall of Jerusalem evolved over time and is a neat, non-identical twin, to Kedar's review of the Latin sources noted earlier.

The subject of relations between the Franks and the indigenous populace is carefully considered in Benjamin Kedar's 'Subjected Muslims of the Frankish Levant', *Muslims under Latin Rule 1100–1300*, ed. J.M. Powell, Princeton University Press, Princeton, NJ, 1990, pp. 135–74. See also Joseph Drory, 'Hanbalis of the Nablus Region in the Eleventh and Twelfth Centuries', *Asian and African Studies* 22 (1988), pp. 93–112. The authority on Frankish rule and settlement in the countryside is Ronnie Ellenblum in his *Frankish Rural Settlement in the Latin Kingdom of Jerusalem*, Cambridge University Press, Cambridge, 1998. Adrian Boas has produced the most up-to-date and effective work on towns in *Crusader Archaeology: Material Culture of the Latin East*, Routledge, London, 1999, and *Jerusalem in the Time of the Crusades*, Routledge, London, 2001.

One could build a mountain out of the misguided, ill-informed and fictitious books on the military orders; ignore everything outside the publications of serious historians. A fine starting point that covers the orders in the Holy Land, Iberia and the Baltic is Nicholas Morton's *The Medieval Military Orders, 1120–1314*, Pearson, Harlow, 2013. Easily the best work on the Templars is Malcolm Barber's *The New Knighthood. A History of the Order of the Templars*, Cambridge University Press, Cambridge, 1994. The Hospitallers have received succinct treatment in Jonathan Riley-Smith's *Hospitallers: The History of the Order of St John*, Hambledon, London, 1999, or greater depth in his *The Knights Hospitaller in the Levant, c.1070–1309*, Palgrave Macmillan, Basingstoke, 2012. An interesting study of the military orders' activities in the West is Dominic Selwood's *Knights of the Cloister*, Boydell, Woodbridge, 1999, while Jochen Schenk's *Templar Families: Landowning Families and the Order of the Temple in France, c.1120–1307*, Cambridge University Press, Cambridge, 2012 is an erudite analysis of the dynamics of the relationship between the order and the noble families of Burgundy, Champagne and the Languedoc.

The Second Crusade has been given comprehensive treatment by Jonathan Phillips in his *The Second Crusade: Extending the Frontiers of Christendom*, Yale University Press, New Haven and London, 2007. Giles Constable's seminal article 'The Second Crusade as Seen by Contemporaries', *Traditio* 9 (1953), pp. 213–79 remains important. Jonathan Phillips and Martin Hoch (eds), *The Second Crusade: Scope and Consequences*, Manchester University Press, Manchester, 2001 includes a range of articles on many aspects of the expedition and its impact. Penny Cole's *The Preaching of the Crusades to the Holy Land, 1095–1274*, Medieval Academy of America, Cambridge, MA, 1991, contains a fine analysis of the ideas of St Bernard and Peter the Venerable.

R.C. (Otto) Smail's fundamental work, *Crusading Warfare 1097–1193*, second edition, Cambridge University Press, Cambridge, 1995, remains a foundation for studies of military history. For a top-line analysis of the tactics and effectiveness of the First Crusade, see John France, *Victory in the East: A Military History of the First Crusade*, Cambridge University Press, Cambridge, 1994. Siege warfare is covered in Randall Rogers's *Latin Siege Warfare in the Twelfth Century*, Clarendon Press, Oxford, 1992, and Muslim military practice is considered in Carole Hillenbrand's *The Crusades: Islamic Perspectives*, 1999, pp. 431–587. John France's essay 'Warfare in the Mediterranean Region in the Age of the Crusades, 1095–1291: A Clash of Contrasts', in Kostick, *Crusades and the Near East*, 2011, pp. 9–26 is a fine overview. Crusader castles are discussed in a lively and well-illustrated form in Hugh Kennedy's *Crusader Castles*, Cambridge University Press, Cambridge, 1994, and in a more thematic manner in Adrian Boas's *Crusader Archaeology*, 1999. Ronnie Ellenblum's *Crusader Castles and Modern Histories*, Cambridge, Cambridge University Press, 2007 is a very important volume that blends archaeology and textual work to analyse the phases of crusader castle building and to show how and why they evolved in form and location.

The complex relations between Byzantium and crusading armies, and Byzantium and the Latin East are astutely dealt with by Jonathan Harris, *Byzantium and the Crusades*, second edition, Bloomsbury, London, 2014, as well as Ralph-Johannes Lilie, *Byzantium and the Crusader States, 1095–1204*, tr. J.C. Morris and J.E. Ridings, Clarendon Press, Oxford, 1993. An article by Chris Wright, 'On the Margins of Christendom: The Impact of the Crusades on Byzantium', in Kostick, *Crusades and the Near East*, 2011, pp. 55–82 is a subtle, shorter analysis.

The impact of the failure of the Second Crusade is examined extensively in Jonathan Phillips, *Defenders of the Holy Land*, 1996. The rise of Nur ad-Din and Saladin is given thoughtful coverage in Nikita Elisséeff, 'The Reaction of the Syrian Muslims after the Foundation of the First Latin Kingdom of Jerusalem', *Crusaders and Muslims in Twelfth-Century Syria*, ed. M. Shatzmiller,

E.J. Brill, Leiden, 1993, pp. 162–72, and Carole Hillenbrand, *The Crusades: Islamic Perspectives*, 1999. Yehoshua Frenkel's 'Muslim Responses to the Frankish Dominion in the Near East, 1098–1291' in: Kostick, *Crusades and the Near East*, 2011, pp. 27–54 is well worth reading, as is Suleiman Mourad and James Lindsay's 'Ibn 'Asakir and the Intensification and Reorientation of Sunni Jihad Ideology in Crusader-Era Syria', *Just Wars, Holy Wars and Jihads: Christian, Jewish and Muslim Encounters and Exchanges*, ed. Sohail H. Hashmi, Oxford University Press, Oxford, 2012, pp. 107–24. A biography of Usama ibn Munqidh is the opportunity for Paul Cobb to pen an interesting and enjoyable insight into the life and times of this prolific writer, *Usama ibn Munqidh: Warrior Poet of the Age of the Crusades*, One World, Oxford, 2005.

The power of the kings of Jerusalem is given provocative, but largely convincing treatment in Steven Tibble's *Monarchy and Lordships in the Latin Kingdom of Jerusalem, 1099–1291*, Oxford University Press, Oxford, 1989. The details of succession to the early kings are considered in Alan Murray, *The Crusader Kingdom of Jerusalem*, 2000.

The role of women on crusade was a subject historians tended to overlook until Natasha R. Hodgson's *Women, Crusading and the Holy Land in Historical Narrative*, Boydell, Woodbridge, 2007, examined perceptions of women in crusading narratives (mostly written by male clerics, of course), to see how they were treated in such texts and to look at their role in these campaigns, and at home and in the Levant. The work of Danielle Park (2013) offers further close analysis of the role of female regents during the absence of their husbands on crusade. Deborah Gerish's article on 'Gender Theory' in H. Nicholson, *Palgrave Advances in the Crusades*, Palgrave Macmillan, Basingstoke, 2005, pp. 130–47 is an important theoretical guide, while the essay collection *Gendering the Crusades*, eds S.B. Edgington and S. Lambert, University of Wales Press, Cardiff, 2001 should also be noted.

Religious life in the Levant is another relatively neglected subject, but Bernard Hamilton's *The Latin Church in the Crusader States*, Variorum, London, 1980, and Andrew Jotischky's *The Perfection of Solitude: Monks and Hermits in the Crusader States*, Pennsylvania State University Press, University Park, PA, 1995, cover two key aspects to good effect. Alan Murray has neatly collated the information on the True Cross in his article 'Mighty against the Enemies of the Christ: The Relic of the True Cross in the Armies of the Kingdom of Jerusalem', *The Crusades and their Sources: Essays Presented to Bernard Hamilton*, eds John France and William Zajac, Ashgate, Aldershot, 1998, pp. 217–38. Denys Pringle's monumental *The Churches of the Crusader Kingdom of Jerusalem. A Corpus*, 4 volumes, Cambridge University Press, Cambridge, 1993–2009, is a benchmark reference work on religious buildings in the Latin kingdom of Jerusalem.

The period 1174–87 has received considerable attention from historians. On the Frankish side, Bernard Hamilton's *The Leper-king and his*

Heirs: Baldwin IV and the Crusader Kingdom of Jerusalem, Cambridge University Press, Cambridge, 2000, is a clear overview. Peter Edbury's article, 'Propaganda and Faction in the Kingdom of Jerusalem: The Background to Hattin', *Crusaders and Muslims in Twelfth-Century Syria*, ed. M. Shatzmiller, E.J. Brill, Leiden, 1993, pp. 173–89, is a very important and effective paper that completely demolishes the old 'hawks' versus 'doves' idea. Jonathan Phillips reveals the settlers' efforts to secure outside help at this time in *Defenders of the Holy Land*, 1996. Malcolm Barber's article, 'Frontier Warfare in the Latin Kingdom of Jerusalem: The Campaign of Jacob's Ford, 1178–9', *The Crusades and their Sources: Essays presented to Bernard Hamilton*, eds John France and William Zajac, Ashgate, Aldershot, 1998, pp. 9–22, deals with an important episode in the conflict. The Muslim angle is covered in huge detail in Malcolm Lyons and D.E.P. Jackson, *Saladin. The Politics of the Holy War*, Cambridge University Press, Cambridge, 1982. This book is, to put it mildly, hard work, but is well worth the effort because it offers the most definitive work on Saladin's career to date, and makes use of narrative and hitherto ignored (and untranslated) documentary evidence. Anne-Marie Eddé's *Saladin*, tr. Jane-Marie Todd, Belknap Harvard, Cambridge MA, 2011, is another weighty and erudite work, albeit one that is extremely well-written and provides a substantial amount of superb contextual material too. Carole Hillenbrand's *The Crusades: Islamic Perspectives*, 1999, is a lighter overview. The Battle of Hattin is best covered in Benjamin Kedar's 'The Battle of Hattin Revisited', *The Horns of Hattin*, ed. B.Z. Kedar, Variorum, London, 1992, pp. 190–207, although see also Smail's *Crusading Warfare 1097–1193*, 1995.

There is no good monograph on the Third Crusade, but the best account is in John Gillingham's *Richard I*, Yale University Press, London, 1999; enormously scholarly and original, yet readable and entertaining at the same time. Lyons and Jackson's, *Saladin*, 1982 and Eddé's *Saladin*, 2011 both carry a full account from the Muslim perspective.

The Fourth Crusade is analysed to best effect by Donald E. Queller and Thomas F. Madden, *The Fourth Crusade: The Conquest of Constantinople*, second edition, University of Pennsylvania Press, Philadelphia, 1997. Jonathan Phillips, *The Fourth Crusade and the Sack of Constantinople*, Jonathan Cape, London, 2004 offers a lively account of the campaign, while Thomas F. Madden provides excellent insight into the Venetian perspective with his *Enrico Dandolo and the Rise of Venice*, Johns Hopkins University Press, 2003. The Byzantine viewpoint is argued by Michael Angold, *The Fourth Crusade: Event and Context*, Pearson Longman, Harlow, 2003.

At the edges of this book, we have seen developments in crusading elsewhere and it is worth signposting a few important starting points. For the Baltic, see E. Christiansen, *The Northern Crusades*, second edition, Penguin, Harmondsworth, 1997; *Jerusalem in the North: Denmark and the Baltic*

Crusades, 1100–1522, eds A.L. Bysted, C.S. Jensen, K.V. Jensen and J.H. Lind, Brepols, Turnhout, 2012, and Iben Fonnesberg-Schmidt, *The Popes and the Baltic Crusades, 1147–1254*, E.J. Brill, Leiden, 2007. For the Children's Crusade, see Gary Dickson's superb *The Children's Crusade*, Palgrave Macmillan, Basingstoke, 2008. For the Albigensian Crusade, see Michael Costen, *The Cathars and the Albigensian Crusade*, Manchester University Press, Manchester, 1997; Lawrence Marvin, *The Occitan War: A Military and Political History of the Albigensian Crusade, 1209–1218*, Cambridge University Press, Cambridge, 2008. For crusading in Iberia, see Purkis, *Crusading Spirituality*, 2008 noted earlier, and Joseph O'Callaghan, *Reconquest and Crusade in Medieval Spain*, University of Pennsylvania Press, Philadephia, 2003. For Frankish Greece, see Nikos Chrissis, *Crusading in Frankish Greece: A Study of Byzantine–Western Relations and Attitudes 1204–1282*, Brepols, Turnout, 2013.

Finally, the important subject of historiography is given a commanding overview by Giles Constable, 'The Historiography of the Crusades', *The Crusades from the Perspective of the Byzantine and Muslim Worlds*, eds A.E. Laiou and R.P. Mottahedeh, Dumbarton Oaks, Washington D.C., 2001, pp. 1–22. Norman Housley's excellent *Contesting the Crusades*, Blackwell, Oxford, 2006 vigorously explores historians' various interpretations of the crusades, while Christopher Tyerman's *The Debate on the Crusades*, Manchester University Press, Manchester, 2011 does much to trace the context for this evolution, as well as evaluating the strengths and weaknesses of various viewpoints.

PRINTED PRIMARY SOURCES

Ambroise, *The History of the Holy War: Ambroise's 'Estoire de la guerre sainte'*, tr. M. Ailes and M.C. Barber, 2 vols, Boydell, Woodbridge, 2003.

Arab Historians of the Crusades, tr. F. Gabrieli, University of California Press, Berkeley, CA, 1969.

Beha ad-Din, *The Rare and Excellent History of Saladin*, tr. D.S. Richards, Scolar Press, Aldershot, 2001.

Bernard of Clairvaux, *The Letters of Saint Bernard of Clairvaux*, tr. B.S. James, Alan Sutton, Gloucester, 1998.

Caffaro of Genoa, *Caffaro, Genoa and the Twelfth Century Crusades*, tr. M.A. Hall and J.P. Phillips, Ashgate, Farnham, 2013.

Cartulaires de l'abbaye de Molesme, ed. J. Laurent, 2 vols, Imprimerie Nationale, Paris, 1907–11.

Chartes et documents de Saint-Bénique de Dijon, eds G. Chevrier and M. Chaume, 2 vols, Dijon, 1943–86.

The Chronicle of the Third Crusade (A translation of the *Itinerarium Peregrinorum et Gesta Regis Ricardi*), tr. H. Nicholson, Ashgate, Aldershot, 1997.

The Conquest of Jerusalem and the Third Crusade, tr. P.W. Edbury, Scolar Press, Aldershot, 1996.

The Conquest of Lisbon (De expugnatione lyxbonensi), ed. and tr. C.W. David, introduction by J.P. Phillips, second edition, Columbia University Press, New York, 2001.

Contemporary Sources for the Fourth Crusade, tr. Alfred Andrea, E.J. Brill, Leiden, 2000.

The Crusade of Frederick Barbarossa: The History of the Expedition of the Emperor Frederick and Related Texts, tr. G.A. Loud, Ashgate, Farnham, 2010.

Eugenius III, *Quantum praedecessores*, Riley-Smith, *The Crusades: Idea and Reality*, pp. 57–59.

Fulcher of Chartres, *A History of the Expedition to Jerusalem, 1095–1127*, tr. F.R. Ryan, ed. H.S. Fink, University of Tennessee Press, Knoxville, TN, 1969. The first section of this account is also in Peters, E. (ed.), *The First Crusade: 'The Chronicle of Fulcher of Chartres' and Other Source Materials*, University of Pennsylvania Press, Philadelphia, 1998.

Geoffrey of Villehardouin, 'The Conquest of Constantinople', *Joinville and Villehardouin: Chronicles of the Crusades*, tr. C. Smith, Penguin, London, 2008, pp. 5–135.

Gerald of Wales, *The Journey through Wales/The Description of Wales*, tr. L. Thorpe, Penguin, Harmondsworth, 1978.

Gesta Francorum et aliorum Hierosolimitanorum, ed. and tr. R.M.T. Hill, Oxford Medieval Texts, Oxford, 1962.

Gregory VIII, *Audita tremendi*, Riley-Smith, *The Crusades: Idea and Reality*, pp. 63–67.

Guibert of Nogent, *The Deeds of God through the Franks*, tr. R. Levine, Boydell, Woodbridge, 1997.

Gunther of Pairis, *The Capture of Constantinople: The 'Hystoria Constantinopolitana'*, ed. and tr. A. Andrea, University of Pennsylvania Press, Philadelphia, 1997.

Ibn al-Athir, 'The Perfect History' extracts in *Arab Historians of the Crusades*, tr. F. Gabrieli, University of California Press, Berkeley, CA, 1969.

—— *The Chronicle of Ibn al-Athir for the Crusading Period*, tr. D.S. Richards, 3 vols (1097–1146; 1146–1193; 1193–1231), Ashgate Publishing, Farnham, 2006–8.

Ibn al-Qalanisi, *The Damascus Chronicles of the Crusades*, tr. H.A.R. Gibb, Luzac, London, 1932.

Ibn Jubayr, *The Travels of Ibn Jubayr*, tr. R.J.C. Broadhurst, Jonathan Cape, London, 1952.

Imad ad-Din, in: *Arab Historians of the Crusades*, tr. F. Gabrieli, University of California Press, Berkeley, CA, 1969.

Jacques de Vitry, *The History of Jerusalem*, tr. A. Stewart, Palestine Pilgrims' Text Society, London, 1896.

Jerusalem Pilgrimage, 1099–1187, tr. J. Wilkinson, Hakluyt Society, Second Series, Vol. 167, London, 1988.

The Jews and the Crusaders, tr. S. Eidelberg, University of Wisconsin Press, Madison, WI, 1977.

John of Salisbury, *Letters*, eds and tr. S.J. and H.E. Butler, W.J. Millor and C.N.L. Brooke, 2 vols, Oxford Medieval Texts, Oxford, 1955–79.

John Kinnamos, *The Deeds of John and Manuel Comnenus*, tr. C.M. Brand, Columbia University Press, New York, 1976.

Letters from the East: Crusaders, Pilgrims and Settlers in the 12th–13th Centuries, ed. and trans. M.C. Barber and K. Bate, Ashgate, Farnham, 2010.

Matthew of Edessa, *Armenia and the Crusades, Tenth to Twelfth Centuries*, tr. A.E. Dostaurian, University Press of America, Lanham, MD, 1993.

Nicholas Mesarites, extracts translated in C.M. Brand, *Byzantium Confronts the West, 1180–1204*, Harvard University Press, Cambridge MA, 1968.

Niketas Choniates, *O City of Byzantium – The Annals of Niketas Choniates*, tr. H.J. Magoulias, Wayne State University Press, Detroit, MI, 1984.

Odo of Deuil, *De profectione Ludovici VII – The Journey of Louis VII to the East*, tr. V.G. Berry, Columbia University Press, New York, 1948.

Orderic Vitalis, *The Ecclesiastical History*, ed. and tr. M. Chibnall, 6 vols, Oxford Medieval Texts, Oxford, 1969–80.

Otto of Freising, *The Deeds of Frederick Barbarossa*, tr. C.C. Mierow, Columbia University Press, New York, 1953.

Ralph of Caen, *The Gesta Tancredi of Ralph of Caen: A History of the Normans on the First Crusade*, tr. B.S. Bachrach and D.S. Bachrach, Ashgate, Aldershot, 2005.

Raymond of Aguilers, *Historia Francorum qui ceperunt Iherusalem*, tr. J.H. Hill and L.L. Hill, American Philosophical Society, Philadelphia, 1968.

Recueil des chartes de l'abbaye de Cluny, eds A. Bernard and A. Bruel, 6 vols, Imprimerie Nationale, Paris, 1876–1903.

Riley-Smith, L. and Riley-Smith, J.S.C., *The Crusades: Idea and Reality 1095–1274*, Edward Arnold, London, 1981.

Robert of Clari, *The Conquest of Constantinople*, tr. E. McNeal, Columbia University Press, New York, 1936.

Robert the Monk, *Robert the Monk's History of the First Crusade: Historia Iherosolimitana*, tr. C. Sweetenham, Ashgate, Aldershot, 2005.

The Rule of the Templars, tr. J. Upton-Ward, Boydell, Woodbridge, 1992.

The Templars, tr. M.C. Barber and K. Bate, Manchester University Press, Manchester, 2002.

Usama ibn Munqidh, *The Book of Contemplation: Islam and the Crusades*, tr. P.M. Cobb, Penguin, London, 2008.

Walter the Chancellor, *A History of the Antiochene Wars*, tr. T.S. Asbridge and
 S.B. Edgington, Ashgate, Aldershot, 1999.
William of Malmesbury, *Gesta Regum Anglorum – The History of the English
 Kings*, ed. and tr. R.A.B. Mynors, R.M. Thomson and M. Winterbottom,
 2 vols, Clarendon Press, Oxford, 1998.
William of Tyre, *A History of Deeds Done Beyond the Sea*, tr. E.A. Babcock and
 A.C. Krey, 2 vols, Columbia University Press, New York, 1943.

SECONDARY WORKS

Angold, M., *The Byzantine Empire, 1095–1204: A Political History*, second
 edition, Pearson Longman, Harlow, 1997.
—— *The Fourth Crusade: Event and Context*, Pearson Longman, Harlow, 2003.
Asbridge, T.S., *The Principality of Antioch, 1098–1130*, Boydell, Woodbridge,
 2000.
—— *The First Crusade: A New History*, The Free Press, London, 2004.
Barber, M., *The New Knighthood. A History of the Order of the Templars*,
 Cambridge University Press, Cambridge, 1994.
—— 'Frontier Warfare in the Latin Kingdom of Jerusalem: The Campaign of
 Jacob's Ford, 1178–79', *The Crusades and their Sources: Essays Presented to
 Bernard Hamilton*, eds J. France and W.G. Zajac, Ashgate, Aldershot,
 1998, pp. 9–22.
—— *The Crusader States*, Yale University Press, New Haven and London, 2012.
Barton, S.F., 'A Forgotten Crusade: Alfonso VII of Léon-Castile and the
 Campaign for Jaen (1148)', *Historical Research* 73 (2000), pp. 312–20.
Boas, A., *Crusader Archaeology: Material Culture of the Latin East*, Routledge,
 London, 1999.
—— *Jerusalem in the Time of the Crusades*, Routledge, London, 2001.
Bull, M.G., *Knightly Piety and the Lay Response to the First Crusade*, Clarendon
 Press, Oxford, 1993a.
—— 'The Roots of Lay Enthusiasm for the First Crusade', *History* 78
 (1993b), pp. 353–72.
—— 'Origins', *The Oxford Illustrated History of the Crusades*, ed. J.S.C. Riley-
 Smith, Oxford University Press, Oxford, 1995, pp. 13–33.
—— 'The Diplomatic of the First Crusade', *The First Crusade: Origins and Impact*,
 ed. J.P. Phillips, Manchester University Press, Manchester, 1997, pp. 35–56.
—— and Kempf, D., (eds), *Historiography, Memory and Transmission: New
 Approaches to the Narratives of the Early Crusade Movement*, Boydell,
 Woodbridge, 2014.
Chrissis, N., *Crusading in Frankish Greece: A Study of Byzantine-Western
 Relations and Attitudes, 1204–1282*, Brepols, Turnhout, 2013.

Christiansen, E., *The Northern Crusades*, second edition, Penguin, Harmondsworth, 1997.

Cobb, P.M., *Usama ibn Munqidh: Warrior Poet of the Age of the Crusades*, One World Press, Oxford, 2005.

Cole, Penny, *The Preaching of the Crusades to the Holy Land, 1095–1274*, Medieval Academy of America, Cambridge, MA, 1991.

Constable, G., 'The Second Crusade as Seen by Contemporaries', *Traditio* 9 (1953), pp. 213–79.

—— 'The Historiography of the Crusades', *The Crusades from the Perspective of the Byzantine and Muslim Worlds*, eds A.E. Laiou and R.P. Mottahedeh, Dumbarton Oaks, Washington D.C., 2001, pp. 1–22.

Costen, M., *The Cathars and the Albigensian Crusade*, Manchester University Press, Manchester, 1997.

Cowdrey, H.E.J., 'Pope Urban II's Preaching of the First Crusade', *History* 55 (1970), pp. 177–88.

—— 'Pope Urban and the Idea of the Crusade', *Studi Medievali* 36 (1995), pp. 721–42.

Dickson, G., *The Children's Crusade: Medieval History and Modern Mythistory*, Palgrave Macmillan, Basingstoke, 2008.

Drory, Joseph, 'Hanbalis of the Nablus Region in the Eleventh and Twelfth Centuries', *Asian and African Studies* 22 (1988), pp. 93–112.

Edbury, P.W., *The Kingdom of Cyprus and the Crusades, 1191–1374*, Cambridge University Press, Cambridge, 1991.

—— 'Propaganda and Faction in the Kindom of Jerusalem: The Background to Hattin', *Crusaders and Muslims in Twelfth-Century Syria*, ed. M. Shatzmiller, E.J. Brill, Leiden, 1993, pp. 173–89.

—— 'Celestine III, the Crusades and the Latin East', *Pope Celestine III (1191–1198): Pastor and Diplomat*, eds J. Doran and D. Smith, Boydell, Woodbridge, 2008, pp. 129–43.

Eddé, A-M., *Saladin*, Harvard Belknap, New York, 2011.

Ellenblum, R., *Frankish Rural Settlement in the Latin Kingdom of Jerusalem*, Cambridge University Press, Cambridge, 1998.

—— *Crusader Castles and Modern Histories*, Cambridge University Press, Cambridge, 2007.

Elisséeff, Nikita, 'The Reaction of the Syrian Muslims after the Foundation of the First Latin Kingdom of Jerusalem', *Crusaders and Muslims in Twelfth-Century Syria*, ed. M. Shatzmiller, E.J. Brill, Leiden, 1993, pp. 162–72.

Erdmann, C., *The Origin of the Idea of the Crusade*, tr. M.W. Baldwin and W. Goffart, University of Princeton Press, Princeton, NJ, 1977.

Folda, Jaroslav, *The Art of the Crusaders in the Holy Land, 1095–1187*, Cambridge University Press, Cambridge, 1995.

Fonnesberg-Schmidt, I., *The Popes and the Baltic Crusades, 1147–1254*, E.J. Brill, Leiden, 2007.

France, J., *Victory in the East: A Military History of the First Crusade*, Cambridge University Press, Cambridge, 1994.

—— 'Warfare in the Mediterranean Region in the Age of the Crusades, 1095–1291: A Clash of Contrasts', in C. Kostick (ed.), *The Crusades and the Near East: Cultural Histories*, Routledge, Abingdon, 2011, pp. 9–26.

Frankopan, P., *The First Crusade: The Call from the East*, Bodley Head, London, 2012.

Frenkel, Y., 'Muslim Responses to the Frankish Dominion in the Near East, 1098–1291', Kostick, C. (ed.), *The Crusades: Cultural Histories*, Routledge, Abingdon, 2011, pp. 27–54.

Gendering the Crusades, eds S.B. Edgington and S. Lambert, University of Wales Press, Cardiff, 2001.

Gerish, D., 'Gender Theory' in H. Nicholson (ed.), *Palgrave Advances in the Crusades*, Palgrave Macmillan, Basingstoke, 2005, pp. 130–47.

Gillingham, J.B., *Richard the Lionheart*, second edition, Weidenfeld and Nicolson, London, 1989.

—— *Richard I*, Yale University Press, London and New Haven, CT, 1999.

Hamblin, W.J., 'Saladin and Muslim Military Theory', *The Horns of Hattin*, ed. B.Z. Kedar, Yad Izhak Ben-Zvi, Jerusalem, 1992, pp. 228–38.

Hamilton, B., 'Women in the Crusader States: The Queens of Jerusalem (1100–90)', *Medieval Women: Studies in Church History, Subsidia 1*, ed. D. Baker, Blackwell, Oxford, 1978, pp. 143–74.

—— *The Latin Church in the Crusader States*, Variorum, London, 1980.

—— *The Leper-king and his Heirs: Baldwin IV and the Crusader Kingdom of Jerusalem*, Cambridge University Press, Cambridge, 2000a.

—— 'Our Lady of Saidnaya: An Orthodox Shrine Revered by Muslims and Knights Templar at the Time of the Crusades', *The Holy Land, Holy Lands and Christian History*, ed. R.N. Swanson, Studies in Church History 36, Boydell, Woodbridge, 2000b, pp. 207–15.

Harris, J., *Byzantium and the Crusades*, second edition, Bloomsbury, London, 2014.

Hillenbrand, C., '*Jihad* Propaganda in Syria from the Time of the First Crusade until the Death of Zengi: The Evidence of Monumental Inscriptions', *The Frankish Wars and their Influence in Palestine*, eds Khaled Athamina and Robin Heacock, Birzeit University Press, Birzeit, 1994, pp. 60–9.

—— 'The First Crusade: The Muslim Perspective', *The First Crusade: Origins and Impact*, ed. J.P. Phillips, Manchester University Press, Manchester, 1997, pp. 130–41.

—— *The Crusades: Islamic Perspectives*, Edinburgh University Press, Edinburgh, 1999.

—— 'Abominable Acts: The Career of Zengi', *The Second Crusade: Scope and Consequences*, eds M. Hoch and J.P. Phillips, Manchester University Press, Manchester, 2001, pp. 111–32.

Hirschler, K., 'The Jerusalem Conquest of 492/1099 in the Medieval Arabic Historiography of the Crusades: From Regional Plurality to Islamic Narrative', *Crusades* 13 (2014).

Hodgson, N.R., *Women, Crusading and the Holy Land in Historical Narrative*, Boydell, Woodbridge, 2007.

Housley, N., *Fighting for the Cross: Crusading to the Holy Land*, Yale University Press, London and New Haven, 2008.

—— *Contesting the Crusades*, Blackwell, Oxford, 2006.

Jacoby, D., 'The Venetian Privileges in the Latin Kingdom of Jerusalem: Twelfth- and Thirteenth-Century Interpretations and Implementation', *Montjoie. Studies in Crusade History in Honour of Hans Eberhard Mayer*, eds B.Z. Kedar, J.S.C. Riley-Smith and R. Hiestand, Variorum, Aldershot, 1997, pp. 155–76.

Jerusalem in the North: Denmark and the Baltic Crusades, 1100–1522, eds A.L. Bysted, C.S. Jensen, K.V. Jensen and J.H. Lind, Brepols, Turnhout, 2012.

Jotischky, A., *The Perfection of Solitude: Hermits and Monks in the Crusader States*, Pennsylvania State University Press, University Park, PA, 1995.

—— *Crusading and the Crusader States*, Longman, Harlow, 2005.

Kedar, B.Z., 'Subjected Muslims of the Frankish Levant', *Muslims under Latin Rule 1100–1300*, ed. J.M. Powell, Princeton University Press, Princeton, NJ, 1990, pp. 135–74.

—— 'The Battle of Hattin Revisited', *The Horns of Hattin*, ed. B.Z. Kedar, Variorum, London, 1992, pp. 190–207.

—— 'On the Origins of the Earliest Laws of Frankish Jerusalem: The Canons of the Council of Nablus, 1120', *Speculum* 74 (1999), pp. 310–35.

—— 'The Jerusalem Massacre of July 1099 in the Western Historiography of the Crusades', *Crusades* 3 (2004), pp. 15–76.

Kennedy, H., *Crusader Castles*, Cambridge University Press, Cambridge, 1994.

Köhler, M., *Alliances and Treaties between Frankish and Muslim Rulers in the Middle East*, tr. P.M. Holt, revised K. Hirschler, E.J. Brill, Leiden, 2013.

Kostick, C., *The Siege of Jerusalem: Crusade and Conquest in 1099*, Continuum Books, London, 2009.

—— (ed.), *The Crusades and the Near East: Cultural Histories*, Routledge, Abingdon, 2011.

Kühnel, B., *Crusader Art of the Twelfth Century: A Geographical, an Historical, or an Art-Historical Notion?* Gebr. Mann Verlag, Berlin, 1994.

La Monte, J.A., *Feudal Monarchy in the Latin Kingdom of Jerusalem, 1100 to 1291*, The Medieval Academy of America, Cambridge, MA, 1932.

Latiff, O., 'Qur'anic Imagery, Jesus and the Creation of a Pious-Warrior Ethos in the Muslim Poetry of the Anti-Frankish Jihad', *Cultural Encounters during the Crusades*, eds K.V. Jensen, K. Salonen and H. Vogt, University Press of Southern Denmark, Odense, 2013, pp. 135–52.

Lilie, R.-J., *Byzantium and the Crusader States, 1095–1204*, tr. J.C. Morris and J.E. Ridings, Clarendon Press, Oxford, 1993.

Livermore, H.V., 'The *Conquest of Lisbon* and its Author', *Portuguese Studies* 6 (1990), pp. 1–16.

Lyons, M.C. and Jackson, D.E.P., *Saladin: The Politics of the Holy War*, Cambridge University Press, Cambridge, 1982.

Mack, M., 'The Merchant of Genoa', unpublished Ph.D. thesis, University of Cambridge, Cambridge, 2003.

——— 'A Genoese Perspective of the Third Crusade', *Crusades* 10 (2011), pp. 45–62.

Madden, T.F., *Enrico Dandolo and the Rise of Venice*, Johns Hopkins University Press, 2003.

Marvin, L., *The Occitan War: A Military and Political History of the Albigensian Crusade, 1209–1218*, Cambridge, Cambridge University Press, 2008.

Mayer, H.E., 'Studies in the History of Queen Melisende of Jerusalem', *Dumbarton Oaks Papers* 26 (1972), pp. 93–182.

——— 'Henry II and the Holy Land', *English Historical Review* 97 (1982), pp. 721–39.

——— *The Crusades*, tr. J.B. Gillingham, second edition, Oxford University Press, Oxford, 1988.

Mitchell, P.D., Y. Nagar and R. Ellenblum, 'Weapon Injuries in the 12th Century Crusader Garrison of Vadum Iacob Castle, Galilee', *International Journal of Osteoarchaeology* 16 (2006), pp. 145–55.

——— *Medicine in the Crusades: Warfare, Wounds and the Medieval Surgeon*, Cambridge University Press, Cambridge, 2007.

Morton, N.E., *The Medieval Military Orders, 1120–1314*, Pearson, Harlow, 2013.

Mourad, S.A. and J.E. Lindsay, 'Ibn 'Asakir and the Intensification and Reorientation of Sunni Jihad Ideology in Crusader-Era Syria', *Just Wars, Holy Wars and Jihads: Christian, Jewish and Muslim Encounters and Exchanges*, ed. Sohail H. Hashmi, Oxford University Press, Oxford, 2012, pp. 107–24.

——— *The Intensification and Reorientation of Sunni Jihad Ideology in the Crusader Period. Ibn 'Asakir of Damascus (1105–1176) and His Age, with an Edition and Translation of Ibn 'Asakir's 'The Forty Hadiths for Inciting Jihad'*, Brill, Leiden, 2013.

Mullinder, A., 'Albert of Aachen and the Crusade of 1101', *From Clermont to Jerusalem: The Crusades and Crusader Societies 1095–1500*, ed. A.V. Murray, Brepols, Turnhout, 1998, pp. 69–77.

Murray, A.V., 'Mighty against the Enemies of the Christ: The Relic of the True Cross in the Armies of the Kingdom of Jerusalem', *The Crusades and their Sources: Essays Presented to Bernard Hamilton*, eds John France and William Zajac, Ashgate, Aldershot, 1998, pp. 217–38.

—— *The Crusader Kingdom of Jerusalem: A Dynastic History, 1099–1125*, Linacre Unit for Prosopographical Research, Volume 4, Oxford, 2000.

—— *The Crusades: An Encyclopaedia*, 4 volumes, ABC-Clio, Santa Barbara CA, 2006.

—— 'Finance and Logistics on the Crusade of Frederick Barbarossa', *In laudem hierosolymitani: Studies in Crusades and Medieval Culture in Honour of Benjamn Z. Kedar*, eds I. Shagrir, R. Ellenblum and J.S.C. Riley-Smith, Crusades Subsidia 1, Ashgate, Farnham, 2007, pp. 357–68.

—— 'National Identity, Language and Conflict in the Crusades to the Holy Land, 1096–1192', *The Crusades and the Near East: Cultural Histories*, ed. C. Kostick, Routledge, Abingdon, 2011, pp. 107–130.

Nicholson, H. (ed.), *Palgrave Advances in the Crusades*, Palgrave Macmillan, Basingstoke, 2005.

O'Callaghan, J.F., *Reconquest and Crusade in Medieval Spain*, University of Pennsylvania Press, Philadephia, 2003.

Park, D., *Under Our Protection, That of the Church and Their Own: Papal and Secular Protection of the Families and Properties the Crusaders Left Behind, c. 1095–1226*, Unpublished Ph.D. thesis, Royal Holloway, University of London, 2013.

Paul, N.L., *To Follow in Their Footsteps: The Crusades and Family Memory in the High Middle Ages*, Cornell University Press, Ithaca, 2012.

Phillips, J.P., *Defenders of the Holy Land: Relations between the Latin East and the West, 1119–87*, Clarendon Press, Oxford, 1996.

—— (ed.), *The First Crusade: Origins and Impact*, Manchester University Press, Manchester, 1997a.

—— 'St Bernard of Clairvaux, the Low Countries and the Lisbon Letter of the Second Crusade', *Journal of Ecclesiastical History* 48 (1997b), pp. 485–97.

—— and Hoch, M., *The Second Crusade: Scope and Consequences*, Manchester University Press, Manchester, 2001.

—— *The Fourth Crusade and the Sack of Constantinople*, Jonathan Cape, London, 2004.

—— *The Second Crusade: Extending the Frontiers of Christendom*, Yale University Press, London and New Haven, 2007.

—— *Holy Warriors: A Modern History of the Crusades*, Bodley Head, London, 2009.

—— 'Caffaro of Genoa and the Motives of the Early Crusaders', *Religion as an Agent of Change*, ed. P. Ingesman, E.J. Brill, Leiden, 2014.

Prawer, J., *Crusader Institutions*, Clarendon Press, Oxford, 1980.

Pringle, D., *The Churches of the Crusader Kingdom of Jerusalem: A Corpus*, 4 vols., Cambridge University Press, 1993–2009.

Purkis, W.J., *Crusading Spirituality in the Holy Land and Iberia, c.1095–c.1187*, Boydell, Woodbridge, 2008.

Queller, D.E., and Madden, T.F., *The Fourth Crusade: The Conquest of Constantinople*, second edition, University of Pennsylvania Press, Philadelphia, 1997.

Richard, J., *The Latin Kingdom of Jerusalem*, tr. J. Shirley, 2 vols, North Holland Co., Amsterdam, 1979.

Riley-Smith, J.S.C., *The Feudal Nobility and the Kingdom of Jerusalem, 1174–1277*, Macmillan, London, 1973.

—— *The First Crusade and the Idea of Crusading*, Athlone Press, London, 1986.

—— *The Crusades. A Short History*, Athlone Press, London, 1987.

—— *Hospitallers: The History of the Order of St John*, Hambledon, London, 1999.

—— *What were the Crusades?* Fourth edition, Macmillan, Basingstoke, 2009.

—— *The First Crusaders 1095–1131*, Cambridge University Press, Cambridge, 1997.

—— *The Knights Hospitaller in the Levant, c.1070–1309*, Palgrave Macmillan, Basingstoke, 2012.

Roche, J., 'Conrad III and the Second Crusade: Retreat from Dorylaion?' *Crusades* 5 (2006), pp. 85–98.

Rogers, Randall, *Latin Siege Warfare in the Twelfth Century*, Clarendon Press, Oxford, 1992.

Rubenstein, J., *Armies of Heaven: The First Crusade and the Quest for Apocalypse*, Basic Books, New York, 2011.

Runciman, S., *A History of the Crusades*, 3 volumes, Cambridge University Press, Cambridge, 1951–54.

Schenk, J., *Templar Families: Landowning Families and the Order of the Temple in France, c.1120–1307*, Cambridge University Press, Cambridge, 2012.

Selwood, D., *Knights of the Cloister*, Boydell, Woodbridge, 1999.

Setton, K.M. (editor-in-chief), *A History of the Crusades*, 6 vols, University of Wisconsin Press, Madison, WI, 1969–89.

Shagrir, I., *Naming Patterns in the Latin Kingdom of Jerusalem*, Linacre Unit for Prosopographical Research, Volume 12, Oxford, 2003.

Smail, R.C., *Crusading Warfare 1097–1193*, second edition, Cambridge University Press, Cambridge, 1995.

Talmon-Heller, D., *Islamic Piety in Medieval Syria. Mosques, Cemeteries and Sermons under the Zangids and Ayyubids (1146–1260)*, Brill, Leiden, 2007.

Tibble, S., *Monarchy and Lordships in the Latin Kingdom of Jerusalem, 1099–1291*, Clarendon Press, Oxford, 1989.

Tsurtsumia, M., 'Commemorations of Crusaders in the Manuscripts of the Monastery of the Holy Cross in Jerusalem', *Journal of Medieval History* 38 (2012), pp. 318–34.

Tyerman, C.J., *Were there any Crusades in the Twelfth Century?* Macmillan, Basingstoke, 1998.

—— *God's War: A New History of the Crusades*, Penguin Allen Lane, London, 2006.

—— *The Debate on the Crusades*, Manchester University Press, Manchester, 2011.

Vertannes, B., *Crusade and Reform: The Language of Christian Martyrdom, c. 1095–1190*, Unpublished Ph.D. thesis, University of Cambridge, 2013.

Whalen, B., 'God's Will or Not? Bohemond's Campaign Against the Byzantine Empire (1105–1108), *Crusades – Medieval Worlds in Conflict*, eds T.F. Madden, J.L. Naus and V. Ryan, Ashgate, Farnham, 2010, pp. 111–25.

Whatley, L.J., 'Visual Self-Fashioning and the Seals of the Knights Hospitaller in England', eds N.L. Paul and S. Yeager, *Remembering the Crusades: Myth, Image, and Identity*, Johns Hopkins University Press, 2012, pp. 252–70.

Williams, J.B., 'The Making of a Crusade: the Genoese Anti-Muslim Attacks in Spain, 1146–48', *Journal of Medieval History* 23 (1997), pp. 29–53.

Wright, C., 'On the Margins of Christendom: The Impact of the Crusades on Byzantium', *The Crusades and the Near East: Cultural Histories*, ed. C. Kostick, Routledge, Abingdon, 2011, pp. 55–82.

Index